# Walter Savage Landor

W. S. Landor aged eighty-four

From a drawing by William Wetmore Story

# Walter Savage Landor
# Selected Poetry and Prose

edited by Keith Hanley

PERSEA BOOKS
NEW YORK

*For my parents, John and Gemma Hanley*

*Persea Books, Inc.*
*225 Lafayette Street*
*New York, N.Y.*

*ISBN 0–89255–045–7*

*Library of Congress*
*Catalogue No 79–91173*

*Copyright © 1981 Keith Hanley*
*Introduction, Notes and selection of the Text*

*First American Edition*

*Printed in Great Britain*

# Contents

## THE POETRY

from *The Poems of Walter Savage Landor* (1795)

from *Gebir* (1798)

from *Poetry by the Author of Gebir* (1802)

from *Simonidea* (1806)

from *Count Julian: A Tragedy* (1812)

## Miscellaneous poems, 1824–29

## from *Gebir, Count Julian, and Other Poems* (1831)

## Miscellaneous poems, 1834

## from *Pericles and Aspasia* (1836)

## from *The Hellenics of Walter Savage Landor* (1847)

## Miscellaneous poems, 1848–52

## Poems published posthumously

# THE PROSE

from *Imaginary Conversations of Literary Men and Statesmen,*
vols. 1 and 2 (1824)

from *Imaginary Conversations of Literary Men and Statesmen,*
vol. 3 (1828)

from *Imaginary Conversations of Literary Men and Statesmen,*
Second Series (1829)

# Acknowledgments

I am indebted to the series of major Landor editors, Charles G. Crump, Stephen Wheeler, Alice Lavonne Prasher and Charles L. Proudfit, for the guidance provided by their impressive work on textual and bibliographical problems and for the information in their annotations. I, of course, am responsible for my interpretation of their work.

My understanding of Landor relies on the three principal biographies: by his friend John Forster, his modern advocate Malcolm Elwin, and the lucid and authoritative R. H. Super. Those critics I have found particularly instructive are referred to in my Introduction.

Mr Brian Richardson of the Department of Italian, Leeds University, has supplied me with much information concerning Landor's references to Italian history and topography, and Professors Len Findlay of the Department of English, University of Saskatchewan, and H. D. Jocelyn of the Department of Latin, University of Manchester, have responded helpfully to my queries over classical references and citations.

I would like warmly to thank the friends who have encouraged me in persevering with this book: Christiane Kegel, Bernard and Heather O'Donoghue, Sara Pearl, Lilian Schmid, John Stachniewski and Annabelle Wilkinson. My greatest obligation is to Roger Holdsworth who, besides bolstering my conviction that this work was worth doing, has made a number of suggestions and corrections to improve it. I alone, however, am responsible for any errors.

I am grateful to Miss Penny Evans who typed the manuscript. My research for this book was completed while I was the Lees Fellow in English at Manchester University.

# Introduction

## I  The Neo-Classical Rôle

Landor was a minor writer working in the diminishing neo-classical tradition. His position in the English Romantic and early Victorian periods was anomalous, but an unusually enlivening intimacy with the works of his greatest predecessors, and his ambition to write as they had in the modern context, prevented it from becoming obviously outmoded. He was consequently able to enjoy with surprisingly little sense of incongruity the afflatus of the apparently unassailable European classical tradition. In the end, however, it is the seriousness with which he approaches the strict demands of his classical art throughout the astonishing span of his writing career (1795–1863) which makes him of permanent importance. In his own lifetime he resigned himself to the inevitability of the slender and eccentric achievement involved in a consistent allegiance to the tradition he tried to sustain, and assumed the discriminating isolation of the literary patrician: 'I shall have as many readers as I desire to have in other times than ours. I shall dine late; but the dining-room will be well-lighted, the guests few and select'.[1]

His highly self-conscious rôle of the classicist developed precociously, and was both temperamental and cultivated. At Rugby, where he boarded from the age of nine to twelve, he channelled his proud unruliness into excelling at the daily exercises in Latin translation and composition, and was, he believed, one of the first schoolboys of his time to attempt a Greek verse. His love of the classics was to provide a line of calming continuity through the otherwise tempestuous course of his education. When in later life he wrote to a young protégée that 'Much of our subsequent life depends on the turn we ourselves give to the expression of our early feelings',[2] he was in effect accounting for the origin of his own sense of style. After he had been withdrawn from school for insubordination, he happily studied Pope and classical authors with a private tutor, and at the age of sixteen was translating Cowley into Latin verse, 'correcting his extravagance'.[3] He composed Latin verses regularly during his life, resorting to them especially in times of stress. Indeed, a number of his longer English poems were originally written in Latin; and he was deterred from making it his chief medium only by the example of Milton and the advice of Southey and Wordsworth. As an old man he remarked, 'I am sometimes at a loss for an English word, for a Latin never'.[4]

Landor resorted to his self-protective concentration on cultural integrity when he was also rusticated from Oxford, and developed his predominant interest in Latin culture both forwards and backwards, taking up the private study of French, Italian and Greek. The forward development climaxed in middle age during his exile in Italy, where his delight in Trecento literature, particularly that of Petrarch and Boccaccio, provided a bridge between the ancient world and the modern world of the Renaissance. It was a wonderfully fruitful period in which his sense of tradition opened out in the ampler dimension of the prose works which he then began to write. Simply living there, he imbibed the Italian passion for all art: 'Nature I loved, and, next to Nature, Art'. (POETRY **130**, 2)

It was in Italy too, when preparing his Imaginary Conversations on classical themes and *Pericles and Aspasia,* that he discovered the imaginative roots of the Latin tradition, and made his first systematic study of Greek literature:

> He who beholds the skies of Italy
> Sees ancient Rome reflected, sees beyond,
> Into more glorious Hellas, nurse of Gods
> And godlike men.[5]

In Periclean Athens he recognized the homogeneity with which he tried to inform his own work – an attempt which won the admiration of Yeats and Pound when they came to study him.[6]

The conception of the artist which Landor evolved is that of the culture-hero who condenses in his art the essence of the whole civilization of his state in the way he suggests, speaking in his own person, in one of the Conversations:

> The temperate greatness and pure eloquence of Pericles formed the moral constitution of Sophocles, who had exercised with him a principal magistracy in the republic; and the demon of Socrates, not always unimportunate, followed Euripides from the school to the theatre.[7]

His English model is Milton, who represented the English Commonwealth period, 'which saw Justice and Poesy thriving together'.[8] But Milton and his age provided only an exceptional native approximation to the homogeneous culture of Greece and Rome – the culture which Landor sees, as his imaginary Marcus Cicero describes it, defined by a succession of commanding figures:

> The memory of those great men who consolidated our republic by their wisdom, exalted it by their valor, and protected and defended it by their constancy, stands not alone nor idly; they draw us after them, they place us with them.[9]

Landor found his contemporary England especially inimical to the spirit of that epoch, to which he himself responded so strongly. He felt it was embodied rather in the 'aristocratical republicanism'[10] which he associated with contemporary liberalizing reformers abroad, such as Garibaldi, Bolivar, Kossuth (the Hungarian nationalist leader) and 'Kosciusko, Hofer, George/The staid Virginian, standing side by side'.[11]

He accordingly sees it as the modern artist's function to determine and maintain as the reward of concentrated study and artistic effort the permanence of the classical 'structure of feeling'.[12] The artist can in this way summon up an ever-present 'society which (he) alone can bring together',[13] made up of personalities from different times and places, but seen in terms of a continuously shared culture. On the one hand, the culture which derives from the past must also reanimate it, as in the early mythological poems ('Gebir', 'Crysaor' and 'The Phocaeans') in which Landor supplies, as it were, a missing link in ancient literature by imaginatively evoking the 'classic land' of ancient Spain which Greek and Latin authors had strangely neglected.[14] Landor himself becomes, in this way, an ancient writer, and is consequently empowered to deal with the historical classics on equal terms, as his close and sometimes high-handed analyses of them in the eighteenth-century vein of classical scholarship demonstrate. On the other hand, he is able also to invest contemporary figures and events with the kudos of the continuing tradition, which had dominated the neo-classical culture of Europe in the second half of the eighteenth century. Surprisingly, he avoided the historical and philosophical methods of the neo-classicising critics and seems to have 'denied himself the privilege of direct access to Winckelmann, Lessing, Herder and Schlegel'.[15] Nevertheless, by the private path of his own enthusiasm, Landor had arrived at the Germans' conviction of the recoverable immediacy of classical civilization.

The political interpretation of Landor's classicism was imparted in boyhood by a family friend, Samuel Parr, the celebrated Latin scholar, political controversialist and zealous supporter of Fox. Landor remained faithful to the broad Whig persuasion of his family during the 'mad Jacobin' phase at Oxford depicted by Southey.[16] After the loss of his revolutionary flair, however, when in 1802 he actually witnessed Napoleon's acclaim as First Consul, and the French submission to a new despotism, he felt increasingly that his political drive was unrepresented by any faction in British politics, and allowed his opinions to run along the grooves of his master principles, in Colvin's phrase, 'the elementary principles of love of freedom and hatred of tyranny'.[17]

His time in Italy (1815–35) fired him with the fervour for national freedom which was springing up there and over half of Europe. After his return to England, such idealism evidently seemed to some observers to be hopelessly bound up with the lovable impetuosity which Dickens fondly sent up in his fictional portrait of Landor as Laurence Boythorn in *Bleak House*; but it also made him, to a later generation of literary devotees such as Browning and Swinburne, something of an inspiration. Having collected his English writings in 1846, Landor began the following year the long-delayed plan of translating the lengthy narrative poems he had been composing in Latin since almost the beginning of the century. He derived from the expanding context of liberal republicanism at this time a sustaining sense of the political relevance of his classicism which had been shown in several of his dedications to contemporary activists. In 1853 he published the only selection he made of the Imaginary Conversations, 'of the Greeks and the Romans'.

It must be admitted that Landor's sense of his rôle could verge on the histrionic. It entailed an element of posturing. As a young heir, he sold off the majority of his family estates to purchase Llanthony Abbey, Monmouthshire, in a disastrous attempt to set up in grand style as a would-be republican senator. In the event, he was abused for his magnanimity and resented for his lordliness by his tenants and the local Welsh peasants. Another exhibition of his rôle was the bravado of his departure for Corunna to aid the Spanish revolt in the Peninsular War. He was prevented from seeing action but disbursed a handsome sum in aid. More generally, it informed the prickly sense of honour manifested in his exaggerated chivalry toward ladies, and the occasionally violent quixoticism of his treatment of foreign officials. It is there, also, in the superb scorn and self-congratulation of some poems.

In the end, however, the theme of 'Gloriae Contemptor',[18] with its typical distinction between local 'celebrity' and 'lasting fame'[19] (originally formulated to accommodate the public neglect of his early poetry from the viewpoint of a self-consoling aloofness) mingles with a Hölderlin-like sense of the classical mystique, with the satisfaction of having scaled the classical heights of Helicon and Sunium for their own sake:

> He who is within two paces of the ninetieth year may sit down and make no excuses; he must be unpopular, he never tried to be much otherwise, he never contended with a contemporary, but walked alone on the far eastern uplands, meditating and remembering.[20]

## II  Landor's Art of Imitation

Landor's imagination is pervaded by 'the historical sense' which Eliot sees as essential for the continuity of the European tradition, and which

> compels a man to write not merely with his own generation in his bones, but with a feeling that the whole of the literature of Europe from Homer and within it the whole of the literature of his own country has a simultaneous existence and composes a simultaneous order.[1]

Though the poetry, in genre and allusion, and the prose, with its many settings in ancient history, explicitly invoke the classical period of Greece and Rome, it is Landor's general preoccupation with a formal sense of style as such which expresses his unspecific sympathy with the whole classical tradition, characterized by its respect for convention, its restraint, clarity and serenity. The highly artificial prose, evident in such Imaginary Conversations as 'Aesop and Rhodopè', and in set pieces such as the apologue of Critobulus in 'Marcus Tullius and Quinctus Cicero' and the dreams of Petrarca and Boccaccio in *The Pentameron*, offers the most pronounced example of this tendency; but the more usual prose style shows more broadly a similar concern. It was formulated as a vehicle for the ceremonial encounter of the eminent in all ages, and was cast from a late eighteenth-century, loosely Ciceronian mould, formed by those writers whom Landor considered the best of the period, 'Johnson in his "Lives of the Poets", Goldsmith, Blackstone, and Sir Joshua Reynolds'.[2]

Despite his 'historical sense', Landor was to Eliot finally 'only a magnificent by-product', because, unlike Wordsworth, whose greatness is integral to 'his place in the pattern of history',[3] Landor resists with impressive single-mindedness the pressures of reformulation and recombination which give significantly new power to a poet, and make him part of history himself. Landor's peculiar talent is the imitation of a diffuse tradition of writing, entirely refabricating it in English; and he is consequently profoundly derivative. He defined his own aim as 'to make men speak/In English as they would in Greek'. (POETRY **182**, 1–2) Yet, as the proviso added by his imaginary Sidney specifies, he tries to imitate the Greeks 'without borrowing a thought or expression from them'. (PROSE **1**, p. 129) His art of imitation is based on the same theory of 'mythical translations' he discovered in 1847 in a remark by Novalis which defines them as

> translations in the highest style: they present the pure, essential, perfect character of the individual work of art. They do not give us the actual work, but its ideal. *As yet I believe there exists no complete model of this kind.* It requires a head thoroughly imbued with both the poetical and the philosophical spirit, in their entire plenitude.[4]

Most of his work is accordingly dominated by the shadow of greater originals, so that he is open to his own criticism of Racine, 'wherever he is great, he is great by the existence of others'.[5] But his vernacularization of the classical structure of feeling into English is effected by the accomplishment of wholly Landorian styles, which – and this is the nature of his achievement – never smack of pastiche. This is true even of specific imitations such as that of Catullus's Carmen XXI, beginning 'AURELIUS, Sire of Hungrinesses!', or the 'Invocation to Sleep' ascribed to Sidney in the Conversation 'Lord Brooke and Sir Philip Sidney', or the poems attributed to Greek authors in *Pericles and*

*Aspasia*, all of which are informed, in different ways appropriate to their contexts, with a recognizably Landorian voice and technique.

The main influences behind Landor's poetry are consistent but unobtrusive. His first 'Heroic Poem', 'Gebir', predictably derives its overall structure from Homeric and Virgilian epic, but its style is affected by an attempt to imitate that of Pindar, whom Landor considered 'of all poets . . . the most accurate and the most laborious'.[6] His reading of Milton had convinced him that blank verse was a heroic medium superior to the classical hexameter in conveying in English an impression of weight and dignity; but 'repeated perusals of Pindar'[7] conditioned the severity of his own style, starkly focusing the imaginative back-drop of the known world of myth and history. Pindar presides in Landor's odes and addresses, and influences his art of allusion generally, especially in its abrupt changes of subject.

Already, in the first book of 'Gebir', Landor couples the pastoral ambience of Theocritan idyll and Virgilian eclogue with touches of Ovidian pictorialism – the combination which was to infuse the Hellenics (the poems on specifically Greek subjects). In fact, this book is also an example of the 'idyl' which, derived expressly from Theocritus, was to become the dominant form of the narrative Hellenics. Landor developed its heroic and dramatic potential by imitating especially Theocritus's epyllia, or miniature epics, and Homeric interludes or Aeschylan scenes. Another influence on the 'idyl' is Catullus's epyllion on the marriage of Peleus and Thetis; and it is this poet, with his Alexandrine formal miniaturism, cult of erudition and use of peripheral myths (together with his unusually personal element of the 'fervid and tender',[8]) who is most recalled in Landor's shorter lyrics. These lyrics, as the title of the 1806 collection, *Simonidea* (after the Greek poet Simonides), suggests, hark back ultimately in simplicity of theme and form to the *Greek Anthology*. In them Landor also occasionally adopts Horatian patrician attitudes.

The prose influences are more tenuous. A major one is the general tradition of the dialogue, to which Landor's invented form of the Imaginary Conversation has been traced.[9] His interest in concrete settings may be associated with the tradition of the philosophical dialogue, particularly as introduced by Plato and developed by Cicero; and his habit of inserting lengthy poems may be compared with that of Boethius. Similarly, from the didactic dialogue tradition there are suggestions of Xenophon and of Galileo in the blending of conversation and didacticism, and also of Xenophon's *Memorabilia* in the diversity of subject matter. The greatest influence in the discursive Conversations, however, is Cicero, especially in the introduction of memorable historical characters and his aim in expounding a particular point of view. There is also a debt to the tradition of 'Dialogues of the Dead', started by Lucian, and practised by Fénélon, Fontenelle, Lyttleton and Bishop Hurd. It was Hurd, in fact, who introduced the term 'Conversation' to denote this form of imaginative literature. Landor's originality rests on his individual combination of a succinct portrayal of character with a fastidious interest in prose style.

These elements in Landor's imitations are always in solution, and are combined by the general structure of feeling which they have cultivated in Landor himself. There is also an inescapably individualizing correspondence between Landor's derived culture and his personality, whereby his culture is invested with moods, ranging from trained sobriety to tremendous gusto, which it also controls. His epicureanism, for instance, stems from an instinctive enjoyment of the Mediterranean experience of peace, pleasure and fecundity seen as the essence of the European quality of life of the past, and the basis of the post-revolutionary society projected in 'Gebir'.[10] For a time, during his years at the Villa Gherardesca, in Fiesole above Florence, when as romping paterfamilias he was disturbed merely by the small dramas of his children's games and obliged only to tend the garden and orchard where Boccaccio's ladies had lain, refined sensation was the very essence of his daily existence. His works convey a strongly personal but highly organized relish for sharp sensuous pleasure, excited by such various stimulants as mutton chops, buck venison, freshly ripened fruit and unashamed eroticism. In a similar way, the constant theme of the brevity of love is invested with a personal plangency delicately coloured by the frustration of his great passion for 'Ianthe',[11] while at the same time this feeling is soothed by the sense of its conventionality.

There is something temperamentally matter-of-fact also about Landor's underlying stoicism. It merges with the Englishness which, as Mrs Browning suggested, made his dogged empiricism indistinguishable from his attraction to Greek naturalism,[12] of which his admiration for Bacon's preference for 'the palpable, the practical, the orderly',[13] and his contempt for Plato, are equally symptomatic. Such personal and English resonances aided the imaginative process of vernacularization and could even get the upper hand, as Emerson recorded, who found him 'well content to impress, if possible, his English whim upon the immutable past'.[14]

His sense of form is itself a development of philosophical realism:

> Whatever stands must fall; the dust alone
> We trample on rises and keeps its form.[15]

This kind of awareness provides the impetus towards continual redefinition and reconstruction in works of art. His own craft should be seen as a refinement of positivism; and Landor was himself conscious of the thoroughly down-to-earth aspect of his artifices, of their belonging to the world of common sense:

> The business of philosophy is to examine and estimate all those things which come within the cognizance of the understanding. Speculations on any that lie beyond are only pleasant dreams, leaving the mind to the lassitude of disappointment. They are easier

than geometry and dialectics; they are easier than the efforts of a well-regulated imagination in the structure of a poem.[16]

The aim of Landor's unique attempt at the art of imitation was not to extend his tradition, but simply to keep it alive. He tried to sustain the real sense of pleasure and satisfaction which he derived from his experience of past culture, and even a conviction of its political urgency, not dwelling on its pastness in order to berate a contemporary decline in civilization, as the French Parnassians were to do, nor using its effeteness as an exponent of his own world-weariness, as did Dowson and the other poets of the Nineties. His contribution had immediate relevance to the Victorian society for which Arnold advocated in 1853 the classical culture of Goethe and Niebuhr, with its concentration on 'the eternal objects of poetry, among all nations, and at all times'[17] – great actions, noble persons, and intense situations – in his appeal against modernity of theme and introspective self-consciousness.

The ostensible cultural contribution of Landor's classicism was, however, marginal. His sensibility was after all a link with a previous, almost pre-industrial society, as his poignant description of the South Wales coast at the very end of the eighteenth century recalls:

> I lived among woods, which are now killed with copper works, and took my walk over sandy sea-coast deserts, then covered with low roses and thousands of nameless flowers and plants, trodden by the naked feet of the Welsh peasantry, and trackless.[18]

But the effect of his technical discipline on such Victorian poets as Tennyson, Browning and Swinburne, and on modern poets such as Yeats and Pound, was considerable. Further, the economy and irony of dramatization in his imaginary characters contributed significantly to the development of the poetic persona in Browning, Pound and Eliot. The permanent influence of his art of classical imitation lies in the artistic strategies it prompted rather than in the overt ethos it promotes.

## III The Classical Structure of Feeling

The classical structure of feeling which emanates from Landor's works is the result of a world-view inalterably defined for all time; and it seeks, both intuitively and strenuously, for the satisfaction to be derived from an appropriate sense of wholeness and completion.

The Dramatic Scenes and Imaginary Conversations usually revolve around some implicit moment of climax which, occurring either just before or soon after the dialogue, defines conclusively the moral structure of the whole. Even the selection of highly significant junctures at which to set the more discursive Conversations is designed to encapsulate the speakers' personalities and life-histories. Landor chooses, for example, the final prolonged meeting between the dying Pitt and his chosen successor, Canning, and the day before Newton's final examination on which the student consults the tutor to whom he owes so much, but whom he is also about to eclipse intellectually.

Landor's enforcement of this firm sense of organization inhibited the flow of action in his attempts at formal drama, resulting, as he recognized, in a series of separate scenes. His own practice caused him to think that 'intricacy, called plot, undermines the solid structure of well-ordered poetry'.[1] In this way, his most successful play, *Count Julian*, moves along simply as the protracted unfolding of a tragic stance already adopted before the beginning of the action: the admission, that is, of the Moors into Christian Spain as a protest against the outrage of private honour.

Yet the effect he admired and imitated in those Theocritan idylls which represent 'a continuity of action in one graven piece', revealing 'not only what is passing, but also what is past and what is to come',[2] is capable of a wealth of dramatic irony. Compression of this kind can summarize the contradictory course of history, as when the second, third and sixth wives of Henry VIII are all encountered in the King's ride through Richmond Chase, or when the ill-fated Menou pushes himself forward at the end of 'General Kleber and French Officers', or when Hannibal's triumph over Marcellus is seen in the light of his unfulfilled expectation to reach Rome.

A similar tendency to stasis governs Landor's visual imagination. Participation in a conversation naturally requires a pause from action, however bristling with a sealed or imminent fate the dialogue may be; but dramatic Conversations such as 'Marcellus and Hannibal' seem to be conceived almost as sculptural tableaux, with the characters caught in attitudes of heroic assertion, grief or death. Landor was well aware of the rigidness which was the result of the sharp definition of personality he sought, and he remarked: 'My Conversations, whatever their demerits, will exhibit more qualities and postures of the human mind than any other book published in my day'.[3] At their barest, his characters tend to the kind of personification of patterns of feeling which is a favourite type of imagery:

> There is a gloom in deep love, as in deep water: there is a silence in it which suspends the foot, and the folded arms and the dejected head are the images it reflects. (PROSE **35**, p. 196)

Such external characterization is to be found particularly in the narrative idylls; and in the prefatory note to *The Hellenics*, 1847, Landor acknowledged that

> The reader . . . will remember that Sculpture and Painting have never ceased to be occupied with the scenes and figures which we venture once more to introduce in poetry.

His concern in the Hellenics is not to recreate vignettes of immutably

great conceptions from past art, though his own imagination is con-
strained by the recollection of impressive examples:

Show me Achilles in his tent,
And Hector drag'd round Troy, show *me*
Where stood and wailed Andromache;
Her tears through ages still flow on,
Still rages, Peleus, thy stern son. (POETRY **182**, 28–32)

What he attempts is to convey throughout his own poems a similar
culture of integrated feeling and complete expression. He tries to create
with the same structure of feeling as he derives from his originals, but
mostly without the security of their instinctive assurance, and only as
the result of painstaking effort, paring away and scaling down to the
characteristic miniaturism of his favoured epigrams, single dramatic
scenes, and the 'idyl', which he defines as 'a small image of something
greater',[4] urged by the knowledge that 'A diamond not larger than a
pea is more valuable than a mountain of granite'.[5]

Like John Flaxman, whose draughtsmanship Landor greatly
admired, he is interested in outline, achieving thereby designs which
can evoke the resonance of a tradition of feeling, unobscured by the
particularity of detail. This is the kind of transparency he attempts in
his own imagery, and which he defined in the Preface to *The Hellenics*,
1859, claiming his own poetry was 'diaphanous' rather than
'prismatic':

they who look into it may see through. If there be anywhere a few
small air-bubbles, it yet leaves to the clear vision a wide expanse of
varied scenery.

A similar kind of naïvety in the icon-like stiffness, definition of line
and uniformalization of colour masses formed Landor's taste for the
fourteenth and fifteenth-century Italian primitive paintings which he
collected.[6] The effect he sought is seen throughout the colourless,
plastic, and conventionalized imagery of the Hellenics:

In spring we garland him with pointed flowers,
Anemone and crocus and jonquil,
And tender hyacinth in clustering curls;
Then with sweet-breathing mountain strawberry;
Then pear and apple blossom, promising
(If he is good) to bring the fruit full-ripe.[7]

In the prose also, the elaborate metaphors never merge together; they
are used illustratively, while the imagery generally recurs to the defin-
able categories of architecture, nature, body, disease, food and drink,
art and the arts of gardening and agriculture.[8]

On the expression of emotion the neo-classical art of simplification
has a homogeneously deadening effect. As Landor half-views his char-
acters from the outside, so he avoids the direct avowal of his own
experience in the lyrical poetry, shaping it into conformity with essen-

tially impersonal themes of youth and love, old age and death. Pluto's underworld of the living dead – Iphigeneia, Ternissa, Dirce and even Southey – provides a fitting ambience for such muted passions, where 'Thoughts . . . repose within the breast half-dead'. (POETRY **151**, 3) Yet his very reticences articulate the discipline of a moral power with which the human mind confronts tragedy, as in the *single* 'night of memories and of sighs' (POETRY **6**, 7) consecrated to Rose Aylmer, or the restrained irony at the end of 'The Death of Artemidora':

> Her head fell back: and now a loud deep sob
> Swell'd thro' the darken'd chamber; 'twas not hers.
> (POETRY 76, 18–19)

Checking sensations, however, can also awaken subtleties of feeling at a low frequency, especially of a sort of submerged sensuousness, and even eroticism, which tingles with tiny restraints:

> She held one forth,
> Whether for me to look at or to take
> She knew not, nor did I; but taking it
> Would best have solved (and this she felt) her doubt.
> I dared not touch it; for it seemed a part
> Of her own self; fresh, full, the most mature
> Of blossoms, yet a blossom; with a touch
> To fall, and yet unfallen. (POETRY **25**, 53–60)

Even when an image engages Landor's personal interest, as does that of human hair, it is precisely its congruity with the overall tenor of his art which fascinates him. Its ambivalent vitality, organic but incorruptible, lends it a quality, neither quite living nor dead, which associates it with the finely wrought artefact, and so with the transmutation of experience involved generally in his work. His imaginary Milton is struck by the consideration that a lock of black hair from the tomb of a Norman 'should remain unchanged in color and substance when body, bones, and brains had become earth';[9] and the lovely hair of his imaginary Godiva has a kind of erotic vitality, partially derived from Milton's lines on Eve,[10] which both enlivens and is contained by a feel for artifice:

> I wish thou hadst not alighted so hastily and roughly: it hath shaken down a sheaf of thy hair: take heed thou sit not upon it, lest it anguish thee. Well done! it mingleth now sweetly with the cloth of gold upon the saddle, running here and there, as if it had life and faculties and business, and were working thereupon some newer and cunninger device. O my beauteous Eve! there is a Paradise about thee! the world is refreshed as thou movest and breathest on it.
> (PROSE 17, p. 180)

In 'On Seeing a Hair of Lucretia Borgia' it almost comes to stand for the essentializing of a human personality into the condition of an *objet d'art*:

All that remains of thee these plaits unfold,
  Calm hair, meandering in pellucid gold. (POETRY **16**, 3–4)

The inherent sense of form which is evident throughout Landor's work creates a powerful illusion of timelessness, opposing a humanist belief in the weight and order of art to a classical apprehension of Fate, a belief voiced by his imaginary Aspasia: 'The Gods themselves will vanish away before their images'.[11] Timeless forms demand a sense of completeness, which, though it entails a loss of vitality, offers the force of conviction – 'the hard verity of Death swept by the rustling masquerade of Life!'[12] They express a stoical tradition of human resilience only defined, as his imaginary Marcus Cicero asserts, by the finality of death, not effaced by it: 'We cannot conquer fate and necessity, yet we can yield to them in such a manner as to be greater than if we could'.[13] This is the moral implication of Landor's own formalism, as his 'rhyme/Holds up these records in the face of Time'. (POETRY **136**, 29–30)

The achievement of this sort of monumentality necessitates a kind of severity towards the pleasure derived from the felt process of creative experience on which Landor insists:

Both the poet and the painter should acquire facility and frankness; but they must be exercised with discretion; they must be sternly regulated, and in great part suppressed.[14]

Like Dryden, who, Landor writes, 'wrestles with and conquers Time' (POETRY **42**, 62), Landor attempts to arrest the enjoyment of live experience, because it threatens the concentrated awareness which, abstracted from the sequential flux, is capable of objectifying its overall moral scheme.

The encroachment of passing pleasure is as seductive as the instinctive response to music:

Few, when light fingers with sweet voices play
And melodies swell, pause, and melt away,
Mind how at every touch, at every tone,
A spark of life hath glisten'd and hath gone. (POETRY **151**, 7–10)

Landor's ear is as exquisitely conscious of this delicious temptation as is that of his imaginary Fra Filippo Lippi:

A bell warbles the more mellifluously in the air when the sound of the stroke is over, and when another swims out from underneath it, and pants upon the element that gave it birth. (PROSE **18**, p. 184)

But he is conscious that, without a detached sense of organization, 'on every human thing,/ Time sprinkles Lethe's water with his wing' (POETRY **77**, 1–2), and he laments the chaotic originality of contemporary Victorian poets who neglect this concern for the virtue of classicism:

Thought erases thought,

As numerous sheep erase each other's print
When spongy moss they press or sterile sand.
Blades thickly sown want nutriment and droop,
Although the seed be sound, and rich the soil;
Thus healthy-born ideas, bedded close,
By dreaming fondness perish overlain. (POETRY **131**, 28–34)

He is particularly apprehensive of such shapelessness because he feels it represents an attack on the politico-moral dimension of his tradition, which opposes acquiescence in the routine of political oppression, and has

Power to show mortals that the kings they serve
Swallow each other like the shapeless forms
And unsubstantial which pursue pursued
In every drop of water, and devour
Devoured, perpetual round the crystal globe.[15]

The kind of satisfaction Landor strives for in his art is won by the illusion of perfection created by having attempted to fit every part into an achieved whole:

Most have an eye for colour, few for form.
Imperfect is the glory to *create*,
Unless on our creations we can look
And see that all is good; we then may rest. (POETRY **131**, 23–6)

It is an art which, expressing a world-view timeless and omniscient, derives a complicated sense of pleasure from the impression of an overall organization, with which every detail harmonizes, as his imaginary Aesop explains: 'the present, like a note in music, is nothing but as it appertains to what is past and what is to come'. (PROSE **19**, p. 186) The nature of the perfection of an epigram like 'Dirce' lies consequently in the accumulating impressions of the force of each line and line-ending acting out the overall structure of a gradual but irrefutable awareness.

In each individual work Landor appeals finally to the symmetry of a traditional structure of feeling. By making his imaginary Sidney express his own aesthetic in a sixteenth-century setting, he obliquely indicates the added element of traditional assurance behind the realization that art absorbs the simple delights of live experience and transforms them into an incomparably more satisfying complex pleasure:

Do you imagine that any contest of shepherds can afford them the same pleasure as I receive from the description of it; or that even in their loves, however innocent and faithful, they are so free from anxiety as I am when I celebrate them? The exertion of intellectual power, of fancy and imagination, keeps from us greatly more than their wretchedness, and affords us greatly more than their enjoyment. (PROSE **1**, p. 128)

## *IV  The Poetic Style*

Landor's poetry may tend towards the condition of the artefact, but, as his imaginary Aspasia points out, it can never, by definition, achieve it: 'Sculpture and Painting are moments of life; Poetry is life itself, and every thing around it and above it'.[1] His Phocion refers to the powerful 'undersong of sense'[2] which is a feature of the best poetry; and the depth of feeling which Landor himself can elicit derives from a highly organized sense of movement in the verse. Pound noted 'the cantabile quality' of the shorter poems, 'even when they are manifestly *inscribed*';[3] and many of the lighter pieces, such as 'Verse for Ianthe' or 'Am I He?', are indeed quite song-like, in a way which recalls the Caroline poets. Landor occasionally wrote poems in Italian for the sense of ease in composition, before translating them into English; and he admired the harmony of Greek lyric verse, one detail of which he picked out: 'Greek poets more frequently than Latin, gave those (epithets) rather which suited the metre than those which conveyed a peculiar representation'.[4]

Pound also described the sense of firm organization in Landor's verse which he terms its 'hardness', and drew attention to the technical control over detail which accompanies 'an intentness on the quality of the emotion to be conveyed'.[5] Robert Pinsky has pointed out the 'most prominent technique' involved in the blank verse of 'Gebir':

> the careful use of the runover line as a sort of substitute for rhyme. The line-endings function very precisely in lending the lines that force which arises from the play of abstract form upon content.[6]

Similar impressions of shaping characterize Landor's verse throughout. Though Landor's metres are fundamentally traditionalist, they accommodate, as his advice to Southey on the subject indicates, numerous effects of delicate interference which compound this impression of 'hardness':

> Poetry is intended to soothe and flatter our prepossessions, not to wound or irritate or contradict them. We are at liberty to choose the best modifications, we are not at liberty to change or subvert.[7]

In his heroic poetry, he renounced the classical hexameter in favour of English blank verse, which he also used in his idylls and addresses. It suited his kind of effect, because, as his imaginary Milton observes about English metres generally, it is 'infinitely more capable of stops and variations'.[8] In his lyric verse he avoided complicated rhyming stanzas, such as the Spenserian and the sonnet. His favourite form for the short lyric is the alternately rhyming quatrain of octosyllabic lines; and he was also fond of octosyllabic couplets for Apologies and Invitations. Unlike his Latin, his English verse only occasionally seems to offer a version of a classical form, as of the Sapphic-derived stanza in, for example, 'Sedater Pleasures'; and even then such examples are nearer to the countless permutations of what Saintsbury refers to as his 'magisterially applied'[9] experiments with simple quatrain-based metres. Yet within the restriction of these lyrics' shorter line, he attempts to achieve the 'power' of Catullus's hendecasyllabics 'in the expression of passion, in its sudden throbs and changes'.[10] Adjustments on this scale had intensity for Landor who believed that 'Passion can alone give the higher beauties of versification'.[11]

The impression of delicate control in Landor's diction owes something to what Arthur Symons referred to as the 'Latin savour'[12] of the verse. It is especially marked in the blank verse of 'Gebir' and the Hellenics, much of which was translated from Latin into English; but it is a pervasive influence throughout the poetry. A number of elliptical figures, such as anaphora, repetend, polyptuton and chiasmus,[13] contribute to the parataxis typical of an inflected language. The effect is compounded by a series of Landorian manipulations which similarly regulate the metrical flow, such as the omission of the connective 'that', and a meticulous disposition of pauses controlled by stops, ellipses and italicizations. As a comparison between the 1847 and 1859 versions of the Hellenic idyls demonstrates, the life-long process of Landor's revision was directed to the end Forster indicates:

> it had been especially his study, with advancing years, to give more and more of a severe and simple character to all his writing after the antique, and . . . this was exclusively the object, here, of the most part of his changes or additions.[14]

The upshot is often a curious kind of lucidity, involving the articulation of slight personal complexities of thought and feeling which ruffle the smooth fluency of the verse into an unlikely impression of depth. It can be the result, for example, of a simple, liquid parenthesis:

> Alas! my voice and lyre alike he flies,
> And only in my dream, nor kindly then, replies.
> (POETRY **53**, 5–6)

Many of the final lines of Landor's lyrics are gently halting in this way. Italicized emphases can similarly detain a point slightly behind the flow of the verse, as can a hint of sententiousness:

> Of all who pass us in life's drear descent
> We grieve the most for those that wisht to die.[15]

The point being made in such cases has to achieve notice by delaying the onward movement without arresting it.

Another element in Landor's diction is that indicated by his imaginary Milton: 'Antiquated words, used sparingly and characteristically, give often a force and always a gravity, to composition'.[16] Pound diagnosed the added kind of formality it represents when he described the technique of a modern poetess:

> There *is* a slight stiffness or old-fashionedness . . . The language is

still literary ('beholds' and 'wenches' are not live speech). All of which is *very* slight, in the given case, but cumulative . . . and damned hard to escape. Landor's marmoreal???[17]

The artificiality of Landor's style led to the charge of 'mannerism' in his own day, and Landor's reply is a guide to the ways in which he was attempting to fabricate a classical style: 'Whose manner? I resemble none of the ancients, and still less the moderns. My merits, if I have any at all, are variety and simplicity'.[18] Only occasionally does Landor seem to be aiming to create the kind of style Pound terms 'classic', which is based on 'the *least possible* variant that would turn the most worn-out and commonest phrases of journalism into something distinguished'.[19] A poem like 'Hegemon to Praxinoe' shows something of this kind of exclusive approach to 'simplicity'. But the 'simplicity' of Landor's diction, especially the syntax, is usually conveyed in a composite idiom of its own, made up of a 'variety' of imitations of figures and constructions drawn from the common poetic tradition of Latin and English. It is inclusive, but blended. His own idiom, achieved with great editorial effort, is quite unspecific, and can finally be described only as the extraordinary formal organization seen in every detail of his verse. The poetic diction he achieves is far removed from colloquial speech and its power of self-expression; it is a new, highly wrought invention of English classical speech.[20]

Landor's poetic style as a whole is consequently allusive to a traditional structure of feeling; and his art of specific allusion invokes this in two important ways. The Hellenics, for example, are filled with references to the appropriate historical culture of the Greek world in which they are set. They elicit, Landor expects, in the manner of Catullus's learned references, a shared recollection in the mind of the cultivated reader of the myth, history and literary achievement of the supreme cultural experience which informs his own effort in English. In addition, such recognitions evoke the imaginative homogeneity of the Greek world-view – the kind of homogeneity, that is, on which the ability to be allusive relies. His art of allusion is consequently another example of imitation, implying the timelessness and omniscience of the classical structure of feeling.

One technique is the loose combination of a series of overlapping associations to effect the kind of splendid obscurity or imaginative density which he himself compares to the Greek choral poetry of Pindar and Aeschylus,[21] and to Dante.[22] Examples are found in the Chorus of 'The Shades of Agamemnon and Iphigeneia' and at the end of 'Icarios and Erigonè', for instance, where Landor amplifies the legendary power of a little known story by involving it in another allusion to the more memorable imagery of carnage associated with the familiar myth of the Feast of the Lapiths and Centaurs.

Occasionally, though rarely, Landor's use of myth carries overtones of his personal psychology, as at the end of 'To My Child Carlino', where he alludes to the Calypso myth of the promise of eternal youth to convey his own wistful sense of the loss of irresponsibility. More commonly he drew on the kind of typological potential he admired in, for instance, Ariosto's description of the palace of Atlantes which he considered 'a wonderful type of the French revolution'.[23] In this way he analyses the evocative power of place-names in the ancient world, like Corinth and Chios, generalizing their associations around some pattern of feeling in which they merge with the urgency of contemporary politics, and thereby redeems the contemporary political reference from mere topicality.[24]

The art of allusion depends on names which arouse memory, 'The mother of the Muses' (POETRY **164**, 1):

> Unconsciously I spoke the name
> And verses in full chorus came.[25]

The succinctness of a name makes it the most precise expression of a classical art in which paradoxically an impersonal structure of feeling is the final implication – in which, as Landor writes, 'The name is graven on the workmanship'. (POETRY **131**, 59) The life of an old name results from its having become synonymous with recognizable configurations of feeling. Otherwise, as Landor insists, it must die out of memory, so as not to obscure the definition of a permanent tradition: 'The monument of the greatest man should be only a bust and a name. If the name alone is insufficient to illustrate the bust, let them both perish'.[26] When such synonymity has been achieved, a name becomes unassailable, and Landor scorns even Catullus's attempt to threaten this kind of survival in his 'In Caesarem'.

The same configurations of feeling, Landor believed, can bestow life on new names, and he accordingly rechristened his own loves 'Iöne' and 'Ianthe' to include them in a conventionality which, he suggests, promises them a version of immortality. Though the name of a dear friend evokes a depth of private reminiscence which makes Landor sympathetic to Petrarch's playing on the name of Laura, because 'there is a true and a pardonable pleasure in cherishing the very sound of what we love',[27] there is a poignancy about the realization that it is precisely the degree of subjectivity involved in the intimate associations of a cherished name which makes the possibility of its survival so fragile, as his imaginary Aesop hints: 'there is no name, with whatever emphasis of passionate love repeated, of which the echo is not faint at last'. (PROSE **19**, p. 186) Landor came nearest to achieving the objectivization of such powerfully personal associations when he revised what became his most finished lyric, 'Ah what avails the sceptred race'. He found the most perfect expression of his kind of art in simply writing the full name, '*Rose* Aylmer', at the beginning of the central fourth and fifth lines, so that it seems to affect the formal implications of the whole poem. The inclusion of the first name, Rose, previously omitted, adds a faintly touching individuality to the poem's overall effort at memorial impersonalization.

## V   The Imaginary Characters

Landor told Browning that in the prose works he found 'more room'[1] than in his poetry. Indeed, he increasingly allowed them to sprawl, according to the easy-going format indicated by his imaginary Milton, who remarks that 'In conversation, as in the country, variety is pleasant and expected',[2] and by his imaginary Marcus Cicero who approves of the dialogue because of 'the facility of turning the cycle of our thoughts to what aspect we wish, as geometers and astronomers the globe'.[3] Writing in prose, Landor naturally tended to relax the effort at tightness of control which is integral to the nature of his poetic style. The major result is, as he also told Browning, that he became 'more of a dramatist in prose than in poetry'.[4]

Landor often practises, in Coleridge's term, 'a sort of ventriloquism',[5] through what his imaginary Diogenes, speaking of Plato's use of Socrates in his Dialogues, calls the 'wide-mouthed mask'[6] of a character, in order to give vent quite inappropriately to his own private hobby-horses of a political, legal, religious or much more trivial nature. Some Conversations become little more than extended essays, and Landor is able symptomatically to transfer speeches from one character to another without any impression of misrepresentation.[7] Yet his creative interest in some of his characters in the Imaginary Conversations and longer works does lead him out of himself, and half-emancipates them from his usually strict control.

Southey referred to the process involved in Landor's dramatic characterization as one of 'consubstantiating',[8] and the term happily conveys the two-way modification which takes place. Landor himself described the method in a letter to Southey describing the composition of *Count Julian*:

> My hours were four or five together, after long walks, in which I brought before me the various characters, the very tones of their voices, their forms, complexions, and step. In the daytime I laboured and at night unburdened my mind, shedding many tears.[9]

It is clear that this kind of sympathetic identification requires both a projection outwards into a variety of other personalities conditioned by other times and countries, and the assimilation of them into the author's own organizing structure of feeling. The tendency towards incorporation of characters, when it is not opposed, pulls them into the kind of frozen stasis desired by Landor's imaginary Dante, who feels that his ability to evoke the same memories as Beatrice, merging her mind with his, gives him a sense of timeless possession:

> Oh! could my thoughts incessantly and eternally dwell among these

recollections, undisturbed by any other voice, – undisturbed by any other presence![10]

Landor's characterization generally is weakened by his refusal to confront the recalcitrance of historical fact. His attitude is that voiced by his imaginary Epicurus, that 'All history is fabulous'.[11] Finding in the preparation for the composition of *Pericles and Aspasia* that 'Few materials are extant', he rejoices that he can give free rein to his own imagination: 'The coast is clear'.[12] There is consequently a tendency to simplify characters towards the condition of archetypes, as Landor's approach to the question in *Count Julian* indicates: 'I will cut all my figures out of one block, under one conception of their characters'.[13] In this way his dramatic characterization becomes an extension of the neo-classical invention which rules all his art, seeking to identify patterns of similarity through the vast range of his varied material.

The sense of characters being used as the orchestration of central concepts was a conscious element in Landor's shaping of the Conversations. He wrote quite plainly that

> Principles and ideas are my objects: they must be reflected from high and low, but they must also be exhibited where people can see them best, and are most inclined to look at them.[14]

Landor doubtless took his brief for the propagandizing of his own pet opinions in the more discursive Conversations from this determination; but the idealization of language and personality is itself intended to subserve the moral design inherent in the structure of the dramatic Conversations. In this way, a sublime structure of feeling informs a Conversation like 'Marcellus and Hannibal', where a shared sense of greatness emerges from an encounter between enemies; and a feeling of intense pathos is intended to imbue the melodramatic oppositions of blood-thirsty tyrants and their martyred victims, as in 'Henry VIII and Anne Boleyn' or 'Peter the Great and Alexis'.

His most interesting characters, however, escape this sense of systematization, and he shows in them an uninhibited delight in the investigation of human personality which is reflected in his eighteenth-century relish for anecdotalism, in his curiosity about local colour and personages in *Citation and Examination of William Shakspeare*, and in his enjoyment of sheer gossip in *The Pentameron*.

His creative delight is most evident in the conception of self-revealing villains of a sort similar to those Browning was to develop in the dramatic monologue, when he established it as a medium in which an absorbing display of human character relativizes moral judgement.[15] Characters like Landor's Pope Leo XII, chatting with his valet, Gigi, or William Pitt the younger, expounding his cynical approach to statecraft, give themselves unblushingly away in a manner which is fascinating, and which may even attract sympathetic engagement on the reader's part. The connection between Landor's tentative 'negative capability'[16] and Browning's method in the dramatic monologues is best gauged by a comparison of Landor's Fra Filippo Lippi (his most charming extension of creative sympathy to moral imperfection) with Browning's similar, though more explicit treatment.[17]

Certain imaginary characters, of course, such as Phocion, Diogenes and Anaxagoras, are bold projections of recognizably Landorian traits, and carry an overt sense of sympathetic identification. Even monsters of egotism, however, such as his Henry VIII, drunkenly abusing the wife he is about to have beheaded, or his Peter the Great, complaining of an empty stomach when he hears of the death of the son he has denounced, are grimly humorous in their egregiousness, and seem sometimes to escape the critical irony with which Landor intends to present them. Certainly, the positive interest which their defects provoke creates an impression of psychological complexity, rather than of caricature.

In the process of succinct characterization, the economy of implication which is a key feature of Landor's neo-classical art has become almost detached from its specific cultural overtones. Of course, his writings do offer the encyclopedic view of European culture and do convey the impression of its ethos which prompted Pound's assertion: 'A set of Landor's collected works will go further towards civilizing a man than any university education now on the market'.[18] The moral dimension of that ethos inheres even in the very fashioning of the prose, most obviously in the control involved in what Nietzsche, accounting for Landor's 'mastership in prose', termed the 'polite warfare with poetry'[19] of its most artificial style. But as his poetic art of imitation contributed to a continuing, but increasingly independent sense of formalism, so his art of characterization pointed towards the irreducible ironies of personality developed by modern poets in the poetic persona. These are the skills, the product of irritable sensitivity and awesome single-mindedness, which ensure Landor's permanence.

# Life and Publications

1775 Walter Savage Landor born at Warwick, January 30; eldest son of Walter Landor, physician, by his second wife, Elizabeth Savage.

1783 Boarder at Rugby School. Removed for rebelliousness, 1791.

1785 His early mentor, Samuel Parr, takes up his curacy near Warwick.

1792 Pupil of Revd William Langley near Ashbourne, Derbyshire. Matriculated at Trinity College, Oxford.

1793 Undergraduate from January. Begins love affair with Nancy Jones ('Iöne') at Tenby, South Wales.

1794 Rusticated from Trinity in June for prevarication over shooting incident. Quarrels with his father. Goes to London; studies French, Italian and Greek.

1795 His first publication, *The Poems of Walter Savage Landor*; also *Moral Epistle, Respectfully Dedicated to Earl Stanhope*. Financial arrangement with his father. Returns to South Wales.

1796 Meets Rose Aylmer at Swansea.

1797 *To the Burgesses of Warwick*. Mostly between Warwick and London till end of 1800.

1798 *Gebir; A Poem, in Seven Books* (2nd edition, 1803).

1800 *Poems from the Arabic and Persian*.

1801 Attempts anti-Pittite journalism. Between London, Oxford and Warwick.

1802 In love with Jane Sophia Swift ('Ianthe') at Bath in spring. Visits Paris after the Peace of Amiens. *Poetry by the Author of Gebir* (printed 1800) published. *Iambi* (anonymous Latin poems) probably published this year.

1803 *Gebirus*, Latin version of *Gebir*. In fashionable circles, mostly at Bath, till marriage, 1811.

1805 Death of father. Succeeds to Landor estates at Rugeley, Staffordshire.

1806 *Simonidea*.

1808 Buys Llanthony Abbey, Monmouthshire. Meets Southey at Bristol. Goes to Corunna to aid the Spanish revolt against Napoleon.

1809 *Three Letters, Written in Spain, to Don Francisco Riquelme*.

1810 'Hints to a Junta' and 'Letter to Sir Francis Burdett', written but not published. *Ode ad Gustavum Regem. Ode ad Gustavum Exulem.*

1811 Meets (January) and marries (May) Julia Thuillier at Bath. Takes up residence at Llanthony.

1812 *Count Julian: A Tragedy*; *Commentary on Memoirs of Mr Fox* (printed but suppressed; 2nd edition, 1907); *Address to the Freeholders of Monmouthshire.*

1813 Leaves Llanthony for Swansea, harassed by lawsuits and debts.

1814 *Letters Addressed to Lord Liverpool, and the Parliament, on the Preliminaries of Peace,* under pseudonym 'Calvus'. *Letter from Mr Landor to Mr Jervis.* Leaves England for France, separating from his wife after a quarrel in Jersey.

1815 *Idyllia Nova Quinque Heroum atque Heroidum.* Rejoined by wife at Tours. Moves to Como, Italy. Visited there by Southey.

1818 Birth of first child, Arnold. Moves to Albaro, near Genoa, and then to Pisa.

1819 *Sponsalia Polyxenae,* a Latin idyll.

1820 Birth of only daughter, Julia. *Idyllia Heroica Decem.*

1821 *Poche Osservazioni* (orations against the Holy Alliance). Moves to Florence. Begins sustained writing of Imaginary Conversations.

1822 Birth of second son, Walter.

1823 First Conversation 'Southey and Porson' appears in *London Magazine,* July.

1824 *Imaginary Conversations of Literary Men and Statesmen,* 2 vols., (2nd edition, 1826).

1825 Birth of third and last son, Charles.

1828 *Imaginary Conversations of Literary Men and Statesmen,* vol. 3.

1829 *Imaginary Conversations of Literary Men and Statesmen,* Second Series, 2 vols. Settles in Villa Gherardesca at Fiesole, above Florence. Death of mother. Twice-widowed 'Ianthe' visits Florence.

1830 Meets Crabb Robinson.

1831 *Gebir, Count Julian, and Other Poems.*

1832 Revisits England, May–October. Meets Wordsworth with whom he had corresponded intermittently since 1820. Visits Southey. Meets Charles and Mary Lamb, also Coleridge.

1833 Visited by Emerson at Fiesole.

1834 *Citation and Examination of William Shakspeare.*

1835 Leaves wife and children at Fiesole after break-down of marriage. Returns to England.

1836 *Pericles and Aspasia,* 2 vols.; *Letters of a Conservative.* Meets Browning, Forster and Elizabeth Barrett. Visits Germany, July–October. *Terry Hogan, An Eclogue*; *A Satire on Satirists, and Admonition to Detractors.*

1837 *High and Low Life in Italy* in *Monthly Repository,* August–April

1838. Settles at Bath for next twenty-one years. *The Pentameron and Pentalogia.*

1839 *Andrea of Hungary, and Giovanna of Naples.*

1840 Meets Tennyson. Becomes friendly with Dickens. *Fra Rupert.*

1842 Contributions to *Foreign Quarterly Review* (also 1843) and to *Blackwood's Edinburgh Magazine* (also 1843).

1843 Death of Southey.

1845 'To Robert Browning' in *Morning Chronicle*, November 22.

1846 *The Works of Walter Savage Landor*, 2 vols.

1847 *Poemata et Inscriptiones* (collected Latin verse and prose); *The Hellenics of Walter Savage Landor* (new edition, enlarged, 1859).

1848 *The Italics of Walter Savage Landor; Savagius Landor Lamartino*, a Latin ode; *Imaginary Conversation of King Carlo-Alberto and the Duchess Belgioioso, on the Affairs and Prospects of Italy; Carmen ad Heroinam* (to Duchess Belgioioso), a Latin ode.

1849 *Epistola ad Pium IX Pontificem; Epistola ad Romanos; Ad Cossuthum et Bemum*, a Latin leaflet containing two poems; *Statement of Occurrences at Llanbedr;* 'To the Author of *Festus* on the Classick and Romantick' in *Examiner*, December 29.

1850 *Two Poems* (attacking J. G. Lockhart, editor of *Quarterly Review*).

1851 *Five Scenes* (on Beatrice Cenci) in *Fraser's Magazine*, January. *Popery: British and Foreign.* Death of 'Ianthe' at Versailles. *On Kossuth's Voyage to America; Tyrannicide.*

1852 *Two Poems* ('On Mrs Southey's Pension' and 'Paraphrase of Horace's Pyrrha').

1853 *Imaginary Conversations of Greeks and Romans; The Last Fruit off an Old Tree.*

1854 *Letters of an American, mainly on Russia and Revolution.*

1855 Letters in *Atlas.*

1856 *Antony and Octavius. Scenes for the Study.* Imaginary Conversations, 'Alfieri and Metastasio' and 'Menander and Epicurus', in *Fraser's Magazine*, April. *Letter from W. S. Landor to R. W. Emerson.* Becomes involved with Geraldine Hooper and Mrs Yescombe. *Selections from the Writings of Walter Savage Landor*, Boston, ed. G. S. Hillard.

1857 Suspects defraudment by Mrs Yescombe. *Walter Savage Landor and the Honourable Mrs Yescombe; Mr Landor Threatened* (2nd edition, same year).

1858 *Dry Sticks, Fagoted by Walter Savage Landor*, including verses leading to a libel writ from Mrs Yescombe issued December 1857. Leaves for Italy before case is won by Mrs Yescombe. At Fiesole.

1859 *Mr Landor's Remarks on a Suit Preferred against Him, at the Summer Assizes in Taunton.* Leaves family villa. Helped by Browning, becomes house-guest of friends; then takes cottage at Marciano, near Siena; then rents house in Florence.

1860 *Savonarola e Il Priore di San Marco.*
1862 *Letters of a Canadian.*
1863 *Heroic Idyls, with Additional Poems.*
1864 Visited by Swinburne, March. Dies at Florence on September 17, aged 89. Buried there in the Protestant Cemetery.

# Principal Editions of Landor

With the assistance of John Forster, Landor prepared a collected edition of his English writings, *The Works of Walter Savage Landor*, 2 vols., London, 1846. *The Hellenics of Walter Savage Landor*, London, 1847, and *Imaginary Conversations of Greeks and Romans*, London, 1853, contain both new works and works previously published. In *The Last Fruit off an Old Tree*, London, 1853, he assembled prose and poetry nearly all of which had been written since the collected edition of 1846. These five volumes present the final revisions of the writings not reprinted in subsequent editions.

He produced four more important volumes of poetry: *Antony and Octavius. Scenes for the Study*, London, 1856, *Dry Sticks, Fagoted by Walter Savage Landor*, Edinburgh, 1858, *The Hellenics of Walter Savage Landor*, new edition, enlarged, Edinburgh, 1859 (which contains new poems and translations of his own Latin originals so different from the previous ones in the first edition of 1847 as to represent new works) and *Heroic Idyls, with Additional Poems*, London, 1863.

His considerable Latin writings (never reprinted) are almost all to be found in the collected edition, *Poemata et Inscriptiones*, London, 1847, and at the end of the volumes *Dry Sticks*, *The Hellenics*, 1859, and *Heroic Idyls*.

The first posthumous collected edition, *The Works and Life of Walter Savage Landor*, 8 vols., London, 1876, was edited by Forster. It is badly incomplete, the texts are uncollated and it is unannotated. Charles G. Crump produced the first scholarly editions in *Imaginary Conversations*, 6 vols., London, 1891; *Poems, Dialogues in Verse, and Epigrams by Walter Savage Landor*, 2 vols., London, 1892; and *The Longer Prose Works of Walter Savage Landor*, 2 vols., London, 1892–3. *Poems* offers only a selection of the poetry and very little annotation, and *The Longer Prose Works* omits many of Landor's longer pieces. Nevertheless, the eight volumes of prose, including pieces omitted by Forster, indicating main variants, and providing introductory notes and a general index, are still the most reliable editions of the collected prose.

*The Complete Works of Walter Savage Landor*, 16 vols., London, 1927–36, is the work of two distinct editors. Vols. 1–12, covering the prose, are edited by T. Earle Welby. Pieces not previously collected are included (as well as the spurious 'John Dryden and Henry Purcell') but variants are unreliably and inconsistently recorded, and there are almost no notes and no index. These volumes also reinstituted a

wrong-headed principle of artificial classification for the Imaginary
Conversations, begun by Forster and Crump, based in this case on
historical chronology and nationality.

Vols. 13–16 (republished as *The Poetical Works of Walter Savage Landor*,
3 vols., Oxford, 1937) contain the collected poems edited by Stephen
Wheeler. They indicate most variants and are well annotated and
indexed, providing the accepted standard text for the poetry. The
defects are editorial over-classification and the suspect decision to
present almost always the first published versions, printing the in-
tended authorial revisions as footnotes to the main texts.

The most important supplements to the Landor corpus are *Charles
James Fox: A Commentary on his Life and Character*, 2nd edition, London,
1907, edited by Stephen Wheeler; and the 'Three Unpublished "Im-
aginary Conversations" by Walter Savage Landor', published by M.
F. Ashley-Montagu in *Nineteenth Century and After*, CVII (1930), 837–
45.

Landor's correspondence remains uncollected. The most substantial
selections are in John Forster, *Walter Savage Landor: a biography*, 2 vols.,
London., 1869; Stephen Wheeler, *Letters and Other Unpublished Writings
of Landor*, London, 1897, and *Letters of Walter Savage Landor, Private and
Public*, London, 1899; H. C. Minchin, *Walter Savage Landor: Last Days,
Letters and Conversations*, London, 1934; R. H. Super, 'Landor's Letters
to Wordsworth and Coleridge', *Modern Philology*, LV (1957), 73–83; A.
Lavonne Ruoff and Edwin Burton Levine, 'Landor's Letters to the
Reverend Walter Birch', *Bulletin of the John Rylands Library*, LI (1968),
200–61; A. Lavonne Ruoff, 'Landor's Letters to His Family: 1802–25',
*Bulletin of the John Rylands Library*, LIII (1971), 465–500, and 'Landor's
Letters to His Family: 1826–29', *Bulletin of the John Rylands Library*,
LIV (1972), 398–433; John F. Mariani, 'The Letters of Walter Savage
Landor to Marguerite Countess of Blessington', unpublished Ph.D.
dissertation, Columbia University, 1973; A. Lavonne Ruoff, 'Walter
Savage Landor's Letters to His Family, 1830–1832', *Bulletin of the John
Rylands Library*, LVIII (1976), 467–507.

The most valuable selections of Landor's writings are: *Selections from
the Writings of Landor*, ed. Sidney Colvin (Golden Treasury Series)
London, 1882; *Imaginary Conversations: a selection*, ed. E. de Selincourt
(World's Classics) Oxford, 1914; *The Shorter Poems of Walter Savage
Landor*, ed., J. B. Sidgwick, Cambridge, 1946; *Landor, Poetry and Prose*,
ed. E. K. Chambers, Oxford, 1946; *Landor: a biographical anthology*, ed.
H. van Thal, with an introduction by Malcolm Elwin, London, 1973.

The most comprehensive modern selection of the poetry is *Poems by
Walter Savage Landor*, London, 1964, edited by Geoffrey Grigson. It
lacks, however, several of the most celebrated pieces, and prints poems
arbitrarily in order of composition, first appearance, or book publi-
cation. It offers no variants (so that substantial revisions are sometimes
printed without indication) and almost no notes.

Selections from the prose have been exhaustively edited and generously annotated in Alice Lavonne Prasher's 'Walter Savage Landor's *Imaginary Conversations*: A Critical Edition of the First Eight Conversations in Volume One', unpublished Ph.D. dissertation, Northwestern University, 1966; Charles L. Proudfit, *Selected Imaginary Conversations of Literary Men and Statesmen by Walter Savage Landor*, Lincoln, Nebraska, 1969, which comprises seven full-length Conversations from the Second Series, 1829; and Charles L. Proudfit, *Landor as Critic*, London, 1979, which contains extracts from prose commentaries, letters, Imaginary Conversations, reviews and poems which exemplify Landor's literary criticism.

# Note on This Edition

The guiding aim of this selection is to put Landor back into print in a way which suggests something of the diversity of his achievement in both poetry and prose, while respecting his rightful, if sometimes pernickety, concern to provide texts representing as far as possible his final intentions.

Landor published books unflaggingly over a period of sixty-eight years, principally in English and Latin, but also in Italian; and he belongs to the group of writers, like Milton and Hardy, unusual for its equal accomplishment in poetry and prose. In a small anthology, such variety calls for clear-cut arrangement and implies enormous gaps.

I have confined selections to the works in English, and have completely separated the poetry and the prose. Within these divisions, the poems are printed in the order of their first published appearance, and in their original order within those publications; the prose is printed in the order of first *book* publication, except that the Imaginary Conversations are grouped together as a coherent unit, so that the later Conversations of 1846 precede excerpts from books published before them. Chronology of publication, as has been authoritatively pointed out,[1] is the only principle of arrangement endorsed by Landor's own practice in the collected edition of 1846.

The particulars of those few instances when Imaginary Conversations were published separately prior to book publication are given in the Notes, as are dates of composition for all items of poetry and prose when they are known to differ materially from those of first publication.

The text of both poetry and prose is the last printed in the author's lifetime, and so incorporates whatever can be assumed to be Landor's final intention as regards his substantive readings. The only exceptions are the excerpts from Landor's earliest important work 'Gebir', which I print according to the second, revised edition of 1803, the corrected version of the form in which it made its contemporary impact on the first generation of English Romantic writers; and the 1847 and 1859 translations of the same originally Latin *Heroica Idyllia*, which I print in one version or the other as separate poems.

The principle behind the text reflects the nature of Landor's art of which the life-long condensing and polishing in the poetry and the process of amplification in the Imaginary Conversations are integral features. All additions and significant earlier versions are indicated in the Notes.

The majority of later revisions involve changes of spelling. Landor had decided, if whimsical, opinions on this subject, reflecting his general concern for linguistic hygiene.[2] Since Forster persuaded Landor to allow him in the collected edition of 1846 to normalize nearly all the words previously spelled idiosyncratically, and since the exceptional forms (more common in the later volumes) are perfectly intelligible, I let all final spellings stand. It might be argued that such eccentricities influence the chiselled 'hardness' of the verse especially.[3]

I retain the final titles Landor gives his poems, or the latest, when he subsequently omits them.[4] I provide titles, in square brackets, for untitled poems. Line numeration and the uniform capitalization of all first words are also editorial. Omissions within the prose extracts are indicated by ellipses and by line-spacing whenever considerable excisions are made.[5]

In making my selections I have kept an eye on the established preferences of a long tradition of anthologies, as well as trying to convey my own sense of Landor's scope. The prose must obviously be the severer casualty in such a process of extraction. Regrettably, only 'General Kleber and French Officers' and 'Marcellus and Hannibal' of the Imaginary Conversations are printed in full. They are short, and have respectively an anecdotal and dramatic unity missing in the longer, meandering kind of Conversation, which I hope the lengthy extract from 'Barrow and Newton' may illustrate. Charles L. Proudfit's recent *Landor as Critic* has reprinted several extracts from Landor's literary criticism which I had intended to include, especially the review 'Francesco Petrarca'. The availability of Landor's most important critical writings in that selection has enabled me to concentrate on his creative prose, touching on the criticism only as it crops up in the course of Imaginary Conversations or longer works.

Landor's writings are crammed with allusions: much of his art depends on them, no less when he is being deliberately obscure. The Notes at the end of the volume are intended to increase the reader's understanding and enjoyment of this art, elucidating references and contexts both overt and implicit.

Readers may wish to pursue some of the points raised in my Introduction in the works listed in the Selected Bibliography.

An index of the first lines and titles of the poetry and an index of the persons referred to in the prose are appended.

[1] Cf. R. H. Super, 'Walter Savage Landor', in *The English Romantic Poets and Essayists*, ed. C. W. Houtchens and J. E. Jordan, New York, 1957, p. 234.

[2] Cf. Charles L. Proudfit, 'Landor's Hobby-horse: A Study in Romantic Orthography', *Studies in Romanticism*, VII (1968), 207–17.

[3] For instance, the spellings he invents to avoid the diphthong ('highths', 'honorable' etc.), and the Miltonic past participles of weak verbs with a final 't'.

[4] The only exceptions are 'To Psyche', 'One Year Ago' and 'Pentheusa: from Myrtis'.

[5] As practised by Charles L. Proudfit in *Landor as Critic*, London, 1979.

*The Poetry*

## from THE POEMS OF WALTER SAVAGE LANDOR (1795)

**1      INVOCATION TO THE MUSE**

>      T HO ' Helicon! I seldom dream
> Aside thy lively limpid stream,
> Nor glory that to me belong
> Or elegance, or nerve of Song,
> Or Hayley's easy-ambling horse,
> Or Peter Pindar's comic force,
> Or Mason's fine majestic flow,
> Or aught that pleases one in Crowe—
> Yet thus a *saucy-suppliant* bard!
> .I court the Muse's kind regard.                         10
> 'O! whether, Muse! thou please to give
> My humble verses long to live;
> Or tell me *The decrees of Fate*
> *Have order'd them a shorter date—*
> I bow: yet O! may every word
> Survive, however, George III.


## from GEBIR (1798)

**2      BOOK I**

> GEBIR, his habitation and habits. Alarms of *Charoba*—imparted to *Dalica—Dalica's* reply. The Queen's expostulation, and compliance —her interview with *Gebir. Gebir* returning, meets his brother *Tamar* —*Tamar* describes his wrestling with a Nymph. *Her* victory, and promise. *His* regret and shame. *Gebir's* sympathy—his determination to remain in *Egypt*, and to restore the city which *Sidad*, his ancestor, had founded.

> WHEN old Silenus call'd the Satyrs home,
> Satyrs then tender-hooft and ruddy-horn'd,
> With Bacchus and the Nymphs, he sometimes rose
> Amidst the tale of pastoral, and shew'd
> The light of purest wisdom; and the God
> Scatter'd with wholesome fruit the pleasant plains.
>       Ye woody vales of Cambria! and ye hills
> That hide in heaven your summits and your fame!
> Your ancient songs, and breezes pure, invite
> Me from my noon-tide rambles, and the force          10
> Of high example influences my lay.
>       I sing the fates of Gebir! how he dwelt
> Among those mountain-caverns, which retain

His labours yet, vast halls, and flowing wells,
Nor have forgotten their old master's name,
Though sever'd from his people: how, incens'd
By meditating on primeval wrongs,
He blew his battle-horn, at which uprose
Whole nations: how, ten thousand, mightiest men,
He call'd aloud; and soon Charoba saw                           20
His dark helm hover o'er the land of Nile.
      What should the damsel do? should royal knees
Bend suppliant? or defenceless hands engage
Men of gigantic force, gigantic arms?
For, 'twas reported, that nor sword sufficed,
Nor shield immense, nor coat of massive mail;
But, that upon their tow'ring heads they bore
Each a huge stone, refulgent as the stars.
This told she Dalica—then earnest cried
'If, on your bosom laying down my head,                         30
I sobb'd away the sorrows of a child;
If I have always, and Heav'n knows I have,
Next to a mother's held a nurse's name,
Succour this one distress! recall those days;
Love me; though 'twere because you lov'd me then.'
      But, whether confident in magic rites;
Or touch'd with sexual pride to stand implored,
Dalica smiled; then spake: 'Away those fears.
Tho' stronger than the strongest of his kind,
He falls; on me devolve that charge; he falls.                 40
Rather than fly him, stoop thou to allure,
Nay, journey to his tents: a city stood
Upon that coast, they say, by Sidad built,
Whose father Gad built Gades; on this ground
Perhaps he sees an ample room for war.
Persuade him to restore the walls himself,
In honor of his ancestors, persuade—
But wherefor this advice? young, unespoused,
Charoba want persuasions! and a queen!'
      'O Dalica!' the shudd'ring maid exclaim'd,                50
'Could I encounter that fierce frightful man?
Could I speak? no, nor sigh!' 'And canst thou reign?'
Cried Dalica; 'yield empire or comply.'
      Unfixt, though seeming fixt, her eyes down-cast,
The wonted buz and bustle of the court
From far, through sculptur'd galleries, met her ear;
Then lifting up her head, the evening sun
Pour'd a fresh splendor on her burnish'd throne,—
The fair Charoba, the young queen, complied.
      But Gebir, when he heard of her approach,                 60

Laid by his orbed shield, his vizor-helm,
His buckler and his corslet he laid by,
And bade that none attend him: at his side
Two faithful dogs that urge the silent course,
Shaggy, deep-chested, crouched: the crocodile,
Crying, oft made them raise their flaccid ears,
And push their heads within their master's hand.
There was a bright'ning paleness in his face,
Such as Diana rising o'er the rocks
Shower'd on the lonely Latmian; on his brow                        70
Sorrow there was, yet nought was there severe.
But when the royal damsel first he saw,
Faint, hanging on her handmaids, and her knees
Tott'ring, as from the motion of the car,
His eyes looked earnest on her; and those eyes
Shew'd, if they had not, that they might have lov'd,
For there was pity in them at that hour.
With gentle speech, and more, with gentle looks,
He sooth'd her; but, lest Pity go beyond,
And crost Ambition lose her lofty aim,                             80
Bending, he kiss'd her garment, and retir'd.
He went: nor slumber'd in the sultry noon,
When viands rich, and generous wines persuade,
And slumber most refreshes; nor at night,
When heavy dews are laden with disease;
And blindness waits not there for lingering age.
Ere morning dawn'd behind him, he arrived
At those rich meadows where young Tamar fed
The royal flocks, entrusted to his care.
Now, said he to himself, will I repose                             90
At least this burden on a brother's breast:
His brother stood before him: he, amaz'd,
Rear'd suddenly his head, and thus began.
'Is it thou, brother! Tamar, is it thou!
Why, standing on the valley's utmost verge,
Lookest thou on that dull and dreary shore
Where many a league Nile blackens all the sand.
And why that sadness? when I passed our sheep
The dew-drops were not shaken off the bar,
Therefor if one be wanting 'tis untold.'                          100
    'Yes! one is wanting, nor is that untold,'
Said Tamar, 'and this dull and dreary shore
Is neither dull nor dreary at all hours.'
Whereon, the tear stole silent down his cheek.
Silent, but not by Gebir unobserv'd:
Wondering he gazed awhile, and pitying spake:—
'Let me approach thee: does the morning light

Scatter this wan suffusion o'er thy brow,
This faint blue lustre under both thine eyes?'
'O, brother, is this pity or reproach,'                                110
Cried Tamar,—'cruel if it be reproach,
If pity—O how vain!'
               'Whate'er it be
That grieves thee, I will pity; thou but speak,
And I can tell thee, Tamar, pang for pang.'
    'Gebir! then more than brothers are we now!
Every thing—take my hand—will I confess.
I neither feed the flock, nor watch the fold;
How can I, lost in love? But, Gebir, why
That anger which has risen in your cheek?
Can other men? Could you? What, no reply!                              120
And still more anger, and still worse conceal'd!
Are these your promises, your pity this?'
    'Tamar, I well may pity what I feel—
Mark me aright—I feel for thee—proceed—
Relate me all.' 'Then will I all relate.'
Said the young shepherd, gladden'd from his heart.
''Twas evening, though not sun-set, and spring-tide
Level with these green meadows, seem'd still higher;
'Twas pleasant: and I loosen'd from my neck
The pipe you gave me, and began to play.                               130
O that I ne'er had learnt the tuneful art!
It always brings us enemies or love!
Well, I was playing—when above the waves
Some swimmer's head methought I saw ascend;
I, sitting still, survey'd it, with my pipe
Awkwardly held before my lips half-clos'd.
Gebir! it was a nymph! a nymph divine!
I cannot wait describing how she came,
How I was sitting, how she first assum'd
The sailor: of what happened, there remains                            140
Enough to say, and too much to forget.
The sweet deceiver stept upon this bank
Before I was aware; for, with surprize
Moments fly rapid as with love itself.
Stooping to tune afresh the hoarsen'd reed,
I heard a rustling; and where that arose
My glance first lighted on her nimble feet.
Her feet resembled those long shells explored
By him who to befriend his steeds' dim sight
Would blow the pungent powder in their eye.—                           150
Her eyes too! O immortal Gods! her eyes
Resembled—what could they resemble—what
Ever resemble those! E'en her attire

Was not of wonted woof nor vulgar art:
Her mantle shew'd the yellow samphire-pod,
Her girdle, the dove-color'd wave serene.
'Shepherd,' said she, 'and will you wrestle now,
And with the sailor's hardier race engage?'
I was rejoiced to hear it, and contrived
How to keep up contention;—could I fail                            160
By pressing not too strongly, still to press.
'Whether a shepherd, as indeed you seem,
Or whether of the hardier race you boast,
I am not daunted, no: I will engage.'
'But first,' said she, 'what wager will you lay?'
'A sheep,' I answered, 'add whate'er you will.'
'I cannot,' she replied, 'make that return:
Our hided vessels, in their pitchy round,
Seldom, unless from rapine, hold a sheep.
But I have sinuous shells, of pearly hue                           170
Within, and they that lustre have imbibed
In the sun's palace porch; where, when unyoked,
His chariot wheel stands midway in the wave.
Shake one, and it awakens; then apply
Its polished lips to your attentive ear,
And it remembers its august abodes,
And murmurs as the ocean murmurs there.
And I have others given me by the nymphs,
Of sweeter sound than any pipe you have.—
But we, by Neptune, for no pipe contend;                           180
This time a sheep I win, a pipe the next.'
Now came she forward, eager to engage;
But, first her dress, her bosom then, survey'd,
And heav'd it, doubting if she could deceive.
Her bosom seem'd, inclos'd in haze like heav'n,
To baffle touch; and rose forth undefined.
Above her knees she drew the robe succinct,
Above her breast, and just below her arms:
'This will preserve my breath, when tightly bound,
If struggle and equal strength should so constrain.'               190
Thus, pulling hard to fasten it, she spoke,
And, rushing at me, closed. I thrill'd throughout
And seem'd to lessen and shrink up with cold.
Again, with violent impulse gushed my blood;
And hearing nought external, thus absorb'd,
I heard it, rushing through each turbid vein,
Shake my unsteady swimming sight in air.
Yet with unyielding though uncertain arms,
I clung around her neck; the vest beneath
Rustled against our slippery limbs entwined:                       200

Often mine, springing with eluded force,
Started aside, and trembled, till replaced.
And when I most succeeded, as I thought,
My bosom and my throat felt so comprest
That life was almost quivering on my lips,
Yet nothing was there painful! these are signs
Of secret arts, and not of human might,
What arts I cannot tell: I only know
My eyes grew dizzy, and my strength decay'd,
I was indeed o'ercome!—with what regret,                              210
And more, with what confusion, when I reached
The fold, and yielding up the sheep, she cried,
'This pays a shepherd to a conquering maid.'
She smil'd, and more of pleasure than disdain
Was in her dimpled chin, and liberal lip,
And eyes that languished, lengthening,—just like love.
She went away: I, on the wicker gate
Lean'd, and could follow with my eyes alone.
The sheep she carried easy as a cloak.
But when I heard its bleating, as I did,                              220
And saw, she hastening on, its hinder feet
Struggle, and from her snowy shoulder slip,
(One shoulder its poor efforts had unveil'd,)
Then, all my passions mingling fell in tears!
Restless then ran I to the highest ground
To watch her; she was gone; gone down the tide;
And the long moon-beam on the hard wet sand
Lay like a jaspar column half uprear'd.'
        'But, Tamar! tell me, will she not return?'
'She will return: but not before the moon                            230
Again is at the full; she promis'd this;
But when she promis'd I could not reply.'
        'By all the Gods! I pity thee! go on—
Fear not my anger, look not on my shame;
For, when a lover only hears of love,
He finds his folly out, and is ashamed.
Away with watchful nights, and lonely days,
Contempt of earth, and aspect up to heaven,
With contemplation, with humility,—
A tatter'd cloak that pride wears when deform'd—                     240
Away with all that hides me from myself,
Parts me from others, whispers I am wise—
From our own wisdom less is to be reaped
Than from the barest folly of our friend.
Tamar! thy pastures, large and rich, afford
Flowers to thy bees, and herbage to thy sheep,
But, battened on too much, the poorest croft

Of thy poor neighbour yields what thine denies.'
    They hastened to the camp; and Gebir there
—Resolved his native country to forego—       250
Ordered, that from those ruins to their right
They forthwith raise a city: Tamar heard
With wonder, though in passing 'twas half-told,
His brother's love; and sigh'd upon his own.


3    *from* BOOK IV

    Description of an embassy—of the *Gadites* reposing in the evening.
Reception of the Egyptian elders at the Iberian tent.

    Meanwhile, with pomp august and solemn, borne
On four white camels, tinkling plates of gold,
Heralds before, and Ethiop slaves behind,
Each with the signs of office in his hand,
Each on his brow the sacred stamp of years,
The four ambassadors of peace proceed.
Rich carpets bear they, corn and generous wine;
The Syrian olive's cheerful gifts they bear:
With stubborn goats that eye the mountain-tops
Askance, and riot with reluctant horn,       10
And steeds and stately camels in their train.
The king, who sat before his tent, descried
The dust rise redden'd from the setting sun:
Through all the plains below the Gadite men
Were resting from their labor: some surveyed
The spacious scite, ere yet obstructed, walls
Already, soon will roofs have, interposed.
Nor is the glory of no price, to take
The royal city in, as these presume.
Some ate their frugal viands on the steps,       20
Contented: some, remembering home, prefer
The cot's bare rafters o'er the high gilded dome,
And sing, for often sighs, too, end in song,
'In smiling meads how sweet the brooks repose,
To the rough ocean and red restless sands!'
But others trip along with hasty steps,
Whistling, and fix too soon on their abodes:
Haply and one among them with his spear
Measures the lintel, if so great its height
As will receive him with his helm unlower'd.       30
    But silence went throughout, e'en thoughts were hushed,
When to full view of navy and of camp
Now first expanded the bare-headed train.

Majestic, unpresuming, unappall'd,
Onward they marched; and neither to the right
Nor to the left, though there the city stood,
Turn'd they their sober eyes: and now they reach'd
Within a few steep paces of ascent
The lone pavilion of the Iberian king.
He saw them, he awaited them, he rose;                    40
He hail'd them, '*Peace be with you.*' They replied
'King of the western world, be with you peace.'


4    *from* BOOK V

DESCRIPTION of the city *Masar*.

ONCE a fair city, courted then by kings,
Mistress of nations, throng'd by palaces,
Raising her head o'er destiny, her face
Glowing with pleasure, and with palms refreshed,
Now, pointed at by Wisdom or by Wealth,
Bereft of beauty, bare of ornaments,
Stood, in the wilderness of woe, Masar.
Ere far advancing, all appear'd a plain.
Treacherous and fearful mountains, far advanced.
Her glory so gone down, at human step              10
The fierce hyæna, frighted from the walls,
Bristled his rising back, his teeth unsheathed,
Drew the long growl and with slow foot retired.


## from POETRY BY THE AUTHOR OF GEBIR (1802)

5    *from* CRYSAOR

Thrown prostrate on the earth, the Sacrilege
Rais'd up his head astounded, and accurst
The stars, the destinies, the gods; his breast
Panted from consternation and dismay,
And pride untoward on himself o'erthrown.
From his distended nostrils issued gore
At intervals, wherewith his wiry locks,
Huge arms, and bulky bosom, shone beslimed:
And thrice he call'd his brethren, with a voice
More dismal than the blasts from Phlegethon        10
Below, that urge along ten thousand ghosts
Wafted loud-wailing o'er the fiery tide.
But answer heard he none: the men of might

Who gather'd round him formerly, the men
Whom frozen at a frown, a smile revived,
Were far: enormous mountains interposed,
Nor ever had the veil-hung pine out-spred
O'er Tethys then her wandering leafless shade:
Nor could he longer under winter stars
Suspend the watery journey, nor repose                    20
Whole nights in Ocean's billowy restless bed;
No longer, bulging through the tempest, rose
That bulky bosom; nor those oarlike hands,
Trusted ere mortal's keenest ken conceived
The bluest shore, threw back opposing tides.
Shrunken mid brutal hair his violent veins
Subsided, yet were hideous to behold
As dragons panting in the noontide brake.
At last, absorbing deep the breath of heaven,
And stifling all within his deadly grasp,                    30
Struggling and tearing up the glebe to turn,
And from a throat that, as it throbb'd and rose,
Seem'd shaking ponderous links of dusky iron,
Uttering one anguish-forced indignant groan,
Fired with infernal rage, the spirit flew.

## from SIMONIDEA (1806)

6    [ROSE AYLMER]

AH what avails the sceptred race,
    Ah what the form divine!
What every virtue, every grace!
    Rose Aylmer, all were thine.
Rose Aylmer, whom these wakeful eyes
    May weep, but never see,
A night of memories and of sighs
    I consecrate to thee.

7    [IMITATION FROM SAPPHO]

MOTHER, I can not mind my wheel;
    My fingers ache, my lips are dry:
Oh! if you felt the pain I feel!
    But Oh, who ever felt as I!
No longer could I doubt him true. .
    All other men may use deceit;
He always said my eyes were blue,
    And often swore my lips were sweet.

8    PROGRESS OF EVENING

FROM yonder wood mark blue-eyed Eve proceed:
First thro' the deep and warm and secret glens,
Thro' the pale-glimmering privet-scented lane,
And thro' those alders by the river-side:
Now the soft dust impedes her, which the sheep
Have hollow'd out beneath their hawthorn shade.
But ah! look yonder! see a misty tide
Rise up the hill, lay low the frowning grove,
Enwrap the gay white mansion, sap its sides
Until they sink and melt away like chalk;                    10
Now it comes down against our village-tower,
Covers its base, floats o'er its arches, tears
The clinging ivy from the battlements,
Mingles in broad embrace the obdurate stone,
(All one vast ocean), and goes swelling on
In slow and silent, dim and deepening waves.

9    [WISH FOR IANTHE]

SHE leads in solitude her youthful hours,
    Her nights are restlessness, her days are pain.
    O when will Health and Pleasure come again,
Adorn her brow and strew her path with flowers,
And wandering wit relume the roseate bowers,
    And turn and trifle with his festive train?
Grant me, O grant this wish, ye heavenly Powers!
    All other hope, all other wish, restrain.

10   [IANTHE AWAITED]

WHILE the winds whistle round my cheerless room,
And the pale morning droops with winter's gloom;
While indistinct lie rude and cultured lands,
The ripening harvest and the hoary sands;
Alone, and destitute of every page
That fires the poet or informs the sage,
Where shall my wishes, where my fancy, rove,
Rest upon past or cherish promist love?
Alas! the past I never can regain,
Wishes may rise and tears may flow . . in vain.             10
Fancy, that brings her in her early bloom,
Throws barren sunshine o'er the unyielding tomb.
What then would passion, what would reason, do?
Sure, to retrace is worse than to pursue.
Here will I sit till heaven shall cease to lour

And happier Hesper bring the appointed hour,
Gaze on the mingled waste of sky and sea,
Think of my love, and bid her think of me.

## 11 [IANTHE IMAGINED]

I OFTEN ask upon whose arm she leans,
 She whom I dearly love,
And if she visit much the crowded scenes
 Where mimic passions move.
There, mighty powers! assert your just control,
 Alarm her thoughtless breast,
Breathe soft suspicion o'er her yielding soul,
 But never break its rest.
O let some faithful lover, absent long,
 To sudden bliss return; 10
Then Landor's name shall tremble from her tongue,
 Her cheek thro' tears shall burn.

## from COUNT JULIAN (1812)

### 12 FOURTH ACT: FIRST SCENE
*Tent of* JULIAN.
RODERIGO *and* JULIAN.

 *Julian* The people had deserted thee, and throng'd
My standard, had I raised it, at the first;
But once subsiding, and no voice of mine
Calling by name each grievance to each man,
They, silent and submissive by degrees,
Bore thy hard yoke, and, hadst thou but opprest,
Would still have borne it: thou hast now deceived;
Thou hast done all a foreign foe could do
And more against them; with ingratitude
Not hell itself could arm the foreign foe; 10
'Tis forged at home and kills not from afar.
Amid whate'er vain glories fell upon
Thy rainbow span of power, which I dissolve,
Boast not how thou conferredst wealth and rank,
How thou preservedst me, my family,
All my distinctions, all my offices,
When Witiza was murder'd; that I stand
Count Julian at this hour by special grace.
The sword of Julian saved the walls of Ceuta,
And not the shadow that attends his name: 20
It was no badge, no title, that o'erthrew

Soldier and steed and engine. Don Roderigo!
The truly and the falsely great here differ:
These by dull wealth or daring fraud advance;
Him the Almighty calls amid his people
To sway the wills and passions of mankind.
The weak of heart and intellect beheld
Thy splendour, and adored thee lord of Spain:
I rose . . Roderigo lords o'er Spain no more.
   *Roderigo* Now to a traitor's add a boaster's name.       30
   *Julian* Shameless and arrogant, dost thou believe
I boast for pride or pastime? forced to boast,
Truth costs me more than falsehood e'er cost thee.
Divested of that purple of the soul,
That potency, that palm of wise ambition,
Cast headlong by thy madness from that high,
That only eminence 'twixt earth and heaven,
Virtue, which some desert, but none despise,
Whether thou art beheld again on earth,
Whether a captive or a fugitive,       40
Miner or galley-slave, depends on me;
But he alone who made me what I am
Can make me greater or can make me less.
   *Roderigo* Chance, and chance only, threw me in thy power;
Give me my sword again and try my strength.
   *Julian* I tried it in the front of thousands.
   *Roderigo*                     Death
At least vouchsafe me from a soldier's hand.
   *Julian* I love to hear thee ask it: now my own
Would not be bitter; no, nor immature.
   *Roderigo* Defy it, say thou rather.
   *Julian*                Death itself       50
Shall not be granted thee, unless from God;
A dole from his and from no other hand.
Thou shalt now hear and own thine infamy.
   *Roderigo* Chains, dungeons, tortures . . but I hear no more.
   *Julian* Silence, thou wretch! live on . . ay, live . . abhorr'd.
Thou shalt have tortures, dungeons, chains enough;
They naturally rise and grow around
Monsters like thee, everywhere, and for ever.
   *Roderigo* Insulter of the fallen! must I endure
Commands as well as threats? my vassal's too?       60
Nor breathe from underneath his trampling feet?
   *Julian* Could I speak patiently who speak to thee,
I would say more: part of thy punishment
It should be, to be taught.
   *Roderigo*            Reserve thy wisdom
Until thy patience come, its best ally:

I learn no lore, of peace or war, from thee.
   *Julian* No, thou shalt study soon another tongue,
And suns more ardent shall mature thy mind.
Either the cross thou bearest, and thy knees
Among the silent caves of Palestine                                    70
Wear the sharp flints away with midnight prayer,
Or thou shalt keep the fasts of Barbary,
Shalt wait amid the crowds that throng the well
From sultry noon till the skies fade again,
To draw up water and to bring it home
In the crackt gourd of some vile testy knave,
Who spurns thee back with bastinaded foot
For ignorance or delay of his command.
   *Roderigo* Rather the poison or the bowstring.
   *Julian*                    Slaves
To others' passions die such deaths as those:                          80
Slaves to their own should die . .
   *Roderigo*          What worse?
   *Julian*                 Their own.
   *Roderigo* Is this thy counsel, renegade?
   *Julian*              Not mine:
I point a better path, nay, force thee on.
I shelter thee from every brave man's sword
While I am near thee: I bestow on thee
Life: if thou die, 'tis when thou sojournest
Protected by this arm and voice no more:
'Tis slavishly, 'tis ignominiously,
'Tis by a villain's knife.
   *Roderigo*       By whose?
   *Julian*           Roderigo's.
   *Roderigo* O powers of vengeance! must I hear? . . endure? . . 90
Live?
   *Julian* Call thy vassals: no? then wipe the drops
Of froward childhood from thy shameless eyes.
So! thou canst weep for passion; not for pity.
   *Roderigo* One hour ago I ruled all Spain! a camp
Not larger than a sheepfold stood alone
Against me: now, no friend throughout the world
Follows my steps or hearkens to my call.
Behold the turns of fortune, and expect
No better: of all faithless men the Moors
Are the most faithless: from thy own experience                       100
Thou canst not value nor rely on them.
   *Julian* I value not the mass that makes my sword,
Yet while I use it I rely on it.
   *Roderigo* Julian, thy gloomy soul still meditates . .
Plainly I see it . . death to me . . pursue

The dictates of thy leaders, let revenge
Have its full sway, let Barbary prevail,
And the pure creed her elders have embraced:
Those placid sages hold assassination
A most compendious supplement to law.                                  110
  *Julian* Thou knowest not the one, nor I the other.
Torn hast thou from me all my soul held dear,
Her form, her voice, all, hast thou banisht from me,
Nor dare I, wretched as I am! recall
Those solaces of every grief erewhile.
I stand abased before insulting crime,
I falter like a criminal myself;
The hand that hurl'd thy chariot o'er its wheels,
That held thy steeds erect and motionless
As molten statues on some palace-gate,                                 120
Shakes as with palsied age before thee now.
Gone is the treasure of my heart for ever,
Without a father, mother, friend, or name.
Daughter of Julian . .  Such was her delight . .
Such was mine too! what pride more innocent,
What surely less deserving pangs like these,
Than springs from filial and parental love!
Debarr'd from every hope that issues forth
To meet the balmy breath of early life,
Her sadden'd days, all cold and colourless,                            130
Will stretch before her their whole weary length
Amid the sameness of obscurity.
She wanted not seclusion to unveil
Her thoughts to heaven, cloister, nor midnight bell;
She found it in all places, at all hours:
While to assuage my labours she indulged
A playfulness that shunn'd a mother's eye,
Still to avert my perils there arose
A piety that even from *me* retired.
  *Roderigo* Such was she! what am I! those are the arms         140
That are triumphant when the battle fails.
O Julian! Julian! all thy former words
Struck but the imbecile plumes of vanity,
These thro' its steely coverings pierce the heart.
I ask not life nor death; but, if I live,
Send my most bitter enemy to watch
My secret paths, send poverty, send pain . .
I will add more . .  wise as thou art, thou knowest
No foe more furious than forgiven kings.
I ask not then what thou wouldst never grant:                          150
May heaven, O Julian, from thy hand receive
A pardon'd man, a chasten'd criminal.

*Julian* This further curse hast thou inflicted; wretch!
I can not pardon thee.
  *Roderigo*        Thy tone, thy mien,
Refute those words.
  *Julian*          No . . I can *not* forgive.
  *Roderigo* Upon my knee, my conqueror, I implore!
Upon the earth, before thy feet . . hard heart!
  *Julian* Audacious! hast thou never heard that prayer
And scorn'd it? 'tis the last thou shouldst repeat.
Upon the earth! upon her knees! O God!                              160
  *Roderigo* Resemble not a wretch so lost as I:
Be better; O! be happier; and pronounce it.
  *Julian* I swerve not from my purpose: thou art mine,
Conquer'd; and I have sworn to dedicate,
Like a torn banner on my chapel's roof,
Thee to that power from whom thou hast rebell'd.
Expiate thy crimes by prayer, by penances.
  *Roderigo* Hasten the hour of trial, speak of peace.
Pardon me not then, but with purer lips
Implore of God, who *would* hear *thee*, to pardon.                170
  *Julian* Hope it I may . . pronounce it . . O Roderigo!
Ask it of him who can; I too will ask,
And, in my own transgressions, pray for thine.
  *Roderigo* One name I dare not . .
  *Julian*              Go; abstain from that;
I do conjure thee, raise not in my soul
Again the tempest that has wreckt my fame;
Thou shalt not breathe in the same clime with her.
Far o'er the unebbing sea thou shalt adore
The eastern star, and may thy end be peace.

**13**   *from* FIFTH ACT: SECOND SCENE

  *Tarik*                  At last
He must be happy; for delicious calm
Follows the fierce enjoyment of revenge.
  *Hernando* That calm was never his, no other will be.
Thou knowest not, and mayst thou never know,
How bitter is the tear that fiery shame
Scourges and tortures from the soldier's eye.
Whichever of these bad reports be true,
He hides it from all hearts to wring his own,
And drags the heavy secret to the grave.                           10
Not victory that o'ershadows him sees he;
No airy and light passion stirs abroad
To ruffle or to soothe him; all are quell'd
Beneath a mightier, sterner stress of mind:

Wakeful he sits, and lonely, and unmoved,
Beyond the arrows, views, or shouts of men;
As oftentimes an eagle, ere the sun
Throws o'er the varying earth his early ray,
Stands solitary, stands immovable
Upon some highest cliff, and rolls his eye,                              20
Clear, constant, unobservant, unabased,
In the cold light above the dews of morn.
He now assumes that quietness of soul
Which never but in danger have I seen
On his staid breast.

## MISCELLANEOUS POEMS, 1824-29

**14**  TO CORINTH

QUEEN of the double sea, beloved of him
Who shakes the world's foundations, thou hast seen
Glory in all her beauty, all her forms;
Seen her walk back with Theseus when he left
The bones of Sciron bleaching to the wind,
Above the ocean's roar and cormorant's flight,
So high that vastest billows from above
Show but like herbage waving in the mead;
Seen generations throng thy Isthmian games,
And pass away; the beautiful, the brave,                                 10
And them who sang their praises. But, O Queen,
Audible still, and far beyond thy cliffs,
As when they first were utter'd, are those words
Divine which praised the valiant and the just;
And tears have often stopt, upon that ridge
So perilous, him who brought before his eye
The Colchian babes. 'Stay! spare him! save the last!
Medea! Is that blood? again! it drops
From my imploring hand upon my feet!
I will invoke the Eumenides no more,                                     20
I will forgive thee, bless thee, bend to thee
In all thy wishes, do but thou, Medea,
Tell me, one lives.' 'And shall I too deceive?'
Cries from the fiery car an angry voice;
And swifter than two falling stars descend,
Two breathless bodies; warm, soft, motionless,
As flowers in stillest noon before the sun,
They lie three paces from him: such they lie
As when he left them sleeping side by side,
A mother's arm round each, a mother's cheeks                             30

Between them, flusht with happiness and love.
He was more changed than they were, doomed to show
Thee and the stranger, how defaced and scarr'd
Grief hunts us down the precipice of years,
And whom the faithless prey upon the last.
    To give the inertest masses of our earth
Her loveliest forms, was thine; to fix the Gods
Within thy walls, and hang their tripods round
With fruits and foliage knowing not decay.
A nobler work remains: thy citadel                                      40
Invites all Greece: o'er lands and floods remote
Many are the hearts that still beat high for thee:
Confide then in thy strength, and unappall'd
Look down upon the plain, while yokemate kings
Run bellowing where their herdsmen goad them on.
Instinct is sharp in them and terror true,
They smell the floor whereon their necks must lie.

## 15   REGENERATION

WE are what suns and winds and waters make us;
The mountains are our sponsors, and the rills
Fashion and win their nursling with their smiles.
But where the land is dim from tyranny,
There tiny pleasures occupy the place
Of glories and of duties; as the feet
Of fabled faeries when the sun goes down
Trip o'er the grass where wrestlers strove by day.
Then Justice, call'd the Eternal One above,
Is more inconstant than the buoyant form                                10
That bursts into existence from the froth
Of ever-varying ocean: what is best
Then becomes worst; what loveliest, most deformed.
The heart is hardest in the softest climes,
The passions flourish, the affections die.
O thou vast tablet of these awful truths,
That fillest all the space between the seas,
Spreading from Venice's deserted courts
To the Tarentine and Hydruntine mole,
What lifts thee up? what shakes thee? 'tis the breath                   20
Of God. Awake, ye nations! spring to life!
Let the last work of his right-hand appear
Fresh with his image, Man. Thou recreant slave
That sittest afar off and helpest not,
O thou degenerate Albion! with what shame
Do I survey thee, pushing forth the spunge
At thy spear's length, in mockery at the thirst

Of holy Freedom in his agony,
And prompt and keen to pierce the wounded side!
Must Italy then wholly rot away                                    30
Amid her slime, before she germinate
Into fresh vigour, into form again?
What thunder bursts upon mine ear! some ile
Hath surely risen from the gulphs profound,
Eager to suck the sunshine from the breast
Of beauteous Nature, and to catch the gale
From golden Hermus and Melena's brow.
A greater thing than ile, than continent,
Than earth itself, than ocean circling earth,
Hath risen there; regenerate Man hath risen.              40
Generous old bard of Chios! not that Jove
Deprived thee in thy latter days of sight
Would I complain, but that no higher theme
Than a disdainful youth, a lawless king,
A pestilence, a pyre, awoke thy song,
When on the Chian coast, one javelin's throw
From where thy tombstone, where thy cradle stood,
Twice twenty self-devoted Greeks assail'd
The naval host of Asia, at one blow
Scatter'd it into air . . and Greece was free . .          50
And ere these glories beam'd, thy day had closed.
Let all that Elis ever saw, give way,
All that Olympian Jove e'er smiled upon:
The Marathonian columns never told
A tale more glorious, never Salamis,
Nor, faithful in the center of the false,
Platea, nor Anthela, from whose mount
Benignant Ceres wards the blessed Laws,
And sees the Amphictyon dip his weary foot
In the warm streamlet of the strait below.                  60
Goddess! altho' thy brow was never rear'd
Among the powers that guarded or assail'd
Perfidious Ilion, parricidal Thebes,
Or other walls whose war-belt e'er inclosed
Man's congregated crimes and vengeful pain,
Yet hast thou touched the extremes of grief and joy;
Grief upon Enna's mead and Hell's ascent,
A solitary mother; joy beyond,
Far beyond, that thy woe in this thy fane:
The tears were human, but the bliss divine.              70

I, in the land of strangers, and deprest
With sad and certain presage for my own,
Exult at hope's fresh dayspring, tho afar,
There where my youth was not unexercised
By chiefs in willing war and faithful song:
Shades as they were, they were not empty shades
Whose bodies haunt our world and blear our sun,
Obstruction worse than swamp and shapeless sands.
Peace, praise, eternal gladness, to the souls
That, rising from the seas into the heavens,           80
Have ransom'd first their country with their blood!
O thou immortal Spartan! at whose name
The marble table sounds beneath my palms,
Leonidas! even thou wilt not disdain
To mingle names august as these with thine;
Nor thou, twin-star of glory, thou whose rays
Stream'd over Corinth on the double sea,
Achaian and Saronic, whom the sons
Of Syracuse, when Death removed thy light,
Wept more than slavery ever made them weep,       90
But shed (if gratitude is sweet) sweet tears;
The hand that then pour'd ashes o'er their heads
Was loosen'd from its desperate chain by thee.
What now can press mankind into one mass
For Tyranny to tread the more secure?
From gold alone is drawn the guilty wire
That Adulation trills: she mocks the tone
Of Duty, Courage, Virtue, Piety,
And under her sits Hope! O how unlike
That graceful form in azure vest array'd,          100
With brow serene, and eyes on heaven alone
In patience fixt, in fondness unobscured!
What monsters coil beneath the spreading tree
Of Despotism! what wastes extend around!
What poison floats upon the distant breeze!
But who are those that cull and deal its fruit?
Creatures that shun the light and fear the shade,
Bloated and fierce, Sleep's mien and Famine's cry.
Rise up again, rise in thy dignity,
Dejected Man! and scare this brood away.       110

## 16    ON SEEING A HAIR OF LUCRETIA BORGIA

BORGIA, thou once wert almost too august
And high for adoration; now thou'rt dust.
All that remains of thee these plaits unfold,
Calm hair, meandering in pellucid gold.

**17**    [BURNS]

HAD we two met, blithe-hearted Burns,
   Tho' water is my daily drink,
   May God forgive me but I think
We should have roared out toasts by turns.

Inquisitive low whispering cares
   Had found no room in either pate,
   Until I asked thee, rather late,
Is there a hand-rail to the stairs!

**18**    [GODIVA]

IN every hour, in every mood,
O lady, it is sweet and good
   To bathe the soul in prayer,
And, at the close of such a day,
When we have ceased to bless and pray,
   To dream on thy long hair.

## from GEBIR, COUNT JULIAN, AND OTHER POEMS (1831)

**19**    [TO A PORTRAIT PAINTER]

O THOU whose happy pencil strays
Where I am call'd, nor dare to gaze,
   But lower my eye and check my tongue;
O, if thou valuest peaceful days,
Pursue the ringlet's sunny maze,
   And dwell not on those lips too long.

What mists athwart my temples fly,
Now, touch by touch, thy fingers tie
   With torturing care her graceful zone!
For all that sparkles from her eye                    10
I could not look while thou art by,
   Nor could I cease were I alone.

**20**    [VERSE FOR IANTHE]

AWAY my verse; and never fear,
   As men before such beauty do;
On you she will not look severe,
   She will not turn her eyes from you.

Some happier graces could I lend
    That in her memory you should live,
Some little blemishes might blend,
    For it would please her to forgive.

## 21   [IANTHE'S NAME]

PAST ruin'd Ilion Helen lives,
    Alcestis rises from the shades;
Verse calls them forth; 'tis verse that gives
    Immortal youth to mortal maids.

Soon shall Oblivion's deepening veil
    Hide all the peopled hills you see,
The gay, the proud, while lovers hail
    These many summers you and me.

## 22   [CAN SHE FORGET?]

SO late removed from him she swore,
    With clasping arms and vows and tears,
In life and death she would adore,
    While memory, fondness, bliss, endears.

Can she forswear? can she forget?
    Strike, mighty Love! strike, Vengeance! Soft!
Conscience must come and bring regret . .
    These let her feel! . . nor these too oft!

## 23   [IANTHE LEAVES]

IANTHE! you are call'd to cross the sea!
    A path forbidden *me*!
Remember, while the Sun his blessing sheds
    Upon the mountain-heads,
How often we have watcht him laying down
    His brow, and dropt our own
Against each other's, and how faint and short
    And sliding the support!
What will succeed it now? Mine is unblest,
    Ianthe! nor will rest          10
But on the very thought that swells with pain.
    O bid me hope again!
O give me back what Earth, what (without you)
    Not Heaven itself can do,
One of the golden days that we have past;
    And let it be my last!

Or else the gift would be, however sweet,
    Fragile and incomplete.

24          [THE PARTING YEAR]

MILD is the parting year, and sweet
    The odour of the falling spray;
Life passes on more rudely fleet,
    And balmless is its closing day.
I wait its close, I court its gloom,
    But mourn that never must there fall
Or on my breast or on my tomb
    The tear that would have sooth'd it all.

25          FIESOLAN IDYL

HERE, where precipitate Spring, with one light bound
Into hot Summer's lusty arms, expires,
And where go forth at morn, at eve, at night,
Soft airs that want the lute to play with 'em,
And softer sighs that know not what they want,
Aside a wall, beneath an orange-tree,
Whose tallest flowers could tell the lowlier ones
Of sights in Fiesolè right up above,
While I was gazing a few paces off
At what they seem'd to show me with their nods,          10
Their frequent whispers and their pointing shoots,
A gentle maid came down the garden-steps
And gathered the pure treasure in her lap.
I heard the branches rustle, and stept forth
To drive the ox away, or mule, or goat,
Such I believed it must be. How could I
Let beast o'erpower them? When hath wind or rain
Borne hard upon weak plant that wanted me,
And I (however they might bluster round)
Walkt off? 'Twere most ungrateful: for sweet scents          20
Are the swift vehicles of still sweeter thoughts,
And nurse and pillow the dull memory
That would let drop without them her best stores.
They bring me tales of youth and tones of love,
And 'tis and ever was my wish and way
To let all flowers live freely, and all die
(Whene'er their Genius bids their souls depart)
Among their kindred in their native place.
I never pluck the rose; the violet's head
Hath shaken with my breath upon its bank          30
And not reproacht me; the ever-sacred cup

Of the pure lily hath between my hands
Felt safe, unsoil'd, nor lost one grain of gold.
I saw the light that made the glossy leaves
More glossy; the fair arm, the fairer cheek
Warmed by the eye intent on its pursuit;
I saw the foot that, altho' half-erect
From its grey slipper, could not lift her up
To what she wanted: I held down a branch
And gather'd her some blossoms; since their hour          40
Was come, and bees had wounded them, and flies
Of harder wing were working their way thro'
And scattering them in fragments under-foot.
So crisp were some, they rattled unevolved,
Others, ere broken off, fell into shells,
For such appear the petals when detacht,
Unbending, brittle, lucid, white like snow,
And like snow not seen thro', by eye or sun:
Yet every one her gown received from me
Was fairer than the first. I thought not so,                 50
But so she praised them to reward my care.
I said, 'You find the largest.'
                                        'This indeed,'
Cried she, 'is large and sweet.' She held one forth,
Whether for me to look at or to take
She knew not, nor did I; but taking it
Would best have solved (and this she felt) her doubt.
I dared not touch it; for it seemed a part
Of her own self; fresh, full, the most mature
Of blossoms, yet a blossom; with a touch
To fall, and yet unfallen. She drew back                     60
The boon she tender'd, and then, finding not
The ribbon at her waist to fix it in,
Dropt it, as loth to drop it, on the rest.

**26**   [FIRST WRINKLES]

WHEN Helen first saw wrinkles in her face
('Twas when some fifty long had settled there
And intermarried and brancht off awide)
She threw herself upon her couch and wept:
On this side hung her head, and over that
Listlessly she let fall the faithless brass
That made the men as faithless.
                                        But when you
Found them, or fancied them, and would not hear
That they were only vestiges of smiles,
Or the impression of some amorous hair                       10

Astray from cloistered curls and roseate band,
Which had been lying there all night perhaps
Upon a skin so soft, 'No, no,' you said,
'Sure, they are coming, yes, are come, are here:
Well, and what matters it, while thou art too!'

### 27    [WILLIAM GIFFORD]

CLAP, clap the double nightcap on!
    Gifford will read you his amours,
Lazy as Scheld and cold as Don;
    Kneel, and thank Heaven they are not yours.

### 28    DIRCE

STAND close around, ye Stygian set,
    With Dirce in one boat convey'd,
Or Charon, seeing, may forget
    That he is old, and she a shade.

### 29    [NEEDWOOD FOREST]

UNDER the hollies of thy breezy glade,
    Needwood, in youth with idle pace I rode,
Where pebbly rills their varied chirrup made,
    Rills which the fawn with tottering knees bestrode.

Twilight was waning, yet I checkt my pace,
    Slow as it was, and longer would remain;
Here first, here only, had I seen the face
    Of Nature free from change and pure from stain.

Here in the glory of her power she lay,
    Here she rejoiced in all the bloom of health;            10
Soon must I meet her faint and led astray,
    Freckled with feverish whims and wasted wealth.

### 30    [TOWARDS FLORENCE]

I LEAVE with unreverted eye the towers
    Of Pisa pining o'er her desert stream.
Pleasure (they say) yet lingers in thy bowers,
    Florence, thou patriot's sigh, thou poet's dream!

O could I find thee as thou once wert known,
    Thoughtful and lofty, liberal and free!
But the pure Spirit from thy wreck has flown,
    And only Pleasure's phantom dwells with thee.

**31   OLD STYLE**

AURELIUS, Sire of Hungrinesses!
Thee thy old friend Catullus blesses,
And sends thee six fine watercresses.
There are who would not think me quite
(Unless we were old friends) polite
To mention whom you should invite.
Look at them well; and turn it o'er
In your own mind . .   I'd have but four . .
Lucullus, Cesar, and two more.

**32   [FIESOLAN MUSINGS]**

LET me sit here and muse by thee
Awhile, aërial Fiesole!
Thy shelter'd walks and cooler grots,
Villas and vines and olive-plots,
Catch me, entangle me, detain me,
And laugh to hear that aught can pain me.
'Twere just, if ever rose one sigh
To find the lighter mount more high,
Or any other natural thing
So trite that Fate would blush to sing,                          10
Of Honour's sport or Fortune's frown,
Clung to my heart and kept it down.
But shunn'd have I on every side
The splash of newly-mounted Pride,
And never riskt my taking cold
In the damp chambers of the old.
    What has the zephyr brought so sweet?
'Tis the vine-blossom round my seat.
Ah! how much better here at ease
And quite alone to catch the breeze,                             20
Than roughly wear life's waning day
On rotten forms with Castlereagh,
'Mid public men for private ends,
A friend to foes, a foe to friends!
Long since with youthful chases warm,
And when ambition well might charm,
And when the choice before me lay,
I heard the din and turn'd away.
Hence oftentimes imperial Seine
Hath listen'd to my early strain,                                30
And past the Rhine and past the Rhone
My Latian muse is heard and known:
Nor is the life of one recluse

An alien quite from public use.
Where alders mourn'd their fruitless beds
A thousand cedars raise their heads,
And from Segovia's hills remote,
My sheep enrich my neighbour's cote.
The wide and easy road I lead
Where never paced the harnest steed,                    40
Where hardly dared the goat look down
Beneath her parent mountain's frown,
Suspended while the torrent-spray
Springs o'er the crags that roll away.
Cares if I had, I turn'd those cares
Toward my partridges and hares,
At every dog and gun I heard
Ill-auguring for some truant bird,
Or whisker'd friend of jet-tipt ear,
Until the frighten'd eld limpt near.                    50
These knew me, and 'twas quite enough,
I paid no *Morning Post* to puff,
Saw others fame and wealth increase,
Ate my own mutton-chop in peace,
Open'd my window, snatcht my glass,
And, from the rills that chirp and pass,
A pure libation pour'd to thee,
Unsoil'd uncitied Liberty!
      Lanthony! an ungenial clime,
And the broad wing of restless Time,                    60
Have rudely swept thy massy walls
And rockt thy abbots in their palls.
I loved thee by thy streams of yore,
By distant streams I love thee more;
For never is the heart so true
As bidding what we love adieu.
Yet neither where we first drew breath,
Nor where our fathers sleep in death,
Nor where the mystic ring was given,
The link from earth that reaches heaven,                70
Nor London, Paris, Florence, Rome,
In his own heart's the wise man's home,
Stored with each keener, kinder, sense,
Too firm, too lofty, for offence,
Unlittered by the tools of state,
And greater than the great world's great.
If mine no glorious work may be,
Grant, Heaven! and 'tis enough for me,
(While many squally sails flit past,
And many break the ambitious mast)                      80

From all that they pursue, exempt,
The stormless bay of deep contempt!

33    [CHILD OF A DAY]

CHILD of a day, thou knowest not
    The tears that overflow thine urn,
The gushing eyes that read thy lot,
    Nor, if thou knewest, couldst return!
And why the wish! the pure and blest
    Watch like thy mother o'er thy sleep.
O peaceful night! O envied rest!
    Thou wilt not ever see her weep.

34    [TO FORTUNE]

WERT thou but blind, O Fortune, then perhaps
Thou mightest always have avoided me;
For never voice of mine (young, middle-aged,
Or going down on tottering knee the shelf
That crumbles with us to the vale of years)
Call'd thee aside, whether thou rannest on
To others who expected, or didst throw
Into the sleeper's lap the unsought prize.
But blind thou art not; the refreshing cup
For which my hot heart thirsted, thou hast ever                10
(When it was full and at the lip) struck down.

35    ON A POET IN A WELSH CHURCH-YARD

KIND souls! who strive what pious hand shall bring
The first-found crocus from reluctant Spring,
Or blow your wintry fingers while they strew
This sunless turf with rosemary and rue,
Bend o'er your lovers first, but mind to save
One sprig of each to trim a poet's grave.

36    ANOTHER URN AT THORESBY PARK

IF in the summer-time, O guest,
Thou comest where these waters rest,
And where these gentle swells of land
Their ever-verdant turf expand,
Not opener these, nor those more clear,
Than was the soul that late dwelt here.
If in the winter thou hast crost
The scene benumb'd with snow and frost,

Ask those thou meetest at the gate
If they are not as desolate.                                    10

37    ON THE DEAD

YES, in this chancel once we sat alone,
O Dorothea! thou wert bright with youth,
Freshness like Morning's dwelt upon thy cheek,
While here and there above the level pews,
Above the housings of the village dames,
The musky fan its groves and zephyrs waved.
I know not why (since we had each our book
And lookt upon it stedfastly) first one
Outran the learned labourer from the desk,
Then tript the other and limpt far behind,                     10
And smiles gave blushes birth, and blushes smiles.
Ah me! where are they flown, my lovely friend!
Two seasons like that season thou hast lain
Cold as the dark-blue stone beneath my feet,
While my heart beats as then, but not with joy.
O my lost friends! why were ye once so dear?
And why were ye not fewer, O ye few?
Must winter, spring, and summer, thus return,
Commemorating some one torn away,
Till half the months at last shall take, with me,              20
Their names from those upon your scatter'd graves!

38    FOR AN EPITAPH AT FIESOLE

LO! where the four mimosas blend their shade,
In calm repose at last is Landor laid;
For ere he slept he saw them planted here
By her his soul had ever held most dear,
And he had lived enough when he had dried her tear.


## MISCELLANEOUS POEMS, 1834

39    TO THE OWLET

WHO, O thou sapient saintly bird!
Thy shouted warnings ever heard
            Unbleached by fear?
The blue-faced blubbering imp, who steals
Yon turnips, thinks thee at his heels,
            Afar or near.

The brawnier churl, who brags at times
To front and top the rankest crimes,
      To paunch a deer,
Quarter a priest, or squeeze a wench,          10
Scuds from thee, clammy as a tench,
      He knows not where.

For this the righteous Lord of all
Consigns to thee the castle-wall,
      When, many a year,
Closed in the chancel-vault, are eyes
Rainy or sunny at the sighs
      Of knight or peer.

**40**    THE MAID'S LAMENT

I LOVED him not; and yet now he is gone
    I feel I am alone.
I check'd him while he spoke; yet could he speak,
    Alas! I would not check.
For reasons not to love him once I sought,
    And wearied all my thought
To vex myself and him: I now would give
    My love, could he but live
Who lately lived for me, and when he found
    'Twas vain, in holy ground          10
He hid his face amid the shades of death.
    I waste for him my breath
Who wasted his for me: but mine returns,
    And this lorn bosom burns
With stifling heat, heaving it up in sleep,
    And waking me to weep
Tears that had melted his soft heart: for years
    Wept he as bitter tears.
*Merciful God!* such was his latest prayer,
    *These may she never share!*          20
Quieter is his breath, his breast more cold,
    Than daisies in the mould,
Where children spell, athwart the churchyard gate,
    His name and life's brief date.
Pray for him, gentle souls, whoe'er you be,
    And oh! pray too for me!

**41**    [LEAVES AND GIRLS]

NATURALLY, as fall upon the ground
The leaves in winter and the girls in spring.

## 42   TO WORDSWORTH

THOSE who have laid the harp aside
    And turn'd to idler things,
From very restlessness have tried
    The loose and dusty strings,
And, catching back some favorite strain,
Run with it o'er the chords again.

But Memory is not a Muse,
    O Wordsworth! though 'tis said
They all descend from her, and use
    To haunt her fountain-head:                            10
That other men should work for me
In the rich mines of Poesie,

Pleases no better than the toil
    Of smoothing under hardened hand,
With attic emery and oil,
    The shining point for Wisdom's wand,
Like those thou temperest 'mid the rills
Descending from thy native hills.

Without his governance, in vain
    Manhood is strong, and Youth is bold.                  20
If oftentimes the o'er-piled strain
    Clogs in the furnace, and grows cold
Beneath his pinions deep and frore,
And swells and melts and flows no more,
That is because the heat beneath,
    Pants in its cavern poorly fed.
Life springs not from the couch of Death,
    Nor Muse nor Grace can raise the dead;
Unturn'd then let the mass remain,
Intractable to sun or rain.                                30

A marsh, where only flat leaves lie,
And showing but the broken sky,
Too surely is the sweetest lay
That wins the ear and wastes the day,
Where youthful Fancy pouts alone
And lets not Wisdom touch her zone.

He who would build his fame up high,
The rule and plummet must apply,
Nor say, 'I'll do what I have plann'd,'
Before he try if loam or sand                              40

Be still remaining in the place
Delved for each polisht pillar's base.
With skilful eye and fit device
Thou raisest every edifice,
Whether in sheltered vale it stand
Or overlook the Dardan strand,
Amid the cypresses that mourn
Laodameia's love forlorn.

We both have run o'er half the space
Listed for mortal's earthly race;                               50
We both have crost life's fervid line,
And other stars before us shine:
May they be bright and prosperous
As those that have been stars for us!
Our course by Milton's light was sped,
And Shakspeare shining overhead:
Chatting on deck was Dryden too,
The Bacon of the rhyming crew;
None ever crost our mystic sea
More richly stored with thought than he;                        60
Tho' never tender nor sublime,
He wrestles with and conquers Time.
To learn my lore on Chaucer's knee,
I left much prouder company;
Thee gentle Spenser fondly led,
But me he mostly sent to bed.

I wish them every joy above
That highly blessed spirits prove,
Save one: and that too shall be theirs,
But after many rolling years,                                   70
When 'mid their light thy light appears.

## from PERICLES AND ASPASIA (1836)

43    CORINNA TO TANAGRA
        FROM ATHENS

TANAGRA! think not I forget
    Thy beautifully-storied streets;
Be sure my memory bathes yet
    In clear Thermodon, and yet greets
The blithe and liberal shepherd-boy,
Whose sunny bosom swells with joy
When we accept his matted rushes
Upheav'd with sylvan fruit; away he bounds, and blushes.

A gift I promise: one I see
    Which thou with transport wilt receive,         10
The only proper gift for thee,
    Of which no mortal shall bereave
In later times thy mouldering walls,
Until the last old turret falls;
A crown, a crown from Athens won,
A crown no God can wear beside Latona's son.

There may be cities who refuse
    To their own child the honours due,
And look ungently on the Muse;
    But ever shall those cities rue         20
The dry, unyielding, niggard breast,
Offering no nourishment, no rest,
To that young head which soon shall rise
Disdainfully, in might and glory, to the skies.

Sweetly where cavern'd Dirce flows
    Do white-arm'd maidens chaunt my lay,
Flapping the while with laurel-rose
    The honey-gathering tribes away;
And sweetly, sweetly Attic tongues
Lisp your Corinna's early songs;         30
To her with feet more graceful come
The verses that have dwelt in kindred breasts at home.

O let thy children lean aslant
    Against the tender mother's knee,
And gaze into her face, and want
    To know what magic there can be
In words that urge some eyes to dance,
While others as in holy trance
Look up to heaven: be such my praise!
Why linger? I must haste, or lose the Delphic bays.         40

**44**    [VERSES FROM MIMNERMUS]

I WISH not Thasos rich in mines,
Nor Naxos girt around with vines,
Nor Crete nor Samos, the abodes
Of those who govern men and gods,
Nor wider Lydia, where the sound
Of tymbrels shakes the thymy ground,
And with white feet and with hoofs cloven
The dedal dance is spun and woven:
Meanwhile each prying younger thing

Is sent for water to the spring,                          10
Under where red Priapus rears
His club amid the junipers.
In this whole world enough for me
Is any spot the Gods decree;
Albeit the pious and the wise
Would tarry where, like mulberries,
In the first hour of ripeness fall
The tender creatures one and all.
To take what falls with even mind
Jove wills, and we must be resign'd.                      20

45    HEGEMON TO PRAXINOE

IS there any season, O my soul,
When the sources of bitter tears dry up,
And the uprooted flowers take their places again
    Along the torrent-bed?

Could I wish to live, it would be for that season,
To repose my limbs and press my temples there.
But should I not speedily start away
    In the hope to trace and follow thy steps!

Thou art gone, thou art gone, Praxinöe!
And hast taken far from me thy lovely youth,             10
Leaving me naught that was desirable in mine.
    Alas! alas! what hast thou left me?

The helplessness of childhood, the solitude of age,
The laughter of the happy, the pity of the scorner,
A colorless and broken shadow am I,
    Seen glancing in troubled waters.

My thoughts too are scattered; thou hast cast them off;
They beat against thee, they would cling to thee,
But they are viler than the loose dark weeds,
    Without a place to root or rest in.                   20

I would throw them across my lyre; they drop from it;
My lyre will sound only two measures;
That Pity will never, never come,
    Or come to the sleep that awakeneth not unto her.

46    [ARTEMIA: FROM MYRTIS]

ARTEMIA, while Arion sighs,
Raising her white and taper finger,

Pretends to loose, yet makes to linger,
   The ivy that o'ershades her eyes.


   'Wait, or you shall not have the kiss,'
Says she; but he, on wing to pleasure,
'Are there not other hours for leisure?
   For love is any hour like this?'


   Artemia! faintly thou respondest,
As falsely deems that fiery youth;              10
A God there is who knows the truth,
   A God who tells me which is fondest.


**47**   [PENTHEUSA: FROM MYRTIS]


FRIENDS, whom she lookt at blandly from her couch
And her white wrist above it, gem-bedewed,
Were arguing with Pentheusa: she had heard
Report of Creon's death, whom years before
She listened to, well-pleas'd; and sighs arose;
For sighs full often fondle with reproofs
And will be fondled by them. When I came
After the rest to visit her, she said,
'Myrtis! how kind! Who better knows than thou
The pangs of love? and my first love was he!'       10
Tell me (if ever, Eros! are reveal'd
Thy secrets to the earth) have they been true
To any love who speak about the first?
What! shall these holier lights, like twinkling stars
In the few hours assign'd them, change their place,
And, when comes ampler splendour, disappear?
Idler I am, and pardon, not reply,
Implore from thee, thus questioned; well I know
Thou strikest, like Olympian Jove, but once.


**48**   [WAR]


WAR is it, O grave heads! that ye
With stern and stately pomp decree?
Inviting all the Gods from far
To join you in the game of war!
Have ye then lived so many years
To find no purer joy than tears?
And seek ye now the highest good
In strife, in anguish, and in blood?
Your wisdom may be more than ours,
But you have spent your golden hours,      10

And have methinks but little right
To make the happier fret and fight.
Ah! when will come the calmer day
When these dark clouds shall pass away?
When (should two cities disagree)
The young, the beauteous, and the free,
Rushing with all their force, shall meet
And struggle with embraces sweet,
Till they who may have suffer'd most
Give in, and own the battle lost.                          20

**49**   [THE RITES OF BACCHUS: FROM ALCAEUS]

WORMWOOD and rue be on his tongue
    And ashes on his head,
Who chills the feast and checks the song
    With emblems of the dead!

By young and jovial, wise and brave,
    Such mummers are derided.
His sacred rites shall Bacchus have,
    Unspared and undivided.

Couch't by my friends, I fear no mask
    Impending from above,                                  10
I only fear the later flask
    That holds me from my love.

**50**   A MORAL

PLEASURES! away; they please no more.
Friends! are they what they were before?
Loves! they are very idle things,
The best about them are their wings.
The dance! 'tis what the bear can do;
Music! I hate your music too.

    Whene'er these witnesses that Time
Hath snatcht the chaplet from our prime,
Are call'd by Nature, as we go
With eye more wary, step more slow,                        10
And will be heard and noted down,
However we may fret or frown,
Shall we desire to leave the scene
Where all our former joys have been?
No, 'twere ungrateful and unwise!
But when die down our charities

For human weal and human woes,
Then is the time our eyes should close.

51    ODE TO MILETUS

> MAIDEN there was whom Jove
> Illuded into love,
>     Happy and pure was she;
> Glorious from her the shore became,
> And Helle lifted up her name
> To shine eternal o'er the river-sea.
>
>  . And many tears are shed
>     Upon thy bridal-bed,
> Star of the swimmer in the lonely night!
>     Who with unbraided hair                    10
>     Wipedst a breast so fair,
> Bounding with toil, more bounding with delight.
>
>     But they whose prow hath past thy straits
>     And, ranged before Byzantion's gates,
> Bring to the God of sea the victim due,
>     Even from the altar raise their eyes,
>     And drop the chalice with surprise,
> And at such grandeur have forgotten you.
>
>     At last there swells the hymn of praise,
>     And who inspires those sacred lays?        20
>        'The founder of the walls ye see.'
>     What human power could elevate
>     Those walls, that citadel, that gate?
>        'Miletos, O my sons! was he.'
>
> Hail then, Miletus! hail beloved town,
>     Parent of me and mine!
> But let not power alone be thy renown,
>     Nor chiefs of ancient line,
>
>     Nor visits of the Gods, unless
>        They leave their thoughts below,        30
>     And teach us that we most should bless
>        Those to whom most we owe.
>
>     Restless is Wealth; the nerves of Power
>        Sink, as a lute's in rain:
>     The Gods lend only for an hour
>        And then call back again

All else than Wisdom; she alone,
   In Truth's or Virtue's form,
Descending from the starry throne
   Thro' radiance and thro' storm,                    40

Remains as long as godlike men
   Afford her audience meet,
Nor Time nor War tread down again
   The traces of her feet.

Always hast thou, Miletus, been the friend,
   Protector, guardian, father, of the wise;
Therefore shall thy dominion never end
   Till Fame, despoil'd of voice and pinion, dies.

With favouring shouts and flowers thrown fast behind,
   Arctinos ran his race,                    50
No wanderer he, alone and blind . .
   And Melesander was untorn by Thrace.

   There have been, but not here,
Rich men who swept aside the royal feast
   On child's or bondman's breast,
Bidding the wise and aged disappear.

   Revere the aged and the wise,
Aspasia! but thy sandal is not worn
   To trample on these things of scorn;
By his own sting the fire-bound scorpion dies.                    60

## 52    ERINNA TO LOVE

WHO breathes to thee the holiest prayer,
   O Love! is ever least thy care.
Alas! I may not ask thee why 'tis so . .
   Because a fiery scroll I see
   Hung at the throne of Destiny,
*Reason with Love and register with Woe.*

   Few question thee, for thou art strong,
   And, laughing loud at right and wrong,
Seizest, and dashest down, the rich, the poor;
   Thy sceptre's iron studs alike                    10
   The meaner and the prouder strike,
And wise and simple fear thee and adore.

53    [FROM SAPPHO]

SWEET girls! upon whose breast that God descends
    Whom first ye pray to come and next to spare,
O tell me whither now his course he bends,
    Tell me what hymn shall thither waft my prayer!
Alas! my voice and lyre alike he flies,
And only in my dreams, nor kindly then, replies.


54    SAPPHO TO HESPERUS

I HAVE beheld thee in the morning hour
    A solitary star, with thankless eyes,
    Ungrateful as I am! who bade thee rise
When sleep all night had wandered from my bower.

    Can it be true that thou art he
    Who shinest now above the sea
Amid a thousand, but more bright?
    Ah yes, the very same art thou
    That heard me then, and hearest now . .
Thou seemest, star of love! to throb with light.                    10


55    [BEAUTY]

BEAUTY! thou art a wanderer on the earth,
    And hast no temple in the fairest isle
Or city over-sea, where Wealth and Mirth
    And all the Graces, all the Muses, smile.

Yet these have always nurst thee, with such fond,
    Such lasting love, that they have followed up
Thy steps thro' every land, and placed beyond
    The reach of thirsty Time thy nectar-cup.

Thou art a wanderer, Beauty! like the rays
    That now upon the platan, now upon                              10
The sleepy lake, glance quick or idly gaze,
    And now are manifold and now are none.

I have call'd, panting, after thee, and thou
    Hast turn'd and look'd and said some pretty word,
Parting the hair, perhaps, upon my brow,
    And telling me none ever was preferr'd.

In more than one bright form hast thou appear'd,
    In more than one sweet dialect hast spoken:

Beauty! thy spells the heart within me heard,
   Griev'd that they bound it, grieves that they are broken.    20

## 56   THE SHADES OF AGAMEMNON AND IPHIGENEIA

   *Iphigeneia* FATHER! I now may lean upon your breast,
And you with unreverted eyes will grasp
Iphigeneia's hand.
               We are not shades
Surely! for yours throbs yet.
                  And did my blood
Win Troy for Greece?
                  Ah! 'twas ill done to shrink,
But the sword gleam'd so sharp, and the good priest
Trembled, and Pallas frown'd above, severe.
   *Agamemnon* Daughter!
   *Iphigeneia*           Beloved father! is the blade
Again to pierce my bosom? 'tis unfit
For sacrifice; no blood is in its veins;           10
No God requires it here; here are no wrongs
To vindicate, no realms to overthrow.
You are standing as at Aulis in the fane,
With face averted, holding (as before)
My hand; but yours burns not, as then it burn'd;
This alone shows that we are with the Blest,
Nor subject to the sufferings we have borne.
I will win back past kindness.
                Tell me then,
Tell how my mother fares who loved me so,
And griev'd, as 'twere for you, to see me part.        20
Frown not, but pardon me for tarrying
Amid too idle words, nor asking how
She prais'd us both (which most?) for what we did.
   *Agamemnon* Ye Gods who govern here! do human pangs
Reach the pure soul thus far below? do tears
Spring in these meadows?
    *Iphigeneia*         No, sweet father, no . .
I could have answered that; why ask the Gods?
   *Agamemnon* Iphigeneia! O my child! the Earth
Has gendered crimes unheard-of heretofore,
And Nature may have changed in her last depths,    30
Together with the Gods and all their laws.
   *Iphigeneia* Father! we must not let you here condemn;
Not, were the day less joyful: recollect
We have no wicked here; no king to judge.
Poseidon, we have heard, with bitter rage
Lashes his foaming steeds against the skies,

And, laughing with loud yell at winged fire
Innoxious to his fields and palaces,
Affrights the eagle from the sceptred hand;
While Pluto, gentlest brother of the three                          40
And happiest in obedience, views sedate
His tranquil realm, nor envies theirs above.
No change have we, not even day for night
Nor spring for summer.
                             All things are serene,
Serene too be your spirit! None on earth
Ever was half so kindly in his house,
And so compliant, even to a child.
Never was snatcht your robe away from me,
Though going to the council. The blind man
Knew his good king was leading him indoors            50
Before he heard the voice that marshall'd Greece.
Therefore all prais'd you.
                             Proudest men themselves
In others praise humility, and most
Admire it in the scepter and the sword.
What then can make you speak thus rapidly
And briefly? in your step thus hesitate?
Are you afraid to meet among the good
Incestuous Helen here?
     *Agamemnon*          Oh! Gods of Hell!
     *Iphigeneia* She hath not past the river.
                                   We may walk
With our hands linkt nor feel our house's shame.        60
     *Agamemnon* Never mayst thou, Iphigeneia, feel it!
Aulis had no sharp sword, thou wouldst exclaim,
Greece no avenger .. I, her chief so late,
Through Erebos, through Elysium, writhe beneath it.
     *Iphigeneia* Come, I have better diadems than those
Of Argos and Mycenai ..  come away,
And I will weave them for you on the bank.
You will not look so pale when you have walkt
A little in the grove, and have told all
Those sweet fond words the widow sent her child.        70
     *Agamemnon* O Earth! I suffered less upon thy shores!
(*Aside.*) The bath that bubbled with my blood, the blows
That spilt it (O worse torture!) must she know?
Ah! the first woman coming from Mycenai
Will pine to pour this poison in her ear,
Taunting sad Charon for his slow advance.
Iphigeneia!
     *Iphigeneia* Why thus turn away?
Calling me with such fondness! I am here,

Father! and where you are, will ever be.
    *Agamemnon* Thou art my child; yes, yes, thou art my child.   80
All was not once what all now is! Come on,
Idol of love and truth! my child! my child!
(*Alone.*) Fell woman! ever false! false was thy last
Denunciation, as thy bridal vow;
And yet even that found faith with me! The dirk
Which sever'd flesh from flesh, where this hand rests,
Severs not, as thou boastedst in thy scoffs,
Iphigeneia's love from Agamemnon:
The wife's a spark may light, a straw consume,
The daughter's not her heart's whole fount hath quencht,   90
'Tis worthy of the Gods, and lives for ever.
    *Iphigeneia* What spake my father to the Gods above?
Unworthy am I then to join in prayer?
If, on the last, or any day before,
Of my brief course on earth, I did amiss,
Say it at once, and let me be unblest;
But, O my faultless father! why should you?
And shun so my embraces?
                     Am I wild
And wandering in my fondness?
                           We are shades!
Groan not thus deeply; blight not thus the season   100
Of full-orb'd gladness! Shades we are indeed,
But mingled, let us feel it, with the blest.
I knew it, but forgot it suddenly,
Altho' I felt it all at your approach.
Look on me; smile with me at my illusion . .
You are so like what you have ever been
(Except in sorrow!) I might well forget
I could not win you as I used to do.
It was the first embrace since my descent
I ever aim'd at: those who love me live,   110
Save one, who loves me most, and now would chide me.
    *Agamemnon* We want not, O Iphigeneia, we
Want not embrace, nor kiss that cools the heart
With purity, nor words that more and more
Teach what we know from those we know, and sink
Often most deeply where they fall most light.
Time was when for the faintest breath of thine
Kingdom and life were little.
    *Iphigeneia*               Value them
As little now.
    *Agamemnon* Were life and kingdom all!
    *Iphigeneia* Ah! by our death many are sad who loved us.   120
The little fond Electra, and Orestes

So childish and so bold! O that mad boy!
They will be happy too.
                              Cheer! king of men!
Cheer! there are voices, songs . .   Cheer! arms advance.
    *Agamemnon* Come to me, soul of peace! These, these alone,
These are not false embraces.
    *Iphigeneia*                    Both are happy!
    *Agamemnon* Freshness breathes round me from some breeze above.
What are ye, winged ones! with golden urns?
        THE HOURS     (*descending*)
            The Hours. To each an urn we bring.
                    Earth's purest gold                          130
                    Alone can hold
            The lymph of the Lethèan spring.
            We, son of Atreus! we divide
            The dulcet from the bitter tide
                That runs athwart the paths of men.
            No more our pinions shalt thou see.
            Take comfort! We have done with thee,
            And must away to earth again.
                    (*Ascending*)
                    Where thou art, thou
                    Of braided brow,                             140
            Thou cull'd too soon from Argive bow'rs,
            Where thy sweet voice is heard among
            The shades that thrill with choral song,
            None can regret the parted Hours.

        CHORUS OF ARGIVES
            Maiden! be thou the spirit that breathes
                Triumph and joy into our song!
            Wear and bestow these amaranth-wreaths,
                Iphigeneia! they belong
            To none but thee and her who reigns
            (Less chaunted) on our bosky plains.               150

        SEMICHORUS
            Iphigeneia! 'tis to thee
            Glory we owe and victory.
            Clash, men of Argos, clash your arms
            To martial worth and virgin charms.

        OTHER SEMICHORUS
            Ye men of Argos! it was sweet
        To roll the fruits of conquest at the feet
        Whose whispering sound made bravest hearts beat fast:
                    This we have known at home,
                    But hither we are come
        To crown the king who ruled us first and last.        160

CHORUS
　　Father of Argos! king of men!
　　　　We chaunt the hymn of praise to thee.
　　In serried ranks we stand again,
　　　　Our glory safe, our country free.
　　Clash, clash the arms we bravely bore
　　Against Scamander's God-defended shore.

SEMICHORUS
　　Blessed art thou who hast repell'd
Battle's wild fury, Ocean's whelming foam;
　　Blessed o'er all, to have beheld
Wife, children, house avenged, and peaceful home!　　　　170

OTHER SEMICHORUS
　　We too, thou seest, are now
　　Among the happy, though the aged brow
From sorrow for us we could not protect,
　　Nor, on the polisht granite of the well
　　Folding our arms, of spoils and perils tell,
Nor lift the vase on the lov'd head erect.

SEMICHORUS
　　What whirling wheels are those behind?
　　What plumes come flaring through the wind,
　　　　Nearer and nearer? From his car
He who defied the heaven-born Powers of war　　　　180
　　　　Pelides springs: Dust, dust are we
　　　　To whom, O king, who bends the knee,
Proud only to be first in reverent praise of thee.

OTHER SEMICHORUS
　　Clash, clash the arms! None other race
　　Shall see such heroes face to face.
　　We too have fought; and they have seen
　　Nor sea-sand grey nor meadow green
　　Where Dardans stood against their men . .
　　Clash! Io Pæan! clash again!
　　Repinings for lost days repress . .　　　　190
　　The flames of Troy had cheer'd us less.

CHORUS
　　Hark! from afar more war-steeds neigh.
　　Thousands o'er thousands rush this way.
　　Ajax is yonder! ay, behold
　　The radiant arms of Lycian gold!
　　Arms from admiring valour won,
　　Tydeus! and worthy of thy son.
　　'Tis Ajax wears them now; for he
　　Rules over Adria's stormy sea.

He threw them to the friend who lost                    200
(By the dim judgment of the host)
Those wet with tears which Thetis gave
The youth most beauteous of the brave.
In vain! the insatiate soul would go
For comfort to his peers below.
Clash! ere we leave them all the plain,
Clash! Io Pæan! once again!

## MISCELLANEOUS POEMS, 1836-39

### 57    FAREWELL TO ITALY

I LEAVE thee, beauteous Italy! no more
From the high terraces, at even-tide,
To look supine into thy depths of sky,
Thy golden moon between the cliff and me,
Or thy dark spires of fretted cypresses
Bordering the channel of the milky-way.
Fiesole and Valdarno must be dreams
Hereafter, and my own lost Affrico
Murmur to me but in the poet's song.
I did believe (what have I not believed?)                    10
Weary with age, but unopprest by pain,
To close in thy soft clime my quiet day
And rest my bones in the Mimosa's shade.
Hope! Hope! few ever cherisht thee so little;
Few are the heads thou hast so rarely raised;
But thou didst promise this, and all was well.
For we are fond of thinking where to lie
When every pulse hath ceast, when the lone heart
Can lift no aspiration . . reasoning
As if the sight were unimpaired by death,                    20
Were unobstructed by the coffin-lid,
And the sun cheered corruption! Over all
The smiles of Nature shed a potent charm,
And light us to our chamber at the grave.

### 58    TO MY CHILD CARLINO

CARLINO! what art thou about, my boy?
Often I ask that question, though in vain,
For we are far apart: ah! therefore 'tis
I often ask it; not in such a tone
As wiser fathers do, who know too well.
Were we not children, you and I together?

Stole we not glances from each other's eyes?
Swore we not secrecy in such misdeeds?
Well could we trust each other. Tell me then
What thou art doing. Carving out thy name,                    10
Or haply mine, upon my favourite seat,
With the new knife I sent thee over sea?
Or hast thou broken it, and hid the hilt
Among the myrtles, starr'd with flowers, behind?
Or under that high throne whence fifty lilies
(With sworded tuberoses dense around)
Lift up their heads at once, not without fear
That they were looking at thee all the while.

   Does Cincirillo follow thee about?
Inverting one swart foot suspensively,                        20
And wagging his dread jaw at every chirp
Of bird above him in the olive-branch?
Frighten him then away! 'twas he who slew
Our pigeons, our white pigeons peacock-tailed,
That fear'd not you and me . . . alas, nor him!
I flattened his striped sides along my knee,
And reasoned with him on his bloody mind,
Till he looked blandly, and half-closed his eyes
To ponder on my lecture in the shade.
I doubt his memory much, his heart a little,                  30
And in some minor matters (may I say it?)
Could wish him rather sager. But from thee
God hold back wisdom yet for many years!
Whether in early season or in late
It always comes high-priced. For thy pure breast
I have no lesson; it for me has many.
Come throw it open then! What sports, what cares
(Since there are none too young for these) engage
Thy busy thoughts? Are you again at work,
Walter and you, with those sly labourers,                     40
Geppo, Giovanni, Cecco, and Poeta,
To build more solidly your broken dam
Among the poplars, whence the nightingale
Inquisitively watch'd you all day long?
I was not of your council in the scheme,
Or might have saved you silver without end,
And sighs too without number. Art thou gone
Below the mulberry, where that cold pool
Urged to devise a warmer, and more fit
For mighty swimmers, swimming three abreast?                  50
Or art thou panting in this summer noon
Upon the lowest step before the hall,

Drawing a slice of watermelon, long
As Cupid's bow, athwart thy wetted lips
(Like one who plays Pan's pipe) and letting drop
The sable seeds from all their separate cells,
And leaving bays profound and rocks abrupt,
Redder than coral round Calypso's cave?

## 59   WALTER TYRREL AND WILLIAM RUFUS

*Rufus* Tyrrel, spur onward! we must not await
The laggard lords: when they have heard the dogs
I warrant they will follow fast enough,
Each for his haunch. Thy roan is mettlesome;
How the rogue sidles up to me, and claims
Acquaintance with young Yorkshire! not afraid
Of wrinkling lip, nor ear laid down like grass
By summer thunder-shower on Windsor mead.
    *Tyrrel* Behold, my liege! hither they troop amain,
Over yon gap.
    *Rufus*      Over my pales? the dolts          10
Have broken down my pales!
    *Tyrrel*          Please you, my liege,
Unless they had, they must have ridden round
Eleven miles.
    *Rufus*    Why not have ridden round
Eleven miles? or twenty, were there need.
By our Lady! they shall be our carpenters
And mend what they have marr'd. At any time
I can make fifty lords; but who can make
As many head of deer, if mine escape?
And sure they will, unless they too are mad.
Call me that bishop . . him with hunting-cap          20
Surcharged with cross, and scarlet above knee.
    *Tyrrel* (*galloping forward*) . Ho! my lord bishop!
    *Bishop*             Who calls *me*?
    *Tyrrel*               Your slave.
    *Bishop* Well said, if toned as well and timed as well.
Who art thou? citizen or hind? what wantest?
    *Tyrrel* My lord! your presence; but before the king;
Where it may grow more placid at its leisure.
The morn is only streakt with red, my lord!
You beat her out and out: how prettily
You wear your stocking over head and ears!
Keep off the gorse and broom! they soon catch fire!          30
    *Bishop* The king shall hear of this: I recognise
Sir Walter Tyrrel.
    *Tyrrel*       And Sir Walter Tyrrel

By the same token duly recognises
The Church's well-begotten son, well-fed,
Well-mounted, and all well, except well-spoken,
The spiritual lord of Winchester.

    *Bishop* Ay, by God's grace! pert losel!
    *Tyrrel*               Prick along
Lord bishop! quicker! catch fresh air! we want it;
We have had foul enough till dinner-time.
    *Bishop* Varlet! I may chastise this insolence.        40
    *Tyrrel* I like those feathers: but there crows no cock
Without an answer. Though the noisiest throat
Sings from the belfrey of snug Winchester,
Yet he from Westminster hath stouter spurs.
    *Bishop* God's blood! were I no bishop ..
    *Tyrrel*              Then thy own
Were cooler.
    *Bishop*     Whip that hound aside! O Christ!
The beast has paw'd my housings! What a day
For dirt!
    *Tyrrel* The scent lies well; pity no more
The housings; look, my lord! here trots the king!
    *Rufus* Which of you broke my palings down?
    *Bishop*               God knows,    50
Most gracious sir.
    *Rufus*        No doubt he does; but you,
Bishop! could surely teach us what God knows.
Ride back and order some score handicrafts
To fix them in their places.
    *Bishop*          The command
Of our most gracious king shall be obeyed.

                            *[Riding off.*

Malisons on the atheist! Who can tell
Where are my squires and other men? confused
Among the servitors of temporal lords!
I must e'en turn again and hail that brute.
Sir Walter! good Sir Walter! one half-word!        60
                  *[*TYRREL *rides toward him.*
Sir Walter! may I task your courtesy
To find me any of my followers?
    *Tyrrel* Willingly.
    *Rufus*         Stay with me; I want thee, Tyrrel!
What does the bishop boggle at?
    *Tyrrel*             At nothing.
He seeks his people, to retrieve the damage.
    *Rufus* Where are the lords?
    *Tyrrel*            Gone past your Grace, bare-headed,
And falling in the rear.

*Rufus*               Well, prick then on.
I care but little for the chase to-day,
Although the scent lies sweetly. To knock down
My paling is vexatious. We must see                                    70
Our great improvements in this forest; what
Of roads blockt up, of hamlets swept away,
Of lurking dens called cottages, and cells,
And hermitages. Tyrrel! thou didst right
And dutifully, to remove the house
Of thy forefathers. 'Twas an odd request
To leave the dovecote for the sake of those
Flea-bitten blind old pigeons. There it stands!
But, in God's name! what mean these hives? the bees
May sting my dogs.
    *Tyrrel*           They hunt not in the summer.          80
    *Rufus* They may torment my fawns.
    *Tyrrel*                        Sir! not unless
Driven from their hives: they like the flowers much better.
    *Rufus* Flowers! and leave flowers too?
    *Tyrrel*                        Only some half-wild,
In tangled knots; balm, clary, marjoram.
    *Rufus* What lies beyond this close briar hedge, that smells
Through the thick dew upon it, pleasantly?
    *Tyrrel* A poor low cottage: the dry marl-pit shields it,
And, frail and unsupported like itself,
Peace-breathing honeysuckles comfort it
In its misfortunes.
    *Rufus*           I am fain to laugh                      90
At thy rank minstrelsy. A poor low cottage!
Only a poor low cottage! where, I ween,
A poor low maiden blesses Walter Tyrrel.
    *Tyrrel* It may be so.
    *Rufus*               No; it may not be so.
My orders were that all should be removed;
And, out of special favour, special trust
In thee, Sir Walter, I consigned the care
Into thy hands, of razing thy own house
And those about it; since thou hast another
Fairer and newer, and more lands around.                      100
    *Tyrrel* Hall, chapel, chamber, cellar, turret, grange,
Are level with the grass.
    *Rufus*               What negligence
To leave the work then incomplete, when little
Was there remaining! Strip that roof, and start
Thy petty game from cover.
    *Tyrrel*               O my liege!
Command not this!

  *Rufus*    Make me no confidant
Of thy base loves.
  *Tyrrel*   Nor you, my liege! nor any:
None such hath Walter Tyrrel.
  *Rufus*     Thou'rt at bay;
Thou hast forgotten thy avowal, man!
  *Tyrrel* My father's house is (like my father) gone:  110
But in that house, and from that father's heart
Mine grew into his likeness, and held thence
Its rich possessions . .  God forgive my boast!
He bade me help the needy, raise the low . .
  *Rufus* And stand against thy king!
  *Tyrrel*      How many yokes
Of oxen, from how many villages
For miles around, brought I, at my own charge,
To bear away the rafters and the beams
That were above my cradle at my birth,
And rang when I was christened, to the carouse  120
Of that glad father and his loyal friends!
  *Rufus* He kept good cheer, they tell me.
  *Tyrrel*     Yonder thatch
Covers the worn-out woman at whose breast
I hung, an infant.
  *Rufus*  Ay! and none beside?
  *Tyrrel* Four sons have fallen in the wars.
  *Rufus*     Brave dogs!
  *Tyrrel* She hath none left.
  *Rufus*   No daughter?
  *Tyrrel*    One.
  *Rufus*     I thought it.
Unkennel her.
  *Tyrrel*  Grace! pity! mercy on her!
  *Rufus* I will not have hot scents about my chase.
  *Tyrrel* A virtuous daughter of a virtuous mother
Deserves not this, my liege!
  *Rufus*   Am I to learn  130
What any subject at my hand deserves?
  *Tyrrel* Happy, who dares to teach it, and who can!
  *Rufus* And thou, forsooth!
  *Tyrrel*   I have done my duty, sire!
  *Rufus* Not half: perform the rest, or bide my wrath.
  *Tyrrel* What, break athwart my knee the staff of age!
  *Rufus* Question me, villain!
  *Tyrrel*   Villain I am none.
  *Rufus* Retort my words! By all the saints! thou diest,
False traitor.
  *Tyrrel*  Sire! no private wrong, no word

Spoken in angriness, no threat against
My life or honour, urge me . .

  *Rufus*       Urge to what?     140
Dismountest?

  *Tyrrel*  On my knees, as best beseems,
I ask . . not pardon, sire! but spare, oh spare
The child devoted, the deserted mother!

  *Rufus* Take her; take both.

  *Tyrrel*       She loves her home; her limbs
Fail her; her husband sleeps in that churchyard;
Her youngest child, born many years the last,
Lies (not half-length) along the father's coffin.
Such separate love grows stronger in the stem
(I have heard say) than others close together,
And that, where pass these funerals, all life's spring   150
Vanishes from behind them, all the fruits
Of riper age are shrivel'd, every sheaf
Husky; no gleaning left. She would die here,
Where from her bed she looks on his; no more
Able to rise, poor little soul! than he.

  *Rufus* Who would disturb them, child or father? where
Is the churchyard thou speakest of?

  *Tyrrel*      Among
Yon nettles: we have level'd all the graves.

  *Rufus* Right: or our horses might have stumbled on them.

  *Tyrrel* Your grace oft spares the guilty; spare the innocent!  160

  *Rufus* Up from the dew! thy voice is hoarse already.

  *Tyrrel* Yet God hath heard it. It entreats again,
Once more, once only; spare this wretched house.

  *Rufus* No, nor thee neither.

  *Tyrrel*      Speed me, God! and judge
O thou! between the oppressor and opprest!

           [*He pierces* RUFUS *with an arrow.*


**60**  [THE MESSAGE]


FATE! I have askt few things of thee,
  And fewer have to ask.
Shortly, thou knowest, I shall be
  No more: then con thy task.


If one be left on earth so late
  Whose love is like the past,
Tell her in whispers, gentle Fate!
  Not even love must last.

Tell her I leave the noisy feast
    Of life, a little tired,                  10
Amid its pleasures few possest
    And many undesired.

Tell her with steady pace to come
    And, where my laurels lie,
To throw the freshest on the tomb,
    When it has caught her sigh.

Tell her to stand some steps apart
    From others on that day,
And check the tear (if tear should start)
    Too precious for dull clay.           20

## 61    [TO PSYCHE]

AGAINST the rocking mast I stand,
    The Atlantic surges swell
To bear me from my native land
    And Psyche's wild farewell.

From billow upon billow hurl'd,
    Again I hear her say,
'Oh! is there nothing in the world
    Worth one short hour's delay?'

Alas, my Psyche! were it thus,
    I should not sail alone,            10
Nor seas nor fates had sever'd us . .
    But are you all my own?

Thus were it, never would burst forth
    These sighs so deep, so true!
But, what to me is little worth,
    The world, is much to you.

And you shall say, when once the dream
    (So hard to break!) is o'er,
My love was very dear to him,
    My fame and peace were more.      20

## 62    TO A PAINTER

CONCEAL not Time's misdeeds, but on my brow
    Retrace his mark:
Let the retiring hair be silvery now

That once was dark:
Eyes that reflected images too bright
        Let clouds o'ercast,
And from the tablet be abolisht quite
        The cheerful past.
Yet Care's deep lines should one from waken'd Mirth
        Steal softly o'er,                                        10
Perhaps on me the fairest of the Earth
        May glance once more.


**63**     HENRY THE EIGHTH AND ANNE BOLEYN
           SCENE IN RICHMOND CHASE
           HENRY, COURTIERS, HOUNDS, &c.


*Henry* Northumberland! pray tell me, if thou canst,
Who is that young one in the green and gold?
Dost thou not see her? hast thou left both eyes
Upon the bushes?
        *Northumberland*     There are many, sir,
In the same livery.
        *Henry*              I mean her yonder
On the iron-gray with yellow round his ears.
Impudent wench! she turns away her cheek!
        *Northumberland*                          [*After inquiring.*
The Lady Katharine Parr, an' please your Highness.
        *Henry* Faith! she *doth* please me. What a sap is rising
In that young bud! how supple! yet how solid!            10
What palpable perfection! ay, Lord Surrey?
        *Surrey* A bloom well worthy of a monarch's bower,
Where only one more lovely smiles beside him.
        *Henry* Though spring is stirring, yet give me the summer . .
I can wait yet. Some day, one not far off,
I would confer with her at Hampton-Court . .
Merely to ask her how she likes the chase:
We shall not have another all this season.
The stag alone can help us on in May:
To-morrow is the twentieth.
                                Hark! the knell              20
From Paul's . .  the Tower-gun, too! I am right enough!
                                        [*Claps his hands.*
I am a widower!                         [*Again claps his hands.*
                By this hour to-morrow
Sunny Jane Seymour's long and laughing eyes
Shall light me to our chamber.
                        Lords! prick on!
The merry hounds are chiding! To the chase
To-day! our coronation for to-morrow.

How sweetly that bell warbled o'er the water.
   *Norfolk* I like it better than the virginals.
   *Suffolk* They are poor music.
   *Norfolk*            Songs but make them worse.
   *Henry* Come; prick we onward. Shall we have a race?     30
   *Surrey* We are well mounted; but the youngest man
Will win, for majesty sits lightly on him.
   *Henry* It may well be. I have lost half my weight
This morning, lithesome as I was before.
Away!
   *Norfolk* His saddle swells its bolstered back
Already full two hundred yards before us.

## 64   ON SEEING A LADY SIT FOR HER PORTRAIT

THE basket upon which thy fingers bend,
   Thou mayst remember in my Tuscan hall,
When the glad children, gazing on a friend,
   From heedless arm let high-piled peaches fall
   On the white marble, splashing to the wall.

Oh, were they present at this later hour!
   Could they behold the form whole realms admire
Lean with such grace o'er cane and leaf and flower,
   Happy once more would they salute their sire,
   Nor wonder that her name still rests upon his lyre.     10

## from FRA RUPERT (1840)

## 65   [ACT V] SCENE IV    CASTLE OF MURO
### GIOVANNA. CHANCELLOR. HIGH STEWARD. CHAMBERLAIN.
### SECRETARIES.

   *Chancellor* Lady! we have heard all, and only ask
(For the realm's weal) your Highness will vouchsafe
To sign this parchment.
   *Giovanna* (*Taking it*). What contains it?
   *Chancellor*            Peace.
   *Giovanna* I then would sign it with my blood; but blood
Running from royal veins never sign'd peace.    (*Reads.*)
It seems I am required to abdicate
In favor of Duke Carlo of Durazzo.
   *Chancellor* Even so.
   *Giovanna* (*To the others*). To you I turn me, gentlemen!
If ever you are told that I admitted
His unjust claims, if ever you behold    10

Sign'd, as you fancy, by my hand the parchment
That waives our kingdom from its rightful heir,
Believe it not: only believe these tears,
Of which no false one ever fell from me
Among the many 'twas my fate to shed.
I want not yours; they come too late, my friends;
Farewell, then! You may live and serve your country;
These walls are mine, and nothing now beyond.

**66**    [ACT V] SCENE V    NAPLES
MAXIMIN. STEPHEN.


*Maximin* Among the idle and the fortunate
Never drops one but catafalc and canopy
Are ready for him: organ raves above,
And songsters wring their hands and push dull rhymes
Into dull ears that worse than wax hath stopt,
And cherubs puff their cheeks and cry half-split
With striding so across his monument.
Name me one honest man for whom such plays
Were ever acted.
                        They will ne'er lay Otho
With kindred clay! no helm, no boot beside                          10
His hurried bier! no stamp of stately soldier
Angry with grief and swearing hot revenge,
Until even the paid priest turns round and winks.
I will away: sick, weary . .
                        (STEPHEN *enters*.)
    *Stephen*                    Hast thou heard
The saddest thing?
    *Maximin*        Heard it? . . committed it,
Say rather. But for thee and thy curst gold,
Which, like magician's, turns to dust, I trow,
I had received him in the gate, and brought
The treasure of his soul before his eyes:
He had not closed them so.
    *Stephen*                    Worst of it all                     20
Is the queen's death.
    *Maximin*        The queen's?
    *Stephen*                        They stifled her
With her own pillow.
    *Maximin*        Who says that?
    *Stephen*                        The man
Runs wild who did it, through the streets, and howls it,
Then imitates her voice, and softly sobs
'*Lay me in Santa Chiara.*'

67   [ACT V] SCENE VI   NAPLES. BEFORE THE PALACE.
     AMONG GUARDS.
     MAXIMIN. DURAZZO.

    *Maximin*               Gallant prince!
Conqueror of more than men, of more than heroes!
What may that soldier merit who deserts
His post, and lets the enemy to the tent?
    *Durazzo* Death is the sentence.
    *Maximin*              Sign that sentence then.
I shall be found beside a new-made grave
In Santa Chiara.
    *Durazzo*     Art thou mad?
    *Maximin*           I shall be
If you delay.
    *Durazzo* (*To Guards*) See this man into Hungary.


# MISCELLANEOUS POEMS, 1841-46

68   [FROM MOSCHUS]

    AH! when the mallow in the croft dies down,
    Or the pale parsley or the crisped anise,
    Again they grow, another year they flourish;
    But we, the great, the valiant, and the wise,
    Once covered over in the hollow earth,
    Sleep a long, dreamless, unawakening sleep.

69   [IMITATION FROM CATULLUS]

    THE vessel which lies here at last
    Had once stout ribs and topping mast,
    And, whate'er wind there might prevail,
    Was ready for a row or sail.
    It now lies idle on its side,
    Forgetful o'er the stream to glide.
    And yet there have been days of yore
    When pretty maids their posies bore
    To crown its prow, its deck to trim,
    And freight it with a world of whim.        10
    A thousand stories it could tell,
    But it loves secrecy too well.
    Come closer, my sweet girl! pray do!
    There may be still one left for you.

**70**   THE HAMADRYAD

RHAICOS was born amid the hills wherefrom
Gnidos the light of Caria is discern'd,
And small are the white-crested that play near,
And smaller onward are the purple waves.
Thence festal choirs were visible, all crown'd
With rose and myrtle if they were inborn;
If from Pandion sprang they, on the coast
Where stern Athenè raised her citadel,
Then olive was intwined with violets
Cluster'd in bosses, regular and large.                          10
For various men wore various coronals;
But one was their devotion: 'twas to her
Whose laws all follow, her whose smile withdraws
The sword from Ares, thunderbolt from Zeus,
And whom in his chill caves the mutable
Of mind, Poseidon, the sea-king, reveres,
And whom his brother, stubborn Dis, hath pray'd
To turn in pity the averted cheek
Of her he bore away, with promises,
Nay, with loud oath before dread Styx itself,                   20
To give her daily more and sweeter flowers
Than he made drop from her on Enna's dell.
     Rhaicos was looking from his father's door
At the long trains that hastened to the town
From all the valleys, like bright rivulets
Gurgling with gladness, wave outrunning wave,
And thought it hard he might not also go
And offer up one prayer, and press one hand,
He knew not whose. The father call'd him in,
And said, 'Son Rhaicos! those are idle games;                   30
Long enough I have lived to find them so.'
And, ere he ended, sighed; as old men do
Always, to think how idle such games are.
'I have not yet,' thought Rhaicos in his heart,
And wanted proof.
                    'Suppose thou go and help
Echeion at the hill, to bark yon oak
And lop its branches off, before we delve
About the trunk and ply the root with axe:
This we may do in winter.'
                          Rhaicos went;
For thence he could see farther, and see more                   40
Of those who hurried to the city-gate.
Echeion he found there, with naked arm
Swart hair'd, strong sinew'd, and his eyes intent

Upon the place where first the axe should fall:
He held it upright. 'There are bees about,
Or wasps, or hornets,' said the cautious eld,
'Look sharp, O son of Thallinos!' The youth
Inclined his ear, afar, and warily,
And cavern'd in his hand. He heard a buzz
At first, and then the sound grew soft and clear,                50
And then divided into what seem'd tune,
And there were words upon it, plaintive words.
He turn'd, and said, 'Echeion! do not strike
That tree: it must be hollow; for some God
Speaks from within. Come thyself near.' Again
Both turn'd toward it: and behold! there sat
Upon the moss below, with her two palms
Pressing it on each side, a maid in form.
Downcast were her long eyelashes, and pale
Her cheek, but never mountain-ash display'd                      60
Berries of colour like her lip so pure,
Nor were the anemones about her hair
Soft, smooth, and wavering, like the face beneath.
    'What dost thou here?' Echeion, half-afraid,
Half-angry, cried. She lifted up her eyes,
But nothing spake she. Rhaicos drew one step
Backward, for fear came likewise over him,
But not such fear: he panted, gaspt, drew in
His breath, and would have turned it into words,
But could not into one.
                          'O send away                           70
That sad old man!' said she. The old man went
Without a warning from his master's son,
Glad to escape, for sorely he now fear'd,
And the axe shone behind him in their eyes.


*Hamadryad* And wouldst thou too shed the most innocent
Of blood? no vow demands it; no God wills
The oak to bleed.
    *Rhaicos*        Who art thou? whence? why here?
And whither wouldst thou go? Among the robed
In white or saffron, or the hue that most
Resembles dawn or the clear sky, is none                         80
Array'd as thou art. What so beautiful
As that gray robe which clings about thee close,
Like moss to stones adhering, leaves to trees,
Yet lets thy bosom rise and fall in turn,
As, toucht by zephyrs, fall and rise the boughs
Of graceful platan by the river-side.
    *Hamadryad* Lovest thou well thy father's house?

*Rhaicos*                                        Indeed
I love it, well I love it, yet would leave
For thine, where'er it be, my father's house,
With all the marks upon the door, that show                          90
My growth at every birth-day since the third,
And all the charms, o'erpowering evil eyes,
My mother nail'd for me against my bed,
And the Cydonian bow (which thou shalt see)
Won in my race last spring from Eutychos.
    *Hamadryad* Bethink thee what it is to leave a home
Thou never yet hast left, one night, one day.
    *Rhaicos* No, 'tis not hard to leave it; 'tis not hard
To leave, O maiden, that paternal home,
If there be one on earth whom we may love                            100
First, last, for ever; one who says that she
Will love for ever too. To say which word,
Only to say it, surely is enough . .
It shows such kindness . . If 'twere possible
We at the moment think she would indeed.
    *Hamadryad* Who taught thee all this folly at thy age?
    *Rhaicos* I have seen lovers and have learnt to love.
    *Hamadryad* But wilt thou spare the tree?
    *Rhaicos*                                        My father wants
The bark; the tree may hold its place awhile.
    *Hamadryad* Awhile! thy father numbers then my days!            110
    *Rhaicos* Are there no other where the moss beneath
Is quite as tufty? Who would send thee forth
Or ask thee why thou tarriest? Is thy flock
Anywhere near?
    *Hamadryad*   I have no flock: I kill
Nothing that breathes, that stirs, that feels the air,
The sun, the dew. Why should the beautiful
(And thou art beautiful) disturb the source
Whence springs all beauty? Hast thou never heard
Of Hamadryads?
    *Rhaicos*        Heard of them I have:
Tell me some tale about them. May I sit                              120
Beside thy feet? Art thou not tired? The herbs
Are very soft; I will not come too nigh;
Do but sit there, nor tremble so, nor doubt.
Stay, stay an instant: let me first explore
If any acorn of last year be left
Within it; thy thin robe too ill protects
Thy dainty limbs against the harm one small
Acorn may do. Here's none. Another day
Trust me; til then let me sit opposite.
    *Hamadryad* I seat me; be thou seated, and content.              130

    *Rhaicos* O sight for gods! Ye men below! adore
The Aphroditè. *Is* she there below?
Or sits she here before me? as she sate
Before the shepherd on those highths that shade
The Hellespont, and brought his kindred woe.
    *Hamadryad* Reverence the higher Powers; nor deem amiss
Of her who pleads to thee, and would repay . .
Ask not how much . . but very much. Rise not:
No, Rhaicos, no! Without the nuptial vow
Love is unholy. Swear to me that none         140
Of mortal maids shall ever taste thy kiss,
Then take thou mine; then take it, not before.
    *Rhaicos* Hearken, all gods above! O Aphroditè!
O Herè! let my vow be ratified!
But wilt thou come into my father's house?
    *Hamadryad* Nay: and of mine I can not give thee part.
    *Rhaicos* Where is it?
    *Hamadryad*        In this oak.
    *Rhaicos*                    Ay; now begins
The tale of Hamadryad: tell it through.
    *Hamadryad* Pray of thy father never to cut down
My tree; and promise him, as well thou mayst,        150
That every year he shall receive from me
More honey than will buy him nine fat sheep,
More wax than we will burn to all the gods.
Why fallest thou upon thy face? Some thorn
May scratch it, rash young man! Rise up; for shame!
    *Rhaicos* For shame I can not rise. Oh pity me!
I dare not sue for love . . but do not hate!
Let me once more behold thee . . not once more,
But many days: let me love on . . unloved!
I aimed too high: on my own head the bolt        160
Falls back, and pierces to the very brain.
    *Hamadryad* Go . . rather go, than make me say I love.
    *Rhaicos* If happiness is immortality,
(And whence enjoy it else the gods above?)
I am immortal too: my vow is heard:
Hark! on the left . . Nay, turn not from me now,
I claim my kiss.
    *Hamadryad* Do men take first, then claim?
Do thus the seasons run their course with them?

  . . Her lips were seal'd, her head sank on his breast.
'Tis said that laughs were heard within the wood:        170
But who should hear them? . . and whose laughs? and why?
    Savoury was the smell, and long past noon,
Thallinos! in thy house; for marjoram,

Basil and mint, and thyme and rosemary,
Were sprinkled on the kid's well roasted length,
Awaiting Rhaicos. Home he came at last,
Not hungry, but pretending hunger keen,
With head and eyes just o'er the maple plate.
'Thou seest but badly, coming from the sun,
Boy Rhaicos!' said the father. 'That oak's bark                    180
Must have been tough, with little sap between;
It ought to run; but it and I are old.'
Rhaicos, although each morsel of the bread
Increast by chewing, and the meat grew cold
And tasteless to his palate, took a draught
Of gold-bright wine, which, thirsty as he was,
He thought not of until his father fill'd
The cup, averring water was amiss,
But wine had been at all times pour'd on kid,
It was religion.
                         He thus fortified                         190
Said, not quite boldly, and not quite abasht,
'Father, that oak is Zeusis' own; that oak
Year after year will bring thee wealth from wax
And honey. There is one who fears the gods
And the gods love . .   that one'
                                        (He blusht, nor said
What one)
                    'Hath promist this, and may do more.
We have not many moons to wait until
The bees have done their best: if then there come
Nor wax nor honey, let the tree be hewn.'
     'Zeus hath bestow'd on thee a prudent mind,'                  200
Said the glad sire: 'but look thou often there,
And gather all the honey thou canst find
In every crevice, over and above
What hath been promist; would they reckon that?'
     Rhaicos went daily; but the nymph was oft
Invisible. To play at love, she knew,
Stopping its breathings when it breathes most soft,
Is sweeter than to play on any pipe.
She play'd on his: she fed upon his sighs;
They pleas'd her when they gently waved her hair,                  210
Cooling the pulses of her purple veins,
And when her absence brought them out they pleas'd.
Even among the fondest of them all,
What mortal or immortal maid is more
Content with giving happiness than pain?
One day he was returning from the wood
Despondently. She pitied him, and said

'Come back!' and twined her fingers in the hem
Above his shoulder. Then she led his steps
To a cool rill that ran o'er level sand                                220
Through lentisk and through oleander, there
Bathed she his feet, lifting them on her lap
When bathed, and drying them in both her hands.
He dared complain; for those who most are loved
Most dare it; but not harsh was his complaint.
'O thou inconstant!' said he, 'if stern law
Bind thee, or will, stronger than sternest law,
Oh, let me know henceforward when to hope
The fruit of love that grows for me but here.'
He spake; and pluckt it from its pliant stem.          230
'Impatient Rhaicos! why thus intercept
The answer I would give? There is a bee
Whom I have fed, a bee who knows my thoughts
And executes my wishes: I will send
That messenger. If ever thou art false,
Drawn by another, own it not, but drive
My bee away: then shall I know my fate,
And, . . for thou must be wretched, . . weep at thine.
But often as my heart persuades to lay
Its cares on thine and throb itself to rest,              240
Expect her with thee, whether it be morn,
Or eve, at any time when woods are safe.'

    Day after day the Hours beheld them blest,
And season after season: years had past,
Blest were they still. He who asserts that Love
Ever is sated of sweet things, the same
Sweet things he fretted for in earlier days,
Never, by Zeus! loved he a Hamadryad.
        The nights had now grown longer, and perhaps
The Hamadryads find them lone and dull              250
Among their woods; one did, alas! She called
Her faithful bee: 'twas when all bees should sleep,
And all did sleep but hers. She was sent forth
To bring that light which never wintry blast
Blows out, nor rain nor snow extinguishes,
The light that shines from loving eyes upon
Eyes that love back, till they can see no more.

    Rhaicos was sitting at his father's hearth:
Between them stood the table, not o'erspread
With fruits which autumn now profusely bore,       260
Nor anise cakes, nor odorous wine; but there
The draft-board was expanded; at which game

Triumphant sat old Thallinos; the son
Was puzzled, vext, discomfited, distraught.
A buzz was at his ear: up went his hand,
And it was heard no longer. The poor bee
Return'd (but not until the morn shone bright)
And found the Hamadryad with her head
Upon her aching wrist, and showed one wing
Half-broken off, the other's meshes marr'd,                    270
And there were bruises which no eye could see
Saving a Hamadryad's.
                        At this sight
Down fell the languid brow, both hands fell down,
A shriek was carried to the ancient hall
Of Thallinos: he heard it not: his son
Heard it, and ran forthwith into the wood.
No bark was on the tree, no leaf was green,
The trunk was riven through. From that day forth
Nor word nor whisper sooth'd his ear, nor sound
Even of insect wing: but loud laments                          280
The woodmen and the shepherds one long year
Heard day and night; for Rhaicos would not quit
The solitary place, but moan'd and died.


Hence milk and honey wonder not, O guest,
To find set duly on the hollow stone.


## 71    TO MY DAUGHTER

BY that dejected city Arno runs
Where Ugolino claspt his famisht sons;
There wert thou born, my Julia! there thine eyes
Return'd as bright a blue to vernal skies;
And thence, sweet infant wanderer! when the Spring
Advanced, the Hours brought thee on silent wing,
Brought (while anemones were quivering round,
And pointed tulips pierced the purple ground)
Where stands fair Florence: there thy voice first blest
My ears, and sank like balm into my breast.                    10
For many griefs had wounded it, and more
Thy little hands could lighten, were in store.
But why revert to griefs? 'thy sculptur'd brow
Dispels from mine its darkest cloud even now.
What then the bliss to see again thy face
And all that rumour has announced of grace!
I urge with fevered breast the coming day . .
O could I sleep and wake again in May!

## 72   ON SOUTHEY'S DEATH

NOT the last struggles of the Sun
Precipitated from his golden throne
    Hold darkling mortals in sublime suspence;
But the calm exod of a man,
Nearer, but far above, who ran
    The race we run, when Heaven recalls him hence.

Thus, O thou pure of mortal taint,
Thus, O my Southey! poet, sage, and saint,
    Thou after saddest silence art removed:
What voice in anguish can we raise,                                10
Or would we, dare we, in thy praise?
    God now does that . . the God thy whole heart loved.


## 73   TO ROBERT BROWNING

THERE is delight in singing, tho' none hear
Beside the singer: and there is delight
In praising, tho' the praiser sit alone
And see the prais'd far off him, far above.
Shakspeare is not our poet, but the world's,
Therefore on him no speech! and brief for thee,
Browning! Since Chaucer was alive and hale,
No man hath walkt along our roads with step
So active, so inquiring eye, or tongue
So varied in discourse. But warmer climes                         10
Give brighter plumage, stronger wing: the breeze
Of Alpine highths thou playest with, borne on
Beyond Sorrento and Amalfi, where
The Siren waits thee, singing song for song.


## 74   [ONE YEAR AGO]

ONE year ago my path was green,
My footstep light, my brow serene;
Alas! and could it have been so
    One year ago?
There is a love that is to last
When the hot days of youth are past:
Such love did a sweet maid bestow
    One year ago!

I took a leaflet from her braid
And gave it to another maid.                              10
Love! broken should have been thy bow
    One year ago.


## from THE WORKS OF WALTER SAVAGE LANDOR (1846)

### 75    [SHAKESPEARE]

HE lighted with his golden lamp on high
The unknown regions of the human heart,
Show'd its bright fountains, show'd its rueful wastes,
Its shoals and headlands; and a tower he rais'd
Refulgent, where eternal breakers roll,
For all to see, but no man to approach.


### 76    THE DEATH OF ARTEMIDORA

'ARTEMIDORA! Gods invisible,
While thou art lying faint along the couch,
Have tied the sandal to thy slender feet
And stand beside thee, ready to convey
Thy weary steps where other rivers flow.
Refreshing shades will waft thy weariness
Away, and voices like thy own come near
And nearer, and solicit an embrace.'
    Artemidora sigh'd, and would have prest
The hand now pressing hers, but was too weak.        10
Iris stood over her dark hair unseen
While thus Elpenor spake. He lookt into
Eyes that had given light and life erewhile
To those above them, but now dim with tears
And wakefulness. Again he spake of joy
Eternal. At that word, that sad word, *joy*,
Faithful and fond her bosom heav'd once more:
Her head fell back: and now a loud deep sob
Swell'd thro' the darken'd chamber; 'twas not hers.


### 77    [LETHE'S WATER]

ON love, on grief, on every human thing,
Time sprinkles Lethe's water with his wing.

**78    THRASYMEDES AND EUNÖE**

WHO will away to Athens with me? who
Loves choral songs and maidens crown'd with flowers,
Unenvious? mount the pinnace; hoist the sail.
I promise ye, as many as are here,
Ye shall not, while ye tarry with me, taste
From unrinsed barrel the diluted wine
Of a low vineyard or a plant ill-pruned,
But such as anciently the Ægæan iles
Pour'd in libation at their solemn feasts:
And the same goblets shall ye grasp, embost          10
With no vile figures of loose languid boors,
But such as Gods have lived with and have led.
    The sea smiles bright before us. What white sail
Plays yonder? what pursues it? Like two hawks
Away they fly. Let us away in time
To overtake them. Are they menaces
We hear? And shall the strong repulse the weak,
Enraged at her defender? Hippias!
Art thou the man? 'Twas Hippias. He had found
His sister borne from the Cecropian port             20
By Thrasymedes. And reluctantly?
Ask, ask the maiden; I have no reply.
    'Brother! O brother Hippias! O, if love,
If pity, ever toucht thy breast, forbear!
Strike not the brave, the gentle, the beloved,
My Thrasymedes, with his cloak alone
Protecting his own head and mine from harm.'
'Didst thou not once before,' cried Hippias,
Regardless of his sister, hoarse with wrath
At Thrasymedes, 'didst not thou, dog-eyed,           30
Dare, as she walkt up to the Parthenon,
On the most holy of all holy days,
In sight of all the city, dare to kiss
Her maiden cheek?'
                'Ay, before all the Gods,
Ay, before Pallas, before Artemis,
Ay, before Aphrodite, before Herè,
I dared; and dare again. Arise, my spouse!
Arise! and let my lips quaff purity
From thy fair open brow.'
              The sword was up,
And yet he kist her twice. Some God withheld         40
The arm of Hippias; his proud blood seeth'd slower
And smote his breast less angrily; he laid
His hand on the white shoulder, and spake thus:

'Ye must return with me. A second time
Offended, will our sire Pisistratos
Pardon the affront? Thou shouldst have askt thyself
This question ere the sail first flapt the mast.'
'Already thou hast taken life from me;
Put up thy sword,' said the sad youth, his eyes
Sparkling; but whether love or rage or grief                    50
They sparkled with, the Gods alone could see.
Piræeus they re-entered, and their ship
Drove up the little waves against the quay,
Whence was thrown out a rope from one above,
And Hippias caught it. From the virgin's waist
Her lover dropt his arm, and blusht to think
He had retain'd it there in sight of rude
Irreverent men: he led her forth, nor spake.
Hippias walkt silent too, until they reacht
The mansion of Pisistratos her sire.                            60
Serenely in his sternness did the prince
Look on them both awhile: they saw not him,
For both had cast their eyes upon the ground.
'Are these the pirates thou hast taken, son?'
Said he. 'Worse, father! worse than pirates they,
Who thus abuse thy patience, thus abuse
Thy pardon, thus abuse the holy rites
Twice over.'
              'Well hast thou performed thy duty,'
Firmly and gravely said Pisistratos.
'Nothing then, rash young man! could turn thy heart            70
From Eunöe, my daughter?'
                        'Nothing, sir,
Shall ever turn it. I can die but once
And love but once. O Eunöe! farewell!'
'Nay, she shall see what thou canst bear for her.'
'O father! shut me in my chamber, shut me
In my poor mother's tomb, dead or alive,
But never let me see what he can bear;
I know how much that is, when borne for me.'
'Not yet: come on. And lag not thou behind,
Pirate of virgin and of princely hearts!                       80
Before the people and before the Goddess
Thou hadst evinced the madness of thy passion,
And now wouldst bear from home and plenteousness
To poverty and exile this my child.'
Then shuddered Thrasymedes, and exclaim'd,
'I see my crime; I saw it not before.
The daughter of Pisistratos was born
Neither for exile nor for poverty,

Ah! nor for me!' He would have wept, but one
Might see him, and weep worse. The prince unmoved 90
Strode on, and said, 'To-morrow shall the people,
All who beheld thy trespasses, behold
The justice of Pisistratos, the love
He bears his daughter, and the reverence
In which he holds the highest law of God.'
    He spake; and on the morrow they were one.

## 79   ICARIOS AND ERIGONÈ

IMPROVIDENT were once the Attic youths,
As (if we may believe the credulous
And testy) various youths have been elsewhere.
But truly such was their improvidence,
Ere Pallas in compassion was their guide,
They never stowed away the fruits of earth
For winter use; nor knew they how to press
Olive or grape: yet hospitality
Sate at the hearth, and there was mirth and song.
Wealthy and generous in the Attic land, 10
Icarios! wert thou; and Erigonè,
Thy daughter, gave with hearty glee the milk,
Buzzing in froth beneath unsteddy goat,
To many who stopt near her; some for thirst,
And some to see upon its back that hand
So white and small and taper, and await
Until she should arise and show her face.
The father wisht her not to leave his house,
Nor she to leave her father; yet there sued
From all the country round both brave and rich; 20
Some, nor the wealthier of her wooers, drove
Full fifty slant-brow'd kingly-hearted swine,
Reluctant ever to be led aright,
Race autocratical, autochthon race,
Lords of the woods, fed by the tree of Jove.
Some had three ploughs; some had eight oxen; some
Had vines, on oak, on maple, and on elm,
In long and strait and gleamy avenues,
Which would have tired you had you reacht the end
Without the unshapen steps that led beyond 30
Up the steep hill to where they leand on poles.
Yet kind the father was, and kind the maid.
And now when winter blew the chaff about,
And hens pursued the grain into the house,
Quarrelsome and indignant at repulse,
And rushing back again with ruffled neck,

They and their brood; and kids blinkt at the brand,
And bee-nosed oxen, with damp nostrils lowered
Against the threshold, stampt the dogs away;
Icarios, viewing these with thoughtful mind,                    40
Said to Erigonè, 'Not scantily
The Gods have given us these birds, and these
Short-bleating kids, and these loose-hided steers.
The Gods have given: to them will we devote
A portion of their benefits, and bid
The youths who love and honor us partake:
So shall their hearts, and so shall ours, rejoice.'
The youths were bidden to the feast: the flesh
Of kid and crested bird was plentiful:
The steam hung on the rafters, where were nail'd          50
Bushes of savory herbs, and figs and dates;
And yellow-pointed pears sent down long stalks
Through nets wide-mesht, work of Erigonè
When night was long and lamp yet unsupplied.
Choice grapes Icarios had; and these, alone
Of all men in the country, he preserved
For festive days; nor better day than this
To bring them from beneath his reed-thatcht roof.
He mounted the twelve stairs with hearty pride,
And soon was heard he, breathing hard: he now            60
Descended, holding in both arms a cask,
Fictile, capacious, bulging: cork-tree bark
Secured the treasure; wax above the mouth,
And pitch above the wax. The pitch he brake,
The wax he scraped away, and laid them by,
Wrenching up carefully the cork-tree bark.
A hum was heard. 'What! are there bees within?'
Euphorbas cried. 'They came then with the grapes,'
Replied the elder, and pour'd out clear juice
Fragrant as flowers, and wrinkled husks anon.               70
'The ghosts of grapes!' cried Phanor, fond of jokes
Within the house, but ever abstinent
Of such as that in woodland and alone,
Where any sylvan God might overhear.
No few were saddened at the ill-omen'd word,
But sniffing the sweet odour, bent their heads,
Tasted, sipt, drank, ingurgitated: fear
Flew from them all, joy rusht to every breast,
Friendship grew warmer, hands were join'd, vows sworn.
From cups of every size, from cups two-ear'd,              80
From ivy-twisted and from smooth alike,
They dash the water; they pour in the wine;
(For wine it was) until that hour unseen.

They emptied the whole cask; and they alone;
For both the father and the daughter sate
Enjoying their delight. But when they saw
Flusht faces, and when angry words arose
As one more fondly glanced against the cheek
Of the fair maiden on her seat apart,
And she lookt down, or lookt another way                    90
Where other eyes caught hers and did the like,
Sadly the sire, the daughter fearfully,
Upon each other fixt wide-open eyes.
This did the men remark, and, bearing signs
Different, as were their tempers, of the wine,
But feeling each the floor reel under him,
Each raging with more thirst at every draught,
Acastor first (sidelong his step) arose,
Then Phanor, then Antyllos:
                              'Zeus above
Confound thee, cursed wretch!' aloud they cried,            100
'Is this thy hospitality? must all
Who loved thy daughter perish at a blow?
Not at a blow, but like the flies and wasps.'
Madness had seiz'd them all. Erigonè
Ran out for help: what help? Before her sprang
Mœra, and howl'd and barkt, and then return'd
Presaging. They had dragg'd the old man out
And murdered him. Again flew Mœra forth,
Faithful, compassionate, and seiz'd her vest,
And drew her where the body lay, unclosed               110
The eyes, and rais'd toward the stars of heaven.
    Thou who hast listened, and stil ponderest,
Raise thine, for thou hast heard enough, raise thine
And view Böotes bright among those stars,
Brighter the Virgin: Mœra too shines there.
But where were the Eumenides? Repress
Thy anger. If the clear calm stars above
Appease it not, and blood must flow for blood,
Harken, and hear the sequel of the tale.
Wide-seeing Zeus lookt down; as mortals knew              120
By the woods bending under his dark eye,
And huge towers shuddering on the mountain tops,
And stillness in the valley, in the wold,
And over the deep waters all round earth.
He lifted up his arm, but struck them not
In their abasement: by each other's blow
They fell; some suddenly; but more beneath
The desperate gasp of long-enduring wounds.

**80**   IPHIGENEIA AND AGAMEMNON

IPHIGENEIA, when she heard her doom
At Aulis, and when all beside the king
Had gone away, took his right-hand, and said,
'O father! I am young and very happy.
I do not think the pious Calchas heard
Distinctly what the Goddess spake. Old-age
Obscures the senses. If my nurse, who knew
My voice so well, sometimes misunderstood
While I was resting on her knee both arms
And hitting it to make her mind my words,                              10
And looking in her face, and she in mine,
Might not he also hear one word amiss,
Spoken from so far off, even from Olympus?'
The father placed his cheek upon her head,
And tears dropt down it, but the king of men
Replied not. Then the maiden spake once more.
'O father! sayst thou nothing? Hear'st thou not
Me, whom thou ever hast, until this hour,
Listen'd to fondly, and awaken'd me
To hear my voice amid the voice of birds,                              20
When it was inarticulate as theirs,
And the down deadened it within the nest?'
He moved her gently from him, silent stil,
And this, and this alone, brought tears from her,
Altho' she saw fate nearer: then with sighs,
'I thought to have laid down my hair before
Benignant Artemis, and not have dimm'd
Her polisht altar with my virgin blood;
I thought to have selected the white flowers
To please the Nymphs, and to have askt of each                         30
By name, and with no sorrowful regret,
Whether, since both my parents will'd the change,
I might at Hymen's feet bend my clipt brow;
And (after these who mind us girls the most)
Adore our own Athena, that she would
Regard me mildly with her azure eyes.
But, father! to see you no more, and see
Your love, O father! go ere I am gone. . '
Gently he moved her off, and drew her back,
Bending his lofty head far over her's,                                 40
And the dark depths of nature heaved and burst.
He turn'd away; not far, but silent stil.
She now first shudder'd; for in him, so nigh,
So long a silence seem'd the approach of death,
And like it. Once again she rais'd her voice.

'O father! if the ships are now detain'd,
And all your vows move not the Gods above,
When the knife strikes me there will be one prayer
The less to them: and purer can there be
Any, or more fervent than the daughter's prayer          50
For her dear father's safety and success?'
A groan that shook him shook not his resolve.
An aged man now enter'd, and without
One word, stept slowly on, and took the wrist
Of the pale maiden. She lookt up, and saw
The fillet of the priest and calm cold eyes.
Then turn'd she where her parent stood, and cried
'O father! grieve no more: the ships can sail.'

81    [PROEM]

O FRIENDS! who have accompanied thus far
My quickening steps, sometimes where sorrow sate
Dejected, and sometimes where valour stood
Resplendent, right before us; here perhaps
We best might part; but one to valour dear
Comes up in wrath and calls me worse than foe,
Reminding me of gifts too ill deserved.
I must not blow away the flowers he gave,
Altho' now faded; I must not efface
The letters his own hand has traced for me.                10
    Here terminates my park of poetry.
Look out no longer for extensive woods,
For clusters of unlopt and lofty trees,
With stately animals coucht under them,
Or grottoes with deep wells of water pure,
And ancient figures in the solid rock:
Come, with our sunny pasture be content,
Our narrow garden and our homestead croft,
And tillage not neglected. Love breathes round;
Love, the bright atmosphere, the vital air,                20
Of youth; without it life and death are one.

82    [THE TORCH OF LOVE]

THE torch of Love dispels the gloom
Of life, and animates the tomb;
But never let it idly flare
On gazers in the open air,
Nor turn it quite away from one
To whom it serves for moon and sun,
And who alike in night or day
Without it could not find his way.

83    [A DREAM]

SHE I love (alas in vain!)
    Floats before my slumbering eyes:
When she comes she lulls my pain,
    When she goes what pangs arise!
Thou whom love, whom memory flies,
    Gentle Sleep! prolong thy reign!
If even thus she soothe my sighs,
    Never let me wake again!

84    [CHILL BEAUTY]

THOU hast not rais'd, Ianthe, such desire
    In any breast as thou hast rais'd in mine.
No wandering meteor now, no marshy fire,
    Leads on my steps, but lofty, but divine:
And, if thou chillest me, as chill thou dost
    When I approach too near, too boldly gaze,
So chills the blushing morn, so chills the host
    Of vernal stars, with light more chaste than day's.

85    [EBBING HOPES]

MY hopes retire; my wishes as before
Struggle to find their resting-place in vain:
The ebbing sea thus beats against the shore;
The shore repels it; it returns again.

86    [LOVE FOR LIFE]

SOON, O Ianthe! life is o'er,
    And sooner beauty's heavenly smile:
Grant only (and I ask no more),
    Let love remain that little while.

87    [I CAN NOT TELL]

I CAN not tell, not I, why she
Awhile so gracious, now should be
So grave: I can not tell you why
The violet hangs its head awry.
It shall be cull'd, it shall be worn,
In spite of every sign of scorn,
Dark look, and overhanging thorn.

88    IANTHE'S TROUBLES

YOUR pleasures spring like daisies in the grass,
    Cut down and up again as blythe as ever;
From you, Ianthe, little troubles pass
    Like little ripples in a sunny river.

89    [THE SOUND OF SPRING]

YOU tell me I must come again
    Now buds and blooms appear:
Ah! never fell one word in vain
    Of yours on mortal ear.
You say the birds are busy now
    In hedgerow, brake, and grove,
And slant their eyes to find the bough
    That best conceals their love:
How many warble from the spray!
    How many on the wing!                                    10
'Yet, yet,' say you, 'one voice away
    I miss the sound of spring.'
How little could that voice express,
    Beloved, when we met!
But other sounds hath tenderness,
    Which neither shall forget.

90    [IANTHE THREATENED]

A TIME will come when absence, grief, and years,
    Shall change the form and voice that please you now,
When you perplext shall ask, 'And fell my tears
    Into his bosom? breath'd I there my vow?'

It must be so, Ianthe! but to think
    Malignant Fate should also threaten *you*,
Would make my heart, now vainly buoyant, sink:
    Believe it not: 'tis what I'll never do.

91    [THE DULLER OLIVE]

ON the smooth brow and clustering hair
    Myrtle and rose! your wreath combine,
The duller olive I would wear,
    Its constancy, its peace, be mine.

92    [HALF EMBRACE]

ALONG this coast I led the vacant Hours
    To the lone sunshine on the uneven strand,
And nipt the stubborn grass and juicier flowers
    With one unconscious inobservant hand,
While crept the other by degrees more near
    Until it rose the cherisht form around,
And prest it closer, only that the ear
    Might lean, and deeper drink some half-heard sound.

93    [NO ANSWERING SMILE]

NO, thou hast never griev'd but I griev'd too;
Smiled thou hast often when no smile of mine
Could answer it. The sun himself can give
But little colour to the desert sands.

94    [TWENTY YEARS HENCE]

TWENTY years hence my eyes may grow
If not quite dim, yet rather so,
Still yours from others they shall know
                    Twenty years hence.
Twenty years hence tho' it may hap
That I be call'd to take a nap
In a cool cell where thunder-clap
                    Was never heard.
There breathe but o'er my arch of grass
A not too sadly sigh'd *Alas*,                          10
And I shall catch, ere you can pass,
                    That winged word.

95    [AGELESS LOVE]

REMAIN, ah not in youth alone,
    Tho' youth, where you are, long will stay,
But when my summer days are gone,
    And my autumnal haste away.
'*Can I be always by your side?*'
    No; but the hours you can, you must,
Nor rise at Death's approaching stride,
    Nor go when dust is gone to dust.

**96   [AM I HE?]**

IS it no dream that I am he
    Whom one awake all night
Rose ere the earliest birds to see,
    And met by dawn's red light;

Who, when the wintry lamps were spent
    And all was drear and dark,
Against the rugged pear-tree leant
    While ice crackt off the bark;

Who little heeded sleet and blast,
    But much the falling snow;           10
*Those* in few hours would sure be past,
    His traces *that* might show;

Between whose knees, unseen, unheard,
    The honest mastiff came,
Nor fear'd he; no, nor was he fear'd:
    Tell me, am I the same?

O come! the same dull stars we'll see,
    The same o'er-clouded moon.
O come! and tell me am I he?
    O tell me, tell me soon.           20

**97   WHAT NEWS**

HERE, ever since you went abroad,
    If there be change, no change I see,
I only walk our wonted road,
    The road is only walkt by me.

Yes; I forgot; a change there is;
    Was it of *that* you bade me tell?
I catch at times, at times I miss
    The sight, the tone, I know so well.

Only two months since you stood here!
    Two shortest months! then tell me why    10
Voices are harsher than they were,
    And tears are longer ere they dry.

98    [LOVE AND ANGER]

> TELL me not things past all belief;
>     One truth in you I prove;
> The flame of anger, bright and brief,
>     Sharpens the barb of Love.

99    [PROUD WORDS]

> PROUD word you never spoke, but you will speak
>     Four not exempt from pride some future day.
> Resting on one white hand a warm wet cheek
>     Over my open volume you will say,
>     'This man loved *me*!' then rise and trip away.

100    FOR AN URN IN THORESBY PARK

> WITH frigid art our numbers flow
> For joy unfelt and fabled woe;
> And listless are the poet's dreams
> Of pastoral pipe and haunted streams.
> All Nature's boundless reign is theirs,
> But most her triumphs and her tears.
> They try, nor vainly try, their power
> To cheer misfortune's lonely hour;
> Whether they raise the laurell'd head,
> Or stoop beneath the peasant's shed,                    10
> They pass the glory they bestow,
> And shine above the light they throw.
> To Valour, in his car of fire,
> Shall Genius strike the solemn lyre:
> A Riou's fall shall Manvers mourn,
> And Virtue raise the vacant urn.

101    [MY NATAL DAY]

> THE day returns, my natal day,
>     Borne on the storm and pale with snow,
> And seems to ask me why I stay,
>     Stricken by Time and bowed by Woe.
>
> Many were once the friends who came
>     To wish me joy; and there are some
> Who wish it now; but not the same;
>     They are whence friend can never come;
>
> Nor are they you my love watcht o'er
>     Cradled in innocence and sleep;                    10

You smile into my eyes no more,
   Nor see the bitter tears they weep.

## 102  [RETURN]

EVERYTHING tells me you are near;
   The hail-stones bound along and melt,
In white array the clouds appear,
   The spring and you our fields have felt.
Paris, I know, is hard to quit;
   But you have left it; and 'twere silly
To throw away more smiles and wit
   Among the forests of Chantilly.
Her moss-paved cell your rose adorns
   To tempt you; and your cyclamen         10
Turns back his tiny twisted horns
   As if he heard your voice again.

## 103  [MOTHER AND GIRL]

'YOU must give back,' her mother said,
To a poor sobbing little maid,
'All the young man has given you,
Hard as it now may seem to do.'
''Tis done already, mother dear!'
Said the sweet girl, 'So, never fear.'
   *Mother* Are you quite certain? Come, recount
(There was not much) the whole amount.
   *Girl* The locket: the kid gloves.
   *Mother*                 Go on.
   *Girl* Of the kid gloves I found but one.      10
   *Mother* Never mind that. What else? Proceed.
You gave back all his trash?
   *Girl*            Indeed.
   *Mother* And was there nothing you would save?
   *Girl* Everything I could give I gave.
   *Mother* To the last tittle?
   *Girl*            Even to that.
   *Mother* Freely?
   *Girl*       My heart went *pit-a-pat*
At giving up . . ah me! ah me!
I cry so I can hardly see . .
All the fond looks and words that past,
And all the kisses, to the last.         20

**104**  [PAST PLEASURES]

WHY, why repine, my pensive friend,
    At pleasures slipt away?
Some the stern Fates will never lend,
    And all refuse to stay.

I see the rainbow in the sky,
    The dew upon the grass,
I see them, and I ask not why
    They glimmer or they pass.

With folded arms I linger not
    To call them back; 'twere vain;                    10
In this, or in some other spot,
    I know they'll shine again.

**105**  [FAVOURITE PAINTERS]

FIRST bring me Raffael, who alone hath seen
In all her purity Heaven's virgin queen,
Alone hath felt true beauty; bring me then
Titian, ennobler of the noblest men;
And next the sweet Correggio, nor chastise
His little Cupids for those wicked eyes.
I want not Rubens's pink puffy bloom,
Nor Rembrandt's glimmer in a dusty room.
With those, and Poussin's nymph-frequented woods,
His templed highths and long-drawn solitudes                10
I am content, yet fain would look abroad
On one warm sunset of Ausonian Claude.

**106**  [THE STATUE]

HE who sees rising from some open down
    A column, stately, beautiful, and pure,
Its rich expansive capital would crown
    With glorious statue, which might long endure,
And bring men under it to gaze and sigh
    And wish that honour'd creature they had known,
Whose name the deep inscription lets not die.
    I raise that statue and inscribe that stone.

**107**  [WAR IN CHINA]

THERE may be many reasons why,
O ancient land of Kong-Fu-Tsi!

Some fain would make the little feet
Of thy indwellers run more fleet.
But while, as now, before my eyes
The steams of thy sweet herb arise,
Amid bright vestures, faces fair,
Long eyes, and closely braided hair,
And many a bridge and many a barge,
And many a child and bird as large,                         10
I can not wish thee wars nor woes . .
And when thy lovely single rose,
Which every morn I haste to see,
Smiles with fresh-opened flower on me,
And when I think what hand it was
Cradled the nursling in its vase,
By all the Gods! O ancient land!
I wish thee and thy laws to stand.

## 108  [TERNISSA]

TERNISSA! you are fled!
I say not to the dead,
But to the happy ones who rest below:
For, surely, surely, where
Your voice and graces are,
Nothing of death can any feel or know.
Girls who delight to dwell
Where grows most asphodel,
Gather to their calm breasts each word you speak:
The mild Persephone                                        10
Places you on her knee,
And your cool palm smoothes down stern Pluto's cheek.

## 109  [WHAT REMAINS]

NO, my own love of other years!
No, it must never be.
Much rests with you that yet endears,
Alas! but what with me?
Could those bright years o'er me revolve
So gay, o'er you so fair,
The pearl of life we would dissolve
And each the cup might share.
You show that truth can ne'er decay,
Whatever fate befals;                                       10
I, that the myrtle and the bay
Shoot fresh on ruin'd walls.

**110**  LINES TO A DRAGON FLY

LIFE (priest and prophet say) is but a dream;
   I wish no happier one than to be laid
   Beneath a cool syringa's scented shade,
Or wavy willow, by the running stream,
   Brimful of moral, where the dragon-fly,
   Wanders as careless and content as I.
Thanks for this fancy, insect king,
Of purple crest and filmy wing,
Who with indifference givest up
The water-lily's golden cup,                                    10
To come again and overlook
What I am writing in my book.
Believe me, most who read the line
Will read with hornier eyes than thine;
And yet their souls shall live for ever,
And thine drop dead into the river!
God pardon them, O insect king,
Who fancy so unjust a thing!

**111**  [MEMORY AND PRIDE]

'DO you remember me? or are you proud?'
Lightly advancing thro' her star-trimm'd crowd,
   Ianthe said, and lookt into my eyes.
'A *yes*, a *yes*, to both: for Memory
Where you but once have been must ever be,
   And at your voice Pride from his throne must rise.'

**112**  TO J. S.

MANY may yet recall the hours
That saw the lover's chosen flowers
Nodding and dancing in the shade
Thy dark and wavy tresses made:
On many a brain is pictured yet
Thy languid eye's dim violet,
But who among them all foresaw
How the sad snows that never thaw
Upon that head one day should lie
And love but glimmer from that eye.                             10

**113**  [SEDATER PLEASURES]

YES; I write verses now and then,
But blunt and flaccid is my pen,

No longer talkt of by young men
    As rather clever:

In the last quarter are my eyes,
You see it by their form and size;
Is it not time then to be wise?
    Or now or never.

Fairest that ever sprang from Eve!
While Time allows the short reprieve,                10
Just look at me! would you believe
    'Twas once a lover?

I can not clear the five-bar gate,
But, trying first its timber state,
Climb stiffly up, take breath, and wait
    To trundle over.

Thro' gallopade I can not swing
The entangling blooms of Beauty's spring:
I can not say the tender thing,
    Be't true or false,                20

And am beginning to opine
Those girls are only half-divine
Whose waists yon wicked boys entwine
    In giddy waltz.

I fear that arm above that shoulder,
I wish them wiser, graver, older,
Sedater, and no harm if colder
    And panting less.

Ah! people were not half so wild
In former days, when, starchly mild,                30
Upon her high-heel'd Essex smiled
    The brave Queen Bess.

## 114 MALVOLIO

THOU hast been very tender to the moon,
Malvolio! and on many a daffodil
And many a daisy hast thou yearn'd, until
The nether jaw quiver'd with thy good heart.
But tell me now, Malvolio, tell me true,
Hast thou not sometimes driven from their play
The village children, when they came too near

Thy study, if hit ball rais'd shouts around,
Or if delusive trap shook off thy muse,
Pregnant with wonders for another age?                    10
Hast thou sat still and patient (tho' sore prest
Hearthward to stoop and warm thy blue-nail'd hand)
Lest thou shouldst frighten from a frosty fare
The speckled thrush, raising his bill aloft
To swallow the red berry on the ash
By thy white window, three short paces off?
If *this* thou hast not done, and hast done *that*,
I do exile thee from the moon twelve whole
Calendar months, debarring thee from use
Of rose, bud, blossom, odour, simile,                     20
And furthermore I do hereby pronounce
Divorce between the nightingale and thee.

## 115  GOOD-BYE

LOVED when my love from all but thee had flown,
Come near me; seat thee on this level stone,
And, ere thou lookest o'er the churchyard-wall
To catch, as once we did, yon waterfall,
Look a brief moment on the turf between
And see a tomb thou never yet hast seen.
My spirit will be sooth'd to hear once more
*Good-bye*, as gently spoken as before.

## 116  [END OF THE YEAR]

SUMMER has doft his latest green,
    And Autumn ranged the barley-mows.
So long away then have you been?
    And are you coming back to close
    The year? It sadly wants repose.

## 117  [THE FIESOLAN VILLA]

WHERE three huge dogs are ramping yonder
    Before that villa with its tower,
No braver boys, no father fonder,
    Ever prolong'd the moonlight hour.

Often, to watch their sports unseen,
    Along the broad stone bench he lies,
The oleander-stems between
    And citron-boughs to shade his eyes.

The clouds now whiten far away,
   And villas glimmer thick below,                    10
And windows catch the quivering ray,
   Obscure one minute's space ago.

Orchards and vine-knolls maple-propt
   Rise radiant round: the meads are dim,
As if the milky-way had dropt
   And fill'd Valdarno to the brim.

Unseen beneath us, on the right,
   The abbey with unfinisht front
Of checker'd marble, black and white,
   And on the left the Doccia's font.                    20

Eastward, two ruin'd castles rise
   Beyond Maiano's mossy mill,
Winter and Time their enemies,
   Without their warder, stately still.

The heaps around them there will grow
   Higher, as years sweep by, and higher,
Till every battlement laid low
   Is seized and trampled by the briar.

That line so lucid is the weir
   Of Rovezzano: but behold                    30
The graceful tower of Giotto there,
   And Duomo's cross of freshen'd gold.

We can not tell, so far away,
   Whether the city's tongue be mute,
We only hear some lover play
   (If sighs be play) the sighing flute.

## 118  [FALLING LEAVES]

   THE leaves are falling; so am I;
The few late flowers have moisture in the eye;
    So have I too.
   Scarcely on any bough is heard
   Joyous, or even unjoyous, bird
    The whole wood through.

   Winter may come: he brings but nigher
His circle (yearly narrowing) to the fire
    Where old friends meet:

Let him; now heaven is overcast,                    10
And spring and summer both are past,
    And all things sweet.

119   [FOR A GRAVE IN WIDCOMBE CHURCH-YARD]

THE place where soon I think to lie,
In its old creviced nook hard-by
    Rears many a weed:
If parties bring you there, will you
Drop slily in a grain or two
    Of wall-flower seed?

I shall not see it, and (too sure!)
I shall not ever hear that your
    Light step was there;
But the rich odour some fine day                    10
Will, what I cannot do, repay
    That little care.

120   FLOWERS SENT IN BAY-LEAVES

I LEAVE for you to disunite
    Frail flowers and lasting bays:
One, let me hope, you'll wear to-night
    The other all your days.

121   PLAYS

HOW soon, alas, the hours are over,
Counted us out to play the lover!
And how much narrower is the stage,
Allotted us to play the sage!
But when we play the fool, how wide
The theater expands; beside,
How long the audience sits before us!
How many prompters! what a chorus!

122   TO JULIUS HARE
WITH 'PERICLES AND ASPASIA'

JULIUS, of three rare brothers, my fast friends,
The latest known to me! Aspasia comes
With him, high-helmeted and trumpet-tongued,
Who loved her. Well thou knowest all his worth,
Valuing him most for trophies rear'd to Peace,
For generous friendships, like thy own, for Arts

Ennobled by protection, not debased.
Hence, worthless ones! throne-cushions, puft, inert,
Verminous, who degrade with patronage
Bargain'd for, ere dealt out! The stone that flew          10
In splinters from the chisel when the hand
Of Phidias wielded it, the chips of stone
Weigh with me more than they do. To thy house
Comes Pericles. Receive the friend of him
Whose horses started from the Parthenon
To traverse seas and neigh upon our strand.
From pleasant Italy my varied page,
Where many men and many ages meet,
Julius! thy friendly hand long since received.
Accept my last of labours and of thanks.                   20
He who held mute the joyous and the wise
With wit and eloquence, whose tomb (afar
From all his friends and all his countrymen)
Saddens the light Palermo, to thy care
Consign'd it; knowing that whate'er is great
Needs not the looming of a darker age,
Nor knightly mail nor scymetar begemm'd.
Stepping o'er all this lumber, where the steel
Is shell'd with rust, and the thin gold worm'd out
From its meandering waves, he took the scroll,             30
And read aloud what sage and poet spake
In sunnier climes; thou heardest it well pleas'd;
For Truth from conflict rises more elate
And lifts a brighter torch, beheld by more.
Call'd to befriend me by fraternal love,
Thou pausedst in thy vigorous march amid
The German forests of wide-branching thought,
Deep, intricate, whence voices shook all France,
Whence Blucher's soldiers heard the trumpet-tongue
And knew the footstep of Tyrtæan Arndt.                    40

## 123   TO SOUTHEY

THERE are who teach us that the depths of thought
Engulph the poet; that irregular
Is every greater one. Go, Southey! mount
Up to those teachers; ask, submissively,
Who so proportioned as the lord of day?
Yet mortals see his stedfast stately course
And lower their eyes before him. Fools gaze up
Amazed at daring flights. Does Homer soar
As hawks and kites and weaker swallows do?
He knows the swineherd; he plants apple-trees              10

Amid Alcinous's cypresses;
He covers with his aged black-vein'd hand
The plumy crest that frighten'd and made cling
To its fond-mother the ill-fated child;
He walks along Olympus with the Gods,
Complacently and calmly, as along
The sands where Simöis glides into the sea.
They who step high and swing their arms, soon tire.
*The glorious Theban then?*

                      The sage from Thebes,
Who sang his wisdom when the strife of cars                                    20
And combatants had paus'd, deserves more praise
Than this untrue one, fitter for the weak,
Who by the lightest breezes are borne up
And with the dust and straws are swept away;
Who fancy they are carried far aloft
When nothing quite distinctly they descry,
Having lost all self-guidance. But strong men
Are strongest with their feet upon the ground.
Light-bodied Fancy, Fancy plover-winged,
Draws some away from culture to dry downs                                     30
Where none but insects find their nutriment;
There let us leave them to their sleep and dreams.
    Great is that poet, great is he alone,
Who rises o'er the creatures of the earth,
Yet only where his eye may well discern
The various movements of the human heart,
And how each mortal differs from the rest.
Although he struggle hard with Poverty,
He dares assert his just prerogative
To stand above all perishable things,                                         40
Proclaiming *this* shall live, and *this* shall die.

## 124 LINES ON THE DEATH OF CHARLES LAMB

ONCE, and once only, have I seen thy face,
Elia! once only has thy tripping tongue
Run o'er my breast, yet never has been left
Impression on it stronger or more sweet.
Cordial old man! what youth was in thy years,
What wisdom in thy levity, what truth
In every utterance of that purest soul!
Few are the spirits of the glorified
I'd spring to earlier at the gate of Heaven.

**125** TO MISS ISABELLA PERCY

> IF that old hermit laid to rest
>     Beneath your chapel-floor,
> Could leave the regions of the blest
>     And visit earth once more:
> If human sympathies could warm
>     His tranquil breast again,
> Your innocence that breast could charm,
>     Perhaps your beauty pain.

**126** TO A BRIDE, FEB. 17, 1846

> A STILL, serene, soft day; enough of sun
> To wreathe the cottage smoke like pine-tree snow,
> Whiter than those white flowers the bride-maids wore;
> Upon the silent boughs the lissom air
> Rested; and, only when it went, they moved,
> Nor more than under linnet springing off.
> Such was the wedding-morn: the joyous Year
> Lept over March and April up to May.
>     Regent of rising and of ebbing hearts,
> Thyself borne on in cool serenity,                              10
> All heaven around and bending over thee,
> All earth below and watchful of thy course!
> Well hast thou chosen, after long demur
> To aspirations from more realms than one.
> Peace be with those thou leavest! peace with thee!
> Is that enough to wish thee? not enough,
> But very much: for Love himself feels pain,
> While brighter plumage shoots, to shed last year's;
> And one at home (how dear that one!) recalls
> Thy name, and thou recallest one at home.                       20
> Yet turn not back thine eyes; the hour of tears
> Is over; nor believe thou that Romance
> Closes against pure Faith her rich domain.
> Shall only blossoms flourish there? Arise,
> Far-sighted bride! look forward! clearer views
> And higher hopes lie under calmer skies.
> Fortune in vain call'd out to thee; in vain
> Rays from high regions darted; Wit pour'd out
> His sparkling treasures; Wisdom laid his crown
> Of richer jewels at thy reckless feet.                          30
> Well hast thou chosen. I repeat the words,
> Adding as true ones, not untold before,
> That incense must have fire for its ascent,
> Else 'tis inert and can not reach the idol.

Youth is the sole equivalent of youth.
Enjoy it while it lasts; and last it will;
Love can prolong it in despite of Years.


## from THE HELLENICS OF WALTER SAVAGE LANDOR (1847)

### 127  PAN AND PITYS

CEASE to complain of what the Gods decree,
Whether by death or (harder!) by the hand
Of one prefer'd thy loves be torn away,
For even against the bourn of Arcady
Beats the sad Styx, heaving its wave of tears,
And nought on earth so high but Care flies higher.
   A maid was wooed by Boreas and by Pan,
Pitys her name, her haunt the wood and wild;
Boreas she fled from; with more placid eye
Lookt she on Pan; yet chided him, and said . .          10
'Ah why should men or clearer-sighted Gods
Propose to link our hands eternally?
That which o'er raging seas is wildly sought
Perishes and is trampled on in port;
And they where all things are immutable
Beside, even they, the very Gods, are borne
Unsteddily wherever love impels;
Even he who rules Olympus, he himself
Is lighter than the cloud beneath his feet.
Lovers are ever an uncertain race,                      20
And they the most so who most loudly sing
Of truth and ardour, anguish and despair,
But thou above them all. Now tell me, Pan,
How thou deceivedst the chaste maid of night
Cynthia, thou keeper of the snow-white flock!
Thy reed had crackled with thy flames, and split
With torture after torture; thy lament
Had fill'd the hollow rocks; but when it came
To touch the sheep-fold, there it paus'd and cool'd.
Wonderest thou whence the story reacht my ear?          30
Why open those eyes wider? why assume
The ignorant, the innocent? prepared
For refutation, ready to conceal
The fountain of Selinos, waving here
On the low water its long even grass,
And there (thou better may'st remember this)
Paved with smooth stones, as temples are. The sheep

Who led the rest, struggled ere yet half-shorn,
And dragged thee slithering after it: thy knee
Bore long the leaves of ivy twined around                    40
To hide the scar, and stil the scar is white.
Dost thou deny the giving half thy flock
To Cynthia? hiding tho' the better half,
Then all begrimed producing it, while stood
Well-washt and fair in puffy wooliness
The baser breed, and caught the unpracticed eye.'
    Pan blusht, and thus retorted.
                    'Who hath told
That idle fable of an age long past?
More just, perhaps more happy, hadst thou been,
Shunning the false and flighty. Heard I have               50
Boreas and his rude song, and seen the goats
Stamp on the rock and lick the affrighted eyes
Of their young kids; and thee too, then averse,
I also saw, O Pitys! Is thy heart,
To what was thy aversion, now inclined?
Believest thou my foe? the foe of all
I hold most dear. Had Cynthia been prefer'd
She would not thus have taunted me: unlike
Thee, Pitys, she looks down with gentle glance
On them who suffer; whether they abide                      60
In the low cottage or the lofty tower
She tends them, and with silent step alike
And watchful eye their aking vigil soothes.
I sought not Cynthia; Cynthia lean'd to me.
Not pleased too easily, unlovely things
She shuns, by lovely (and none else) detain'd.
Sweet, far above all birds, is philomel
To her; above all scenes the Padan glades
And their soft-whispering poplars; sweet to her
The yellow light of box-tree in full bloom                  70
Nodding upon Cytoros. She delights
To wander thro' the twinkling olive-grove,
And where in clusters on Lycæan knolls
Redden the berries of the mountain-ash;
In glassy fountain, and grey temple-top,
And smooth sea-wave, when Hesperus hath left
The hall of Tethys, and when liquid sounds
(Uncertain whence) are wafted to the shore . .
Never in Boreas.'
                  'What a voice is thine!'
She said, and smiled. 'More roughly not himself            80
Could sound with all his fury his own name.
But come, thou cunning creature! tell me how

Thou couldst inveigle Goddesses without
Thinning thy sheepfold.'
                       'What! again' cried he
'Such tart and cruel twitting? She received,
Not as belov'd, but loving me, my gift.
I gave her what she askt, and more had given,
But half the flock was all that she required;
Need therefor was it to divide in twain
The different breeds, that she might have her choice.     90
One, ever meager, with broad bony front,
Shone white enough, but harder than goat's hair
The wool about it; and loud bleatings fill'd
The plains it battened on . .   for only plains
It trod; and smelt . .  as all such coarse ones smell.
Avarice urged the Goddess: she sprang forth
And took, which many more have done, the worse.
    'Why shake thy head? Incredulous! Ah why,
When none believe the truth, should I confess?
Why, one who hates and scorns the lover, love?     100
Once thou reposedst on the words I spake,
And, when I ceast to speak, thou didst not cease
To ponder them, but with thy cool plump palm
Unconsciously didst stroke that lynx-skin down
Which Bacchus gave me, toucht with virgin shame
If any part slipt off and bared my skin.
I then could please thee, could discourse, could pause,
Could look away from that sweet face, could hide
All consciousness that any hand of mine
Had crept where lifted knee would soon unbend.     110
Ah then how pleasant was it to look up
(If thou didst too) from the green glebe supine,
And drink the breath of all sweet herbs, and watch
The last rays run along the level clouds,
Until they kindle into living forms
And sweep with golden net the western sky.
Meanwhile thou notedst the dense troop of crows
Returning on one track and at one hour
In the same darkened intervals of heaven.
Then mutual faith was manifest, but glad     120
Of fresh avowal; then securely lay
Pleasure, reposing on the crop she reapt.
    'The oleaster of the cliff; the vine
Of leaf pellucid, clusterless, untamed;
The tufts of cytisus that half-conceal'd
The craggy cavern, narrow, black, profound;
The scantier broom below it, that betray'd
Those two white fawns to us . .  what now are they?

How the pine's whispers, how the simpering brook's,
How the bright vapour trembling o'er the grass          130
Could I enjoy, unless my Pitys took
My hand and show'd me them; unless she blew
My pipe when it was hoarse; and, when my voice
Fail'd me, took up, and so inspired, my song.'
   Thus he, embracing with brown brawny arm
Her soft white neck, not far from his declined,
And with sharp finger parting her smooth hair.
He paus'd.
        'Take now that pipe,' said she 'and since
Thou findest joyance in things past, run o'er
The race-course of our pleasures: first will I          140
The loves . . of Boreas I abhor . . relate.
He his high spirit, his uprooted oaks,
And heaven confused with hailstones, may sing on:
How into thine own realms his breath has blown
The wasting flames, until the woods bow'd low
Their heads with heavy groans, while he alert
Shook his broad pinions and scream'd loud with joy.
He may sing on, of shattered sails, of ships
Sunk in the depths of ocean, and the sign
Of that wide empire from Jove's brother torn;          150
And how beneath the rocks of Ismaros
Deluded he with cruel sport the dream
That brought the lost one back again, and heard
The Manes clap their hands at her return.
Always his pastime was it, not to shake
Light dreams away, but change them into forms
Horrific; churl, from peace and truth averse.
What in such rival ever couldst thou fear?'
   Boreas heard all she spoke, amid the brake
Conceal'd: rage seiz'd him: the whole mountain shook.          160
'Contemn'd!' said he, and as he said it, split
A rock, and from the summit with his foot
Spurn'd it on Pitys. Ever since, beneath
That rock sits Pan: her name he calls; he waits
Listening, to hear the rock repeat it; wipes
The frequent tear from his hoarse reed, and wears
Henceforth the pine, her pine, upon his brow.

## 128 SILENUS

SILENUS, when he led the Satyrs home,
Young Satyrs, tender-hooft and ruddy-horn'd,
With Bacchus equal-aged, sat down sometimes
Where softer herbs invited, then releast

From fawn-skin pouch a well-compacted pipe,
And sprinkled song with wisdom.
                              Some admired
The graceful order of unequal reeds;
Others cared little for the melody
Or what the melody's deep bosom bore,
And thought Silenus might have made them shine.          10
They whisper'd this: Silenus overheard,
And mildly said "Twere easy: thus I did
When I was youthful: older, I perceive
No pleasure in the buzzes of the flies,
Which like what *you* like, O my little ones!'
     Some fancied he reproved them, and stood still,
Until they saw how grave the Satyr boys
Were looking; then one twitcht an upright ear
And one a tail recurv'd, or stroked it down.
Audacious innocence! A bolder cried                      20
'Sound us a song of war;' a timider,
'Tell us a story that will last til night.'
     Silenus smiled on both, and thus replied.
'Chromis hath sung fierce battles, swords of flame,
Etherial arrows wing'd with ostrich-plumes,
Chariots of chrysolite and ruby reins,
And horses champing pearls and quaffing blood.
Mnasylos tells wide stories: day is short,
Night shorter; they thro months and years extend.
When suns are warm, my children, let your hearts        30
Beat, but not beat for battles; when o'ercast,
Mnasylos and his tepid fogs avoid.
     'I hear young voices near us; they are sweet;
Go where they call you; I am fain to rest;
Leave me, and ask for no more song to-day.'


## MISCELLANEOUS POEMS, 1848-52

**129** TO VERONA

VERONA! thy tall gardens stand erect
Beckoning me upward. Let me rest awhile
Where the birds whistle hidden in the boughs,
Or fly away when idlers take their place,
Mated as well, conceal'd as willingly;
Idlers whose nest must not swing there, but rise
Beneath a gleamy canopy of gold,
Amid the flight of Cupids, and the smiles

Of Venus ever radiant o'er their couch.
Here would I stay, here wander, slumber here,                    10
Nor pass into that theater below
Crowded with their faint memories, shades of joy.
But ancient song arouses me: I hear
Cœlius and Aufilena; I behold
Lesbia, and Lesbia's linnet at her lip
Pecking the fruit that ripens and swells out
For him whose song the Graces loved the most,
Whatever land, east, west, they visited.
Even he must not detain me: one there is
Greater than he, of broader wing, of swoop                      20
Sublimer. Open now that humid arch
Where Juliet sleeps the quiet sleep of death,
And Romeo sinks aside her.
                                    Fare ye well,
Lovers! Ye have not loved in vain: the hearts
Of millions throb around ye. This lone tomb
One greater than yon walls have ever seen,
Greater than Manto's prophet eye foresaw
In her own child or Rome's, hath hallowed;
And the last sod or stone a pilgrim knee
Shall press (Love swears it, and swears true) is here.          30

## 130  DYING SPEECH OF AN OLD PHILOSOPHER

I STROVE with none, for none was worth my strife;
    Nature I loved, and, next to Nature, Art;
I warmed both hands before the fire of Life;
    It sinks, and I am ready to depart.

## 131  TO THE AUTHOR OF 'FESTUS'
### ON THE CLASSICK AND ROMANTICK

PHILIP! I know thee not, thy song I know:
It fell upon my ear among the last
Destined to fall upon it; but while strength
Is left me, I will rise to hail the morn
Of the stout-hearted who begin a work
Wherin I did but idle at odd hours.
    The Faeries never tempted me away
From higher fountains and severer shades;
Their rings allured me not from deeper track
Left by Olympick wheel on ampler plain;                         10
Yet could I see them and can see them now
With pleasurable warmth, and hold in bonds
Of brotherhood men whom their gamesome wreath

In youth's fresh slumber caught, and stil detains.
I wear no cestus; my right-hand is free
To point the road few seem inclined to take.
Admonish thou, with me, the starting youth,
Ready to seize all nature at one grasp,
To mingle earth, sea, sky, woods, cataracts,
And make all nations think and speak alike.     20
  Some see but sunshine, others see but gloom,
Others confound them strangely, furiously;
Most have an eye for colour, few for form.
Imperfect is the glory to *create*.
Unless on our creation we can look
And see that all is good; we then may rest.
In every poem train the leading shoot;
Break off the suckers. Thought erases thought,
As numerous sheep erase each other's print
When spungy moss they press or sterile sand.    30
Blades thickly sown want nutriment and droop,
Although the seed be sound, and rich the soil;
Thus healthy-born ideas, bedded close,
By dreaming fondness perish overlain.
A rose or sprig of myrtle in the hair
Pleases me better than a far-sought gem.
I chide the flounce that checks the nimble feet,
Abhor the cruel piercer of the ear,
And would strike down the chain that cuts in two
The beauteous column of the marble neck.    40
Barbarous and false are all such ornaments,
Yet such hath poesy in whim put on.
Classical hath been deem'd each Roman name
Writ on the roll-call of each pedagogue
In the same hand, in the same tone pronounced;
Yet might five scanty pages well contain
All that the Muses in fresh youth would own
Between the grave at Tomos, wet with tears
Rolling amain down Getick beard unshorn,
And that grand priest whose purple shone afar   50
From his own Venice o'er the Adrian sea.
We talk of schools . . unscholarly; if schools
Part the romantick from the classical.
The classical like the heroick age
Is past; but Poetry may reassume
That glorious name with Tartar and with Turk,
With Goth or Arab, Sheik or Paladin,
And not with Roman and with Greek alone.
The name is graven on the workmanship.
The trumpet-blast of *Marmion* never shook    60

The God-built walls of Ilion; yet what shout
Of the Achaians swells the heart so high?
Nor fainter is the artillery-roar that booms
From *Hohenlinden* to the *Baltick* strand.
Shakespeare with majesty benign call'd up
The obedient classicks from their marble seat,
And led them thro dim glen and sheeny glade,
And over precipices, over seas
Unknown by mariner, to palaces
High-archt, to festival, to dance, to joust,                     70
And gave them golden spur and vizor barred,
And steeds that Pheidias had turn'd pale to see.
The mighty man who open'd Paradise,
Harmonious far above Homerick song,
Or any song that human ears shall hear,
Sometimes was classical and sometimes not:
Rome chain'd him down; the younger Italy
Dissolved (not fatally) his Sampson strength.

 I leave behind me those who stood around
The throne of Shakespeare, sturdy, but unclean,                  80
To hurry past the opprobrious courts and lanes
Of the loose pipers at the Belial feast,
Past mime obscene and grinder of lampoon . .
Away the petty wheel, the callous hand!
Goldsmith was classical, and Gray almost;
So was poor Collins, heart-bound to Romance:
Shelley and Keats, those southern stars, shone higher.
Cowper had more variety, more strength,
Gentlest of bards! stil pitied, stil beloved!
Shrewder in epigram than polity                                  90
Was Canning; Frere more graceful; Smith more grand;
A genuine poet was the last alone.
Romantick, classical, the female hand
That chain'd the cruel Ivan down for ever,
And follow'd up, rapt in his fiery car,
The boy of Casabianca to the skies.
Other fair forms breathe round us, which exert
With Paphian softness Amazonian power,
And sweep in bright array the Attick field.
 To *men* turn now, who stand or lately stood              100
With more than Royalty's gilt bays adorn'd.
Wordsworth, in sonnet, is a classick too,
And on that grass-plot sits at Milton's side;
In the long walk he soon is out of breath
And wheezes heavier than his friends could wish.
Follow his pedlar up the devious rill,
And, if you faint not, you are well repaid.

Large lumps of precious metal lie engulpht
In gravely beds, whence you must delve them out
And thirst sometimes and hunger; shudder not                    110
To wield the pickaxe and to shake the sieve,
Well shall the labour be (tho hard) repaid.
Too weak for ode and epick, and his gait
Somewhat too rural for the tragick pall,
Which never was cut out of duffel grey,
He fell entangled, 'on the grunsel-edge'
Flat on his face, 'and shamed his worshipers.'
    Classick in every feature was my friend
The genial Southey: none who ruled around
Held in such order such a wide domain . .                       120
But often too indulgent, too profuse.
    The ancients see us under them, and grieve
That we are parted by a rank morass,
Wishing its flowers more delicate and fewer.
Abstemious were the Greeks; they never strove
To look so fierce: their Muses were sedate,
Never obstreperous: you heard no breath
Outside the flute; each sound ran clear within.
The Fauns might dance, might clap their hands, might shout,
Might revel and run riotous; the Nymphs                         130
Furtively glanced, and fear'd, or seem'd to fear;
Descended on the lightest of light wings,
The graceful son of Maia mused apart,
Graceful, but strong; he listen'd; he drew nigh;
And now with his own lyre and now with voice
Temper'd the strain; Apollo calmly smiled.

## 132 TO THE REVEREND CUTHBERT SOUTHEY

CUTHBERT! whose father first in all our land
Sate in calm judgment on poetic peer,
Whom hatred never, friendship seldom, warpt . .
Agen I read his page and hear his voice;
I heard it ere I knew it, ere I saw
Who utter'd it, each then to each unknown.
Twelve years had past, when upon Avon's cliff,
Hard-by his birth-place, first our hands were join'd;
After three more he visited my home.
Along Lantony's ruin'd ailes we walkt                           10
And woods then pathless, over verdant hill
And ruddy mountain, and aside the stream
Of sparkling Hondy. Just at close of day
There by the comet's light we saw the fox
Rush from the alders, nor relax in speed

Until he trod the pathway of his sires
Under the hoary crag of Comioy.
Then both were happy.
                              War had paused: the Loire
Invited me. Agen burst forth fierce War.
I minded not his fury: there I staid,                          20
Sole of my countrymen, and foes abstain'd
(Tho sore and bleeding) from my house alone.
But female fear impell'd me past the Alps,
Where, loveliest of all lakes, the Lario sleeps
Under the walls of Como.
                              There he came
Agen to see me; there agen our walks
We recommenced . . less pleasant than before.
Grief had swept over him; days darken'd round:
Bellagio, Valintelvi, smiled in vain,
And Monterosa from Helvetia far                                30
Advanced to meet us, mild in majesty
Above the glittering crests of giant sons
Station'd around . . in vain too! all in vain!
    Perhaps the hour may come when others, taught
By him to read, may read my page aright
And find what lies within it; time enough
Is there before us in the world of thought.
The favor I may need I scorn to ask.
What sovran is there able to reprieve,
How then to grant, the life of the condemn'd              40
By Justice, where the Muses take their seat?
Never was I impatient to receive
What any man could give me: when a friend
Gave me my due, I took it, and no more . .
Serenely glad because that friend was pleas'd.
I seek not many, many seek not me.
If there are few now seated at my board,
I pull no children's hair because they munch
Gilt gingerbread, the figured and the sweet,
Or wallow in the innocence of whey;                            50
Give *me* wild-boar, the buck's broad haunch give *me*,
And wine that time has mellow'd, even as time
Mellows the warrior hermit in his cell.


**133** [IN MEMORY OF LADY BLESSINGTON]

AGEN, perhaps and only once agen,
I turn my steps to London. Few the scenes
And few the friends that there delighted me
Will now delight me: some indeed remain,

Tho changed in features . . friend and scene . . both changed!
I shall not watch my lilac burst her bud
In that wide garden, that pure fount of air,
Where, risen ere the morns are warm and bright,
And stepping forth in very scant attire,
Timidly, as became her in such garb,                                     10
She hasten'd prompt to call up slumbering Spring.
White and dim-purple breathed my favorite pair
Under thy terrace, hospitable heart,
Whom twenty summers more and more endear'd;
Part on the Arno, part where every clime
Sent its most graceful sons to kiss thy hand,
To make the humble proud, the proud submiss,
Wiser the wisest, and the brave more brave.
Never, ah never now, shall we alight
Where the man-queen was born, or, higher up                              20
The nobler region of a nobler soul,
Where breathed his last the more than kingly man.
      Thou sleepest, not forgotten, nor unmourn'd,
Beneath the chestnut shade by Saint Germain;
Meanwhile I wait the hour of my repose,
Not under Italy's serener sky,
Where Fiesole beheld me from above
Devising how my head most pleasantly
Might rest ere long, and how with such intent
I smooth'd a platform for my villagers,                                   30
(Tho stood against me stubborn stony knoll
With cross-grain'd olives long confederate)
And brought together slender cypresses
And bridal myrtles, peering up between,
And bade the modest violet bear her part.
      Dance, youths and maidens! tho around my grave
Ye dance not, as I wisht: bloom, myrtles! bend
Protecting arms about them, cypresses!
I must not come among you; fare ye well!

## 134  REMONSTRANCE AND REPLY

SO then, I feel not deeply! if I did,
I should have seized the pen, and pierced therewith
The passive world!
                              And thus thou reasonest?
Well hast thou known the lover's, not so well
The poet's heart: while that heart bleeds, the hand
Presses it close. Grief must run on and pass
Into near Memory's more quiet shade
Before it can compose itself in song.

He who is agonised, and turns to show
His agony to those who sit around,                                   10
Seizes the pen in vain: thought, fancy, power,
Rush back into his bosom; all the strength
Of genius can not draw them into light
From under mastering Grief; but Memory,
The Muse's mother, nurses, rears them up,
Informs, and keeps them with her all her days.

## 135  TO AGE

WELCOME, old friend! These many years
   Have we lived door by door:
The Fates have laid aside their shears
   Perhaps for some few more.

I was indocil at an age
   When better boys were taught,
But thou at length hast made me sage,
   If I am sage in aught.

Little I know from other men,
   Too little they from me,                                   10
But thou hast pointed well the pen
   That writes these lines to thee.

Thanks for expelling Fear and Hope,
   One vile, the other vain;
One's scourge, the other's telescope,
   I shall not see again:

Rather what lies before my feet
   My notice shall engage . .
He who hath braved Youth's dizzy heat
   Dreads not the frost of Age.                              20

## 136  ON SWIFT JOINING AVON NEAR RUGBY

SILENT and modest Brook! who dippest here
Thy foot in Avon as if childish fear
Witheld thee for a moment, wend along;
   Go, follow'd by my song,
Sung in such easy numbers as they use
Who turn in fondness to the Tuscan Muse,
And such as often have flow'd down on me
   From my own Fiesole.
I watch thy placid smile, nor need to say

That Tasso wove one looser lay,                                          10
And Milton took it up to dry the tear
   Dropping on Lycidas's bier.
In youth how often at thy side I wander'd!
What golden hours, hours numberless, were squander'd
   Among thy sedges, while sometimes
   I meditated native rhymes,
And sometimes stumbled upon Latian feet;
     Then, where soft mole-built seat
     Invited me, I noted down
     What must full surely win the crown,          20
But first impatiently vain efforts made
On broken pencil with a broken blade.
     Anon, of lighter heart, I threw
     My hat where circling plover flew,
And once I shouted til, instead of plover,
There sprang up half a damsel, half a lover.
I would not twice be barbarous; on I went . .
And two heads sank amid the pillowing bent.
     Pardon me, gentle Stream, if rhyme
Holds up these records in the face of Time:                               30
Among the falling leaves some birds yet sing,
And Autumn hath his butterflies like Spring.
Thou canst not turn thee back, thou canst not see
     Reflected what hath ceast to be:
     Haply thou little knowest why
     I check this levity, and sigh.
Thou never knewest her whose radiant morn
   Lighted my path to Love; she bore thy name,
She whom no Grace was tardy to adorn,
   Whom one low voice pleas'd more than louder fame:    40
She now is past my praises: from her urn
     To thine, with reverence due, I turn.
O silver-braided Swift! no victim ever
     Was sacrificed to thee,
Nor hast thou carried to that sacred River
Vases of myrrh, nor hast thou run to see
A band of Mænads toss their timbrels high
Mid *io-evohes* to their Deity.
But holy ashes have bestrewn thy stream
     Under the mingled gleam                         50
Of swords and torches, and the chaunt of Rome,
     When Wiclif's lowly tomb
     Thro its thick briars was burst
     By frantic priests accurst;
For he had enter'd and laid bare the lies
That pave the labyrinth of their mysteries.

>             We part . .  but one more look!
>             Silent and modest Brook!

## from LAST FRUIT OFF AN OLD TREE (1853)

### 137  [POET! I LIKE NOT MEALY FRUIT]

>     POET! I like not mealy fruit; give me
>     Freshness and crispness and solidity;
>     Apples are none the better over-ripe,
>     And prime buck-venison I prefer to tripe.

### 138  ON CATULLUS

>     TELL me not what too well I know
>     About the bard of Sirmio . .
>         Yes, in Thalia's son
>     Such stains there are . .  as when a Grace
>     Sprinkles another's laughing face
>         With nectar, and runs on.

### 139  [PURE PLEASURES]

>     THE crysolites and rubies Bacchus brings
>         To crown the feast where swells the broad-vein'd brow,
>     Where maidens blush at what the minstrel sings,
>         They who have coveted may covet now.
>
>     Bring me, in cool alcove, the grape uncrusht,
>         The peach of pulpy cheek and down mature,
>     Where every voice (but bird's or child's) is husht,
>         And every thought, like the brook nigh, runs pure.

### 140  [IRELAND]

>     IRELAND never was contented . .
>     Say you so? you are demented.
>     Ireland was contented when
>     All could use the sword and pen,
>     And when Tara rose so high
>     That her turrets split the sky,
>     And about her courts were seen
>     Liveried Angels robed in green,
>     Wearing, by Saint Patrick's bounty,
>     Emeralds big as half a county.

**141**   [TO MAZZINI]

IN summer when the sun's mad horses pass
    Thro more than half the heavens, we sink to rest
In Italy, nor tread the crackling grass,
    But wait until they plunge into the west:
And could not you, Mazzini! wait awhile?
    The grass is wither'd, but shall spring agen;
The Gods, who frown on Italy, will smile
    As in old times, and men once more be men.

**142**   [DEATH'S LANGUAGE]

DEATH stands above me, whispering low
    I know not what into my ear:
Of his strange language all I know
    Is, there is not a word of fear.

**143**   [MUTABILITY]

ULYSSES-LIKE had Myrrha known,
Aye, many a man in many a town:
At last she swore that she would be
Constant to one alone, to me.
She fails a trifle: I reprove:
Myrrha no longer swears her love;
One falsehood honest Myrrha spares,
And argues better than she swears.
'Look now,' says she, 'o'er these fair plains,
What find you there that long remains?                              10
The rocks upon yon ugly hill
Are hard and cold and changeless stil.'

**144**   [LIFE'S DECLINE]

OUR youth was happy: why repine
That, like the Year's, Life's days decline?
'Tis well to mingle with the mould
When we ourselves alike are cold,
And when the only tears we shed
Are of the dying on the dead.

**145**   [SPRING IN AGE]

IN early spring, ere roses took
A matronly unblushing look,
Or lilies had begun to fear

A stain upon their character,
I thought the cuckoo more remote
Than ever, and more hoarse his note.
The nightingale had dropt one half
Of her large gamut, and the laugh
Of upright nodding woodpecker
Less petulantly struck my ear.                    10
Why have the birds forgot to sing
In this as in a former spring?
Can it be that the days are cold.
Or (surely no) that I am old.
Strange fancy! how could I forget
That I have not seen eighty yet!

## 146 [AUTUMN]

ALL is not over while the shade
    Of parting life, if now aslant,
Rests on the scene whereon it play'd
    And taught a docile heart to pant.
Autumn is passing by; his day
    Shines mildly yet on gather'd sheaves,
And, tho the grape be pluckt away,
    Its colour glows amid the leaves.

## 147 AGE

DEATH, tho I see him not, is near
And grudges me my eightieth year.
Now, I would give him all these last
For one that fifty have run past.
Ah! he strikes all things, all alike,
But bargains: those he will not strike.

## 148 [THE EAGLE]

A BIRD was seen aloft in air; the sun
Shone brightly round him, yet few eyes could see
His colour, few could scan his size; his form
Appear'd to some like a huge bow unbent,
To others like a shapeless stake hurl'd by,
With a stiff breeze against it in its flight.
It was an eagle all the while: he swoopt
Steddily onward, careless of the gang
Below him, talkative, disquisitive,
But all agreeing 'twas a bird on wing,            10
Some said nine inches, some said ten across.

There were old people who could recollect
That market-day, the crowd, that questioning,
Those outcries to drive off the fearless bird.
One of them I accosted; he replied,
'Yea, I have seen him, and must say for him
Now he is dead (and well it was for us)
He liked a coney or a lamb too much,
But never settled on dead carcases
To pluck out eye or tug at putrid tongue.                          20
They who reviled him while he swept the air
Are glad enough to wear a feather now
Of that strong wing, and boast to have observ'd
Its sunny soaring on that market-day.'

## 149  [THE GENIUS OF GREECE]

WHY do I praise a peach
Not on my wall, no, nor within my reach?
Because I see the bloom
And scent the fragrance many steps from home.
Permit me stil to praise
The higher Genius of departed days.
Some are there yet who, nurst
In the same clime, are vigorous as the first,
And never waste their hours
(Ardent for action) among meadow flowers.                          10
Greece with calm eyes I see,
Her pure white marbles have not blinded me,
But breathe on me the love
Of earthly things as bright as things above:
There is (where is there not?)
In her fair regions many a desart spot;
Neither is Dircè clear,
Nor is Ilissus full throughout the year.

## 150  TO VERONA

TO violate the sanctitude of song,
Of love, of sepulture, have I abstain'd,
Verona! nor would let just wrath approach
Garden or theater: but wrongs are heapt
On thy fair head: my pen must help the sword
To sweep them off.
                         Shall Austria hatch beneath
Thy sunny citadel her mealworm brood?
Shall Austria pluck thy olives, press thy grapes,
Garner thy corn, thy flocks and herds consume?

Enough 'tis surely that Parthenopè                              10
Bends under the false Bourbon. Foren force
Crushes, and let it crush, the unmanly race,
Degenerate even from Sybarites; but thine
The warlike Gaul and Rome's austerer son
Rear'd up to manhood and begirt in arms.
Rise then, Verona! Lift the wave of war,
As Nature lifts Benacus at thy side,
Tempestuous in its surges, while the banks
Are blithe around, and heaven above serene.
The toad's flat claws hold not the dolphin down,             20
Nor sinks and sewers pollute the Adrian wave.

## 151  ON MUSIC

MANY love music but for music's sake,
Many because her touches can awake
Thoughts that repose within the breast half-dead,
And rise to follow where she loves to lead.
What various feelings come from days gone by!
What tears from far-off sources dim the eye!
Few, when light fingers with sweet voices play
And melodies swell, pause, and melt away,
Mind how at every touch, at every tone,
A spark of life hath glisten'd and hath gone.                 10

## 152  TO SHELLEY

SHELLEY! whose song so sweet was sweetest here,
We knew each other little; now I walk
Along the same green path, along the shore
Of Lerici, along the sandy plain
Trending from Lucca to the Pisan pines,
Under whose shadow scatter'd camels lie,
The old and young, and rarer deer uplift
Their knotty branches o'er high-feather'd fern.
Regions of happiness! I greet ye well;
Your solitudes, and not your cities, stay'd                   10
My steps among you; for with you alone
Converst I, and with those ye bore of old.
He who beholds the skies of Italy
Sees ancient Rome reflected, sees beyond,
Into more glorious Hellas, nurse of Gods
And godlike men: dwarfs people other lands.
Frown not, maternal England! thy weak child
Kneels at thy feet and owns in shame a lie.

# MISCELLANEOUS POEMS, 1854-55

## 153 MARCH 24

SHARP crocus wakes the froward Year;
In their old haunts birds re-appear;
From yonder elm, yet black with rain,
The cushat looks deep down for grain
Thrown on the gravel-walk: here comes
The redbreast to the sill for crumbs.
Fly off! fly off! I can not wait
To welcome ye, as she of late.
The earliest of my friends is gone,
Alas! almost my only one!                                    10
The few as dear, long wafted o'er,
Await me on a sunnier shore.

## 154 APOLOGY FOR GEBIR

SIXTY the years since Fidler bore
My grouse-bag up the Bala moor;
Above the lake, along the lea
Where gleams the darkly yellow Dee;
Thro' crags, o'er cliffs, I carried there
My verses with paternal care,
But left them, and went home again,
To wing the birds upon the plain.
With heavier luggage half forgot,
For many months they followed not.                          10
When over Tawey's sands they came,
Brighter flew up my winter flame;
And each old cricket sang alert
With joy that they had come unhurt.
Gebir! men shook their heads in doubt
If we were sane: few made us out,
Beside one stranger; in his heart
We after held no niggard part.
The songs of every age he knew,
But only sang the pure and true.                            20
Poet he was, yet was his smile
Without a tinge of gall or guile.
Such lived, 'tis said, in ages past;
Who knows if Southey was the last?
Dapper, who may perhaps have seen
My name in some late magazine,
Among a dozen or a score
Which interest wise people more,

Wonders if I can be the same
To whom poor Southey augured fame; 30
Erring as usual in his choice
Of one who mocks the public voice,
And fancies two or three are worth
Far more than all the rest on earth.
Dapper, in tones benign and clear,
Tells those who treasure all they hear,
   'Landor would have done better far,
Had he observed the northern star;
Or Bloomfield might have shown the way
To one who always goes astray; 40
He might have tried his pen upon
The living, not the dead and gone.
Are turban'd youths and muffled belles
Extinct along the Dardanelles?
Is there no scimitar, no axe?
Daggers and bow-strings, mutes and sacks,
Are they all swept away for ever
From the sky-blue resplendent river?
Do heroes of old times surpass
Cardigan, Somerset, Dundas? 50
Do the Sigæan mounds inclose
More corses than Death swept from those?'
   No, no: but let me ask in turn
Whether, whene'er Corinthian urn,
With ivied Faun upon the rim
Invites, I may not gaze on him?
I love all beauty: I can go
At times from Gainsboro' to Watteau;
Even after Milton's thorough-bass
I bear the rhymes of Hudibras, 60
And find more solid wisdom there
Than pads professor's easy chair:
But never sit I quiet long
Where broidered cassock floats round Young;
Whose pungent essences perfume
And quirk and quibble trim the tomb;
Who thinks the holy bread too plain,
And in the chalice pours champagne.
I love old places and their climes,
Nor quit the syrinx for the chimes. 70
Manners have changed; but hearts are yet
The same, and will be while they beat.
Ye blame not those who wander o'er
Our earth's remotest wildest shore,
Nor scoff at seeking what is hid

Within one-chambered pyramid;
Let me then, with my coat untorn
By your acacia's crooked thorn,
Follow from Gades to the coast
Of Egypt men thro' ages lost.                                    80
Firm was my step on rocky steeps;
Others slipt down loose sandhill heaps.
I knew where hidden fountains lay;
Hoarse was their thirsty camels' bray;
And presently fresh droves had past
The beasts expiring on the waste.

## 155  THE GEORGES

GEORGE the First was always reckoned
Vile, but viler George the Second;
And what mortal ever heard
Any good of George the Third?
When from earth the Fourth descended
(God be praised!) the Georges ended.

# from DRY STICKS, FAGOTED BY WALTER SAVAGE LANDOR (1858)

## 156  EUROPA AND HER MOTHER

*Mother* Daughter! why roamest thou again so late
Along the damp and solitary shore?
  *Europa* I know not. I am tired of distaf, woof,
Everything.
  *Mother*  Yet thou culledst flowers all morn,
And idledst in the woods, mocking shrill birds,
Or clapping hands at limping hares, who stampt
Angrily, and scour'd off.
  *Europa*        I am grown tired
Of hares and birds. O mother! had you seen
That lovely creature! It was not a cow,
And, if it was an ox, it was unlike                                    10
My father's oxen with the hair rubb'd off
Their necks.
  *Mother*    A cow it was.
  *Europa*          Cow it might be . .
And yet . .  and yet . .  I saw no calf, no font
Of milk: I wish I had; how pleasant 'twere
To draw it and to drink!
  *Mother*          Europa! child!

Have we no maiden for such offices?
No whistling boy? Kings' daughters may cull flowers,
To place them on the altar of the Gods
And wear them at their festivals. Who knows
But some one of those very Gods may deign                    20
To wooe thee? maidens they have wooed less fair.
    *Europa* The Gods are very gracious: some of them
Not very constant.
    *Mother*        Hush!
    *Europa*            Nay, Zeus himself
Hath wandered, and deluded more than one.
    *Mother* Fables! profanest fables!
    *Europa*             Let us hope so.
But I should be afraid of him, and run
As lapwings do when we approach the nest.
    *Mother* None can escape the Gods when they pursue.
    *Europa* They know my mind, and will not follow me.
    *Mother* Consider: some are stars whom they have loved,     30
Others, the very least of them, are flowers.
    *Europa* I would not be a star in winter nights,
In summer days I would not be a flower;
Flowers seldom live thro' half their time, torn off,
Twirl'd round, and indolently cast aside.
Now, mother, can you tell me what became
Of those who were no flowers, but bent their heads
As pliantly as flowers do?
    *Mother*           They are gone
To Hades.
    *Europa* And left there by Gods they loved
And were beloved by! Be not such my doom!                   40
Cruel are men, but crueler are Gods.
    *Mother* Peace! peace! Some royal, some heroic, youth
May ask thy father for thy dower and thee.
    *Europa* I know not any such, if such there live;
Royal there may be, but heroic . . where?
O mother! look! look! look!
    *Mother*            Thou turnest pale;
What ails thee?
    *Europa*     Who in all the house hath dared
To winde those garlands round that grand white brow?
So mild, so loving! Mother! let me run
And tear them off him: let me gather more                   50
And sweeter.
    *Mother*    Truly 'tis a noble beast.
See! he comes forward! see, he rips them off,
Himself!
    *Europa* He should not wear them if he would.

Stay there, thou noble creature! Woe is me!
There are but sandrose, tyme, and snapdragon
Along the shore as far as I can see.
O mother! help me on his back; he licks
My foot. Ah! what sweet breath! Now on his side
He lies on purpose for it. Help me up.
    *Mother* Well, child! Indeed he is gentle. Gods above!          60
He takes the water! Hold him tight, Europa!
'Tis well that thou canst swim.
                       Leap off, mad girl!
She laughs! He lows so loud she hears not me . .
But she looks sadder, or my sight is dim . .
Against his nostril fondly hangs her hand
While his eye glistens over it, fondly too.
It will be night, dark night, ere she returns.
And that new scarf! the spray will ruin it!


## 157 VOYAGE TO ST IVES, CORNWALL, FROM PORT-EINON, GLAMORGAN, 1794

HOW gladsome yet how calm are ye
White birds that dip into the sea!
How sportive those bright fins below
Which through green alga-meadows glow!
How soft the lustrous air around,
And the red sail's is all the sound,
While me my heart's fierce tempest drives
On from Port-Einon to St Ives.


## 158 DEATH OF THE DAY

MY pictures blacken in their frames
    As night comes on,
And youthful maids and wrinkled dames
    Are now all one.

Death of the day! a sterner Death
    Did worse before;
The fairest form, the sweetest breath,
    Away he bore.


## 159 A CRITIC

WITH much ado you fail to tell
The requisites for writing well;
But, what bad writing is, you quite
Have proved by every line you write.

**160**  MY HOMES

HOME! I have changed thee often: on the brink
Of Arrowe early I began to think,
Where the dark alders, closing overhead,
Across the meadow but one shadow shed.
Lantony then received me for a while
And saw me musing in the ruin'd aile:
Then loitered I in Paris; then in Tours,
Where Ronsard sang erewhile his loose amours,
And where the loftier Beranger retires
To sing what Freedom, and what Mirth, inspires.                    10
From France to Italy my steps I bent
And pitcht at Arno's side my household tent.
Six years the Medicæan palace held
My wandering Lares; then they went afield,
Where the hewn rocks of Fiesole impend
O'er Doccia's dell, and fig and olive blend.
There the twin streams of Affrico unite,
One dimly seen, the other out of sight,
But ever playing in his smoothen'd bed
Of polisht stone, and willing to be led                           20
Where clustering vines protect him from the sun,
Never too grave to smile, too tired to run.
Here, by the lake, Boccaccio's *Fair Brigade*
Beguiled the hours and tale for tale repaid.
    How happy! O how happy! had I been
With friends and children in this quiet scene!
Its quiet was not destined to be mine;
'Twas hard to keep, 'twas harder to resign.
Now seek I (now Life says, *My gates I close*)
A solitary and a late repose.                                     30


from **THE HELLENICS OF WALTER SAVAGE LANDOR
     (1859)**


**161**  CORESUS AND CALLIRHOË

WITH song and dance the maids of Calydon
Had met to celebrate the yearly rites
Of Bacchus. Where two taller whirl around
The rope, and call another to run in,
A wanton one pusht forward her who stood
Aside her; when she stumbled they all laught
To see her upright heels and scattered hair.

'Twas then, Callirhoë, that thy mother fail'd
Even with prayer to bring thee back again
Before the altar: it is said a tear                                    10
Roll'd down thy cheek from shame, and not without
A blush of anger . .   who on earth can vouch
For this? since both thy hands hid both thy cheeks.
    Rising from his high seat the youthful priest
Came forward, pitying her: of graceful mien
Coresus was, and worthy of his God.
Ah poor Coresus! luckless was the hour
Of his first meeting her; there might have been
Hour more propitious; she perhaps had loved
Distractedly the youth she now abhor'd;                              20
He too, unless her blushes and her tears
Had penetrated deep his generous heart,
Might have loved on and sung his woes away.
Now neither butting goat nor honeyed must
Pourd by the straining boys between his horns
Regarded he; no, nor with wonted cheer
Appeard to him the God of gamesome glee.
Not even when Hesper call'd his winking train
Around him, and when shook the lower shrubs
More than the breeze had shaken them erewhile,                       30
Would he decline his aking eyes to sleep;
But out of the inclosure, where the grass
Was rank with fallen leaves and heavy dew,
Lonely he stood beneath an ilex shade,
And meditated long and soon forgot
The words he had to say: he could recall
(He thought) her features, but before him rose
A face less beautiful, not less severe.
Many the days he sought the maid in vain,
Many the nights he stood before the house;                           40
She waits not even to be seen; no foot
Passes her door, and the dog barks, but strait
Up springs she from her chair; she surely hears
And knows his tread; what other can it be?
When she would break a thread off with her teeth
She stops, and holds it in a trembling hand
Suspended, just above the humid lip
White now with fear; and often her loose locks
She dashes back to place a surer ear
Against the hinge: is any footfall heard                             50
Passing the portico, he steps that way;
If soft the sound, he stands there, none but he:
If none, he certainly is close behind.
    The reed grows harder from perpetual winds,

From fears perpetual harder grows the maid.
At first Callirhoë scarcely would confess
To her own mother, scarcely to herself;
Now she is ready, now she is resolved
With savage speech his fondness to repay,
Words she would gather for his punishment,                    60
And is more angry when she finds not one;
An aggravation of his past offence.
   Flexible is the coral branch beneath
The Erythræan sea; to air exposed
It stiffens, no strong hand can bend it back:
Such was her nature: she had laid aside
Her former manners; its ingenuous shame
Quitted that cheek it lately discomposed;
Crouds she avoided not, nor greatly cared
If others knew what she but yesterday                         70
Was vext at knowing: she rejoiced to hear
A name she loath'd so late. Vainglory caught
And made a plaything of an empty heart.
When she hears footsteps from behind, she checks
Her own, to let him either stop or pass;
She would not wish his love nor him away,
Conscious that she is walking over fire
Unwounded, on a level with the Gods,
And rendering null the noblest gifts they gave.
   Where grows a dittany that heals the smart           80
Love's broken arrow leaves within the breast?
He loves not who such anguish can endure,
He who can burst asunder such a bond
Loves not.
          Hard-breathing from his inmost soul
Coresus siez'd her hand, then threw it back
And pour'd forth with stern look these bitter words.
'No longer ask I pity on my grief,
Callirhoë! tis unworthy of us both,
But there is one who knows it, one above,
And will avenge it. Thou hast seen the last                   90
Of all the tears these eyes will ever shed;
This grieves me, and this only . .   Pestilence
Now stalks in darkness on from street to street,
And slow steps follow: wasted, worn away,
The aged are gone forth to learn the will
Of those we worship; and their late return,
Lookt for since dawn from all the higher roofs,
In vain is lookt for. Thro the city lie
Children whom dying parents would embrace,
Innocent children! they have not been spared,                 100

And shall the guilty before heaven escape?
   I was contemn'd, and I deserv'd contempt,
I loved imprudently; yet throughout life
Those arts I cherisht which lead youth aright,
And strengthen manhood and adorn old-age.
Old-age! for me there will be none: my brow
Hath worn its crown .. for what? that festal songs
May rise around the altar, sung by thee.
Worthy I was to woo, and woo I did;
I am unworthy now, and now abstain,                        110
Subjected to the levity of all,
Even my own friends: and yet might I have stood
Above those equal-aged, whether the prize
Were olive, given by heroes, whether bay
Which only Gods, and they on few, bestow,
Or whether, O Callirhoë! in thy love.
   Let kings throw largesses around, let earth
And ocean be explored that vulgar eyes
May gaze at vulgar heads rais'd somewhat higher,
The Gods alone give genius, they alone                     120
Give beauty .. why so seldom to unite!
She shines her hour, and then the worshiper
Rises and goes. Genius stands cold, apart,
Like Saturn in the skies; his aspect seems,
To mortal men below, oblique, malign ...'
   While he was speaking and about to pause,
Downcast, with silent and slow step approacht
They who went forth to touch with purest hands
The altar, and appease the offended Powers.
The virgin saw them coming; soon she heard                 130
A croud's tumultuous outcries and turned pale;
But paler was Coresus who presaged
The impending evil; paler when he heard
Curses and (painfuller) immodest speech.
He hastened to withdraw her; but aloud
Palæmon cried,
               'Stay here! stay here thou too
O wretched girl! and take the words I bring,
The God's own words: no longer shall the throng
Around thee rise infuriate, nor shall maids
And matrons turn on thee their dying look                  140
Or call the torch funereal by thy name.'
   Impatient and exultant sprang the youth;
Wildly he threw his arms around her neck,
Then, falling on his knees,
                         'Hail thou' he cried,
'Who fillest with thy deity the grove

Of high Dodona, and with brow serene
Hast clear'd the troubled sky!
                            She lives! she lives!
The source of sorrow to none else than me:
Neither my dreams nor Bacchus promist this.'
Palæmon, after solemn silence, spake:                          150
    'Alas! how sadly do young hopes decieve!
The sight of future things was granted thee
In vain: Love lowers his saffron veil, runs off,
And thro the dimness thou seest only Love.
    Forward, ye youths! since Jupiter ordains,
And since the son of Semele hath deign'd
To honor and avenge his chosen priest,
Lead the peace-offering, the pure victim, forth . .
Lead forth Callirhoë.'
                            Thro the maiden's veins
The blood crept cold: she staggered, fell . . upheav'd          160
And drag'd away by some strong arm, she reacht
The temple: consciousness (not soon) return'd
Thro the loud tramplings, on the marble floor,
Of those who carried incense fresh-alight,
And the salt sprinklings from the frigid font.
    'Take' said Palæmon, trembling as he spake,
'Take thou this sword, Coresus! 'tis thy part.
Often hast thou the avenging Gods invoked,
And wouldst thou cast aside the vows they grant?
Impious! impossible! no grace is this                          170
To thee, but sign to all that in his priest
Wrong'd and offended is the God he serves,
Warning to all that vows be wisely vow'd.
But if among this concourse there stand one
Who pities so the victim, that for hers
He yields his life, then shall the pestilence,
Under Jove's saving son, our Bacchus, cease.'
    With his veind hand a tear the youth swept off:
Less mournfully than scornfully said he,
    'Listen! how swift, how still, their steps retreat!          180
Now then, Callirhoë! now my breast is firm;
None stand before me: in a father's place
And in a lover's I will here discharge
No empty duty.'
                            Cries and groans are heard,
And seen upon the pavement where he stood
His writhing limbs.
                            With sudden terror flies
The croud bewildered, dreading lest a blood
So sacred should run on and reach their feet.

The temple and the grove around it moan,
And other murmurs, other cries, than rose                    190
So lately, fill the city and the plain.
    First flies the rumor that the priest had fallen
By his own hand; it gathered force, and soon
That both were smitten by the wrathful Gods.
From its own weight is that vast multitude
Pusht onward, driven back, conglomerated,
Broken, disperst, like waves on stormy seas.

**162** LEONTION, ON TERNISSA'S DEATH
(EPICUROS ALSO DEPARTED)

BEHOLD, behold me, whether thou
Art dwelling with the Shades below
        Or with the Gods above:
With thee were even the Gods more blest . .
I wish I could but share thy rest
        As once I shared thy love.

'Twas in this garden where I lean
Against thy tombstone, once the scene
        Of more than mortal bliss,
That loiter'd our Ternissa; sure                            10
She left me that her love was pure;
        It gave not kiss for kiss.

Faint was the blush that overspred
Thro' loosen'd hair her dying head;
        One name she utter'd, one
She sigh'd and wept at; so wilt thou,
If any sorrows reach thee now . .
        'Twas not *Leontion*.

Wert thou one earth thou wouldst not chide
The gush of tears I could not hide                          20
        Who ne'er hid aught from thee.
Willing thou wentest on the way
She went . .   and am I doom'd to stay?
        No; we soon meet, all three.

The flowers she cherisht I will tend,
Nor gather, but above them bend
        And think they breathe her breath.
Ah, happy flowers! ye little know
Your faithful nurse lies close below,
        Close as in life in death.                          30

## from **HEROIC IDYLS (1863)**

**163**  A FRIEND TO THEOCRITOS IN EGYPT

DOST thou not often gasp with longdrawn sighs,
Theocritos, recalling Sicily?
Glorious is Nile, but rather give me back
Our little rills, which fain would run away
And hide themselves from persecuting suns
In summer, under oleander boughs,
And catch its roses as they flaunt above.
Here are no birds that sing, no sweeter flower
Than tiny fragile weak-eyed resida,
Which faints upon the bosom it would cool.                10
Altho' the royal lotos sits aloof
On his rich carpet, spred from wave to wave,
I throw myself more gladly where the pine
Protects me, loftier than the palace-roof,
Or where the linden and acacia meet
Across my path, in fragrance to contend.
Bring back the hour, Theocritos, when we
Shall sit together on a thymy knoll,
With few about us, and with none too nigh,
And when the songs of shepherds and their glee         20
We may repeat, perchance and gaily mock,
Until one bolder than the rest springs up
And slaps us on the shoulder for our pains.
Take thou meanwhile these two papyrus-leaves,
Recording, one the loves and one the woes
Of Pan and Pitys, heretofore unsung.
Aside our rivers and within our groves
The pastoral pipe hath dropt its mellow lay,
And shepherds in their contests only try
Who best can puzzle.                                   30
                    Come, Theocritos,
Come, let us lend a shoulder to the wheel
And help to lift it from the depth of sand.

**164**  MEMORY

THE mother of the Muses, we are taught,
Is Memory: she has left me; they remain,
And shake my shoulder, urging me to sing
About the summer days, my loves of old.
*Alas! alas!* is all I can reply.
Memory has left with me that name alone,
Harmonious name, which other bards may sing,

But her bright image in my darkest hour
Comes back, in vain comes back, call'd or uncall'd.
Forgotten are the names of visitors                                          10
Ready to press my hand but yesterday;
Forgotten are the names of earlier friends
Whose genial converse and glad countenance
Are fresh as ever to mine ear and eye;
To these, when I have written, and besought
Remembrance of me, the word *Dear* alone
Hangs on the upper verge, and waits in vain.
A blessing wert thou, O oblivion,
If thy stream carried only weeds away,
But vernal and autumnal flowers alike                                        20
It hurries down to wither on the strand.

## 165   AN OLD POET TO SLEEP

NO God to mortals oftener descends
Than thou, O Sleep! yet thee the sad alone
Invoke, and gratefully thy gift receive.
Some thou invitest to explore the sands
Left by Pactolos, some to climb up higher,
Where points Ambition to the pomp of War;
Others thou watchest while they tighten robes
Which Law throws round them loose, and they meanwhile
Wink at a judge, and he the wink returns.
Apart sit fewer, whom thou lovest more                                       10
And leadest where unruffled rivers flow,
Or azure lakes neath azure skies expand.
These have no wider wishes, and no fears,
Unless a fear, in turning, to molest
The silent, solitary, stately swan,
Disdaining the garrulity of groves
Nor seeking shelter there from sun or storm.
      Me also hast thou led among such scenes,
Gentlest of Gods! and Age appear'd far off
While thou wast standing close above the couch,                              20
And whispered'st, in whisper not unheard,
'I now depart from thee, but leave behind
My own twin-brother, friendly as myself,
Who soon shall take my place; men call him Death.
Thou hearest me, nor tremblest, as most do,
In sooth why shouldst thou? what man hast thou wrong'd
By deed or word? few dare ask this within.'
There was a pause; then suddenly said Sleep
'He whom I named approacheth, so farewell.'

**166** ON THE DEATH OF ADMIRAL SIR SIDNEY SMITH

I AM invited (why?) in latin phrase
To write thy epitaph.
          Two glorious men,
Sydney, have borne thy name through distant lands,
But here no sailor, here no orphan, lifts
His mournful head to read what Rome would write
And place among the noblest, wert thou hers.
   Children, in earlier or in later life,
May play grave follies in the sculptured aisle,
And lengthen out in it the stiffer tongue;
It suits not me to make the rustic stare          10
And ask what booby never learnt to spell
A name that every cabin-boy has chalkt,
And every sunday-school-girl has prickt out
Upon her sampler for the brighter silk,
The name of Sidney; of that Admiral
Who left his ship and stood on Acre's tower
Tottering beneath him, and drove back dismayed
The renegate of honor and of God.
   More than one realm by that one blow he saved;
Some by their weakness are about to fall,       20
Some by their violence . . may these fall the first!

**167** [SHAKESPEARE]

WITH frowning brow o'er pontif-kings elate,
Stood Dante, great the man, the poet great.
Milton in might and majesty surpast
The triple world, and far his shade was cast.
On earth he sang amid the Angelic host,
And Paradise to him was never lost.
But there was one who came these two between
With larger light than yet our globe had seen.
Various were his creations, various speech
Without a Babel he bestow'd on each.       10
Raleigh and Bacon towered above that earth
Which in their day had given our Shakespeare birth,
And neither knew his presence! they half-blind
Saw not in him the grandest of mankind.

**168** [YE WHO HAVE TOIL'D UPHILL]

YE who have toil'd uphill to reach the haunt
Of other men who lived in other days,
Whether the ruins of a citadel

Rais'd on the summit by Pelasgic hands,
Or chamber of the distaff and the song . . .
Ye will not tell what treasure there ye found,
But I will.
                    Ye found there the viper laid
Full-length, flat-headed, on a sunny slab,
Nor loth to hiss at ye while crawling down.
Ye saw the owl flap the loose ivy leaves                    10
And, hooting, shake the berries on your heads.
    Now, was it worth your while to mount so high
Merely to say ye did it, and to ask
If those about ye ever did the like?
Believe me, O my friends, 'twere better far
To stretch your limbs along the level sand
As they do, where small children scoop the drift,
Thinking it must be gold, where curlews soar
And scales drop glistening from the prey above.

## 169  [UNRULY PEGASUS]

OFT, when the Muses would be festive,
Unruly Pegasus runs restive,
And, over the Pierian fount
Flies upward to their sacred mount;
Aware that marshes rot the hoof
He proudly wings his way aloof.
He loves the highest ground the best,
And takes where eagles soar his rest.

## 170  [IANTHE'S NAME ON SAND]

WELL I remember how you smiled
    To see me write your name upon
The soft sea-sand . .  'O! what a child!
    You think you're writing upon stone!'
I have since written what no tide
    Shall ever wash away, what men
Unborn shall read o'er ocean wide
    And find Ianthe's name agen.

## 171  [NEW AUTHORS]

THAT critic must indeed be bold
Who pits new authors against old.
Only the ancient coin is prized,
The dead alone are canonized:
What was even Shakespeare until then?

A poet scarce compared with Ben:
And Milton in the streets no taller
Than sparkling easy-ambling Waller.
Waller now walks with rhyming crowds,
While Milton sits above the clouds,                    10
Above the stars, his fixed abode,
And points to men their way to God.

## 172    INVITATION OF PETRONIUS TO GLYCON

TRYPHOENA says that you must come
To dine with us at Tusculum.
She has invited few to share
Her delicate but frugal fare.
Contrive the dinner to make out
With venison, ortolans, and trout;
These may come after haunch of boar,
Or neck, which wise men relish more;
And, Glycon, 'twould not be unpleasant
To see among them spring a pheasant.                  10
I voted we should have but two
At dinner, these are quite enow.
One of them, worth half Rome, will meet us,
Low-station'd high-soul'd Epictetus.
He told his mind the other day
To ruby-finger'd Seneca,
Who, rich and proud as Nero, teaches
The vanity of pomp and riches.
Just Epictetus can assure us
How continent was Epicurus,                            20
How gorged and staggering Romans claim
With hiccups that immortal name.

## 173    [TO JULIUS HARE: ON FAME]

JULIUS, dear Julius, never think
My spirits are inclined to sink
Because light youths are swimming by
Upon their bladders; so did I.
When in our summer we swam races
I splasht the water in their faces;
And little hands, now only bone,
Clapt me, and call'd the prize my own.

**174** TIBULLUS

> ONLY one poet in the worst of days
> Disdain'd the usurper in his pride to praise.
> Ah, Delia! was it wantonness or whim
> That made thee, once so tender, false to him?
> To him who follow'd over snows and seas
> Messala storming the proud Pyrenees.
> But Nemesis avenged him, and the tear
> Of Rome's last poet fell upon his bier.

**175** [THE LAUREL BEARS A THORN]

> LATELY our poets loiter'd in green lanes,
> Content to catch the ballads of the plains;
> I fancied I had strength enough to climb
> A loftier station at no distant time,
> And might securely from intrusion doze
> Upon the flowers thro' which Ilissus flows.
> In those pale olive grounds all voices cease,
> And from afar dust fills the paths of Greece.
> My slumber broken and my doublet torn,
> I find the laurel also bears a thorn.                                     10

## POEMS PUBLISHED POSTHUMOUSLY

**176** [AT WORDSWORTH'S DESIRE]

> GLORIOUS the names that cluster here
>     The loftiest of our lofty ile;
> Who can approach them void of fear
>     Tho Genius urge & Friendship smile?
>
> To lay one stone upon the hill,
>     And shew that I have climb'd so high,
> Is what they bid me . . Wordsworth's will
>     Is law, and Landor must comply.

**177** [AN INVITATION]

> I AM, but would not be, a hermit;
>     Forster! come hither and confirm it.
> I may not offer 'beechen bowl,'
>     But I can give you soup and sole,
> Sherry and (grown half-mythic) port . .
>     Wise men would change their claret for't;

Quince at dessert, and apricot . .
   In short, with you what have I not?

**178** [SMILES AND TEARS]

I WOULD not see thee weep but there are hours
   When smiles may be less beautiful than tears,
Some of those smiles, some of those tears were ours;
   Ah! why should either now give place to fears?

**179** [ON THE HEIGHTS]

THE cattle in the common field
   Toss their flat heads in vain,
And snort and stamp; weak creatures yield
   And turn back home again.

My mansion stands beyond it, high
   Above where rushes grow;
Its hedge of laurel dares defy
   The heavy-hooft below.

**180** [THOMAS PAINE]

MOBS I abhor, yet bear a crowd
Which speaks its mind, if not too loud.
Willingly would I hear again
The honest words of pelted Payne.
Few dared such homely truths to tell,
Or wrote our English half so well.

**181** [DANIEL DEFOE]

FEW will acknowledge all they owe
To persecuted, brave Defoe.
Achilles, in Homeric song,
May, or he may not, live so long
As Crusoe; few their strength had tried
Without so staunch and safe a guide.
What boy is there who never laid
Under his pillow, half afraid,
That precious volume, lest the morrow
For unlearnt lesson might bring sorrow?
But nobler lessons he has taught
Wide-awake scholars who fear'd naught:
A Rodney and a Nelson may
Without him not have won the day.

10

## 182  [APOLOGY FOR THE *HELLENICS*]

NONE had yet tried to make men speak
In English as they would in Greek.
In Italy one chief alone
Made all the Hellenic realms his own;
He was Alfieri, proud to teach
In equally harmonious speech.
Soon, wondering Romans heard again
Brutus, who had been dumb, speak plain.
Corneille stept forth, and taught to dance
The wigs and furbelows of France.                          10
In long-drawn sighs the soft Racine
Bestrewed with perfumed flowers the scene.
I wish *our* bard, our sole dramatic,
Had never overlookt the attic:
Tho' dried the narrow rill whereby
The bards of Athens loved to lie,
Yet Avon's broader, deeper stream
Might have brought down some distant dream,
Nor left for trembling hand like mine
To point out forms and feats divine.                       20
Children, when they are tired with play,
Make little figures out of clay,
And many a mother then hath smiled
At the rare genius of her child;
But neither child nor man will reach
The godlike power of giving speech.
Fantastic forms weak brains invent . . .
Show me Achilles in his tent,
And Hector drag'd round Troy, show *me*
Where stood and wail'd Andromache;                         30
Her tears through ages still flow on,
Still rages, Peleus, thy stern son.

*The Prose*

# from *Imaginary Conversations of Literary Men and Statesmen,* vols. 1 and 2 (1824)

## 1   Lord Brooke and Sir Philip Sidney

*Brooke* . . . The herbs, elastic with health, seem to partake of sensitive and animated life, and to feel under my hand the benediction I would bestow on them. What a hum of satisfaction in God's creatures! How is it, Sidney, the smallest do seem the happiest?

*Sidney* Compensation for their weaknesses and their fears; compensation for the shortness of their existence. Their spirits mount upon the sunbeam above the eagle; and they have more enjoyment in their one summer than the elephant in his century.

*Brooke* Are not also the little and lowly in our species the most happy?

*Sidney* I would not willingly try nor over-curiously examine it. We, Greville, are happy in these parks and forests: we were happy in my close winter-walk of box and laurustine. In our earlier days did we not emboss our bosoms with the daffodils, and shake them almost unto shedding with our transport! Ay, my friend, there is a greater difference, both in the stages of life and in the seasons of the year, than in the conditions of men: yet the healthy pass through the seasons, from the clement to the inclement, not only unreluctantly but rejoicingly, knowing that the worst will soon finish, and the best begin anew; and we are desirous of pushing forward into every stage of life, excepting that alone which ought reasonably to allure us most, as opening to us the *Via Sacra,*[1] along which we move in triumph to our eternal country. We[2] labour to get through the moments of our life, as we would to get through a crowd. Such is our impatience, such our hatred of procrastination, in everything but the amendment of our practices and the adornment of our nature, one would imagine we were dragging Time along by force, and not he us. We may in some measure frame our minds for the reception of happiness, for more or for less; we should however well consider to what port we are steering in search of it, and that even in the richest its quantity is but too exhaustible. It[3] is easier to alter the modes and qualities of it, than to increase its stores. There is a sickliness in the firmest of us, which induceth us to change our side, though reposing ever so softly; yet, wittingly or unwittingly, we turn again soon into our old position. Afterward,[4] when we have fixed, as we imagine, on the object most desirable, we start extravagantly; and, blinded by the rapidity of our course toward the treasure we would seize and dwell with, we find another hand upon the lock . . . the hand of one standing in shade . . . 'tis Death!

*Brooke*[5]   There is often a sensibility in poets which precipitates 'em thither.

> The winged head of Genius snakes surround,
> As erewhile poor Medusa's.[6]

We however have defences against the shafts of the vulgar, and such as no position could give.

*Sidney*   God hath granted unto both of us hearts easily contented, hearts fitted for every station, because fitted for every duty. What appears the dullest may contribute most to our genius: what is most gloomy may soften the seeds and relax the fibres of gaiety. We enjoy the solemnity of the spreading oak[7] above us: perhaps we owe to it in part the mood of our minds at this instant: perhaps an inanimate thing supplies me, while I am speaking, with whatever I possess of animation. Do you imagine that any contest of shepherds[8] can afford them the same pleasure as I receive from the description of it;[9] or that even in their loves, however innocent and faithful, they are so free from anxiety as I am while I celebrate them? The exertion of intellectual power, of fancy and imagination, keeps from us greatly more than their wretchedness, and affords us greatly more than their enjoyment. We are motes in the midst of generations: we have our sunbeams to circuit and climb. Look at the summits of the trees around us, how they move, and the loftiest the most: nothing is at rest within the compass of our view, except the grey moss on the park-pales. Let it eat away the dead oak, but let it not be compared with the living one.

Poets are in general prone to melancholy; yet the most plaintive ditty hath imparted a fuller joy, and of longer duration, to its composer, than the conquest of Persia to the Macedonian.[10] A bottle of wine bringeth as much pleasure as the acquisition of a kingdom, and not unlike it in kind: the senses in both cases are confused and perverted.

*Sidney* . . . Religions, languages, races of men, rise up, flourish, decay; and just in the order I assign to them. O my friend! is it nothing to think that this hand of mine, over which an insect is creeping, and upon which another more loathsome one ere long will pasture, may hold forth to my fellow men, by resolution of heart in me and perseverance, those things which shall outlive the least perishable in the whole dominion of mortality? Creatures, of whom the best and weightiest part are the feathers in their caps, and of whom the lightest are their words and actions, curl their whiskers and their lips in scorn upon similar meditations.

Let us indulge in them; they are neither weak nor idle, having been suckled by Wisdom and taught to walk by Virtue. We[11] have never thrown away the keepsakes that Nature has given us, nor bartered them for toys easily broken in the public paths of life.

*Brooke*   Argue then no longer about courts and discontents: I would rather hear a few more verses; for a small draught increases the thirst of the thirsty.

*Sidney*   To write as the ancients have written, without borrowing a thought or expression from them, is the most difficult thing we can achieve in poetry. I attempt no composition which I foresee will occupy more than an hour or two, so that I can hardly claim any rank among the poets;[12] yet having once collected, in my curiosity, all the *Invocations to Sleep*, ancient and modern, I fancied it possible to compose one very differently;[13] which, if you consider the simplicity of the subject and the number of those who have treated it, may appear no easy matter.

> Sleep! who contractest the waste realms of Night,
>     None like the wretched can extol thy powers:
> We think of thee when thou art far away,
> We hold thee dearer than the light of day,
>     And most when Love forsakes us wish thee ours:
>         Oh hither bend thy flight!
>
> Silent and welcome as the blessed shade
>     Alcestis to the dark Thessalian hall,
> When Hercules and Death and Hell obey'd
>     Her husband's desolate despondent call.[14]
>
> What fiend would persecute thee, gentle Sleep,
>     Or beckon thee aside from man's distress?
> Needless it were to warn thee of the stings
> That pierce my pillow, now those waxen wings
>     Which bore me to the sun of happiness,
>         Have dropt into the deep.[15]

*Sidney*[16]   So little am I ashamed of the hours I spend in poetry, even a consciousness that the poetry itself is bad never leads me to think the occupation is. Foliage, herbage, pebbles, may put in motion the finer parts of the mind; and although the first things it throws off be verses, and indifferent ones, we are not to despise the cultivator of them, but to consider him as possessing the garden of innocence, at which the great body of mankind looks only through the gate.

In the corner formed by the court-wall, sheltered and sunny, I found, earlier in the season than usual, a little rose-bud, which perhaps owed its existence to my cutting the plant in summer, when it began to intrude on the path, and had wetted the legs of the ladies with the rain it held. None but trifling poetry could be made out of this, yet other than trifling pleasure was.

*Sidney*   ... Let us now dismiss until evening comes (which is much the best time for them) all these disquisitions, and let us talk about absent friends.

*Brooke*   We must sit up late if I am to tell you of all yours.

*Sidney*   While the weather is so temperate and genial, and while I can be out-of-doors, I care not how late I tarry among

Night airs that make tree-shadows walk, and sheep
Washed white in the cold moonshine on grey cliffs.

Our last excess of this nature was nearer the sea, where, when our conversation paused awhile in the stillness of midnight, we heard the distant waves break heavily. Their sound, you remarked, was such as you could imagine the sound of a giant might be, who, coming back from travel unto some smooth and level and still and solitary place, with all his armour and all his spoils about him, casts himself slumberously down to rest.

# 2   Southey and Porson

*Porson*[1]   There are folks who, when they read my criticism, say, "*I do not think so.*" It is because they do not think so, that I write. Men entertain some opinions which it is indeed our duty to confirm, but many also which it is expedient to eradicate, and more which it is important to correct. They read less willingly what may improve their understanding and enlarge their capacity, than what corroborates their prejudices and establishes their prepossessions. I never bear malice toward those who try to reduce me to their own dimensions. A narrow mind cannot be enlarged, nor can a capacious one be contracted. Are we angry with a phial for not being a flask? or do we wonder that the skin of an elephant sits unwieldily on a squirrel?

*Southey*   Great men will always pay deference to greater: little men will not; because the little are fractious; and the weaker they are, the more obstinate and crooked.

*Porson*   To proceed on our inquiry. I will not deny that to compositions of a new kind, like Wordsworth's,[2] we come without scales and weights, and without the means of making an assay.

*Southey*   Mr Porson, it does not appear to me that anything more is necessary in the first instance, than to interrogate our hearts in what manner they have been affected. If the ear is satisfied; if at one moment a tumult is aroused in the breast, and tranquillized at another, with a perfect consciousness of equal power exerted in both cases; if we rise up from the perusal of the work with a strong excitement to thought, to imagination, to sensibility; above all, if we sat down with some propensities toward evil and walk away with much stronger toward good, in the midst of a world which we never had entered and of which we never had dreamed before, shall we perversely put on again the *old man* of criticism,[3] and dissemble that we have been conducted by a most beneficent and most potent genius? Nothing proves to me so manifestly in what a pestiferous condition are its lazarettos,[4] as when I observe how little hath been objected against those who have substituted words for things, and how much against those who have reinstated things for words.

*Porson*[5]  I find, however, much to censure in our modern poets; I mean those who have written since Milton. But praise is due to such as threw aside the French models. Percy[6] was the first: then came the Wartons,[7] and then Cowper;[8] more diversified in his poetry and more classical than any since.

*Southey*  I wonder you admire an author so near your own times, indeed contemporary.

*Porson*  There is reason for wonder. Men in general do so in regard both to liberty and poetry.

*Southey*  I know not whether the Gauls had this latter gift before they assaulted the temple of Apollo at Delphi;[9] certainly from that time downward the god hath owed them a grudge, and hath been as unrelenting as he was with the dogs and mules before Troy.[10] The succeeding race, nevertheless, has tightened and gilded and gallantly tagged the drum of tragic declamation. Surely not Cowper nor any other is farther from it than Wordsworth.

*Porson*  But his drum is damp; and his tags are none the better for being of hemp, with the broken stalks in.

*Southey*  Let Wordsworth prove to the world that there may be animation without blood and broken bones, and tenderness remote from the stews. Some will doubt it; for even things the most evident are often but little perceived and strangely estimated. Swift ridiculed the music of Handel and the generalship of Marlborough,[11] Pope the perspicacity and the scholarship of Bentley,[12] Gray the abilities of Shaftesbury and the eloquence of Rousseau.[13] Shakespeare hardly found those who would collect his tragedies;[14] Milton was read from godliness; Virgil was antiquated and rustic; Cicero Asiatic. What a rabble has persecuted my friend![15] An elephant is born to be consumed by ants in the midst of his unapproachable solitudes: Wordsworth is the prey of Jeffrey.[16] Why repine? Let us rather amuse ourselves with allegories, and recollect that God in the creation left his noblest creature at the mercy of a serpent.

*Porson*  In[17] our authors of the present day I would recommend principally, to reduce the expenditure of words to the means of support, and to be severe in style without the appearance of severity. But this advice is more easily given than taken. Your friend is verbose; not indeed without something for his words to rest upon, but from a resolution to gratify and indulge his capacity. He pursues his thoughts too far; and considers more how he may show them entirely than how he may show them advantageously. Good men may utter whatever comes uppermost, good poets may not. It is better, but it is also more difficult, to make a selection of thoughts than to accumulate them. He who has a splendid sideboard, should have an iron chest with a double lock upon it, and should hold in reserve a greater part than he displays.

I[18] know not why two poets so utterly dissimilar as your author and

Coleridge[19] should be constantly mentioned together. In the one I find diffuseness, monotony, not indistinctness, but uninteresting expanse, and such figures and such colouring as Morland's;[20] in the other, bright colours without form, sublimely void. In his prose he talks like a madman, when he calls Saint Paul's Epistle to the Ephesians "the sublimest composition of man."[21]

*Southey* This indeed he hath spoken, but he has not yet published it in his writings: it will appear in his *Table Talk*, perhaps.

*Porson* Such table-talk may be expected to come forth very late in the evening, when the wine and candles are out, and the body lies horizontally underneath. He believes he is a believer; but why does he believe that the Scriptures are best reverenced by bearing false witness to them? . . .

Wordsworth goes out of his way to be attacked: he picks up a piece of dirt, throws it on the carpet in the midst of the company, and cries *This is a better man than any of you.* He does indeed mould the base material into what form he chooses; but why not rather invite us to contemplate it than challenge us to condemn it? Here surely is false taste.

*Southey* The principal and the most general accusation against him is, that the vehicle of his thoughts is unequal to them. Now did ever the judges at the Olympic games[22] say, "We would have awarded to you the meed of victory, if your chariot had been equal to your horses: it is true they have won; but the people is displeased at a car neither new nor richly gilt, and without a gryphon or sphinx engraved on the axle?" You admire simplicity in Euripides;[23] you censure it in Wordsworth; believe me, sir, it arises in neither from penury of thought, which seldom has produced it, but from the strength of temperance, and at the suggestion of principle. Some[24] of his critics are sincere in their censure, and are neither invidious nor unlearned; but their optics have been exercised on other objects, altogether dissimilar, and they are (permit me an expression not the worse for daily use) entirely out of their element. His very clearness puzzles and perplexes them, and they imagine that straightness is distortion, as children on seeing a wand dipped in limpid and still water. Clear[25] writers, like clear fountains, do not seem so deep as they are: the turbid look the most profound.

*Porson* Fleas know not whether they are upon the body of a giant or upon one of ordinary size, and bite both indiscriminately.

*Southey* Our[26] critics are onion-eaters by the Pyramids of Poetry. They sprawl along the sands, without an idea how high and wonderful are the edifices above, whose base is solid as the earth itself, and whose summits are visible over a hundred ages. . . .

*Southey* . . . As you call upon me to return with you to the point we set out from, I hope I may assert without a charge of paradox, that whatever is good in poetry is common to all good poets, however wide may be the diversity of manner. Nothing can be more dissimilar than the three Greek tragedians:[27] but would you prefer the closest and best copier of Homer to the worst (whichever he be) among them? Let us avoid what is indifferent or doubtful, and embrace what is good, whether we see it in another or not; and if we have contracted any peculiarity while our muscles and bones were softer, let us hope finally to outgrow it. Our feelings and modes of thinking forbid and exclude a very frequent imitation of the old classics, not to mention our manners, which have a nearer connexion than is generally known to exist with the higher poetry. When the occasion permitted it, Wordsworth has not declined to treat a subject as an ancient poet of equal vigour would have treated it. Let me repeat to you his *Laodamia*.[28]

*Porson*    After your animated recital of this classic poem, I begin to think more highly of you both. It is pleasant to find two poets living as brothers, and particularly when the palm lies between them, with hardly a third in sight. Those who have ascended to the summit of the mountain, sit quietly and familiarly side by side; it is only those who are climbing with briers about their legs, that kick and scramble. Yours is a temper found less frequently in our country than in others. The French poets indeed must stick together to keep themselves warm. By employing courteous expressions mutually, they indulge their vanity rather than their benevolence, and bring the spirit of contest into action gaily and safely. Among the Romans we find Virgil, Horace, and several of their contemporaries, intimately united and profuse of reciprocal praise. Ovid, Cicero, and Pliny, are authors the least addicted to censure, and the most ready to offer their testimony in favour of abilities in Greek or countryman. These are the three Romans, the least amiable of nations, and (one excepted) the least sincere, with whom I should have liked best to spend an evening.

*Southey*    Ennius[29] and old Cato,[30] I am afraid, would have run away with your first affections.

*Porson*    Old Cato! he, like a wafer, must have been well wetted to be good for anything. Such gentlemen as old Cato we meet every day in St Mary Axe,[31] and wholesomer wine than his wherever there are sloes and turnips. Ennius could converse without ignorance about Scipio, and without jealousy about Homer.

*Southey*    And I think he would not have disdained to nod his head on reading *Laodamia*.

*Porson*    You have recited a most spirited thing indeed: and now to give you a proof that I have been attentive, I will remark two passages that offend me. In the first stanza,

> With sacrifice before the rising morn
> *Performed*, my slaughtered lord *have I required*;
> And in thick darkness, amid shades forlorn,
> Him of the infernal Gods *have I desired*.[32]

I do not see the necessity of *Performed*, which is dull and cumbersome.

The second line and the fourth terminate too much alike, and express to a tittle the same meaning: *have I required* and *have I desired* are worse than prosaic; beside which there are four words together of equal length in each.

*Southey*   I have seen a couplet oftener than once in which every word of the second verse corresponds in measure to every one above it.

*Porson*   The Scotch have a scabby and a frost-bitten ear for harmony, both in verse and prose: and I remember in *Douglas*[33] two such as you describe.

> This is the place . . the centre of the grove,
> Here stands the oak . . the monarch of the wood.

After this whiff of vapour I must refresh myself with a draught of pure poetry, at the bottom of which is the flake of tartar I wish away.

> He spake of love, such love as spirits feel
> In worlds whose course is equable and pure;
> No fears to beat away, no strife to heal,
> The past unsighed for, and the future sure;
> Spake, as a witness, of a second birth
> For all that is most perfect upon earth.[34]

How unseasonable is the allusion to *witness* and *second birth*! which things, however holy and venerable in themselves, come stinking and reeking to us from the conventicle. I desire to find Laodamia in the silent and gloomy mansion of her beloved Protesilaus; not elbowed by the godly butchers in Tottenham-court-road, nor smelling devoutly of ratafia[35] among the sugar-bakers' wives at Blackfriars.

Mythologies should be kept distinct: the fire-place of one should never be subject to the smoke of another. The gods of different countries, when they come together unexpectedly, are jealous gods, and, as our old women say, *turn the house out of windows*.

*Southey*   A[36] current of rich and bright thoughts runs through the poem. Pindar[37] himself would not on that subject have braced one to more vigour, nor Euripides have breathed into it more tenderness and passion. The first part of the stanza you have just now quoted might have been heard with shouts of rapture in the regions it describes.

*Porson*   I am not insensible to the warmly chaste morality which is the soul of it, nor indifferent to the benefits that literature on many occasions has derived from Christianity. But poetry is a luxury to which, if she tolerates and permits it, she accepts no invitation: she beats down your gates and citadels, levels your high places, and eradicates your groves. For which reason I dwell more willingly with those authors who cannot mix and confound the manners they represent. The hope that we may rescue at Herculaneum[38] a great number of them, hath, I firmly believe, kept me alive. . . .

# 3 Aeschines and Phocion

*Aeschines*  O Phocion, again I kiss the hand that hath ever raised up the unfortunate.

*Phocion*  I know not, Aeschines, to what your discourse would tend.

*Aeschines*  Yesterday,[1] when the malice of Demosthenes[2] would have turned against me the vengeance of the people; by pointing me out as him whom the priestess of Apollo had designated, in declaring the Athenians were unanimous, one excepted; did you not cry aloud, *I am the man*; *I approve of nothing you do*? That I see you again, that I can express to you my gratitude, these are your gifts.

*Phocion*  And does Aeschines then suppose that I should not have performed my duty, whether he were alive or dead? To have removed from the envy of an ungenerous rival, and from the resentment of an inconsiderate populace, the citizen who possesses my confidence, the orator who defends my country, and the soldier who has fought by my side,[3] was among those actions which are always well repaid. The line is drawn across the account: let us close it.

*Aeschines*  I am not insensible, nor have ever been, to the afflicted; my compassion hath been excited in the city and in the field; but when have I been moved, as I am now, to weeping? Your generosity is more pathetic than pity; and at your eloquence, stern as it is, O Phocion, my tears gush like those warm fountains which burst forth suddenly from some convulsion of the earth.

Immortal gods! that Demades[4] and Polyeuctus[5] and Demosthenes should prevail in the council over Phocion! that even their projects for a campaign should be adopted, in preference to that general's who hath defeated Philip in every encounter,[6] and should precipitate the war against the advice of a politician, by whose presages, and his only, the Athenians have never been deceived.

*Phocion*  It is true, I am not popular.

*Aeschines*  Become so.

*Phocion*  It has been frequently and with impunity in my power to commit base actions; and I abstained: would my friend advise me at last to commit the basest of all? to court the suffrages of people I despise!

*Aeschines*  You court not even those who love and honor you. Thirty times and oftener[7] have you been chosen to lead our armies, and never once were present at the election. Unparalleled glory! when have the Gods shown anything similar among men! Not Aristides[8] nor Epaminondas,[9] the most virtuous of mortals, not Miltiades[10] nor Cimon,[11] the most glorious in their exploits, enjoyed the favour of Heaven so uninterruptedly. No presents, no solicitations, no flatteries, no concessions: you never even asked a vote, however duly, customarily, and gravely.

*Phocion*  The highest price we can pay for anything is, to ask it: and to solicit a vote appears to me as unworthy an action as to solicit a place in a will: it is not ours, and might have been another's.

# 4  King James I and Isaac Casaubon

Casaubon here finished his discourse, and James made no farther observation. Such was his simplicity, he really had imagined that reason and truth, urged so forcibly by him, would alter the system and conciliate the goodwill of the papal court, and that it would resign a wide dominion for a weighty argument. He stroked his beard, licked softly the extremities of his whiskers, ejaculated, sighed, and sate down quietly. He was, notwithstanding, in a frame of mind capable of receiving with satisfaction whatever could derogate from the dignity of the Roman Catholic rites, when Archibald Pringle, one of his pages, entered the apartment.

"Archy," said his Majesty, who was fond of such abbreviations, "I remember to have chidden you for a wicked little story you told me last winter, touching a Japanese at Rouen.[1] Come now, if you can divest it of irreverence, I would fain hear it repeated. I think it a subject for the disquisition of my bishops, whether the pagan sinned or not, or whether, if he sinned, his faith was of a nature to atone for it."

Such were really, if not the first thoughts, those however which now arose in the king's mind. The page thus began his narration.

"A young Japanese was brought over to Rouen on the day of Pentecost. He had expressed in the voyage a deep regret at the death of the chaplain, who might have instructed him in the mysteries, and who, the only time he conversed with him, recommended to him zealously the worship of the living God. He was constant in his desire to be edified, and immediately on his debarkation was conducted to the cathedral. He observed the elevation of the Host with imperturbable devotion, and an utter indifference to the flattering whispers of the fairest among the faithful; such as, 'O the sweet jonquil-coloured skin! Oh the pretty piercing black eyes! O the charming long twisted tail! and how finely those flowers and birds and butterflies are painted upon his trowsers! and look at that leopard in the centre! it seems alive.'

When the service was over, and the archbishop was mounting his carriage-step, he ran after him, and, with eyes half-closed, bit him gently by the calf of the leg. Vociferations were raised by the attendants, the soldiers, and the congregation, ill accordant with sanctity, and wronging the moral character and pious disposition of the Japanese. These however the good prelate quieted, by waving his hand and smiling with affability. The neophyte was asked what induced him to bite the archbishop by the leg: he answered, that he wished to pay the living God the same reverence and adoration as the living God had paid the dead one.

"See now," cried James, "the result of proclaiming that the pope is God upon earth. It led this poor heathen, who amid such splendour and prostrations might well mistake an archbishop for a pope, to the verge of an abyss, dark, precipitous, and profound, as any that superstition hath opened in his own deplorable country."

# 5   General Kleber and French Officers

An English officer was sitting with his back against the base of the Great Pyramid. He sometimes looked toward those of elder date and ruder materials before him, sometimes was absorbed in thought, and sometimes was observed to write in a pocket-book with great rapidity.

"If he were not writing" said a French naturalist[1] to a young ensign "I should imagine him to have lost his eyesight by the ophthalmia.[2] He does not see us: level your rifle: we cannot find a greater curiosity."

The Arts prevailed: the officer slided with extended arms from his resting-place: the blood, running from his breast, was audible as a swarm of insects in the sand. No other sound was heard. Powder had exploded; life had passed away; not a vestige remained of either.

"Let us examine his papers," said the naturalist.

"Pardon me, sir," answered the ensign; "my first inquiry on such occasions is *what's o'clock*? and afterward I pursue my mineralogical researches."

At these words he drew forth the dead man's watch, and stuck it into his sash, while with the other hand he snatched out a purse containing some zecchins: every part of the dress was examined, and not quite fruitlessly.

"See! a locket with a miniature of a young woman!" Such it was: a modest and lovely countenance.

"Ha! ha!" said the ensign; "a few touches, a very few touches; I can give them; and Adela will take this for me. Two inches higher, and the ball had split it: what a thoughtless man he was! There is gold in it too: it weighs heavy. Peste! an old woman at the back! grey as a cat."

It was the officer's mother, in her old age, as he had left her. There was something of sweet piety, not unsaddened by presage, in the countenance. He severed it with his knife, and threw it into the bosom of her son. Two foreign letters and two pages in pencil were the contents of the pocket-book. Two locks of hair had fallen out: one rested on his eyelashes, for the air was motionless, the other was drawn to the earth by his blood.

The papers were taken to General Kleber by the naturalist and his associate, with a correct recital of the whole occurrence, excepting the appendages of watch, zecchins, and locket.

"Young man," said Kleber gravely, "is this a subject of merriment to you? Who knows whether you or I may not be deprived of life as suddenly and unexpectedly? He was not your enemy: perhaps he was writing to a mother or sister. God help them! these suffer most from war. The heart of the far-distant is the scene of its most cruel devastations. Leave the papers: you may go: call the interpreter."

He entered.

"Read this letter."

> *My adored Henry . . .*

"Give it me," cried the general; he blew a strong fire from his pipe and consumed it.

"Read the other."

> *My kind-hearted and beloved son . . .*

"Stop: read the last line only."

The interpreter answered, "It contains merely the name and address."

"I ask no questions: read them, and write them down legibly."

He took the paper, tore off the margin, and placed the line in his snuff-box.

"Give me that paper in pencil, with the mark of sealing-wax on it."

He snatched it, shook some snuff upon it, and shrunk back. It was no sealing-wax: it was a drop of blood; one from the heart; one only; dry, but seeming fresh.

"Read."

> 'Yes, my dear mother, the greatest name that exists among mortals is that of Sydney.[3] He who now bears it in the front of battle, could not succour me: I had advanced too far: I am however no prisoner. Take courage, my too fond mother: I am among the Arabs, who detest the French: they liberated me. They report, I know not upon what authority, that Bonaparte has deserted his army, and escaped from Egypt.'

"Stop instantly," cried Kleber, rising. "Gentlemen," added he to his staff-officers, "my duty obliges me to hear this unbecoming language on your late commander-in-chief: retire you a few moments . . . Continue."

> 'He hates every enemy according to his courage and his virtues: he abominates what he can not debase, at home or abroad.'

"Oh!" whispered Kleber to himself, "he knows the man so well."

> 'The first then are Nelson[4] and Sir Sydney Smith, whose friends could expect no mercy at his hands. If the report be anything better than an Arabian tale, I will surrender myself to his successor as prisoner of war, and perhaps may be soon exchanged. How will this little leaf reach you? God knows how and when!'

"Is there nothing else to examine?"

"One more leaf."

"Read it."

WRITTEN IN ENGLAND ON THE BATTLE OF

ABOUKIR[5]

Land of all marvels in all ages past,
    Egypt, I hail thee from a far-off shore;
I hail thee, doom'd to rise again at last,
    And flourish, as in early youth, once more.

How long hast thou lain desolate! how long
    The voice of gladness in thy halls hath ceast!
Mute, e'en as Memnon's lyre,[6] the poet's song,
    And half-suppress'd the chant of cloister'd priest.

Even he, loquacious as a vernal bird,
    Love, in thy plains and in thy groves is dumb,
Nor on thy thousand Nile-fed streams is heard
    The reed that whispers happier days to come.

O'er cities shadowing some dread name divine
    Palace and fane return the hyena's cry,
And hoofless camels in long single line
    Stalk slow, with foreheads level to the sky.

No errant outcast of a lawless isle,
    Mocker of heaven and earth, with vows and prayers,
Comes thy confiding offspring to beguile,
    And rivet to his wrist the chain he wears.

Britain speaks now; her thunder thou hast heard;
    Conqueror in every land, in every sea;
Valour and Truth proclaim the almighty word,
    And all thou ever hast been, thou shalt be.

"Defender and passionate lover of thy country," cried Kleber, "thou art less unfortunate than thy auguries. Enthusiastic Englishman! to which of your conquests have ever been imparted the benefits of your laws? Your governors have not even communicated their language to their vassals. Nelson and Sydney are illustrious names: the vilest have often been preferred to them, and severely have they been punished for the importunity of their valour.[7] We Frenchmen have undergone much: but throughout the whole territory of France, throughout the range of all her new dominions, not a single man of abilities has been neglected. Remember this, ye who triumph in our excesses. Ye who dread our example, speak plainly; is not this among the examples ye are the least inclined to follow?

"Call my staff and a file of soldiers.

"Gentlemen, he who lies under the pyramid, seems to have possessed a vacant mind and full heart, qualities unfit for a spy: indeed he was not one. He was the friend and companion of that Sydney Smith who did all the mischief at Toulon, when Elliot fled from the city, and who lately, you must well remember, broke some of our pipes before Acre[8]

. . . a ceremony which gave us to understand, without the formalities of diplomacy, that the Grand Signor declined the honour of our company to take our coffee with him at Constantinople."[9]

Then turning to the file of soldiers, "A body lies under the Great Pyramid: go, bury it six feet deep. If there is any man among you capable of writing a good epitaph, and such as the brave owe to the brave, he shall have my authority to carve it upon the Great Pyramid, and his name may be brought back to me."

"Allow me the honour," said a lieutenant, "I fly to obey." .

"Perhaps," replied the commander-in-chief, "it may not be amiss to know the character, the adventures, or at least the name" . . .

"No matter, no matter, my general."

"Take them however," said Kleber, holding a copy, "and try your wits."

"General," said Menou[10] smiling, "you never gave a command more certain to be executed. What a blockhead was that king, whoever he was, who built so enormous a monument for a wandering Englishman!"

# 6    Middleton and Magliabechi

*Magliabechi* . . . I will inform you of some facts I know, proving the efficacy of prayer to saints.

Giacomo Pastrani of Genoa, a citizen not abundant in the gifts of fortune, had however in his possession two most valuable and extremely rare things, a virtuous wife and a picture of his patron Saint Giacomo by Leonardo. The wife had long been ill: her malady was expensive: their substance was diminishing: still no offers had tempted him, although many had been made, to sell the picture. At last he refused to alienate it otherwise than in favour of a worthy priest, and only as the price of supplications to the Virgin. "Who knows how many it may require?" said the holy man; "and it is difficult to make a prayer which the Virgin has not heard before; perhaps fifty will hardly do. Now fifty crowns would be little for such protection." The invalid, who heard the conversation, wept aloud. "Take it, take it," said the husband, and wept too, lifting it from the nail, and kissing for the last time the glass that covered it. The priest made a genuflexion, and did the same. His supplications prevailed; the wife recovered. The priest, hearing that the picture was very valuable, although the master was yet uncertain, and that in Genoa there was no artist who could clean it, waited for that operation until he went to Milan. Here it was ascertained to be the work of Leonardo, and a dealer gave him four thousand crowns for it. He returned in high glee at what had happened, and communicated it to all his acquaintance. The recovered woman, on hearing it, fell sick again immediately, and died. Wishing to forget the sacrifice of her picture, she had prayed no more to Saint Giacomo;

and the Virgin, we may presume, on that powerful saint's intercession, had abandoned her.

Awful fact! Mr Middleton. Now mark another perhaps more so. I[1] could overwhelm you with a crowd of witnesses.

*Middleton*   My dear sir, I do perceive you could.

*Magliabechi*   The saints in general are more vindictive than our Lady; of whose forbearance, not unaccompanied at last by chastisement, I will relate to you a memorable example. I have indeed no positive proof that he of whom I am about to speak had neglected his prayers to the Virgin; but, from what he certainly did, it is by no means uncharitable to suppose it. He moreover, by this action, as you will remark, was the cause why others were constrained to omit the salutary act of supplication as they went along.

*Middleton*   I am in suspense.

*Magliabechi*   Contiguous to my own villa there is one belonging to Signor Anco-Marzio Natale del Poggio. At the corner of the road was inserted in the garden-wall an image of the blessed Virgin, with the *bambino* in her arms. Anco-Marzio had been heard to call it, somewhat hastily, an ugly one, and to declare that he would take it down. The threat however, for several years, was not carried into execution: at last it was accomplished. Behold the consequence! Robbers climbed over the wall (would you believe it?) in the very place whence the effigy had been removed, and upon the very night too of its removal: and Anco-Marzio lost not only the whole crop of his lemons, none of which had ever been stolen in former years, but also a pair of knee-buckles, which his maid servant had taken that occasion of polishing with quick lime, and of which he deeply lamented the loss, not because a crown could scarcely have replaced them, but because they were his father's, and he had bequeathed them by his last will and testament to a very dear old friend.

No reply, no reasoning, can affect this. I know the fact: I visited the spot the next morning: I saw the broken wall: I saw the leaves of the lemon-trees under the vases, without a lemon the size of a filbert on the plants. Who delayed the mad project so long? Who permitted it at last? who punished it? and for what end? Never afterward did Anco-Marzio pass an effigy of the blessed Virgin, but he kissed it again and again with due reverence, although it were wet with whitewash or paint. Every day did he renew the flowers before the one whose tabernacle he had violated, placing them where he could bend his head over them in humble adoration as he returned at night from his business in the city. It has indeed been suspected that he once omitted this duty; certain it is, that he once was negligent in it. He acknowledged to me that, coming home later than usual, and desirous of turning the corner and reaching the villa as soon as might be, it being dusk, he was inclined to execute his duty too perfunctorily, and encountered, instead of the flowers, a bunch of butchers-broom. None grows thereabout. I do not insist on this: but the lemons, Mr Middleton! the thieves, Mr Middleton! the breach in the garden-wall, made for an irreligious purpose, and serving to punish irreligion. Well may you ponder. These things can not occur among you Englishmen.

# 7 Henry VIII and Anne Boleyn

*Henry*  Dost thou know me, Nanny, in this yeoman's dress? 'S blood! does it require so long and vacant a stare to recollect a husband after a week or two? No tragedy-tricks with me! a scream, a sob, or thy kerchief a trifle the wetter, were enough. Why, verily the little fool faints in earnest. These whey faces, like their kinsfolk the ghosts, give us no warning. (*Sprinkling water over her*) Hast had water enough upon thee? take that then ... art thyself again?

*Anne*  Father of mercies! do I meet again my husband, as was my last prayer on earth! do I behold my beloved lord ... in peace ... and pardoned, my partner in eternal bliss! It was his voice. I can not see him ... why can not I? O why do these pangs interrupt the transports of the blessed!

*Henry*  Thou openest thy arms: faith! I came for that: Nanny, thou art a sweet slut:[1] thou groanest, wench: art in labour? Faith! among the mistakes of the night, I am ready to think almost that thou hast been drinking, and that I have not.

*Anne*  God preserve your highness: grant me your forgiveness for one slight offence. My eyes were heavy; I fell asleep while I was reading; I did not know of your presence at first, and when I did I could not speak. I strove for utterance; I wanted no respect for my liege and husband.

*Henry*  My pretty warm nestling, thou wilt then lie! Thou wert reading and aloud too, with thy saintly cup of water by thee, and ... what! thou art still girlishly fond of those dried cherries!

*Anne*  I had no other fruit to offer your highness the first time I saw you, and you were then pleased to invent for me some reason why they should be acceptable. I did not dry these: may I present them, such as they are? We shall have fresh next month.

*Henry*  Thou art always driving away from the discourse. One moment it suits thee to know me, another not.

*Anne*  Remember, it is hardly three months since I miscarried;[2] I am weak and liable to swoons.

*Henry*  Thou hast however thy bridal cheeks, with lustre upon them when there is none elsewhere, and obstinate lips resisting all impression: but now thou talkest about miscarrying, who is the father of that boy?

*Anne*  The father is yours and mine; he who hath taken him to his own home, before (like me) he could struggle or cry for it.

*Henry*    Pagan, or worse, to talk so! He did not come into the world alive: there was no baptism.

*Anne*    I thought only of our loss: my senses are confounded. I did not give him my milk, and yet I loved him tenderly; for I often fancied, had he lived, how contented and joyful he would have made you and England.

*Henry*    No subterfuges and escapes. I warrant, thou canst not say whether at my entrance thou wert waking or wandering.

*Anne*    Faintness and drowsiness came upon me suddenly.

*Henry*    Well, since thou really and truly sleepedst, what didst dream of?

*Anne*    I begin to doubt whether I did indeed sleep.

*Henry*    Ha! false one . . . never two sentences of truth together . . . but come, what didst think about, asleep or awake?

*Anne*    I thought that God had pardoned me my offences, and had received me unto him.

*Henry*    And nothing more?

*Anne*    That my prayers had been heard and my wishes were accomplishing: the angels alone can enjoy more beatitude than this.

*Henry*    Vexatious little devil! she says nothing now about me, merely from perverseness. . . .

# 8   Lord Chesterfield and Lord Chatham

*Chatham*    Our own language contains in it a greater quantity and a greater variety of wit and humour, than all the rest of all ages and countries; closing only Cervantes,[1] the Homer of irony, and not only of sharper and better-tempered wit than he who lies before me, but even of an imagination more vivid and poetical, a sounder too and shrewder philosopher. The[2] little volume of Bacon's *Essays*,[3] in my opinion, exhibits not only more strength of mind, not only more true philosophy, but more originality, more fancy, more imagination, than all these volumes of Plato;[4] supposing even that he drew nothing from others; whereas we must receive the authority of antiquity, and believe that he owed to them the greater part, and almost the whole. Without this authority, we should perceive it in the absence of fixed principles, and in the jarring of contradictory positions. It must be conceded that we moderns are but slovens in composition, or ignorant for the most part of its regulations and laws; yet we may insist that there have been among us those to whom, in all the higher magistratures of intellect, the gravest of the ancients would have risen up, and have placed with proper deference at their side.

*Chesterfield*[5]    I never have found anyone so unprejudiced and so unprepossessed on Plato.

*Chatham*    My lord, I do not know that I am entirely.

*Chesterfield*    How! my lord.

*Chatham* I know that everything I have said is just and incontrovertible, and that I could add ten times as much and as fairly; but I can not take to myself a praise that does not belong to me, any more than I could a purse. I dislike, not to say detest, the character of Plato, as I collect it from his works, and the worst part of it I conceive to be his coldness and insincerity in friendship. He pretended to have been sick during the imprisonment of Socrates: was he so very sick that he could not have been carried to receive the last words of his departing friend? the last counsels of a master so affectionate and impressive? He was never sick when a prince was to be visited on his throne, insolent and tyrannical as that prince might be.

*Chesterfield* A throne is to few so frightful a thing as a death-bed.

*Chatham* My lord, it is a more frightful thing to any man who knows it well, than the death-couch of Socrates was to himself, or to those who from their hearts could reason as he did on it.

*Chesterfield* I am happy, my lord, and grateful to you, that the conversation has taken a different turn from what I had expected. I came to receive some information from you on what might be profitable in the education of the young, and you have given me some which would be greatly so in that of the old. My system, I know, can not be quite according to your sentiments; but as no man living hath a nobler air or a more dignified demeanour than your Lordship, I shall be flattered by hearing that what I have written on politeness meets in some degree your approbation.

*Chatham* I believe you are right, my lord. What is superficial in politeness, what we see oftenest and what people generally admire most, must be laid upon a cold breast or will not stand: so far we agree: but whatever is most graceful in it can be produced only by the movements of the heart.

*Chesterfield* These movements, I contend, are to be imitated, and as easily as those of the feet; and that good actors must beware of being moved too much from within. My lord, I do not inquire of you whether that huge quarto is the Bible: for I see the letters on the back. Permit me.

*Chatham* I did not imagine your Lordship was such an enthusiast in religion: I am heartily glad to witness your veneration for a book, which, to say nothing of its holiness or authority, contains more specimens of genius than any other volume in existence.

*Chesterfield* I kissed it from no such motive: I kissed it preparatorily to swearing on it, as your Lordship's power and credit is from time forward at my mercy, that I never will divulge the knowledge I possess of your reading Greek and philosophy.

# 9  Marcus Tullius and Quinctus Cicero

*Marcus* . . . You remember the apologue of Critobulus?[1]

*Quinctus*  No, I do not.

*Marcus*  It was sent to me by Pomponius Atticus[2] soon after my marriage: I must surely have shown it to you.

*Quinctus*  Not you, indeed; and I should wonder that so valuable a present, so rare an accession to Rome as a new Greek volume, could have come into your hands, and not out of them into mine, if you had not mentioned that it was about the time of your nuptials. Let me hear the story.

*Marcus*  "I was wandering," says Critobulus, "in the midst of a forest, and came suddenly to a small round fountain or pool, with several white flowers (I remember) and broad leaves in the center of it, but clear of them at the sides, and of a water the most pellucid. Suddenly a very beautiful figure came from behind me, and stood between me and the fountain. I was amazed. I could not distinguish the sex, the form being youthful and the face toward the water, on which it was gazing and bending over its reflection, like another Hylas or Narcissus.[3] It then stopped and adorned itself with a few of the simplest flowers, and seemed the fonder and tenderer of those which had borne the impression of its graceful feet: and having done so, it turned round and looked upon me with an air of indifference and unconcern. The longer I fixed my eyes on her, for I now discovered it was a female, the more ardent I became and the more embarrassed. She perceived it, and smiled. Her eyes were large and serene; not very thoughtful, as if perplexed, nor very playful, as if easily to be won; and her countenance was tinged with so delightful a colour, that it appeared an effluence from an irradiated cloud passing over it in the heavens. She gave me the idea, from her graceful attitude, that, although adapted to the perfection of activity, she felt rather an inclination for repose. I would have taken her hand: 'You shall presently,' said she; and never fell on mortal a diviner glance than on me. I told her so. She replied, 'You speak well.' I then fancied she was simple, and weak, and fond of flattery, and began to flatter her. She turned her face away from me, and answered nothing. I declared my excessive love: she went some paces off. I swore it was impossible for one who had ever seen her to live without her: she went several paces farther. 'By the immortal gods!' I cried, 'you shall not leave me.' She turned round and looked benignly; but shook her head. 'You are another's then! Say it! say it! utter the word once from your lips . . and let me die.' She smiled, more melancholy than before, and replied, 'O Critobulus! I am indeed another's; I am a God's.' The air of the interior heavens seemed to pierce me as she spoke; and I trembled as impassioned men may tremble once. After a pause, 'I might have thought it!' cried I: 'why then come before me and torment me?' She began to play and trifle with me, as became her age (I fancied) rather than her engagement, and she placed my hand upon the flowers in her lap without a blush. The whole fountain would not at that moment have assuaged my thirst. The sound of the breezes and of the birds around us, even the sound of her own voice, were all confounded in my ear, as colours are in the fulness and intensity of light. She said many pleasing things to me, to the earlier and greater part of which I was insensible; but in the midst of those which I could hear and was listening to attentively, she began to pluck out the grey hairs from my head, and to tell me that the others too were of a hue not very agreeable. My heart sank within me. Presently there was hardly a limb or feature without its imperfection. 'O!' cried I in despair, 'you have been used to the Gods: you must think so: but among men I do not believe I am considered as ill-made or unseemly.' She paid little attention to my words or my vexation; and when she had gone on with my defects for some time longer, in the same calm tone and with the same sweet countenance, she began to declare that she had much affection for me, and was desirous of inspiring it in return. I was about to answer her with rapture, when on a sudden, in her girlish humour she stuck a thorn, wherewith she had been playing, into that part of the body which supports us when we sit. I know not whether it went deeper than she intended, but catching at it, I leaped up in shame and anger, and at the same moment felt something upon my shoulder. It was an armlet inscribed with letters of bossy adamant, 'Jove to his daughter Truth.'

"She stood again before me at a distance, and said gracefully, 'Critobulus! I am too young and simple for you; but you will love me stil, and not be made unhappy by it in the end. Farewell.' "

*Quinctus* Certainly[4] you have much to look back upon, of what is most proper and efficacious to console you. Consciousness of desert protects the mind against obloquy, exalts it above calamity, and scatters into utter invisibility the shadowy fears of death. Nevertheless, O Marcus! to leave behind us our children, if indeed it will be permitted them to stay behind, is painful.

*Marcus* Among the contingencies of life, it is that for which we ought to be best prepared, as the most regular and ordinary in the course of nature. In[5] dying, and leaving our friends, and saying, "I shall see you no more," which is thought by the generous man the painfullest thing in the change he undergoes, we speak as if we shall continue to feel the same desire and want of seeing them. An inconsistency so common as never to have been noticed: and my remark, which you would think too trivial, startles by its novelty before it conciliates by its truth. We bequeathe to our children a field illuminated by our glory and enriched by our example: a noble patrimony, and beyond the jurisdiction of praetor or proscriber.[6] Nor indeed is our fall itself without its fruit to them: for violence is the cause why that is often called a calamity which is not, and repairs in some measure its injuries by exciting to commiseration and tenderness. The pleasure a man receives from his children resembles that which, with more propriety than any other, we may attribute to the Divinity: for to suppose that his chief satisfaction and delight should arise from the contemplation of what he has done or can do, is to place him on a level with a runner or a wrestler. The formation of a world, or of a thousand worlds, is as easy to him as the formation of an atom. Virtue and intellect are equally his production; yet he subjects them in no slight degree to our volition. His benevolence is gratified at seeing us conquer our wills and rise superior to our infirmities; and at tracing day after day a nearer resemblance in our moral features to his. We can derive no pleasure but from exertion: he can derive none from it: since exertion, as we understand the word, is incompatible with omnipotence.

*Quinctus*   Proceed, my brother! for in every depression of mind, in every excitement of feeling, my spirits are equalised by your discourse; and that which you said with too much brevity of our children, soothes me greatly.

*Marcus*   I am persuaded of the truth in what I have spoken; and yet .. ah Quinctus! there is a tear that Philosophy can not dry, and a pang that will rise as we approach the Gods.

Two[7] things tend beyond all others, after philosophy, to inhibit and check our ruder passions as they grow and swell in us, and to keep our gentler in their proper play: and these two things are, seasonable sorrow and inoffensive pleasure, each moderately indulged. Nay, there is also a pleasure, humble, it is true, but graceful and insinuating, which follows close upon our very sorrows, reconciles us to them gradually, and sometimes renders us at last undesirous altogether of abandoning them. If ever you have remembered the anniversary of some day whereon a dear friend was lost to you, tell me whether that anniversary was not purer and even calmer than the day before. The sorrow, if there should be any left, is soon absorbed, and full satisfaction takes place of it, while you perform a pious office to Friendship, required and appointed by the ordinances of Nature. When my Tulliola[8] was torn away from me, a thousand plans were in readiness for immortalising her memory, and raising a monument up to the magnitude of my grief. The grief itself has done it: the tears I then shed over her assuaged it in me, and did everything that could be done for her, or hoped, or wished. I called upon Tulliola; Rome and the whole world heard me: her glory was a part of mine and mine of hers; and when Eternity had received her at my hands, I wept no longer. The tenderness wherewith I mentioned and now mention her, though it suspends my voice, brings what consoles and comforts me: it is the milk and honey left at the sepulcher, and equally sweet ( I hope) to the departed.

The Gods who have given us our affections, permit us surely the uses and the signs of them. Immoderate grief, like everything else immoderate, is useless and pernicious; but if we did not tolerate and endure it, if we did not prepare for it, meet it, commune with it, if we did not even cherish it in its season, much of what is best in our faculties, much of our tenderness, much of our generosity, much of our patriotism, much also of our genius, would be stifled and extinguished.

When I hear any one call upon another to be manly and to restrain his tears, if they flow from the social and kind affections I doubt the humanity and distrust the wisdom of the counsellor. Were he humane, he would be more inclined to pity and to sympathise than to lecture and reprove; and were he wise, he would consider that tears are given us by nature as a remedy to affliction, although, like other remedies, they should come to our relief in private. Philosophy, we may be told, would prevent the tears by turning away the sources of them, and by raising up a rampart against pain and sorrow. I am of opinion that philosophy, quite pure and totally abstracted from our appetites and passions, instead of serving us the better, would do us little or no good at all. We may receive so much light as not to see, and so much philosophy as to be worse than foolish. I[9] have never had leisure to write all I could have written on the subjects I began to meditate and discuss too late. And where, O Quinctus! where are those men gone, whose approbation would have stimulated and cheered me in the course of them? Little is entirely my own in the *Tusculan Disputations;*[10] for I went rather in search of what is useful than of what is specious, and sat down oftener to consult the wise than to argue with the ingenious. In order to determine what is fairly due to me, you will see, which you may easily, how large is the proportion of the impracticable, the visionary, the baseless, in the philosophers who have gone before me; and how much of application and judgment, to say nothing of temper and patience, was requisite in making the selection. Aristoteles[11] is the only one of the philosophers I am intimate with (except you extort from me to concede you Epicurus)[12] who never is a dreamer or a trifler, and almost the only one whose language, varying with its theme, is yet always grave and concise, authoritative and stately, neither running into wild dithyrambics, nor stagnating in vapid luxuriance. I have not hesitated, on many occasions, to borrow largely from one who, in so many provinces, hath so much to lend. The whole of what I collected, and the whole of what I laid out from my own, is applicable to the purposes of our political, civil, and domestic state. And my eloquence, whatever (with Pollio's leave)[13] it may be, would at least have sufficed me to elucidate and explore those ulterior tracts, which the Greeks have coasted negligently and left unsettled. Although I think I have done somewhat more than they, I am often dissatisfied with the scantiness of my store and the limit of my excursion. Every question has given me the subject of a new one, which has always been better treated than the preceding; and, like Archimedes,[14] whose tomb appears now before me as when I first discovered it at Syracuse, I could almost ask of my enemy time to solve my problem.

Quinctus! Quinctus! let us exult with joy: there is no enemy to be appeased or avoided. We are moving forward, and without exertion, thither where we shall know all we wish to know, and how greatly more than, whether in Tusculum or in Formiae,[15] in Rome or in Athens, we could ever hope to learn!

## from *Imaginary Conversations of Literary Men and Statesmen*, vol. 3 (1828)
## 10   Marcellus and Hannibal

*Hannibal*   Could a Numidian horseman ride no faster? Marcellus! ho! Marcellus! He moves not . . he is dead. Did he not stir his fingers? Stand wide, soldiers . . wide, forty paces . . give him air . . bring water . . halt! Gather those broad leaves, and all the rest, growing under the brushwood . . unbrace his armour. Loose the helmet first . . his breast rises. I fancied his eyes were fixed on me . . they have rolled back again. Who presumed to touch my shoulder? This horse? It was surely the horse of Marcellus! Let no man mount him. Ha! ha! the Romans too sink into luxury: here is gold about the charger.

*Gaulish Chieftain*   Execrable thief! The golden chain of our king under a beast's grinders![1] The vengeance of the gods hath overtaken the impure . . .

*Hannibal*   We will talk about vengeance when we have entered Rome, and about purity among the priests, if they will hear us. Sound for the surgeon. That arrow may be extracted from the side, deep as it is. . . The conqueror of Syracuse lies before me. . . Send a vessel off to Carthage. Say Hannibal is at the gates of Rome . . . Marcellus, who stood alone between us, fallen. Brave man! I would rejoice and can not . . . How awfully serene a countenance! Such as we hear are in the ilands of the Blessed.[2] And how glorious a form and stature! Such too was theirs! They also once lay thus upon the earth wet with their blood . . few other enter there. And what plain armour!

*Gaulish Chieftain*   My party slew him . . indeed I think I slew him myself. I claim the chain: it belongs to my king: the glory of Gaul requires it. Never will she endure to see another take it: rather would she lose her last man. We swear! we swear!

*Hannibal*   My friend, the glory of Marcellus did not require him to wear it. When he suspended the arms of your brave king in the temple, he thought such a trinket unworthy of himself and of Jupiter. The shield he battered down, the breast-plate he pierced with his sword, these he showed to the people and to the gods; hardly his wife and little children saw this, ere his horse wore it.

*Gaulish Chieftain*   Hear me, O Hannibal!

*Hannibal*   What! when Marcellus lies before me? when his life may perhaps be recalled? when I may lead him in triumph to Carthage? when Italy, Sicily, Greece, Asia, wait to obey me? Content thee! I will give thee mine own bridle, worth ten such.

*Gaulish Chieftain*   For myself?

*Hannibal*   For thyself.

*Gaulish Chieftain*   And these rubies and emeralds, and that scarlet . .

*Hannibal*   Yes, yes.

*Gaulish Chieftain*   O glorious Hannibal! unconquerable hero! O my happy country! to have such an ally and defender. I swear eternal gratitude . . yes, gratitude, love, devotion, beyond eternity.

*Hannibal*   In all treaties we fix the time: I could hardly ask a longer. Go back to thy station . . I would see what the surgeon is about, and hear what he thinks. The life of Marcellus! the triumph of Hannibal! what else has the world in it? only Rome and Carthage: these follow.[3]

*Surgeon*   Hardly an hour of life is left.

*Marcellus*   I must die then! The gods be praised! The commander of a Roman army is no captive.

*Hannibal (to the Surgeon)*   Could not he bear a sea-voyage? Extract the arrow.

*Surgeon*   He expires that moment.

*Marcellus*   It pains me: extract it.

*Hannibal*   Marcellus, I see no expression of pain on your countenance, and never will I consent to hasten the death of an enemy in my power. Since your recovery is hopeless, you say truly you are no captive.

(*To the Surgeon*)   Is there nothing, man, that can assuage the mortal pain? for, suppress the signs of it as he may, he must feel it. Is there nothing to alleviate and allay it?

*Marcellus*   Hannibal, give me thy hand . . thou hast found it and brought it me, compassion.

(*To the Surgeon*)   Go, friend; others want thy aid; several fell around me.

*Hannibal*   Recommend to your country, O Marcellus, while time permits it, reconciliation and peace with me, informing the Senate of my superiority in force, and the impossibility of resistance. The tablet is ready: let me take off this ring . . try to write, to sign it at least. O! what satisfaction I feel at seeing you able to rest upon the elbow, and even to smile!

*Marcellus*   Within an hour or less, with how severe a brow would Minos[4] say to me, "Marcellus, is this thy writing?"

Rome loses one man: she hath lost many such, and she stil hath many left.

*Hannibal*   Afraid as you are of falsehood, say you this? I confess in shame the ferocity of my countrymen. Unfortunately too the nearer posts are occupied by Gauls, infinitely more cruel. The Numidians are so in revenge; the Gauls both in revenge and in sport. My presence is required at a distance, and I apprehend the barbarity of one or other, learning, as they must do, your refusal to execute my wishes for the common good, and feeling that by this refusal you deprive them of their country, after so long an absence.

*Marcellus*   Hannibal, thou art not dying.

*Hannibal*   What then? What mean you?

*Marcellus*   That thou mayest, and very justly, have many things yet to apprehend: I can have none. The barbarity of thy soldiers is nothing to me: mine would not dare be cruel. Hannibal is forced to be absent; and his authority goes away with his horse. On this turf lies defaced the semblance of a general; but Marcellus is yet the regulator of his army. Dost thou abdicate a power conferred on thee by thy nation? Or wouldst thou acknowledge it to have become, by thy own sole fault, less plenary than thy adversary's?

I have spoken too much: let me rest: this mantle oppresses me.

*Hannibal*   I placed my mantle on your head when the helmet was first removed, and while you were lying in the sun. Let me fold it under, and then replace the ring.

*Marcellus*   Take it, Hannibal. It was given me by a poor woman who flew to me at Syracuse, and who covered it with her hair, torn off in desperation that she had no other gift to offer. Little thought I that her gift and her words should be mine. How suddenly may the most powerful be in the situation of the most helpless! Let that ring and the mantle under my head be the exchange of guests at parting. The time may come, Hannibal, when thou (and the gods alone know whether as conqueror or conquered) mayest sit under the roof of my children, and in either case it shall serve thee. In thy adverse fortune, they will remember on whose pillow their father breathed his last; in thy prosperous (heaven grant it may shine upon thee in some other country) it will rejoice thee to protect them. We feel ourselves the most exempt from affliction when we relieve it, although we are then the most conscious that it may befall us.

There is one thing here which is not at the disposal of either.

*Hannibal*   What?

*Marcellus*   This body.

*Hannibal*   Whither would you be lifted? Men are ready.

*Marcellus*   I meant not so. My strength is failing. I seem to hear rather what is within than what is without. My sight and my other senses are in confusion. I would have said, This body, when a few bubbles of air shall have left it, is no more worthy of thy notice than of mine; but thy glory will not let thee refuse it to the piety of my family.

*Hannibal*   You would ask something else. I perceive an inquietude not visible til now.

*Marcellus*   Duty and Death make us think of home sometimes.

*Hannibal*   Thitherward the thoughts of the conqueror and of the conquered fly together.

*Marcellus*   Hast thou any prisoners from my escort?

*Hannibal*   A few dying lie about . . and let them lie . . they are Tuscans. The remainder I saw at a distance, flying, and but one brave man among them . . he appeared a Roman . . a youth who turned back, though wounded. They surrounded and dragged him away, spurring his horse with their swords. These Etrurians measure their courage carefully, and tack it well together before they put it on, but throw it off again with lordly ease.

Marcellus, why think about them? or does aught else disquiet your thoughts?

*Marcellus*   I have suppressed it long enough. My son . . my beloved son!

*Hannibal*   Where is he? Can it be? Was he with you?

*Marcellus*   He would have shared my fate . . and has not. Gods of my country! beneficent throughout life to me, in death surpassingly beneficent, I render you, for the last time, thanks.

# 11   Peter the Great and Alexis

*Peter*   And so, after flying from thy father's house, thou hast returned again from Vienna. After this affront in the face of Europe, thou darest to appear before me?

*Alexis*   My emperor and father! I am brought before your majesty, not at my own desire.

*Peter*   I believe it well.

*Alexis*   I would not anger you.

*Peter*   What hope hadst thou, rebel, in thy flight to Vienna?

*Alexis*   The hope of peace and privacy; the hope of security; and above all things, of never more offending you.

*Peter*   That hope thou hast accomplished.

Thou imaginedst then that my brother of Austria[1] would maintain thee at his court . . speak!

*Alexis*   No, sir! I imagined that he would have afforded me a place of refuge.

*Peter*   Didst thou then take money with thee?

*Alexis*   A few gold pieces.

*Peter*   How many?

*Alexis*   About sixty.

*Peter*   He would have given thee promises for half the money; but the double of it does not purchase a house: ignorant wretch!

*Alexis*   I knew as much as that; although my birth did not appear to destine me to purchase a house anywhere; and hitherto your liberality, my father, hath supplied my wants of every kind.

*Peter*   Not of wisdom, not of duty, not of spirit, not of courage, not of ambition. I have educated thee among my guards and horses, among my drums and trumpets, among my flags and masts. When thou wert a child, and couldst hardly walk, I have taken thee into the arsenal, though children should not enter, according to regulations; I have there rolled cannon-balls before thee over iron plates; and I have shown thee bright new arms, bayonets and sabres; and I have pricked the back of my hands until the blood came out in many places; and I have made thee lick it; and I have then done the same to thine. Afterward, from thy tenth year, I have mixed gunpowder in thy grog; I have peppered thy peaches; I have poured bilge-water (with a little good wholesome tar in it) upon thy melons; I have brought out girls to mock thee and cocker thee, and talk like mariners, to make thee braver. Nothing would do. Nay, recollect thee! I have myself led thee forth to the window when fellows were hanged and shot; and I have shown thee every day the halves and quarters of bodies; and I have sent an orderly or chamberlain for the heads; and I have pulled the cap up from over the eyes; and I have made thee, in spite of thee, look stedfastly upon them; incorrigible coward!

And now another word with thee about thy scandalous flight from the palace; in time of quiet too! To the point! did my brother of Austria invite thee? Did he, or did he not?

*Alexis*  May I answer without doing an injury or disservice to his Imperial Majesty?

*Peter*  Thou mayest. What injury canst thou or any one do, by the tongue, to such as he is?

*Alexis*  At the moment, no; he did not. Nor indeed can I assert that he at any time invited me: but he said he pitied me.

*Peter*  About what? hold thy tongue: let that pass. Princes never pity but when they would make traitors: then their hearts grow tenderer than tripe. He pitied thee, kind soul, when he would throw thee at thy father's head; but finding thy father too strong for him, he now commiserates the parent, laments the son's rashness and disobedience, and would not make God angry for the world. At first, however, there must have been some overture on his part; otherwise thou art too shame-faced for intrusion. Come .. thou hast never had wit enough to lie .. tell me the truth, the whole truth.

*Alexis*  He said that, if ever I wanted an asylum, his court was open to me.

*Peter*  Open! so is the tavern; but folks pay for what they get there. Open truly! and didst thou find it so?

*Alexis*  He received me kindly.

*Peter*  I see he did.

*Alexis*  Derision, O my father, is not the fate I merit.

*Peter*  True, true! it was not intended.

*Alexis*  Kind father! punish me then as you will.

*Peter*  Villain! wouldst thou kiss my hand too? Art thou ignorant that the Austrian threw thee away from him, with the same indifference as he would the outermost leaf of a sandy sunburnt lettuce?

*Alexis*  Alas! I am not ignorant of this.

*Peter*  He dismissed thee at my order. If I had demanded from him his daughter, to be the bed-fellow of a Kalmuc,[2] he would have given her, and praised God.

*Alexis*  Father! father! my heart is broken! If I have offended, forgive me!

*Peter*  The state requires thy signal punishment.

*Alexis*  If the state requires it, be it so: but let my father's anger cease!

*Peter*  The world shall judge between us. I will brand thee with infamy.

*Alexis*  Until now, O father! I never had a proper sense of glory. Hear me, O Czar! let not a thing so vile as I am stand between you and the world! Let none accuse you!

*Peter*  Accuse me! rebel! Accuse me! traitor!

*Alexis*  Let none speak ill of you, O my father! The public voice shakes the palace; the public voice penetrates the grave; it precedes the chariot of Almighty God, and is heard at the judgment-seat.

*Peter*  Let it go to the devil! I will have none of it here in Petersburgh. Our church says nothing about it; our laws forbid it. As for thee, unnatural brute, I have no more to do with thee neither!

Ho there! chancellor! What! come at last! Wert napping, or counting thy ducats?

*Chancellor*  Your majesty's will and pleasure!

*Peter*  Is the senate[3] assembled in that room?

*Chancellor*  Every member, sire.

*Peter*  Conduct this youth with thee, and let them judge him: thou understandest me.

*Chancellor*  Your majesty's commands are the breath of our nostrils.

*Peter*  If these rascals are remiss, I will try my new cargo of Livonian hemp[4] upon 'em.

*Chancellor* (returning).  Sire! sire!

*Peter*  Speak, fellow! Surely they have not condemned him to death, without giving themselves time to read the accusation, that thou comest back so quickly.

*Chancellor*  No, sire! Nor has either been done.

*Peter*  Then thy head quits thy shoulders.

*Chancellor*  O sire!

*Peter*  Curse thy silly *sires!* what art thou about?

*Chancellor*  Alas! he fell.

*Peter*  Tie him up to thy chair then. Cowardly beast! what made him fall?

*Chancellor*  The hand of Death; the name of father.

*Peter*  Thou puzzlest me; prythee speak plainlier.

*Chancellor*  We told him that his crime was proven and manifest; that his life was forfeited.

*Peter*  So far, well enough.

*Chancellor*  He smiled.

*Peter*   He did! did he! Impudence shall do him little good. Who could have expected it from that smock-face! Go on: what then?

*Chancellor*   He said calmly, but not without sighing twice or thrice, "Lead me to the scaffold: I am weary of life: nobody loves me." I condoled with him, and wept upon his hand, holding the paper against my bosom. He took the corner of it between his fingers, and said, "Read me this paper: read my death-warrant. Your silence and tears have signified it; yet the law has its forms. Do not keep me in suspense. My father says, too truly, I am not courageous: but the death that leads me to my God shall never terrify me."

*Peter*   I have seen these white-livered knaves die resolutely: I have seen them quietly fierce like white ferrets, with their watery eyes and tiny teeth. You read it?

*Chancellor*   In part, sire! When he heard your majesty's name, accusing him of treason and attempts at rebellion and parricide, he fell speechless. We raised him up: he was motionless: he was dead!

*Peter*   Inconsiderate and barbarous varlet as thou art, dost thou recite this ill accident to a father! And to one who has not dined! Bring me a glass of brandy.

*Chancellor*   And it please your majesty, might I call a. . a . .

*Peter*   Away, and bring it: scamper! All equally and alike shall obey and serve me.

Harkye! bring the bottle with it: I must cool myself . . . and . . . harkye! a rasher of bacon on thy life! and some pickled sturgeon, and some krout and caviar, and good strong cheese.

## from *Imaginary Conversations of Literary Men and Statesmen*, Second Series (1829)
## 12   Lucullus and Caesar

*Lucullus*   Repose yourself, and touch with the ebony wand, beside you, the sphynx on either of those obelisks, right or left.

*Caesar*   Let me look at them first.

*Lucullus*   The contrivance was intended for one person, or two at most, desirous of privacy and quiet. The blocks of jasper in my pair, and of porphyry in yours, easily yield in their grooves, each forming one partition. There are four, containing four platforms. The lower holds four dishes, such as sucking forest-boars, venison, hares, tunnies, sturgeons, which you will find within; the upper three, eight each, but diminutive. The confectionary is brought separately: for the steam would spoil it, if any should escape. The melons are in the snow thirty feet under us: they came early this morning from a place in the vicinity of Luni,[1] so that I hope they may be crisp, independently of their coolness.

*Caesar*   I wonder not at anything of refined elegance in Lucullus:

but really here Antiochia and Alexandria[2] seem to have cooked for us, and magicians to be our attendants.

*Lucullus*   The absence of slaves from our repast is the luxury: for Marcipor[3] alone enters, and he only when I press a spring with my foot or wand. When you desire his appearance, touch that chalcedony, just before you.

*Caesar*   I eat quick, and rather plentifully: yet the valetudinarian (excuse my rusticity, for I rejoice at seeing it) appears to equal the traveler in appetite, and to be contented with one dish.

*Lucullus*   It is milk: such, with strawberries, which ripen on the Apennines many months in continuance, and some other berries[4] of sharp and grateful flavour, has been my only diet since my first residence here. The state of my health requires it; and the habitude of nearly three months renders this food not only more commodious to my studies and more conducive to my sleep, but also more agreeable to my palate, than any other.

*Caesar*   Returning to Rome or Baiae,[5] you must domesticate and tame them. The cherries you introduced from Pontus[6] are now growing in Cisalpine and Transalpine Gaul, and the largest and best in the world perhaps are upon the more sterile side of Lake Larius.[7]

*Lucullus*   There are some fruits, and some virtues, which require a harsh soil and bleak exposure for their perfection.

*Caesar*   In such a profusion of viands, and so savoury, I perceive no odour.

*Lucullus*   A flue conducts heat through the compartments of the obelisks; and if you look up, you may observe that those gilt roses, between the astragals in the cornice, are prominent from it half a span. Here is an aperture in the wall, between which and the outer is a perpetual current of air. We are now in the dog-days; and I have never felt in the whole summer more heat than at Rome in many days of March.

*Caesar*   Usually you are attended by troops of domestics and of dinner-friends, not to mention the learned and scientific, nor your own family, your attachment to which, from youth upward, is one of the higher graces in your character. Your brother was seldom absent from you.[8]

*Lucullus*   Marcus was coming: but the vehement heats along the Arno, in which valley he has a property he never saw before, inflamed his blood; and he now is resting for a few days at Faesulae,[9] a little town destroyed by Sylla within our memory,[10] who left it only air and water, the best in Tuscany. The health of Marcus, like mine, has been declining for several months: we are running our last race against each other: and never was I, in youth along the Tiber, so anxious of first reaching the goal. I would not outlive him: I should reflect too painfully on earlier days, and look forward too despondently on future. As for friends, lampreys and turbots beget them, and they spawn not amid the solitude of the Apennines. To dine in company with more than two, is a Gaulish and German thing. I can hardly bring myself to believe that I have eaten in concert with twenty; so barbarous and herdlike a practice does it now appear to me: such an incentive to drink much and talk loosely; not to add, such a necessity to speak loud: which is clownish and odious in the extreme. On this mountain-summit I hear no noises, no voices, not even of salutation: we have no flies about us, and scarcely an insect or reptile.

# 13  Mr Pitt and Mr Canning

*Pitt*  Dear Canning, my constitution is falling to pieces, as fast as your old friend Sheridan[1] would tell you, the constitution of the country is, under my management. Of all men living, you are the person I am most desirous to appoint my successor. My ambition is unsatisfied, while any doubt of my ability to accomplish it remains upon my mind. Nature has withholden from me the faculty of propagating my species: nor do I at all repine at it, as many would do: since every great man must have some imbecile one very near him, if not next to him, in descent.

*Canning*  I am much flattered, sir, by your choice of me, there being so many among your relatives who might expect it for themselves. However, this is only another instance of your great disinterestedness.

*Pitt*  You may consider it in that light if you will: but you must remember that those who have exercised power long together and without control, seldom care much about affinities. The Mamelukes[2] do not look out for brothers and cousins: they have favourite slaves who leap into their saddles when vacant.

*Canning*  Among the rich families, or the ancient aristocracy of the kingdom . . .

*Pitt*  Hold your tongue! prythee hold your tongue! I hate and always hated these. I do not mean the rich: they served me. I mean the old houses: they overshadowed me. There is hardly one however that I have not disgraced or degraded; and I have filled them with smoke and sore eyes by raising a vassal's hut above them.

I desire to be remembered as the founder of a new system in England: I desire to bequeath my office by will, a verbal one: and I intend that you, and those who come after you, shall do the same!

As you are rather more rash than I could wish, and allow your words to betray your intentions; and as sometimes you run counter to them in your hurry to escape from them, having thrown them out foolishly where there was no occasion nor room; I would advise you never to speak until you have thoroughly learnt your sentences. Do not imagine that, because I have the gift of extempory eloquence, you have the same. No man ever possessed it in the same degree, excepting the two fanatics, Wesley[3] and Whitfield.[4]

*Canning*  In the same degree certainly not; but many in some measure.

*Pitt*  Some measure is not enough.

*Canning*  Excuse me: Mr Fox[5] possessed it greatly, though not equally with you, and found it enough for his purpose.

*Pitt*  Fox foresaw, as any man of acuteness may do, the weaker parts of the argument that would be opposed to him, and he always learnt his replies: I had not time for it. I owe everything to the facility and fluency of my speech, excepting the name bequeathed me by my father: and, although I have failed in everything I undertook, and have cast in solid gold the clay colossus of France,[6] people will consider me after my death as the most extraordinary man of my age.

*Canning*  Do you groan at this? or does the pain in your bowels grow worse? Shall I lift up the cushion of your other chair yonder?

*Pitt*  Oh! oh!

*Canning*  I will make haste, and then soften by manipulation those two or three letters of condolence.

*Pitt*  Oh! oh! . . . next to that cursed fellow who foiled me with his broken weapon, and befooled me with his half-wit, Bonaparte.

*Canning*  Be calmer, sir! be calmer.

*Pitt*  The gout and stone be in him! Port wine and Cheltenham-water! An Austrian wife, Italian jealousy,[7] his country's ingratitude, and his own ambition, dwell with him everlastingly.

*Canning*  Amen! let us pray!

*Pitt*  Upon my soul, we have little else to do. I hardly know where we can turn ourselves.

*Canning*  Hard indeed! when we can not do that!

Be comforted, sir! The worse the condition of the country, the greater is the want of us; the more power we shall possess, the more places we shall occupy and distribute.

*Pitt*  Statesmanlike reflection.

*Canning*  Those who have brought us into danger can alone bring us out, has become a maxim of the English people.

*Pitt*  If they should ever be strong again, they would crush us.

*Canning*  We have lightened them; and, having less ballast, they sail before the wind at the good pleasure of the pilot.

*Pitt*  A little while ago I would have made you chancellor or speaker, for composing and singing that capital song of the *Pilot*:[8] so I thought it: at present I never hear the word but it gives me the sea-sickness, as surely as would a fishing-boat in the Channel. It sounds like ridicule.

*Canning*  *We* have weathered the storm.

*Pitt*  I have not. I never believed in any future state; but I have made a very damnable one of the present, both for myself and others. We never were in such danger from without or from within. Money-lenders and money-voters are satisfied: the devil must be in them if they are not: but we have taken the younger children's fortunes from every private gentleman in Great Britain.

*Canning* Never think about it.

*Pitt* I have formerly been in their houses: I have relatives and connections among them: if you had, you would sympathise. I feel as little as any man can feel for others, you excepted. And this utter indifference, this concentration, which inelegant men call selfishness, is among the reasons why I am disposed to appoint you my successor. You are aware that, should the people recover their senses, they would drive us in a dungcart to the scaffold: *me* they can not: I shall be gone.

*Canning* Condescend to give me some precepts, which, if your disease should continue, it might be painfuller to deliver at any other time. Do not, however, think that your life is at all in danger, or that the supreme power can remain long together in any hands but yours.

*Pitt* Attempt not to flatter me, Canning, with the prospect of much longer life. The doctors of physic have hinted that it is time I should divert my attention from the affairs of Europe to my own: and the doctors of divinity drive oftener to the chancellor's door than to mine. The flight of these sable birds portends a change of season and a fall of bones.

I have warned you against some imprudences of yours: now let me warn you against some of mine. You are soberer than I am: but when you are rather warm over claret, you prattle childishly. For a successful minister three things are requisite on occasion; to speak like an honest man, to act like a dishonest one, and to be indifferent which you are called. Talk of God as gravely as if you believed in him. Unless you do this, I will not say what our Church does, you will be damned; but, what indeed is a politician's true damnation, you will be dismissed. Most very good men are stout partisans of some religion, and nearly all very bad ones. The old women about the prince,[9] are as notorious for praying as for prostitution; and if you lose the old women, you lose him. He is their prophet, he is their champion, and they are his Houris.[10]

*Canning* I shall experience no difficulty in observing this commandment. In our days, only men who have some unsoundness of conscience and some latent fear, reason against religion; and those only scoff at it who are pushed back and hurt by it.

*Pitt* Canning! you must have brought this with you from Oxford:[11] the sentiment is not yours even by adoption: it is too profound for you, and too well expressed. You are brilliant by the multitude of flaws, and not by the clearness nor the quantity of light.

*Canning* On second thoughts, I am not quite sure, not perfectly satisfied, that it is, as one may say, altogether mine.

*Pitt* This avowal suggests another counsel.

Prevaricate as often as you can defend the prevarication, being close

pressed: but, my dear Canning! never . . I would say . . . come, come,
let me speak it plainly: my dear fellow, never lie.

*Canning*  How sir! what, sir! pardon me, sir! But, sir! do you imagine
I ever lied in my lifetime?

*Pitt*  The certainty that you never did, makes me apprehensive that
you would do it awkwardly, if the salvation of the country (the only
case in question) should require it.

*Canning*  I ought to be satisfied: and yet my feelings . . . If you
profess that you believe me incapable . . .

*Pitt*  What is my profession? what is my belief? If a man believes
a thing of me, how can I prevent or alter his belief? or what right have
I to be angry at it? Do not play the fool before me. I sent for you to
give you good advice. If you apprehend any danger of being thought,
what it is impossible any man alive should ever think you, I am ready
to swear in your favour as solemnly as I swore at Tooke's trial.[12] I am
presuming that you will become prime minister; you will then have
plenty of folks ready to lie for you; and it would be as ungentlemanly
to lie yourself as to powder your own hair or tie your own shoe-string.
I usually had Dundas[13] at my elbow, who never lied but upon his
honour, or supported the lie but upon his God. As for the more delicate
duty of prevarication, take up those letters of inquiry and condolence,
whether you have rubbed the seals off or not in your promptitude to
serve me, and lay them carefully by; and some years hence, when
anyone exclaims, "What would Mr Pitt have said!" bring out one from
your pocket, and cry, "This is the last letter his hand, stricken by
death, could trace." Another time you may open one from Burke,[14]
some thirty years after the supposed receipt of it, and say modestly,
"Never but on this momentous occasion did that great man write to
me. He foretold, in the true spirit of prophecy, all our difficulties."
But remember; do not quote him upon finance, else the House will
laugh at you. For Burke was unable to cast up a tailor's bill, as
Sheridan is to pay it.

I was about to give you another piece of advice, which on recollection
I find to be superfluous. Surely my head sympathises very powerfully
with my stomach, which the physicians tell me is always the case,
though not so much with us in office as with the honourable gentlemen
out. I was on the point of advising you never to neglect the delivery
of long speeches: the minister who makes short speeches enjoys short
power. Now, although I have constantly been in the habit of saying
a great deal more than was requisite to the elucidation of my subject,
for the same reason as hares, when pursued, run over more ground
than would bring them into their thickets, I would have avoided it
with you, principally to save my breath. You can no more stop when
you are speaking, than a ball can stop on an inclined plane. You
bounce at every impediment, and run on; often with the very thing in
your mouth that the most malicious of your adversaries would cast
against you; and showing what you would conceal, and concealing
what you would show.[15] This is of no ill consequence to a minister: it

goes for sincerity and plain dealing. It would never have done at Christ-Church or Eton:[16] for boys dare detect anything, and laugh with all their hearts. I think it was my father who told me (if it was not my father I forget who it was) that a minister must have two gifts: the gift of places and the gift of the gab. Perfectly well do I remember his defence of this last expression, which somebody at table, on another occasion, called a vulgarism. At the end of the debate on it, he asked the gentleman whether all things ought not to have names; whether there was any better for this; and whether the learning and ingenuity of the company could invent one. The importance of the faculty was admirably exhibited, he remarked, by the word *gift*: he then added, with a smile, "The alliteration itself has its merit: these short sayings are always the better for it: a pop-gun must have a pellet at both ends."

Ah, Canning! why have I not remembered my father as perfectly in better things? I have none of his wit, little of his wisdom: but all his experience, all his conduct, were before me and within my reach. I will not think about him now, when it would vex and plague me.

*Canning*    Unless it should fatigue you, sir, will you open your views of domestic polity a little wider before me?

*Pitt*    Willingly. Never choose colleagues for friendship or wisdom. If friends, they will be importunate: if wise, they may be rivals. Choose them for two other things quite different; for tractability and connections. A few men of business, quite enough for you, may be picked up anywhere on the road-side. Be particular in selecting for all places and employments the handsomest young men, and those who have the handsomest wives, mothers, and sisters. Every one of these brings a large party with him; and it rarely happens that any such is formidable for mental prowess. The man who can bring you three votes, is preferable to him who can bring you thrice your own quantity of wisdom. For, although in private life we may profit much by the acquisition of so much more of it than we had ourselves, yet in public we know not what to do with it. Often it stands in our way; often it hides us; sometimes we are oppressed by it. Oppose in all elections the man, whatever may be his party or principles, who is superior to yourself in attainments, particularly in ratiocination and eloquence. Bring forward, when places are found for all the men of rank who present themselves, those who believe they resemble you; young declaimers, young poets, young critics, young satirists, young journalists, young magazine-men, and young lampooners and libellers: that is, those among them who have never been more than ducked and cudgelled. Every soul of them will hope to succeed you by adoption.

My father made this remark,[17] in his florid way. When an insect dips into the surface of a stream, it forms a circle round it, which catches a quick radiance from the sun or moon, while the stiller water on every side flows without any; in like manner a small politician may attract the notice of the king or people, by putting into motion the pliant element about him; while quieter men pass utterly away, leaving not even this weak impression, this momentary sparkle. . . .

*Pitt* . . . As you must return to London in the morning, and as I may not be disposed or able to talk much at another time, what remains to be said I will say now.

Never be persuaded to compose a mixed administration of whigs and tories:[18] for, as you can not please them equally, each will plot eternally to supplant you by some leader of its party.

Employ[19] men of less knowledge and perspicacity than yourself, if you can find them. Do not let any stand too close or too much above; because in both positions they may look down into your shallows and see the weeds at the bottom. Authors may be engaged by you; but never pamper them; keep them in wind and tractability by hard work. Many of them are trusty while they are needy: enrich them only with promised lands, enjoying the most extensive prospect and most favourable exposure. For my part, I little respect any living author. The only one, ancient or modern, I ever read with attention, is Bolingbroke,[20] who was recommended to me for a model. His principles, his heart, his style, have formed mine exclusively: everything sits easy upon him: mostly I like him because he supersedes inquiry: the thing best to do and to inculcate. We should have been exterminated long ago, if the House of Commons had not thought so, and had not voted us a Bill of Indemnity:[21] which I was certain I could obtain as often as I should find it necessary, be the occasion what it might. Neither free governments nor arbitrary have such security: ours is constituted for evasion. I hope nobody may ever call me the *Pilot of the Escape-boat.* In Turkey I should have been strangled; in Algiers I should have been impaled; in America I should have mounted the gallows in the market-place; in Sweden I should have been pistoled at a public dinner or court-ball: in England I am extolled above my father.

Ah Canning! how delighted, how exultant was I, when I first heard this acclamation! When I last heard it, how sorrowful! how depressed! He was always thwarted, and always succeeded: I was always seconded, and always failed. He left the country flourishing; I leave it impoverished, exhausted, ruined. He left many able statesmen; I leave *you.*

Excuse me: dying men are destined to feel and privileged to say unpleasant things.

Good night! I retire to rest.

# 14 Diogenes and Plato

*Diogenes* Stop! stop! come hither! Why lookest thou so scornfully and askance upon me?

*Plato*    Let me go; loose me; I am resolved to pass.

*Diogenes*    Nay then, by Jupiter and this tub![1] thou leavest three good ells of Milesian[2] cloth behind thee. Whither wouldst thou amble?

*Plato*    I am not obliged in courtesy to tell you.

*Diogenes*    Upon whose errand? Answer me directly.

*Plato*    Upon my own.

*Diogenes*    O! then I will hold thee yet awhile. If it were upon another's, it might be a hardship to a good citizen, though not to a good philosopher.

*Plato*    That can be no impediment to my release: you do not think me one.

*Diogenes*    No, by my father Jove!

*Plato*    Your father!

*Diogenes*    Why not? Thou shouldst be the last man to doubt it. Hast not thou declared it irrational to refuse our belief to those who assert that they are begotten by the gods, though the assertion (these are thy words) be unfounded on reason or probability?[3] In me there is a chance of it: whereas in the generation of such people as thou art fondest of frequenting, who claim it loudly, there are always too many competitors to leave it probable.

*Plato*    Those who speak against the great, do not usually speak from morality, but from envy.

*Diogenes*    Thou hast a glimpse of the truth in this place; but as thou hast already shown thy ignorance in attempting to prove to me what a *man* is,[4] ill can I expect to learn from thee what is a *great man*.

*Plato*    No doubt your experience and intercourse will afford me the information.

*Diogenes*    Attend, and take it. The great man is he who hath nothing to fear and nothing to hope from another. It is he who, while he demonstrates the iniquity of the laws, and is able to correct them, obeys them peaceably. It is he who looks on the ambitious both as weak and fraudulent. It is he who hath no disposition or occasion for any kind of deceit, no reason for being or for appearing different from what he is. It is he who can call together the most select company when it pleases him.

*Plato*    Excuse my interruption. In the beginning of your definition I fancied that you were designating your own person, as most people do in describing what is admirable; now I find that you have some other in contemplation.

*Diogenes*    I thank thee for allowing me what perhaps I *do* possess, but what I was not then thinking of; as is often the case with rich possessors: in fact, the latter part of the description suits me as well as any portion of the former.

*Plato*    You may call together the best company, by using your hands in the call, as you did with me; otherwise I am not sure that you would succeed in it.

*Diogenes*    My thoughts are my company: I can bring them together, select them, detain them, dismiss them. Imbecile and vicious men can not do any of these things. Their thoughts are scattered, vague, uncertain, cumbersome: and the worst stick to them the longest; many indeed by choice, the greater part by necessity, and accompanied, some by weak wishes, others by vain remorse.

*Plato* Is there nothing of greatness, O Diogenes! in exhibiting how cities and communities may be governed best, how morals may be kept the purest, and power become the most stable?

*Diogenes* *Something* of greatness does not constitute the great man. Let me however see him who hath done what thou sayest: he must be the most universal and the most indefatigable traveller, he must also be the oldest creature upon earth.

*Plato* How so?

*Diogenes* Because he must know perfectly the climate, the soil, the situation, the peculiarities, of the races, of their allies, of their enemies: he must have sounded their harbours, he must have measured the quantity of their arable land and pasture, of their woods and mountains: he must have ascertained whether there are fisheries on their coasts, and even what winds are prevalent.[5] On these causes, with some others, depend the bodily strength, the numbers, the wealth, the wants, the capacities, of the people.

*Plato* Such are low thoughts.

*Diogenes* The bird of wisdom flies low, and seeks her food under hedges: the eagle himself would be starved if he always soared aloft and against the sun. The sweetest fruit grows near the ground, and the plants that bear it require ventilation and lopping. Were this not to be done in thy garden,[6] every walk and alley, every plot and border, would be covered with runners and roots, with boughs and suckers. We want no poets or logicians or metaphysicians to govern us: we want practical men, honest men, continent men, unambitious men, fearful to solicit a trust, slow to accept, and resolute never to betray one. Experimentalists may be the best philosophers: they are always the worst politicians. Teach people their duties, and they will know their interests. Change as little as possible, and correct as much. . . .

*Plato* . . . I may trust you, I hope, O Diogenes!

*Diogenes* Thou mayest lower the gods in my presence, as safely as men in the presence of Timon.[7]

*Plato* I would not lower them: I would exalt them.

*Diogenes* More foolish and presumptuous stil!

*Plato* Fair words, O Sinopean![8] I protest to you my aim is truth.

*Diogenes* I can not lead thee where of a certainty thou mayest always find it; but I will tell thee what it is. Truth is a point; the subtilest and finest; harder than adamant; never to be broken, worn away, or blunted. Its only bad quality is, that it is sure to hurt those who touch it; and likely to draw blood, perhaps the life-blood, of those who press earnestly upon it. Let us away from this narrow lane skirted with hemlock,[9] and pursue our road again through the wind and dust, toward the *great* man and the *powerful*. Him I would call the powerful one, who controls the storms of his mind, and turns to good account the worst accidents of his fortune. The great man, I was going on to demonstrate, is somewhat more. He must be able to do this, and he must have an intellect which puts into motion the intellect of others.

*Plato*  Socrates[10] then was your great man.

*Diogenes*  He was indeed; nor can all thou hast attributed to him ever make me think the contrary.[11] . . .

*Diogenes*  . . . I meddle not at present with infinity or eternity: when I can comprehend them I will talk about them. You metaphysicians kill the flower-bearing and fruit-bearing glebe with delving and turning over and sifting, and never bring up any solid and malleable mass from the dark profundity in which you labor. The intellectual world, like the physical, is inapplicable to profit and incapable of cultivation a little way below the surface . . of which there is more to manage, and more to know, than any of you will undertake.

*Plato*  It happens that we do not see the stars at even-tide, sometimes because there are clouds intervening, but oftener because there are glimmerings of light: thus many truths escape us from the obscurity we stand in; and many more from that crepuscular state of mind, which induceth us to sit down satisfied with our imaginations and unsuspicious of our knowledge.

*Diogenes*  Keep[12] always to the point, or with an eye upon it, and instead of saying things to make people stare and wonder, say what will withhold them hereafter from wondering and staring. This is philosophy; to make remote things tangible, common things extensively useful, useful things extensively common, and to leave the least necessary for the last. I have always a suspicion of sonorous sentences. The full shell sounds little, but shows by that little what is within. A bladder swells out more with wind than with oil.

*Plato*  Diogenes! you are the only man that admires not the dignity and stateliness of my expressions.

*Diogenes*  Thou[13] hast many admirers; but either they never have read thee, or do not understand thee, or are fond of fallacies, or are incapable of detecting them. I would rather hear the murmur of insects in the grass than the clatter and trilling of cymbals and timbrels over-head. The tiny animals I watch with composure, and guess their business: the brass awakes me only to weary me: I wish it underground again, and the parchment on the sheep's back.

*Plato*  My sentences, it is acknowledged by all good judges, are well constructed and harmonious.

*Diogenes*  I admit it: I have also heard it said that thou art eloquent.

*Plato*  If style, without elocution, can be.

*Diogenes*  Neither without nor with elocution is there eloquence, where there is no ardour, no impulse, no energy, no concentration. Eloquence raises the whole man: thou raisest our eyebrows only. We wonder, we applaud, we walk away, and we forget. Thy eggs are very prettily speckled; but those which men use for their sustenance are plain white ones. People do not every day put on their smartest dresses; they are not always in trim for dancing, nor are they practising their steps in all places. I profess to be no weaver of fine words, no dealer in the plumes of phraseology, yet every man and every woman I speak to understands me.

*Plato* Which would not always be the case if the occulter operations of the human mind were the subject.

*Diogenes* If what is occult must be occult for ever, why throw away words about it? Employ on every occasion the simplest and easiest, and range them in the most natural order. Thus they will serve thee faithfully, bringing thee many hearers and readers from the intellectual and uncorrupted. All popular orators, victorious commanders, crowned historians, and poets above crowning, have done it. Homer, for the glory of whose birthplace none but the greatest cities dared contend,[14] is alike the highest and the easiest in poetry. Herodotus,[15] who brought into Greece more knowledge of distant countries than any or indeed than all before him, is the plainest and gracefulest in prose. Aristoteles, thy scholar,[16] is possessor of a long and lofty treasury, with many windings and many vaults at the sides of them, abstruse and dark. He is unambitious of displaying his wealth; and few are strong-wristed enough to turn the key of his iron chests. Whenever he presents to his reader one full-blown thought, there are several buds about it which are to open in the cool of the study; and he makes you learn more than he teaches.

*Plato* I can never say that I admire his language.

*Diogenes* Thou wilt never say it; but thou dost. His language, where he wishes it to be harmonious, is highly so; and there are many figures of speech exquisitely beautiful, but simple and unobtrusive. You see what a fine head of hair he might have if he would not cut it so short. Is there as much true poetry in all thy works, prose and verse, as in that *Scolion* of his on Virtue?[17]

*Diogenes* Thou remindest me of a cavern I once entered.[18] The mouth was spacious; and many dangling weeds and rampant briers caught me by the hair above, and by the beard below, and flapped my face on each side. I found it in some places flat and sandy; in some rather miry; in others I bruised my shins against little pointed pinnacles, or larger and smoother round stones. Many were the windings, and deep the darkness. Several men came forward with long poles and lighted torches on them, promising to show innumerable gems, on the roof and along the sides, to some ingenious youths whom they conducted. I thought I was lucky, and went on among them. Most of the gems turned out to be drops of water; but some were a little more solid. These however in general gave way and crumbled under the touch; and most of the remainder lost all their brightness by the smoke of the torches underneath. The farther I went in, the fouler grew the air and the dimmer the torchlight. Leaving it, and the youths, and the guides and the long poles, I stood a moment in wonder at the vast number of names and verses graven at the opening, and forbore to insert the ignoble one of Diogenes.

The vulgar indeed and the fashionable do call such language as thine the noblest and most magnificent: the scholastic bend over it in paleness, and with the right hand upon the breast, at its unfathomable depth: but what would a man of plain simple sound understanding say upon it? what would a metaphysician? what would a logician? what would Pericles?[19] Truly, he had taken thee by the arm, and kissed that broad well-perfumed forehead, for filling up with light (as thou wouldst say) the dimple in the cheek of Aspasia,[20] and for throwing such a gadfly in the current of her conversation. She was of a different sect from thee both in religion and in love, and both her language and her dress were plainer.

# 15  Barrow and Newton

*Newton*  I come, sir, before you with fear and trembling, at the thoughts of my examination to-morrow. If the masters are too hard upon me, I shall never take my degree. How I passed as bachelor I can not tell: it must surely have been by especial indulgence.

*Barrow*  My dear Isaac! do not be dispirited. The less intelligent of the examiners will break their beaks against the gravel, in trying to cure the indigestions and heart-burnings your plenteousness has given them: the more intelligent know your industry, your abilities, and your modesty: they would favour you, if there were need of favour, but you, without compliment, surpass them all.

*Newton*  Oh sir! forbear, forbear! I fear I may have forgotten a great deal of what you taught me.

*Barrow*  I wonder at that. I am older than you by many years; I have many occupations and distractions; my memory is by nature less retentive; and yet I have not forgotten any thing *you* taught *me*.

*Newton*  Too partial tutor, too benevolent friend! this unmerited praise confounds me. I can not calculate the powers of my mind, otherwise than by calculating the time I require to compass anything.

*Barrow*  Quickness is among the least of the mind's properties, and belongs to her in almost her lowest state: nay, it doth not abandon her when she is driven from her home, when she is wandering and insane. The mad often retain it: the liar has it, the cheat has it: we find it on the race-course and at the card-table: education does not give it, and reflection takes away from it.

*Newton*   I am slow; and there are many parts of ordinary learning yet unattained by me.

*Barrow*   I had an uncle, a sportsman, who said that the light dog beats over most ground, but the heavier finds the covey.

*Newton*   Oftentimes indeed have I submitted to you problems and possibilities. .

*Barrow*   And I have made you prove them.

*Newton*   You were contented with me; all may not be.

*Barrow*   All will not be: many would be more so if you could prove nothing. Men, like dogs and cats, fawn upon you while you leave them on the ground; if you lift them up they bite and scratch; and if you show them their own features in the glass, they would fly at your throat and tear your eyes out. This between ourselves: for we must not indulge in unfavourable views of mankind, since by doing it we make bad men believe that they are no worse than others, and we teach the good that they are good in vain. Philosophers have taken this side of the question to show their ingenuity: but sound philosophers are not ingenious. If philosophy can render us no better and no happier, away with it! There are things that can; and let us take them.

What dost thou sigh at, Isaac?

*Newton*   At my ignorance, in some degree, of their writings.

*Barrow*   At your ignorance of the ignorant? No man ever understood the things that are most admired in Plato[1] and Aristoteles.[2] In Plato there are incoherencies that fall to pieces at a touch: and Aristoteles lost himself in the involutions of his own web. What must we think of a philosopher, who promised to teach one pupil that which he withheld from the rest, although these were more familiar with him, and more instructed? And what must we think of a pupil, who was indignant that any others should partake in his sentiments and his knowledge? Yet such men have guided the scientific, such men have ruled the world.

*Newton*   Not such was Bacon.[3]

*Barrow*   No indeed. I told you, and I repeat it, I think the small volume of *Essays* in your hand, contains more wisdom and more genius than we can find in all the philosophers of antiquity; with one exception, Cicero.[4] On which I desired you to peruse it attentively, and to render me an account of it according to your opinion.

*Newton*   Sir, I have been induced to believe, but rather from the authority of my elders than from my own investigation, that Bacon is the more profound of the two, although not the more eloquent.

*Barrow*   If Bacon had written as easily and harmoniously as Cicero, he would have lost a portion of his weight with the generality of the learned, who are apt to conceive that in easy movement there is a want of solidity and strength. We must confess that antiquity has darkened colleges and has distorted criticism. Very wise men, and very wary and inquisitive, walk over the earth, and are ignorant not only

what minerals lie beneath, but what herbs and foliage they are tread-
ing. Some time afterward, and probably some distant time, a specimen
of ore is extracted and exhibited; then another; lastly the bearing and
diameter of the vein are observed and measured. Thus it is with writers
who are to have a currency through ages. In the beginning they are
confounded with most others; soon they fall into some secondary class;
next, into one rather less obscure and humble; by degrees they are
liberated from the dross and lumber that hamper them; and, being
once above the heads of contemporaries, rise slowly and waveringly,
then regularly and erectly, then rapidly and majestically, till the vision
strains and aches as it pursues them in their ethereal elevation. . . .

*Newton*  Although I could not in conscience disclaim the small merit
there may be in application, since I owe it to the encouragement of
my tutor, I surely have no right or title to invention.

*Barrow*  You have already given proofs of it beyond any man I
know. Your questions lead to great discoveries: whether it please God
that you hereafter make them, or some one following you, is yet
uncertain. We are silly enough to believe that the quality of invention,
as applied to literature, lies in poetry and romance, mostly or alto-
gether. I dare to speculate on discoveries in the subjects of your studies,
every one far greater, every one far more wonderful, than all that lie
within the range of fiction. In our days the historian is the only
inventor: and it is ludicrous to see how busily and lustily he beats
about, with his string and muzzle upon him. I wish we could drag
him for a moment into philosophical life: it would be still more amusing
to look at him, as he runs over this loftier and dryer ground, throwing
up his nose and whimpering at the prickles he must pass through.

Few men are contented with what is strictly true concerning the
occurrences of the world: it neither heats nor soothes. The body itself,
when it is in perfect health, is averse to a state of rest. We wish our
prejudices to be supported, our animosities to be increased, as those
who are inflamed by liquor would add materials to the inflammation.

*Newton*  The simple verities, important perhaps in their conse-
quences, which I am exploring, not only abstract me from the daily
business of society, but exempt me from the hatred and persecution to
which every other kind of study is exposed. In poetry a good pastoral
would raise against one as vehement enemies as a good satire. A great
poet in our country, like the great giant in Sicily,[5] can never move
without shaking the whole island; while the mathematician and astron-
omer may pursue their occupations, and rarely be hissed or pelted
from below. You spoke of historians: it would ill become a person of
my small experience to discourse on them after you.

*Barrow*  Let me hear, however, what you have to say, since at least
it will be dispassionate.

*Newton*  Those who now write history do certainly write it to gratify
a party, and to obtain notoriety and money. The materials lie in the

cabinet of the statesman, whose actions and their consequences are to be recorded. If you censure them, you are called ungrateful for the facilities he has afforded you; and if you commend them, venal. No man, both judicious and honest, will subject himself to either imputation.

*Barrow* Not only at the present day, but always, the indulgence of animosity, the love of gain, and the desire of favour, have been the inducements of an author to publish in his lifetime the history of his contemporaries. But there have been, and let us hope there may be, judicious and virtuous men, so inflamed by the glory of their country in their days, that, leaving all passions and prejudices, they follow this sole guide, and are crowned by universal consent for commemorating her recent exploits.

*Newton* Here are reasons enough for me rather to apply my mind as you direct it, than to the examination of facts which never can be collected by one person; or to poetry, for which I have no call; or to the composition of essays, such as those of Montaigne[6] and Bacon; or dialogues, such as those of Cicero and Plato, and, nearer our times, of Erasmus[7] and Galileo.[8] You had furnished me before with arguments in abundance; convincing me that, even if I could write as well as they did, the reward of my labours would be dilatory and posthumous.

*Barrow* I should entertain a mean opinion of myself, if all men or the most-part praised and admired me: it would prove me to be somewhat like them. Sad and sorrowful is it to stand near enough to people for them to see us wholly; for them to come up to us and walk round us leisurely and idly, and pat us when they are tired and going off. That lesson which a dunce can learn at a glance, and likes mightily, must contain little, and not good. Unless it can be proved that the majority are not dunces, are not wilful, presumptuous, and precipitate, it is a folly to care for popularity. There are indeed those who must found their fortunes upon it; but not with books in their hands. After the first start, after a stand among the booths and gauds and prostitutes of party, how few have lived contentedly, or died calmly! One hath fallen the moment when he had reached the last step of the ladder, having undersawed it for him who went before, and forgotten that knavish act: another hath wasted away more slowly, in the fever of a life externally sedentary, internally distracted: a third, unable to fulfill the treason he had stipulated, and haunted by the terrors of detection, snaps the thread under the shears of the Fates, and makes even those who frequented him believe in Providence.

Isaac! Isaac! the climbing plants are slender ones. Men of genius have sometimes been forced away from the service of society into the service of princes; but they have soon been driven out, or have retired. When shall we see again, in the administration of any country, so accomplished a creature as Wentworth,[9] the favourite of Charles? Only light men recover false steps: his greatness crushed him. Aptitude for serving princes is no proof or signification of genius, nor indeed of any elevated or extensive knowledge. The interests of many require a multiplicity of talents to comprehend and accomplish them. Mazarin[10] and Richelieu[11] were as little able as they were little disposed to promote the well-being of the community; both of them had keen eyes, and kept them on one object, aggrandisement. We find the most trivial men in the streets pursuing an object through as many intricacies, and attaining it; and the schemes of children, though sooner dropped, are frequently as ingenious and judicious. No person can see more clearly than you do, the mortifications to which the ambitious are subject: but some may fall into the snares of ambition whose nature was ever averse to it, and whose wisdom would almost reach anything, and only seems too lofty to serve them watchfully as a guard. It may thus happen to such as have been accustomed to study and retirement, and fall unexpectedly on the political world by means of recommendations. There are those, I doubt not, who would gladly raise their name and authority in the state, by pushing you forward, as the phrase is, into parliament. They seize any young man who has gained some credit at college, no matter for what, whether for writing an epigram or construing a passage in Lycophron;[12] and, if he succeeds to power, they and their family divide the patronage. The ambitious heart is liable to burst in the emptiness of its elevation: let yours, which is sounder, lie lower and quieter. Think how much greater is the glory you may acquire by opening new paths to science, than by widening old ones to corruption. I would not whisper a syllable in the ear of Faction: but the words of the intelligent, in certain times and on certain occasions, do not vary with parties and systems. The royalist and republican meet; the difference lies merely in the intent, the direction, and the application. Do not leave the wise for the unwise, the lofty for the low, the retirement of a college for the turbulence of a House of Commons. Rise, but let no man lift you: leave that to the little and to the weak. Think within yourself, I will not say how impure are the sources of election to our Parliament, but how inconsiderable a distinction is conferred on the representative, even where it is not an individual who nominates, or only a few who appoint him, but where several hundreds are the voters. For who are they, and who direct them? The roughest bearguard, the most ferocious bull-baiter, the most impudent lawyer, the tinker that sings loudest, and the parson that sits latest at the alehouse, hitting them all by turns with his tobacco-pipe, calling them all sad dogs, and swearing till he falls asleep he will hear no more filthy toasts. Show me the borough where such people as these are not the most efficient in returning a candidate to parliament; and then tell me which of them is fit to be the associate . . it would be too ludicrous to say the patron . . of a Euclid[13] or an Archimedes?[14] My dear Newton! the best thing is to stand above the world; the next is, to stand apart from it on any side. You *may* attain the first: in trying to attain it, you are certain of the second.

*Barrow*  . . . You will become an author ere long; and every author must attend to the means of conveying his information. The plainness of your style is suitable to your manners and your studies. Avoid, which many grave men have not done, words taken from sacred subjects and from elevated poetry: these we have seen vilely prostituted. Avoid too the society of the barbarians who misemploy them: they are vain, irreverent, and irreclaimable to right feelings. The dialogues of Galileo, which you have been studying, are written with much propriety and precision. I do not urge you to write in dialogue, although the best writers of every age have done it: the best parts of Homer and Milton are speeches and replies, the best parts of every great historian are the same: the wisest men of Athens and of Rome converse together in this manner, as they are shown to us by Xenophon,[15] by Plato, and by Cicero. Whether you adopt such a form of composition, which, if your opinions are new, will protect you in part from the hostility all novelty (unless it is vicious) excites; or whether you choose to go along the unbroken surface of the didactic; never look abroad for any kind of ornament. Apollo, either as the God of day or the slayer of Python,[16] had nothing about him to obscure his clearness or to impede his strength. To one of your mild manners, it would be superfluous to recommend equanimity in competition, and calmness in controversy. How easy is it for the plainest things to be misinterpreted by men not unwise, which a calm disquisition sets right! and how fortunate and opportune is it to find in ourselves that calmness which almost the wisest have wanted, on urgent and grave occasions! If others for a time are preferred to you, let your heart lie sacredly still! and you will hear from it the true and plain oracle, that not for ever will the magistracy of letters allow the rancid transparencies of coarse colourmen to stand before your propylaea.[17] It is time that Philosophy should have her share in our literature; that the combinations and appearances of matter be scientifically considered and luminously displayed. Frigid conceits on theological questions, heaps of snow on barren crags, compose at present the greater part of our domain: volcanoes of politics burst forth from time to time, and vary, without enlivening, the scene.

Do not fear to be less rich in the productions of your mind at one season than at another. Marshes are always marshes, and pools are pools; but the sea, in those places where we admire it most, is sometimes sea and sometimes dry land; sometimes it brings ships into port, and sometimes it leaves them where they can be refitted and equipt. The capacious mind neither rises nor sinks, neither labours nor rests, in vain. Even in those intervals when it loses the consciousness of its powers, when it swims as it were in vacuity, and feels not what is external nor internal, it acquires or recovers strength, as the body does by sleep. Never try to say things admirably; try only to say them plainly; for your business is with the considerate philosopher, and not with the polemical assembly. If a thing can be demonstrated two ways, demonstrate it in both: one will please this man best, the other that;

and pleasure, if obvious and unsought, is never to be neglected by those appointed from above to lead us into knowledge. Many will readily mount stiles and gates to walk along a footpath in a field, whom the very sight of a bare public road would disincline and weary; and yet the place whereto they travel lies at the end of each. Your studies are of a nature unsusceptible of much decoration: otherwise it would be my duty and my care to warn you against it, not merely as idle and unnecessary, but as obstructing your intent. The fond of wine are little fond of the sweet or of the new: the fond of learning are no fonder of its must than of its dregs. Something of the severe hath always been appertaining to order and to grace: and the beauty that is not too liberal is sought the most ardently and loved the longest. The Graces[18] have their zones,[19] and Venus her cestus.[20] In the writings of the philosopher are the frivolities of ornament the most ill-placed; in you would they be particularly, who, promising to lay open before us an infinity of worlds, should turn aside to display the petals of a double pink.

It is dangerous to have any intercourse or dealing with small authors. They are as troublesome to handle, as easy to discompose, as difficult to pacify, and leave as unpleasant marks on you, as small children. Cultivate on the other hand the society and friendship of the higher; first that you may learn to reverence them, which of itself is both a pleasure and a virtue, and then that on proper occasions you may defend them against the malevolent, which is a duty. And this duty can not be well and satisfactorily performed with an imperfect knowledge or with an inadequate esteem. Habits of respect to our superiors are among the best we can attain, if we only remove from our bosom the importunate desire of unworthy advantages from them. They belong to the higher department of justice, and will procure for us in due time our portion of it. Beside, O Isaac! in this affair our humanity is deeply concerned. Think, how gratifying, how consolatory, how all-sufficient, are the regards and attentions of such wise and worthy men as you, to those whom inferior but more powerful ones, some in scarlet, some in purple, some (it may be) in ermine, vilify or neglect. Many are there to whom we are now indifferent, or nearly, whom, if we had approached them as we ought to have done, we should have cherished, loved, and honoured. Let not this reflection, which on rude and unequal minds may fall without form and features, and pass away like the idlest cloud-shadow, be lost on you. Old literary men, beside age and experience, have another quality in common with Nestor:[21] they, in the literature of the country, are praisers of times past, partly from moroseness, and partly from custom and conviction. The illiterate, on the contrary, raise higher than the steeples, and dress up in the gaudiest trim, a maypole of their own, and dance round it while any rag flutters. So tenacious are Englishmen of their opinions, that they would rather lose their franchises and almost their lives. And this tenacity hath not its hold upon letters only, but likewise upon whatever is public. I have witnessed it in men guilty of ingratitude, of fraud, of peculation, of prevarication, of treachery to friends, of insolence to patrons, of misleading of colleagues, of abandonment of party, of renunciation of principles, of arrogance to honester men and wiser, of humiliation to strumpets for the obtainment of place and profit, of every villany in short which unfits not only for the honours of public, but rejects from the confidence of private life. And there have been people so maddened by faction, that they would almost have erected a monument to such persons, hoping to spite and irritate their adversaries, and unconscious or heedless that the inscription must be their own condemnation. Those who have acted in this manner will repent of it; but they will hate you for ever if you foretell them of their repentance. It is not the fact nor the consequence, it is the motive that turns and pinches them; and they would think it straightforward and natural to cry out against you, and a violence and a malady to cry out against themselves. The praises they have given they will maintain, and more firmly than if they were due; as perjurers stick to perjury more hotly than the veracious to truth. Supposing there should be any day of your life unoccupied by study, there will not be one without an argument why parties, literary or political, should be avoided. You are too great to be gregarious; and were you to attempt it, the gregarious in a mass would turn their heads against you. The greater who enter into public life are disposed at last to quit it: *retirement with dignity* is their device: the meaning of which is, retirement with as much of the public property as can be amassed and carried away. This race of great people is very numerous. I want before I die to see one or two ready to believe, and to act on the belief, that there is as much dignity in retiring soon as late, with little as with loads, with quiet minds and consciences as with ulcerated or discomposed. I have already seen some hundred sectaries of that pugnacious pope,[22] who, being reminded that Christ commanded Peter to put up his sword, replied, "Yes, when he had cut the ear off."

To be in right harmony, the soul not only must be never out of time, but must never lose sight of the theme its Creator's hand hath noted. . . .

# 16   Epicurus, Leontion, and Ternissa

*Leontion*   It is as wise to moderate our belief as our desires.

*Epicurus*   Some minds require much belief, some thrive on little. Rather an exuberance of it is feminine and beautiful. It acts differently on different hearts: it troubles some, it consoles others: in the generous it is the nurse of tenderness and kindness, of heroism and self-devotion: in the ungenerous it fosters pride, impatience of contradiction and appeal, and, like some waters, what it finds a dry stick or hollow straw, it leaves a stone.

*Ternissa*  We want it chiefly to make the way of death an easy one.

*Epicurus*  There is no easy path leading out of life, and few are the easy ones that lie within it. I would adorn and smoothen the declivity, and make my residence as commodious as its situation and dimensions may allow: but principally I would cast underfoot the empty fear of death.[1]

*Ternissa*  O! how can you?

*Epicurus*  By many arguments already laid down: then by thinking that some perhaps, in almost every age, have been timid and delicate as Ternissa; and yet have slept soundly, have felt no parent's or friend's tear upon their faces, no throb against their breasts: in short, have been in the calmest of all possible conditions, while those around were in the most deplorable and desperate.

*Ternissa*  It would pain me to die, if it were only at the idea that anyone I love would grieve too much for me.

*Epicurus*  Let the loss of our friends be our only grief, and the apprehensions of displeasing them our only fear.

*Leontion*  No apostrophes! no interjections! Your argument was unsound; your means futile.

*Epicurus*  Tell me then, whether the horse of a rider on the road should not be spurred forward if he started at a shadow.

*Leontion*  Yes.

*Epicurus*  I thought so: it would however be better to guide him quietly up to it, and to show him that it was one. Death is less than a shadow: it represents nothing, even imperfectly.

*Leontion*  Then at the best what is it? why care about it, think about it, or remind us that it must befall us? Would you take the same trouble, when you see my hair entwined with ivy, to make me remember that, although the leaves are green and pliable, the stem is fragile and rough, and that before I go to bed I shall have many knots and intanglements to extricate? Let me have them; but let me not hear of them until the time is come.

*Epicurus*  I would never think of death as an embarrassment, but as a blessing.

*Ternissa*  How! a blessing?

*Epicurus*  What, if it makes our enemies cease to hate us? what, if it makes our friends love us the more?

*Leontion*  Us? According to your doctrine, we shall not exist at all.

*Epicurus*  I spoke of that which is consolatory while we are here, and of that which in plain reason ought to render us contented to stay no longer. You, Leontion, would make others better: and better they certainly will be, when their hostilities languish in an empty field, and their rancour is tired with treading upon dust. The generous affections stir about us at the dreary hour of death, as the blossoms of the Median apple swell and diffuse their fragrance in the cold.[2]

*Ternissa*  I can not bear to think of passing the Styx,[3] lest Charon[4] should touch me: he is so old and wilful, so cross and ugly.

*Epicurus* Ternissa! Ternissa! I would accompany you thither, and stand between. Would not you too, Leontion?

*Leontion* I don't know.

*Ternissa* O! that we could go together!

*Leontion* Indeed!

*Ternissa* All three, I mean . . I said . . or was going to say it. How ill-natured you are, Leontion! to misinterpret me; I could almost cry.

*Leontion* Do not, do not, Ternissa! Should that tear drop from your eyelash you would look less beautiful.

*Epicurus* Whenever[5] I see a tear on a beautiful young face, twenty of mine run to meet it. If it is well to conquer a world, it is better to conquer two.

*Ternissa* That is what Alexander of Macedon wept because he could not accomplish.

*Epicurus* Ternissa! we three can accomplish it; or any one of us.

*Ternissa* How? pray!

*Epicurus* We can conquer this world and the next: for you will have another, and nothing should be refused you.

*Ternissa* The next by piety: but this, in what manner?

*Epicurus* By indifference to all who are indifferent to us; by taking joyfully the benefit that comes spontaneously; by wishing no more intensely for what is a hair's breadth beyond our reach than for a draught of water from the Ganges; and by fearing nothing in another life.

*Ternissa* This, O Epicurus! is the grand impossibility.

*Epicurus* Do you believe the gods to be as benevolent and good as you are? or do you not?[6]

*Ternissa* Much kinder, much better in every way.

*Epicurus* Would you kill or hurt the sparrow that you keep in your little dressing-room with a string around the leg, because he hath flown where you did not wish him to fly?

*Ternissa* No: it would be cruel: the string about the leg of so little and weak a creature is enough.

*Epicurus* You think so; I think so; God thinks so. This I may say confidently: for whenever there is a sentiment in which strict justice and pure benevolence unite, it must be his.

*Ternissa* O Epicurus! when you speak thus . . .

*Leontion* Well, Ternissa! what then?

*Ternissa* When Epicurus teaches us such sentiments as this, I am grieved that he has not so great an authority with the Athenians as some others have.

*Leontion* You will grieve more, I suspect, my Ternissa, when he possesses that authority.

*Ternissa* What will he do?

*Leontion* Why turn pale? I am not about to answer that he will forget or leave you. No; but the voice comes deepest from the sepulcher, and a great name hath its root in the dead body. If you invited a company to a feast, you might as well place round the table live sheep and oxen, and vases of fish and cages of quails, as you would invite a company of friendly hearers to the philosopher who is yet living.[7] One would imagine that the iris of our intellectual eye were lessened by the glory of his presence, and that, like eastern kings, he could be looked at near only when his limbs are stiff, by waxlight, in closed curtains.

*Epicurus*   One of whom we know little leaves us a ring or other token of remembrance, and we express a sense of pleasure and of gratitude; one of whom we know nothing writes a book, the contents of which might (if we would let them) have done us more good and might have given us more pleasure, and we revile him for it. The book may do what the legacy can not; it may be pleasurable and serviceable to others as well as ourselves: we would hinder this too. In fact, all other love is extinguished by self-love: beneficence, humanity, justice, philosophy, sink under it. While we insist that we are looking for Truth, we commit a falsehood. It never was the first object with anyone, and with few the second.

Feed unto replenishment your quieter fancies, my sweetest little Ternissa! and let the gods, both youthful and aged, both gentle and boisterous, administer to them hourly on these sunny downs: what can they do better?

# 17   Leofric and Godiva

*Godiva*   There is a dearth in the land, my sweet Leofric! Remember how many weeks of drought we have had, even in the deep pastures of Leicestershire; and how many Sundays we have heard the same prayers for rain, and supplications that it would please the Lord in his mercy to turn aside his anger from the poor pining cattle. You, my dear husband, have imprisoned more than one malefactor for leaving his dead ox in the public way; and other hinds have fled before you out of the traces, in which they and their sons and their daughters, and haply their old fathers and mothers, were dragging the abandoned wain homeward. Although we were accompanied by many brave spearmen and skilful archers, it was perilous to pass the creatures which the farm-yard dogs, driven from the hearth by the poverty of their masters, were tearing and devouring; while others, bitten and lamed, filled the air either with long and deep howls or sharp and quick barkings, as they struggled with hunger and feebleness or were exasperated by heat and pain. Nor could the thyme from the heath, nor the bruised branches of the fir-tree, extinguish or abate the foul odour.

*Leofric*   And now, Godiva my darling, thou art afraid we should be eaten up before we enter the gates of Coventry; or perchance that in the gardens there are no roses to greet thee, no sweet herbs for thy mat and pillow.

*Godiva* Leofric, I have no such fears. This is the month of roses: I find them everywhere since my blessed marriage: they, and all other sweet herbs, I know not why, seem to greet me wherever I look at them, as though they knew and expected me. Surely they can not feel that I am fond of them.

*Leofric* O light laughing simpleton! But what wouldst thou? I came not hither to pray; and yet if praying would satisfy thee, or remove the drought, I would ride up straightway to Saint Michael's[1] and pray until morning.

*Godiva* I would do the same, O Leofric! but God hath turned away his ear from holier lips than mine. Would my own dear husband hear me, if I implored him for what is easier to accomplish? what he can do like God.

*Leofric* How! what is it!

*Godiva* I would not, in the first hurry of your wrath, appeal to you, my loving lord, in behalf of these unhappy men who have offended you.

*Leofric* Unhappy! is that all?

*Godiva* Unhappy they must surely be, to have offended you so grievously. What a soft air breathes over us! how quiet and serene and still an evening! how calm are the heavens and the earth! shall none enjoy them? not even we, my Leofric! The sun is ready to set: let it never set, O Leofric, on your anger.[2] These are not my words; they are better than mine; should they lose their virtue from my unworthiness in uttering them!

*Leofric* Godiva, wouldst thou plead to me for rebels?

*Godiva* They have then drawn the sword against you! Indeed, I knew it not.

*Leofric* They have omitted to send me my dues, established by my ancestors, well knowing of our nuptials, and of the charges and festivities they require, and that in a season of such scarcity my own lands are insufficient.

*Godiva* If they were starving as they said they were . . .

*Leofric* Must I starve too? Is it not enough to lose my vassals?

*Godiva* Enough! O God! too much! too much! may you never lose them! Give them life, peace, comfort, contentment. There are those among them who kissed me in my infancy, and who blessed me at the baptismal font. Leofric, Leofric! the first old man I meet I shall think is one of those; and I shall think on the blessing he gave, and (ah me!) on the blessing I bring back to him. My heart will bleed, will burst . . and he will weep at it! he will weep, poor soul! for the wife of a cruel lord who denounces vengeance on him, who carries death into his family.

*Leofric* We must hold solemn festivals.

*Godiva* We must, indeed.

*Leofric* Well then.

*Godiva*   Is the clamorousness that succeeds the death of God's dumb creatures, are crowded halls, are slaughtered cattle, festivals? are maddening songs and giddy dances, and hireling praises from party-coloured coats? Can the voice of a minstrel tell us better things of ourselves than our own internal one might tell us; or can his breath make our breath softer in sleep? O my beloved! let everything be a joyance to us: it will, if we will. Sad is the day, and worse must follow, when we hear the blackbird in the garden and do not throb with joy. But, Leofric, the high festival is strown by the servant of God upon the heart of man. It is gladness, it is thanksgiving; it is the orphan, the starveling, pressed to the bosom, and bidden as its first commandment to remember its benefactor. We will hold this festival; the guests are ready: we may keep it up for weeks, and months, and years together, and always be the happier and the richer for it. The beverage of this feast, O Leofric, is sweeter than bee or flower or vine can give us: it flows from heaven; and in heaven will it abundantly be poured out again, to him who pours it out here unsparingly.

*Leofric*   Thou art wild.

*Godiva*   I have indeed lost myself. Some Power, some good kind Power, melts me (body and soul and voice) into tenderness and love. O, my husband, we must obey it. Look upon me! look upon me! lift your sweet eyes from the ground! I will not cease to supplicate; I dare not.

*Leofric*   We may think upon it.

*Godiva*   Never say that! What! think upon goodness when you can be good? Let not the infants cry for sustenance! The mother of our blessed Lord will hear them; us never, never afterward.

*Leofric*   Here comes the bishop: we are but one mile from the walls. Why dismountest thou? no bishop can expect it. Godiva! my honour and rank among men are humbled by this: Earl Godwin[3] will hear of it: up! up! the bishop hath seen it: he urgeth his horse onward: dost thou not hear him now upon the solid turf behind thee?

*Godiva*   Never, no, never will I rise, O Leofric, until you remit this most impious tax, this tax on hard labour, on hard life.

*Leofric*   Turn round: look how the fat nag canters, as to the tune of a sinner's psalm, slow and hard-breathing. What reason or right can the people have to complain, while their bishop's steed is so sleek and well caparisoned? Inclination to change, desire to abolish old usages ... Up! up! for shame! They shall smart for it, idlers! Sir bishop, I must blush for my young bride.

*Godiva*   My husband, my husband! will you pardon the city?

*Leofric*   Sir bishop! I could not think you would have seen her in this plight. Will I pardon? yea, Godiva, by the holy rood, will I pardon the city, when thou ridest naked at noontide through the streets.

*Godiva*   Say, dearest Leofric, is there indeed no other hope, no other mediation?

*Leofric*   I have sworn: beside, thou hast made me redden and turn my face away from thee, and all the knaves have seen it: this adds to the city's crime.

*Godiva*   I have blushed too, Leofric, and was not rash nor obdurate.

*Leofric*   But thou, my sweetest, art given to blushing; there is no conquering it in thee. I wish thou hadst not alighted so hastily and roughly: it hath shaken down a sheaf of thy hair: take heed thou sit not upon it, lest it anguish thee. Well done! it mingleth now sweetly with the cloth of gold upon the saddle, running here and there, as if it had life and faculties and business, and were working thereupon some newer and cunninger device. O my beauteous Eve! there is a Paradise about thee! the world is refreshed as thou movest and breathest on it. I can not see or think of evil where thou art. I could throw my arms even here about thee. No signs for me! no shaking of sunbeams! no reproof or frown or wonderment ... I *will* say it ... now then for worse ... I could close with my kisses thy half-open lips, ay, and those lovely and loving eyes, before the people.

*Godiva*   To-morrow you shall kiss me, and they shall bless you for it. I shall be very pale, for to-night I must fast and pray.

## from *The Works of Walter Savage Landor* (1846)
## 18   Fra Filippo Lippi and Pope Eugenius the Fourth

*Filippo*   Abdul is by no means deficient in a good opinion of his own capacity and his Prophet's all-sufficiency, but he never took me to task about my faith or his own.

*Eugenius*   How wert thou mainly occupied?

*Filippo*   I will give your Holiness a sample both of my employments and of his character. He was going one evening to a country-house, about fifteen miles from Tunis; and he ordered me to accompany him. I found there a spacious garden, overrun with wild-flowers and most luxuriant grass, in irregular tufts, according to the dryness or the humidity of the spot. The clematis overtopped the lemon and orange-trees; and the perennial pea, sent forth here a pink blossom, here a purple, here a white one, and, after holding (as it were) a short conversation with the humbler plants, sprang up about an old cypress, played among its branches, and mitigated its gloom. White pigeons, and others in colour like the dawn of day, looked down on us and ceased to coo, until some of their companions, in whom they had more confidence, encouraged them loudly from remoter boughs, or alighted on the shoulders of Abdul, at whose side I was standing. A few of them examined me in every position their inquisitive eyes could take;

displaying all the advantages of their versatile necks, and pretending querulous fear in the midst of petulant approaches.

*Eugenius*    Is it of pigeons thou art talking, O Filippo? I hope it may be.

*Filippo*    Of Abdul's pigeons. He was fond of taming all creatures; men, horses, pigeons, equally; but he tamed them all by kindness. In this wilderness is an edifice not unlike our Italian chapter-houses built by the Lombards, with long narrow windows, high above the ground. The centre is now a bath, the waters of which, in another part of the inclosure, had supplied a fountain, at present in ruins, and covered by tufted canes, and by every variety of aquatic plants. The structure has no remains of roof: and, of six windows, one alone is unconcealed by ivy. This had been walled up long ago, and the cement in the inside of it was hard and polished. "Lippi!" said Abdul to me, after I had long admired the place in silence, "I leave to thy superintendence this bath and garden. Be sparing of the leaves and branches: make paths only wide enough for me. Let me see no mark of hatchet or pruning-hook, and tell the labourers that whoever takes a nest or an egg shall be impaled."

*Eugenius*    Monster! so then he would really have impaled a poor wretch for eating a bird's egg? How disproportionate is the punishment to the offence!

*Filippo*    He efficiently checked in his slaves the desire of transgressing his command. To spare them as much as possible, I ordered them merely to open a few spaces, and to remove the weaker trees from the stronger. Meanwhile I drew on the smooth blank window the figure of Abdul and of a beautiful girl.

*Eugenius*    Rather say handmaiden: choicer expression; more decorous.

*Filippo*    Holy Father! I have been lately so much out of practice, I take the first that comes in my way. Handmaiden I will use in preference for the future.

*Eugenius*    On then! and God speed thee!

*Filippo*    I drew Abdul with a blooming handmaiden. One of his feet is resting on her lap, and she is drying the ancle with a saffron robe, of which the greater part is fallen in doing it. That she is a bondmaid is discernible, not only by her occupation, but by her humility and patience, by her loose and flowing brown hair, and by her eyes expressing the timidity at once of servitude and of fondness. The countenance was taken from fancy, and was the loveliest I could imagine: of the figure I had some idea, having seen it to advantage in Tunis. After seven days Abdul returned. He was delighted with the improvement made in the garden. I requested him to visit the bath. "We can do nothing to that," answered he impatiently. "There is no sudatory, no dormitory, no dressing-room, no couch. Sometimes I sit an hour there in the summer, because I never found a fly in it; the principal curse of hot countries, and against which plague there is neither prayer nor amulet, nor indeed any human defence." He went away into the house. At dinner he sent me from his table some quails and ortolans,[1] and tomatas and honey and rice, beside a basket of fruit covered with moss and bay-leaves, under which I found a verdino fig,[2] deliciously ripe, and bearing the impression of several small teeth, but certainly no reptile's.

*Eugenius*  There might have been poison in them, for all that.

*Filippo*  About two hours had passed, when I heard a whirr and a crash in the windows of the bath (where I had dined and was about to sleep), occasioned by the settling and again the flight of some pheasants. Abdul entered. "Beard of the Prophet! what hast thou been doing? That is myself! No, no, Lippi! thou never canst have seen her: the face proves it: but those limbs! thou hast divined them aright: thou hast had sweet dreams then! Dreams are large possessions: in them the possessor may cease to possess his own. To the slave, O Allah! to the slave is permitted what is not his! . . I burn with anguish to think how much . . yea, at that very hour. I would not another should, even in a dream . . But, Lippi! thou never canst have seen above the sandal?" To which I answered, "I never have allowed my eyes to look even on that. But if anyone of my lord Abdul's fair slaves resembles, as they surely must all do, in duty and docility, the figure I have represented, let it express to him my congratulation on his happiness." "I believe," said he, "such representations are forbidden by the Koran; but as I do not remember it, I do not sin. There it shall stay, unless the angel Gabriel[3] comes to forbid it." He smiled in saying so.

*Eugenius*  There is hope of this Abdul. His faith hangs about him more like oil than pitch.

*Filippo*  He inquired of me whether I often thought of those I loved in Italy, and whether I could bring them before my eyes at will. To remove all suspicion from him, I declared I always could, and that one beautiful object occupied all the cells of my brain by night and day. He paused and pondered, and then said, "Thou dost not love deeply." I thought I had given the true signs. "No, Lippi! we who love ardently, we, with all our wishes, all the efforts of our souls, can not bring before us the features which, while they were present, we thought it impossible we ever could forget. Alas! when we most love the absent, when we most desire to see her, we try in vain to bring her image back to us. The troubled heart shakes and confounds it, even as ruffled waters do with shadows. Hateful things are more hateful when they haunt our sleep: the lovely flee away, or are changed into less lovely."

*Eugenius*  What figures now have these unbelievers?

*Filippo*  Various in their combinations as the letters or the numerals; but they all, like these, signify something. Almeida (did I not inform your Holiness?) has large hazel eyes . .

*Eugenius*  Has she? thou never toldest me that. Well, well! and what else has she? Mind! be cautious! use decent terms.

*Filippo*    Somewhat pouting lips.

*Eugenius*    Ha! ha! What did they pout at?

*Filippo*    And she is rather plump than otherwise.

*Eugenius*    No harm in that.

*Filippo*    And moreover is cool, smooth, and firm as a nectarine gathered before sunrise.

*Eugenius*    Ha! ha! do not remind me of nectarines. I am very fond of them; and this is not the season! Such females as thou describest, are said to be among the likeliest to give reasonable cause for suspicion. I would not judge harshly, I would not think uncharitably; but, unhappily, being at so great a distance from spiritual aid, peradventure a desire, a suggestion, an inkling . . ay? If she, the lost Almeida, came before thee when her master was absent . . which I trust she never did . . . But those flowers and shrubs and odours and alleys and long grass and alcoves, might strangely hold, perplex, and entangle, two incautious young persons . . ay?

*Filippo*    I confessed all I had to confess in this matter, the evening I landed.

*Eugenius*    Ho! I am no candidate for a seat at the rehearsal of confessions: but perhaps my absolution might be somewhat more pleasing and unconditional. Well! well! since I am unworthy of such confidence, go about thy business . . paint! paint!

*Filippo*    Am I so unfortunate as to have offended your Beatitude?

*Eugenius*    Offend *me*, man! who offends *me*? I took an interest in thy adventures, and was concerned lest thou mightest have sinned; for by my soul! Filippo! those are the women that the devil hath set his mark on.

*Filippo*    It would do your Holiness's heart good to rub it out again, wherever he may have had the cunning to make it.

*Eugenius*    Deep! deep!

*Filippo*    Yet it may be got at; she being a Biscayan[4] by birth, as she told me, and not only baptised, but going by sea along the coast for confirmation, when she was captured.

*Euginius*    Alas! to what an imposition of hands was this tender young thing devoted! Poor soul!

*Filippo*    I sigh for her myself when I think of her.

*Eugenius*    Beware lest the sigh be mundane, and lest the thought recur too often. I wish it were presently in my power to examine her myself on her condition. What thinkest thou! Speak.

*Filippo*    Holy Father! she would laugh in your face.

*Eugenius*    So lost!

*Eugenius*    . . . Thy residence among the Mahometans, I am afraid, hath rendered thee more favourable to them than beseems a Catholic, and thy mind, I do suspect, sometimes goes back into Barbary[5] unreluctantly.

*Filippo*    While I continued in that country, although I was well treated, I often wished myself away, thinking of my friends in Florence, of music, of painting, of our villegiatura[6] at the vintage-time; whether in the green and narrow glades of Pratolino,[7] with lofty trees above us, and little rills unseen, and little bells about the necks of sheep and goats, tinkling together ambiguously; or amid the grey quarries or under the majestic walls of ancient Fiesole;[8] or down in the woods of the Doccia,[9] where the cypresses are of such girth that, when a youth stands against one of them, and a maiden stands opposite, and they clasp it, their hands at the time do little more than meet. Beautiful scenes, on which Heaven smiles eternally, how often has my heart ached for you! He who hath lived in this country, can enjoy no distant one. He breathes here another air; he lives more life; a brighter sun invigorates his studies, and serener stars influence his repose. Barbary hath also the blessing of climate; and although I do not desire to be there again, I feel sometimes a kind of regret at leaving it. A bell warbles the more mellifluously in the air when the sound of the stroke is over, and when another swims out from underneath it, and pants upon the element that gave it birth. In like manner the recollection of a thing is frequently more pleasing than the actuality; what is harsh is dropped in the space between. . . .

*Eugenius*  It appears then really that the Infidels have some semblances of magnanimity and generosity?

*Filippo*  I thought so when I turned over the many changes of fine linen; and I was little short of conviction when I found at the bottom of my chest two hundred Venetian zecchins.

*Eugenius*  Corpo di Bacco! Better things, far better things, I would fain do for thee, not exactly of this description; it would excite many heart-burnings. Information has been laid before me, Filippo, that thou art attached to a certain young person, by name Lucrezia, daughter of Francesco Buti, a citizen of Prato.[10]

*Filippo*  I acknowledge my attachment: it continues.

*Eugenius*  Furthermore, that thou hast offspring by her.[11]

*Filippo*  Alas 'tis undeniable.

*Eugenius*  I will not only legitimatize the said offspring by *motu proprio*[12] and rescript to consistory and chancery. .

*Filippo*  Holy Father! Holy Father! For the love of the Virgin, not a word to consistory or chancery, of the two hundred zecchins. As I hope for salvation, I have but forty left: and thirty-nine would not serve them.

*Eugenius*  Fear nothing. Not only will I perform what I have promised, not only will I give the strictest order that no money be demanded by any officer of my courts, but, under the seal of Saint Peter, I will declare thee and Lucrezia Buti man and wife.

*Filippo*  Man and wife!

*Eugenius*  Moderate thy transport.

*Filippo*  O Holy Father! may I speak?

*Eugenius*    Surely she is not the wife of another?

*Filippo*    No indeed.

*Eugenius*    Nor within the degrees of consanguinity and affinity?

*Filippo*    No, no, no. But . . man and wife! Consistory and chancery are nothing to this fulmination.

*Eugenius*    How so?

*Filippo*    It is man and wife the first fortnight, but wife and man ever after. The two figures change places: the unit is the decimal and the decimal is the unit.

*Eugenius*    What then can I do for thee?

*Filippo*    I love Lucrezia: let me love her: let her love me. I can make her at any time what she is not: I could never make her again what she is.

*Eugenius*    The only thing I can do then is to promise I will forget that I have heard anything about the matter. But, to forget it, I must hear it first.

*Filippo*    In the beautiful little town of Prato, reposing in its idleness against the hill that protects it from the north, and looking over fertile meadows, southward to Poggio Cajano, westward to Pistoja, there is the convent of Santa Margarita. I was invited by the sisters to paint an altar-piece for the chapel. A novice of fifteen, my own sweet Lucrezia, came one day alone to see me work at my Madonna. Her blessed countenance had already looked down on every beholder lower by the knees. I myself who made her could almost have worshipped her.

*Eugenius*    Not while incomplete: no half-virgin will do.

*Filippo*    But there knelt Lucrezia! there she knelt! first looking with devotion at the Madonna, then with admiring wonder and grateful delight at the artist. Could so little a heart be divided? 'Twere a pity! There was enough for me: there is never enough for the Madonna. Resolving on a sudden that the object of my love should be the object of adoration to thousands, born and unborn, I swept my brush across the maternal face, and left a blank in heaven. The little girl screamed: I pressed her to my bosom.

*Eugenius*    In the chapel?

*Filippo*    I knew not where I was: I thought I was in Paradise.

*Eugenius*    If it was not in the chapel, the sin is venial. But a brush against a Madonna's mouth is worse than a beard against her votary's.

*Filippo*    I thought so too, Holy Father!

*Eugenius*    Thou sayest thou hast forty zecchins: I will try in due season to add forty more. The fisherman[13] must not venture to measure forces with the pirate. Farewell! I pray God, my son Filippo, to have thee alway in his holy keeping.

# 19 Aesop and Rhodopè

*Rhodopè* ... But, Aesop, you should never say the thing that is untrue.

*Aesop* We say and do and look no other all our lives.

*Rhodopè* Do we never know better?

*Aesop* Yes; when we cease to please, and to wish it; when death is settling the features, and the cerements are ready to render them unchangeable.

*Rhodopè* Alas! alas!

*Aesop* Breathe, Rhodopè, breathe again those painless sighs: they belong to thy vernal season. May thy summer of life be calm, thy autumn calmer, and thy winter never come!

*Rhodopè* I must die then earlier.

*Aesop* Laodameia[1] died; Helen[2] died; Leda,[3] the beloved of Jupiter, went before. It is better to repose in the earth betimes than to sit up late; better, than to cling pertinaciously to what we feel crumbling under us, and to protract an inevitable fall. We may enjoy the present while we are insensible of infirmity and decay: but the present, like a note in music, is nothing but as it appertains to what is past and what is to come. There are no fields of amaranth on this side of the grave: there are no voices, O Rhodopè, that are not soon mute, however tuneful: there is no name, with whatever emphasis of passionate love repeated, of which the echo is not faint at last.

*Rhodopè* O Aesop! let me rest my head on yours: it throbs and pains me.

*Aesop* What are these ideas to thee?

*Rhodopè* Sad, sorrowful.

*Aesop* Harrows that break the soil, preparing it for wisdom. Many flowers must perish ere a grain of corn be ripened. And now remove thy head: the cheek is cool enough after its little shower of tears.

# 20 Second Conversation

*Rhodopè* Never shall I forget the morning when my father, sitting in the coolest part of the house, exchanged his last measure of grain for a chlamys[1] of scarlet cloth fringed with silver. He watched the merchant out of the door, and then looked wistfully into the corn-chest. I, who thought there was something worth seeing, looked in also, and, finding it empty, expressed my disappointment, not thinking however about the corn. A faint and transient smile came over his countenance at the sight of mine. He unfolded the chlamys, stretched it out with both hands before me, and then cast it over my shoulders. I looked down on the glittering fringe and screamed with joy. He then went out; and I know not what flowers he gathered, but he gathered many; and some he placed in my bosom, and some in my hair. But I told him with captious pride, first that I could arrange them better, and again that I would have only the white. However, when he had selected all the white, and I had placed a few of them according to my fancy, I told him (rising in my slipper) he might crown me with the remainder. The splendour of my apparel gave me a sensation of authority. Soon as the flowers had taken their station on my head, I expressed a dignified satisfaction at the taste displayed by my father, just as if I could have seen how they appeared! But he knew that there was at least as much pleasure as pride in it, and perhaps we divided the latter (alas! not both) pretty equally. He now took me into the market-place, where a concourse of people was waiting for the purchase of slaves. Merchants came and looked at me; some commending, others disparaging; but all agreeing that I was slender and delicate, that I could not live long, and that I should give much trouble. Many would have bought the chlamys, but there was something less saleable in the child and flowers.

*Aesop* Had thy features been coarse and thy voice rustic, they would all have patted thy cheeks and found no fault in thee.

*Rhodopè* As it was, every one had bought exactly such another in time past, and been a loser by it. At these speeches I perceived the flowers tremble slightly on my bosom, from my father's agitation. Although he scoffed at them, knowing my healthiness, he was troubled internally, and said many short prayers, not very unlike imprecations, turning his head aside. Proud was I, prouder than ever, when at last several talents were offered for me, and by the very man who in the beginning had undervalued me the most, and prophesied the worst of me. My father scowled at him, and refused the money. I thought he was playing a game, and began to wonder what it could be, since I never had seen it played before. Then I fancied it might be some celebration because plenty had returned to the city, insomuch that my father had bartered the last of the corn he hoarded. I grew more and more delighted at the sport. But soon there advanced an elderly man, who said gravely, "Thou hast stolen this child: her vesture alone is worth above a hundred drachmas. Carry her home again to her parents, and do it directly, or Nemesis[2] and the Eumenides[3] will overtake thee." Knowing the estimation in which my father had always been holden by his fellow-citizens, I laughed again, and pinched his ear. He, although naturally choleric, burst forth into no resentment at these reproaches, but said calmly, "I think I know thee by name, O guest! Surely thou art Xanthus the Samian. Deliver this child from famine."

Again I laughed aloud and heartily; and, thinking it was now my part of the game, I held out both my arms and protruded my whole body toward the stranger. He would not receive me from my father's neck, but he asked me with benignity and solicitude if I was hungry: at which I laughed again, and more than ever: for it was early in the morning, soon after the first meal, and my father had nourished me most carefully and plentifully in all the days of the famine. But Xanthus, waiting for no answer, took out of a sack, which one of his slaves carried at his side, a cake of wheaten bread and a piece of honey-comb, and gave them to me. I held the honey-comb to my father's mouth, thinking it the most of a dainty. He dashed it to the ground; but, seizing the bread, he began to devour it ferociously. This also I thought was in play; and I clapped my hands at his distortions. But Xanthus looked on him like one afraid, and smote the cake from him, crying aloud, "Name the price." My father now placed me in his arms, naming a price much below what the other had offered, saying, "The Gods are ever with thee, O Xanthus! therefor to thee do I consign my child." But while Xanthus was counting out the silver, my father seized the cake again, which the slave had taken up and was about to replace in the wallet. His hunger was exasperated by the taste and the delay. Suddenly there arose much tumult. Turning round in the old woman's bosom who had received me from Xanthus, I saw my beloved father struggling on the ground, livid and speechless. The more violent my cries, the more rapidly they hurried me away; and many were soon between us. Little was I suspicious that he had suffered the pangs of famine long before: alas! and he had suffered them for me. Do I weep while I am telling you they ended? I could not have closed his eyes; I was too young: but I might have received his last breath; the only comfort of an orphan's bosom. Do you now think him blamable, O Aesop?

## from *Citation and Examination of William Shakspeare* (1834)
## 21  [Dr Glaston's Warning]

Then did William Shakspeare resume Dr. Glaston's discourse.

" 'Ethelbert![1] I think thou walkest but little; otherwise I should take thee with me, some fine fresh morning, as far as unto the first hamlet on the Cherwell.[2] There lies young Wellerby, who, the year before, was wont to pass many hours of the day poetising amid the ruins of Godstow nunnery.[3] It is said that he bore a fondness toward a young maiden in that place, formerly a village, now containing but two old farm-houses. In my memory there were still extant several dormitories. Some love-sick girl had recollected an ancient name, and had engraven on a stone with a garden-nail, which lay in rust near it,

POORE ROSAMUND.[4]

I entered these precincts, and beheld a youth of manly form and countenance, washing and wiping a stone with a handful of wet grass; and on my going up to him, and asking what he had found, he showed it to me. The next time I saw him was near the banks of the Cherwell. He had tried, it appears, to forget or overcome his foolish passion, and had applied his whole mind unto study. He was foiled by his competitor; and now he sought consolation in poetry. Whether this opened the wounds that had closed in his youthful breast, and malignant Love, in his revenge, poisoned it; or whether the disappointment he had experienced in finding others preferred to him, first in the paths of fortune, then in those of the muses; he was thought to have died broken-hearted.

" 'About half a mile from St John's College is the termination of a natural terrace, with the Cherwell close under it, in some places bright with yellow and red flowers glancing and glowing through the stream, and suddenly in others dark with the shadows of many different trees, in broad overbending thickets, and with rushes spear-high, and party-coloured flags.

" 'After a walk in Midsummer, the immersion of our hands into the cool and closing grass is surely not the least among our animal delights. I was just seated, and the first sensation of rest vibrated in me gently, as though it were music to the limbs, when I discovered by a hollow in the herbage that another was near. The long meadow-sweet and blooming burnet[5] half concealed from me him whom the earth was about to hide totally and for ever.

" 'Master Batchelor!' said I, 'it is ill sleeping by the water-side.'

" 'No answer was returned. I arose, went to the place, and recognised poor Wellerby. His brow was moist, his cheek was warm. A few moments earlier, and that dismal lake whereunto and wherefrom the waters of life, the buoyant blood, ran no longer, might have received one vivifying ray reflected from my poor casement. I might not indeed have comforted: I have often failed: but there is one who never has; and the strengthener of the bruised reed should have been with us.

" 'Remembering that his mother did abide one mile further on, I walked forward to the mansion, and asked her what tidings she lately had received of her son. She replied, that having given up his mind to light studies, the fellows of the college would not elect him. The master had warned him before-hand to abandon his selfish poetry, take up manfully the quarterstaff of logic, and wield it for St John's, come who would into the ring. "We want our man," said he to me, "and your son hath failed us in the hour of need. Madam, he hath been foully beaten in the schools by one he might have swallowed, with due exercise." I rated him, told him I was poor, and he knew it. He was stung, and threw himself upon my neck, and wept. Twelve days have passed since, and only three rainy ones. I hear he has been seen upon the knoll yonder, but hither he hath not come. I trust he knows at last the value of time, and I shall be heartily glad to see him after this accession of knowledge. Twelve days, it is true, are rather a chink than a gap in time; yet, O gentle sir! they are that chink which makes the vase quite valueless. There are light words which may never be shaken off the mind they fall on. My child, who was hurt by me, will not let me see the marks." "Lady!" said I, "none are left upon him. Be comforted! thou shalt see him this hour. All that thy God hath not taken is yet thine."

" 'She looked at me earnestly, and would have then asked some-
thing, but her voice failed her. There was no agony, no motion, save
in the lips and cheeks. Being the widow of one who fought under
Hawkins,[6] she remembered his courage and sustained the shock, saying
calmly, "God's will be done! I pray that he find me as worthy as he
findeth me willing to join them."

" 'Now, in her unearthly thoughts, she had led her only son to the
bosom of her husband; and in her spirit (which often is permitted to
pass the gates of death with holy love) she left them both with their
Creator.

" 'The curate of the village sent those who should bring home the
body; and some days afterward he came unto me, beseeching me to
write the epitaph. Being no friend to stone-cutters' charges, I entered
not into biography, but wrote these few words:

"JOANNES WELLERBY

LITERARUM QUÆSIVIT GLORIAM,

VIDET DEI." ' "[7]

## from *Pericles and Aspasia* (1836)
## 22  IV Aspasia to Cleone

I was determined to close my letter when your curiosity was at the
highest,[1] that you might flutter and fall from the clouds like Icarus.[2]
I wanted two things; first, that you should bite your lip, an attitude
in which you alone look pretty; and secondly, that you should say
half-angrily, "This now is exactly like Aspasia." I will be remembered;
and I will make you look as I would have you.

How fortunate! to have arrived at Athens at dawn on the twelfth of
Elaphebolion.[3] On this day begin the festivals of Bacchus,[4] and the
theatre is thrown open at sunrise.

What a theatre! what an elevation! what a prospect of city and port,
of land and water, of porticoes and temples, of men and heroes, of
demi-gods and gods!

It was indeed my wish and intention, when I left Ionia, to be present
at the first of the Dionysiacs; but how rarely are wishes and intentions
so accomplished, even when winds and waters do not interfere!

I will now tell you all. No time was to be lost: so I hastened on
shore in the dress of an Athenian boy who came over with his mother
from Lemnos.[5] In the giddiness of youth he forgot to tell me that, not
being yet eighteen years old, he could not be admitted; and he left me
on the steps. My heart sank within me; so many young men stared
and whispered; yet never was stranger treated with more civility.
Crowded as the theatre was (for the tragedy had begun) every one
made room for me. When they were seated, and I too, I looked toward

the stage; and behold there lay before me, but afar off, bound upon a rock, a more majestic form, and bearing a countenance more heroic, I should rather say more divine, than ever my imagination had conceived! I know not how long it was before I discovered that as many eyes were directed toward me as toward the competitor of the gods. I was neither flattered by it nor abashed. Every wish, hope, sigh, sensation, was successively with the champion of the human race, with his antagonist Zeus, and his creator Aeschylus.[6] How often, O Cleone, have we throbbed with his injuries! how often hath his vulture torn our breasts! how often have we thrown our arms around each other's neck, and half-renounced the religion of our fathers! Even your image, inseparable at other times, came not across me then; Prometheus stood between us. He had resisted in silence and disdain the cruellest tortures that Almightiness could inflict; and now arose the Nymphs of ocean, which heaved its vast waves before us; and now they descended with open arms and sweet benign countenances, and spake with pity; and the insurgent heart was mollified and quelled.

I sobbed; I dropt.

# 23 .IX Aspasia to Cleone

Epimedea[1] has been with me in my chamber. She asked me whether the women of Ionia had left off wearing ear-rings. I answered that I believe they always had worn them, and that they were introduced by the Persians, who received them from nations more remote.

"And do you think yourself too young" said she "for such an ornament?" producing at the same instant a massy pair, inlaid with the largest emeralds. "Alas! alas!" said she, "your mother neglected you strangely. There is no hole in the ear, right or left! We can mend that, however; I know a woman who will bring us the prettiest little pan of charcoal, with the prettiest little steel rod in it; and, before you can cry out, one ear lets light through. These are yours," said she, "and so shall everything be when I am gone . . house, garden, quails, leveret."

"Generous Epimedea!" said I, "do not say things that pain me. I will accept a part of the present; I will wear these beautiful emeralds on one arm. Thinking of nailing them in my ears, you resolve to make me steady; but I am unwilling they should become dependencies of Attica."

"All our young women wear them; the Goddesses too."

"The Goddesses are in the right," said I; "their ears are marble; but I do not believe any one of them would tell us that women were made to be the settings of pearls and emeralds."

I had taken one, and was about to kiss her, when she said, "Do not leave me an odd ear-ring: put the other in the hair."

"Epimedea," said I, "I have made a vow never to wear on the head any thing but one single flower, a single wheat-ear, green or yellow, and ivy or vine-leaves: the number of these are not mentioned in the vow."

"Rash child!" said Epimedea, shaking her head: "I never made but two vows; one was when I took a husband."

"And the other? Epimedea!"

"No matter," said she; "it might be, for what I know, never to do the like again."

# 24   XX Xeniades to Aspasia[1]

Aspasia! Aspasia! have you forgotten me? have you forgotten *us*? Our childhood was one, our earliest youth was undivided. Why should you not see me? Did you fear that you would have to reproach me for any fault I have committed? This would have pained you formerly; ah, how lately!

Your absence . . not absence . . flight . . has broken my health, and left me fever and frenzy. Eumedes is certain I can only recover my health by composure. Foolish man! as if composure were more easy to recover than health. Was there ever such a madman as to say, "You will never have the use of your limbs again unless you walk and run!"

I am weary of advice, of remonstrance, of pity, of everything; above all, of life.

Was it anger (how dared I be angry with you?) that withheld me from imploring the sight of you? Was it pride? Alas! what pride is left me? I am preferred no longer; I am rejected, scorned, loathed. Was it always so? Well may I ask the question; for everything seems uncertain to me but my misery. At times I know not whether I am mad or dreaming. No, no, Aspasia! the past was a dream, the present is a reality. The mad and the dreaming do not shed tears as I do. And yet in these bitter tears are my happiest moments; and some angry demon knows it, and presses my temples that there shall fall but few.

You refused to admit me. I asked too little, and deserved the refusal. Come to me. This you will not refuse, unless you are bowed to slavery. Go, tell your despot this, with my curses and defiance.

I am calmer, but insist. Spare yourself, Aspasia, one tear, and not by an effort, but by a duty.

# 25   XXI Aspasia to Cleone[1]

Of all men living, what man do you imagine has come to Athens? Insensate! now you know. What other, so beloved, would ever have left Miletus! I wish I could be convinced that your coldness or indifference had urged him to this extravagance. I can only promise you we will not detain him. Athens is not a refuge for the perfidious or the flighty. But if he is unfortunate; what shall we do with him? Do? I will tell him to return. Expect him hourly.

# 26   XXII Aspasia to Xeniades

I am pained to my innermost heart that you are ill.

Pericles is not the person you imagine him. Behold his billet! And can not you think of me with equal generosity?

True, we saw much of each other in our childhood, and many childish things we did together. This is the reason why I went out of your way as much as I could afterward. There is another too. I hoped you would love more the friend that I love most. How much happier would she make you than the flighty Aspasia! We resemble each other too much, Xeniades! we should never have been happy, so ill-mated. Nature hates these alliances: they are like those of brother and sister. I never loved anyone but Pericles: none else attracts the admiration of the world. I stand, O Xeniades! not only above slavery, but above splendour, in that serene light which Homer describes as encompassing the Happy on Olympus.[1] I will come to visit you within the hour; be calm, be contented! love me, but not too much, Xeniades!

# 27   XXIII Aspasia to Pericles

Xeniades, whom I loved a little in my childhood, and (do not look serious now, my dearest Pericles!) a very little afterward, is sadly ill. He was always, I know not how, extravagant in his wishes, although not so extravagant as many others; and what do you imagine he wishes now? He wishes . . but he is very ill, so ill he can not rise from his bed, . . that I would go and visit him. I wonder whether it would be quite considerate: I am half inclined to go, if you approve of it.

Poor youth! he grieves me bitterly.

I shall not weep before him; I have wept so much here. Indeed, indeed, I wept, my Pericles, only because I had written too unkindly.

# 28   XXIV Pericles to Aspasia

Do what your heart tells you: yes, Aspasia, do *all* it tells you. Remember how august it is: it contains the temple, not only of Love, but of Conscience; and a whisper is heard from the extremity of the one to the extremity of the other.

Bend in pensiveness, even in sorrow, on the flowery bank of youth, whereunder runs the stream that passes irreversibly! let the garland drop into it, let the hand be refreshed by it; but may the beautiful feet of Aspasia stand firm!

## 29   XXV Xeniades to Aspasia

You promised you would return. I thought you only broke hearts, not promises.

It is now broad daylight: I see it clearly, although the blinds are closed. A long sharp ray cuts off one corner of the room, and we shall hear the crash presently.

Come; but without that pale silent girl: I hate her. Place her on the other side of you, not on mine.

And this plane-tree gives no shade whatever. We will sit in some other place.

No, no; I will not have you call her to us. Let her play where she is . . the notes are low . . she plays sweetly.

## 30   XXVI Aspasia to Pericles

See what incoherency! He did not write it; not one word. The slave who brought it, told me that he was desired by the guest to write his orders, whenever he found his mind composed enough to give any.

About four hours after my departure, he called him mildly, and said, "I am quite recovered."

He gave no orders however, and spake nothing more for some time. At last he raised himself up, and rested on his elbow, and began (said the slave) like one inspired. The slave added, that finding he was indeed quite well again, both in body and mind, and capable of making as fine poetry as any man in Athens, he had written down every word with the greatest punctuality; and that, looking at him for more, he found he had fallen into as sound a slumber as a reaper's.

"Upon this I ran off with the verses," said he.

## 31   XXVII Cleone to Aspasia

Comfort him. But you must love him, if you do. Well! comfort him. Forgive my inconsiderateness. You will not love him now. You would not receive him when your bosom was without an occupant. And yet you saw him daily. Others, all others, pine away before him. I wish I could solace my soul with poetry, as you have the power of doing. In all the volumes I turn over, I find none exactly suitable to my condition: part expresses my feelings, part flies off from them to something more light and vague. I do not believe the best writers of love-poetry ever loved. How could they write if they did? where could they collect the thoughts, the words, the courage? Alas! alas! men can find all these, Aspasia, and leave us after they have found them. But in Xeniades there is no fault whatever: he never loved me: he never said he did: he fled only from my immodesty in loving him. Dissembler as

I was, he detected it. Do pity him, and help him: but pity me too, who am beyond your help.

## 32   XXVIII Pericles to Aspasia

Tears, O Aspasia, do not dwell long upon the cheeks of youth. Rain drops easily from the bud, rests on the bosom of the maturer flower, and breaks down that one only which hath lived its day.

Weep, and perform the offices of friendship. The season of life, leading you by the hand, will not permit you to linger at the tomb of the departed; and Xeniades, when your first tear fell upon it, entered into the number of the blessed.

## 33   XXIX Aspasia to Cleone

What shall I say to you, tender and sweet Cleone! The wanderer is in the haven of happiness; the restless has found rest.

Weep not; I have shed all your tears .. not all .. they burst from me again.

## 34   XXX Cleone to Aspasia

O! he was too beautiful to live! Is there anything that shoots through the world so swiftly as a sunbeam! Epialtes has told me everything. He sailed back without waiting at the islands; by your orders, he says.

What hopes could I, with any prudence, entertain? The chaplet you threw away would have cooled and adorned my temples; but how could he ever love another who had once loved you? I am casting my broken thoughts before my Aspasia: the little shells upon the shore, that the storm has scattered there, and that heedless feet have trampled on.

I have prayed to Venus; but I never prayed her to turn toward me the fondness that was yours. I fancied, I even hoped, you might accept it; and my prayer was, "Grant I may never love! Afar from me, O Goddess! be the malignant warmth that dries up the dews of friendship."

## 35   *from* XLVII Cleone to Aspasia

... Could Sappho[1] be ignorant how infantinely inarticulate is early love? Could she be ignorant that shame and fear seize it unrelentingly by the throat, while hard-hearted impudence stands at ease, prompt at opportunity, and profuse in declarations!

There is a gloom in deep love, as in deep water: there is a silence in it which suspends the foot, and the folded arms and the dejected head are the images it reflects. No voice shakes its surface: the Muses themselves approach it with a tardy and a timid step, and with a low and tremulous and melancholy song.

The best Ode of Sappho, the Ode to Anactoria,[2]
"Happy as any God is he," &c.,
shows the intemperance and disorder of passion. The description of her malady may be quite correct, but I confess my pleasure ends at the first strophe, where it begins with the generality of readers. I do not desire to know the effects of the distemper on her body, and I run out of the house into the open air, although the symptoms have less in them of contagion than of unseemliness. Both Sophocles and Euripides[3] excite our sympathies more powerfully and more poetically. . . .

# 36  XCIX Aspasia to Cleone

Thanks for the verses! I hope Leuconöe was as grateful as I am, and as sensible to their power of soothing.

Thanks too for the perfumes! Pericles is ashamed of acknowledging he is fond of them; but I am resolved to betray one secret of his: I have caught him several times *trying* them, as he called it.

How many things are there that people pretend to dislike, without any reason, as far as we know, for the dislike or the pretence!

I love sweet odours. Surely my Cleone herself must have breathed her very soul into these! Let me smell them again: let me inhale them into the sanctuary of my breast, lighted up by her love for their reception.

But, ah Cleone! what an importunate and exacting creature is Aspasia! Have you no willows fresh-peeled? none lying upon the bank for baskets, white, rounded, and delicate, as your fingers! How fragrant they were formerly! I have seen none lately. Do you remember the cross old Hermesionax! how he ran to beat us for breaking his twigs? and how, after looking in our faces, he seated himself down again, finished his basket, disbursed from a goat-skin a corroded clod of rancid cheese, put it in, pushed it to us, forced it under my arm, told us to carry it home *with the Gods*! and lifted up both hands and blest us.

I do not wish *that* one exactly; cheese is the cruellest of deaths to me; and Pericles abhors it.

I am running over trifling occurrences which you must have forgotten. You are upon the spot, and have no occasion to recall to memory how the munificent old basket-maker looked after us, not seeing his dog at our heels; how we coaxed the lean, shaggy, suspicious animal; how many devices we contrived to throw down, or let slip, so that the good man might not observe it, the pestilence you insisted on carrying;

how many names we called the dog by, ere we found the true one, *Cyrus*; how, when we had drawn him behind the lentisk, we rewarded him for his assiduities, holding each an ear nevertheless, that he might not carry back the gift to his master; and how we laughed at our fears, when a single jerk of the head served at once to engulf the treasure and to disengage him.

I shall always love the smell of the peeled willow. Have you none for me? Is there no young poplar then, with a tear in his eye on bursting into bud? I am not speaking by metaphor and Asiatically. I want the poplars, the willows, the water-lilies, and the soft green herbage. How we enjoyed it on the Maeander![1] what liberties we took with it! robbing it of the flowers it had educated, of those it was rearing, of those that came confidently out to meet us, and of those that hid themselves. None escaped us. For those remembrances, green is the colour I love best. It brings me to the *Fortunate Island*[2] and my Cleone; it brings me back to Childhood, the proud little nurse of Youth, brighter of eye and lighter of heart than Youth herself.

These are not regrets, Cleone; they are respirations, necessary to existence. You may call them half-wishes if you will. We are poor indeed when we have no half-wishes left us. The heart and the imagination close the shutters the instant they are gone.

Do not chide me then for coming to you after the blossoms and buds and herbage: do not keep to yourself all the grass on the Maeander. We used to share it; we will now. I love it wherever I can get a glimpse of it. It is the home of the eyes, ever ready to receive them, and spreading its cool couch for their repose.

# 37 *from* Oration of Pericles to the Soldiers round Samos

Little time is now left us, O Athenians, between the consideration and the accomplishment of our duties. The justice of the cause, when it was first submitted to your decision in the Agora,[1] was acknowledged with acclamations; the success of it you have insured by your irresistible energy. The port of Samos is in our possession, and we have occupied all the eminences round her walls. Patience is now as requisite to us as to the enemy: for, although every city which can be surrounded, can be captured, yet in some, where courage and numbers have been insufficient to drive off the besieger, Nature and Art may have thrown up obstacles to impede his progress. Such is Samos; the strongest fortress in Europe, excepting only Byzantion.[2] But Byzantion fell before our fathers; and unless she become less deaf to the reclamations of honour, less indifferent to the sanctitude of treaties, unless she prefer her fellow-soldiers to her common enemy, freedom to aristocracy, friends to strangers, Greeks to Asiatics, she shall abase her Thracian fierceness before *us*. However, we will neither spurn the suppliant nor punish the repentant: our arms we will turn for ever, as we turn them now, against the malicious rival, the alienated relative, the apostate confederate, and the proud oppressor. Where a sense of dignity is faint and feeble, and where reason hath lain unexercised and inert, many nations have occasionally been happy and even flourishing under kings: but oligarchy hath ever been a curse to all, from its commencement to its close. To remove it eternally from the vicinity of Miletus, and from the well-disposed of that very city by which hostilities are denounced against her, is at once our interest and our duty. For oligarchs in every part of the world are necessarily our enemies, since we have always shown our fixed determination to aid and support with all our strength the defenders of civility and freedom. It is not in our power (for against our institutions and consciences we Athenians can do nothing), it is not in our power, I repeat it, to sit idly by, while those who were our fellow-combatants against the Persian, and who suffered from his aggression even more than we did, are assailed by degenerate Ionians, whose usurpation rests on Persia.[3] We have enemies wherever there is injustice done to Greeks; and we will abolish that injustice, and we will quell those enemies. Wherever there are equal laws we have friends; and those friends we will succour, and those laws we will maintain. On which side do the considerate and religious look forward to the countenance of the Gods? Often have they deferred indeed their righteous judgments, but never have they deserted the long-suffering and the brave. Upon the ground where we were standing when you last heard my appeal to you, were not Xerxes[4] and his myriads encamped? What drove them from it? The wisdom, force, and fortitude, breathed into your hearts by the immortal Gods. Preserve them with equal constancy; and your return, I promise you, shall not have been more glorious from Salamis[5] than from Samos.

# 38   CLVIII  Oration of Pericles,
*On the approach of the Lacedaemonians to Athens*[1]

Long ago, and lately, and in every age intervening, O Athenians! have you experienced the jealousy and insolence of Lacedaemon. She listens now to the complaints of Corinth,[2] because the people of Corcyra[3] will endure no longer her vexations, and because their navy, in which the greater part of the mariners have fought and conquered by the side of ours, seek refuge in the Piraeus.[4] A little while ago she dared to insist that we should admit the ships of Megara[5] to our harbour, her merchandise to our markets, when Megara had broken her faith with us, and gone over to the Spartans. Even this indignity we might perhaps have endured. We told the Lacedaemonians that we would admit the Megaraeans to that privilege, if the ports of Sparta would admit us

and our allies: although we and our allies were never in such relation-
ship with her, and therefore could never have fallen off from her. She
disdained to listen to a proposal so reasonable, to a concession so little
to be expected from us. Resolved to prove to her that generosity, and
not fear, dictated it, we chastised the perfidious Megara.

The king of the Lacedaemonians, Archidamos,[6] a wiser and honester
man than any of his people, is forced to obey the passions he would
control; and an army of sixty thousand men is marching under his
command to ravage Attica. The braver will rather burn their harvests
than transfer to a sanguinary and insatiable enemy the means of
inflicting evil on their relatives and friends. Few, I trust, are base
enough, sacrilegious enough, to treat as guests, those whom you before
men and Gods denounce as enemies. We will receive within our walls
the firm and faithful. And now let the orators who have blamed our
expenditure in the fortification of the city, tell us again that it was
improvident.[7] They would be flying in dismay had not those bulwarks
been raised effectually. Did it require any sagacity to foresee that
Athens would be the envy of every state around? Was there any man
so ignorant as not to know that he who has lost all his enemies will
soon lose all his energy? and that men are no more men when they
cease to act, than rivers are rivers when they cease to run? The forces
of our assailants must be broken against our walls.[8] Our fleets are our
farms henceforward, until the Spartans find that, if they can subsist
on little, they can not so well subsist on stones and ashes. Their forces
are vast; but vast forces have never much hurt us. Marathon[9] and
Plataea[10] were scarcely wide enough for our trophies; a victorious
army, an unvanquished fleet, Miltiades[11] himself, retired unsuccessful
from the rock of Paros.[12] Shall we tremble then before a tumultuous
multitude, ignorant how cities are defended or assailed? Shall we
prevent them from coming to their discomfiture and destruction?
Firmly do I believe that the Protectress of our city[13] leads them against
it to avenge her cause. They may ravage the lands; they can not
cultivate, they can not hold them. Mischief they will do, and great;
much of our time, much of our patience, much of our perseverance,
and something of our courage, are required. At present I do not
number this event among our happiest. We must owe our glory partly
to ourselves and partly to our enemies. They offer us the means of
greatness; let us accept their offer. Brief danger is the price of long
security. The countryman, from the mists of the morning, not only
foretells the brightness of the day, but discerns in them sources of
fertility; and he remembers in his supplications to the immortal Gods
to thank them alike for both blessings. It is thus, O men of Athens,
that you have constantly looked up at calamities. Never have they
depressed you: always have they chastened your hearts, always have
they exalted your courage. Impelled by the breath of Xerxes, the
locusts of Asia consumed your harvests; your habitations crumbled
away as they swarmed along: the temples of the Gods lay prostrate;

the Gods themselves bowed and fell: the men of Athens rose higher than ever. They had turned their faces in grief from the scene of devastation and impiety; but they listened to a provident valour, and the myriads of insects that had plagued them were consumed.

There is affront in exhortation. I have spoken.

# 39 CLXXIV Anaxagoras[1] to Aspasia

The gratitude and love I owe to Pericles induces me to write the very day I have landed at Lampsacos.[2] You are prudent, Aspasia! and your prudence is of the best quality; instinctive delicacy. But I am older than you, or than Pericles, although than Pericles by only six years; and, having no other pretext to counsel you, will rest upon this. Do not press him to abstain from public business: for, supposing he is by nature no obstinate man, yet the long possession of authority has accustomed him to grasp the tighter what is touched; as shell-fish contract the claws at an atom. The simile is not an elegant one, but I offer it as the most apposite. He might believe that you fear for him, and that you wish him to fear: this alone would make him pertinacious. Let everything take its season with him. Perhaps it is necessary that he should control the multitude: if it is, he will know it; even you could not stir him, and would only molest him by the attempt. Age is coming on. This will not loosen his tenacity of power . . it usually has quite the contrary effect . . but it will induce him to give up more of his time to the studies he has always delighted in, which however were insufficient for the full activity of his mind. Mine is a sluggard: I have surrendered it entirely to philosophy, and it has made little or no progress: it has dwelt pleased with hardly anything it has embraced, and has often run back again from fond prepossessions to startling doubts: it could not help it.

But as we sometimes find one thing while we are looking for another, so, if truth escaped me, happiness and contentment fell in my way, and have accompanied me even to Lampsacos.

Be cautious, O Aspasia! of discoursing on philosophy. Is it not in philosophy as in love? the more we have of it, and the less we talk about it, the better. Never touch upon religion with anybody. The irreligious are incurable and insensible; the religious are morbid and irritable: the former would scorn, the latter would strangle you. It appears to me to be not only a dangerous, but, what is worse, an indelicate thing, to place ourselves where we are likely to see fevers and phrenzies, writhings and distortions, debilities and deformities. Religion at Athens is like a fountain near Dodona,[3] which extinguishes a lighted torch, and which gives a flame of its own to an unlighted one held down to it. Keep yours in your chamber; and let the people run about with theirs; but remember, it is rather apt to catch the skirts. Believe me, I am happy: I am not deprived of my friends. Imagination is little less strong in our later years than in our earlier. True, it alights on fewer objects, but it rests longer on them, and sees them better. Pericles first, and then you, and then Meton,[4] occupy my thoughts. I am with you still; I study with you, just as before, although nobody talks aloud in the schoolroom.

This is the pleasantest part of life. Oblivion throws her light coverlet over our infancy; and, soon after we are out of the cradle we forget how soundly we had been slumbering, and how delightful were our dreams. Toil and pleasure contend for us almost the instant we rise from it: and weariness follows whichever has carried us away. We stop awhile, look around us, wonder to find we have completed the circle of existence, fold our arms, and fall asleep again.

# 40   CCVII Anaxagoras to Aspasia

Did I tell you, O Aspasia, we were free and remote from the calamities of war? we were. The flute and the timbrel and the harp alone were heard along our streets; and the pavement was bestrewn with cistus and lavender and myrtle, which grow profusely on the rocks behind us. Melanthos had arrived from the Chersonese[1] to marry Eurycleia; and his friend Sosigenes of Corinth had determined to be united on the same day with her sister Phanera.

Those who have seen them say that they were the prettiest girls in the city: they were also the happiest; but less happy than their lovers, who however owed at present but a part of the happiness to either. They were sworn friends from early youth, and had not met since, but always had corresponded.

Why can not men draw a line against war as against plague, and shut up the infected? Instead of which, they are proud of being like the dogs in the worst feature; rushing forth into every affray, and taking part in it instantly with equal animosity. I wish we had arrived at such a degree of docility, and had advanced so many steps in improvement, that by degrees we might hope to acquire anything better of these good creatures. We have the worst of every beast, and the best of none.

This is not, O Aspasia! my usual tone of thinking and discoursing: nor is what has happened here among the usual occurrences of my life. The generous heart needs little to be reminded what are the embraces of young and ardent friends; and the withered one could ill represent them.

Eurycleia, in the silence of fondness, in the fulness of content, was holding the hand of her Melanthos. Love has few moments more sweet, Philosophy none more calm. That moment was interrupted by the entrance of Sosigenes; and composure was exchanged for rapture by the friendly soul of Melanthos. Yes, yes, Aspasia! friendship, even in the young, may be more animated than love itself. It was not long, however.

"Where is Phanera?"

"I will call her," said Eurycleia, and went out.

Phanera, fond of ornament, it may be, and ambitious to surpass her sister and enchant her lover, came not speedily, nor indeed did Eurycleia very soon, for it was not at first that she could find her. Conversation had begun in the meanwhile about the war. Melanthos was a little more vehement than the mildness of his nature, it is said, ever allowed him before, and blamed the Corinthians for inciting so many states to hostility. Often had Sosigenes been looking toward the door, expecting his Phanera, and now began to grow impatient. The words of Melanthos, who felt the cruelty of war chiefly because it would separate the two sisters and the two friends, touched the pride of Sosigenes. Unable to moderate his temper, now excited by the absence of Phanera after the sister had some time returned, he said fiercely,

"It is well to blame the citizens of the noblest city upon earth, for not enduring an indignity. It is well; but in slaves alone, or viler dependents."

"Sosigenes! Sosigenes!" cried Melanthos, starting up and rushing toward him. At that instant the impetuous Sosigenes, believing violence was about to follow affront, struck him with his dagger to the heart.

"I could not then calm thy anger with an embrace! my too unhappy friend!" while the blood gurgled through the words, sobbed forth Melanthos.

# 41   CCXXXV Pericles to Aspasia

It is right and orderly, that he who has partaken so largely in the prosperity of the Athenians, should close the procession of their calamities. The fever that has depopulated our city, returned upon me last night,[1] and Hippocrates and Acron[2] tell me that my end is near.

When we agreed, O Aspasia, in the beginning of our loves, to communicate our thoughts by writing, even while we were both in Athens, and when we had many reasons for it, we little foresaw the more powerful one that has rendered it necessary of late. We never can meet again: the laws forbid it, and love itself enforces them. Let wisdom be heard by you as imperturbably, and affection as authoritatively, as ever: and remember that the sorrow of Pericles can arise but from the bosom of Aspasia. There is only one word of tenderness we could say, which we have not said oftentimes before; and there is no consolation in it. The happy never say, and never hear said, farewell.

Reviewing the course of my life, it appears to me at one moment as if we met but yesterday; at another as if centuries had past within it; for within it have existed the greater part of those who, since the origin of the world, have been the luminaries of the human race. Damon[3] called me from my music to look at Aristides[4] on his way to exile: and my father pressed the wrist by which he was leading me along, and whispered in my ear,

"Walk quickly by; glance cautiously; it is there Miltiades is in prison."

In my boyhood Pindar[5] took me up in his arms, when he brought to our house the dirge he had composed for the funeral of my grandfather: in my adolescence I offered the rites of hospitality to Empedocles:[6] not long afterward I embraced the neck of Aeschylus,[7] about to abandon his country. With Sophocles I have argued on eloquence; with Euripides on polity and ethics; I have discoursed, as became an inquirer, with Protagoras[8] and Democritus,[9] with Anaxagoras and Meton. From Herodotus[10] I have listened to the most instructive history, conveyed in a language the most copious and the most harmonious; a man worthy to carry away the collected suffrages of universal Greece; a man worthy to throw open the temples of Egypt, and to celebrate the exploits of Cyrus.[11] And from Thucydides,[12] who alone can succeed to him, how recently did my Aspasia hear with me the energetic praises of his just supremacy!

As if the festival of life were incomplete, and wanted one great ornament to crown it, Phidias[13] placed before us, in ivory and gold, the tutelary Deity of this land, and the Zeus of Homer and Olympus.[14]

To have lived with such men, to have enjoyed their familiarity and esteem, overpays all labours and anxieties. I were unworthy of the friendships I have commemorated, were I forgetful of the latest. Sacred it ought to be, formed as it was under the portico of Death, my friendship with the most sagacious, the most scientific, the most beneficent of philosophers, Acron and Hippocrates. If mortal could war against Pestilence and Destiny, they had been victorious. I leave them in the field: unfortunate he who finds them among the fallen!

And now, at the close of my day, when every light is dim and every guest departed, let me own that these wane before me, remembering, as I do in the pride and fulness of my heart, that Athens confided her glory, and Aspasia her happiness, to me.

Have I been a faithful guardian? do I resign them to the custody of the Gods undiminished and unimpaired? Welcome then, welcome, my last hour! After enjoying for so great a number of years, in my public and my private life, what I believe has never been the lot of any other, I now extend my hand to the urn, and take without reluctance or hesitation what is the lot of all.

from *The Pentameron and Pentalogia* (1837)
## 42   *from* Second Day's Interview

*Boccaccio*  . . . Probably, so near as I am to Florence, and so dear as Florence hath always been to me, I shall see that city no more. The last time I saw it, I only passed through. Four years ago, you remember, I lost my friend Acciaioli.[1] Early in the summer of the preceding, his kindness had induced him to invite me again to Naples, and I undertook a journey to the place where my life had been too happy.[2] There are many who pay dearly for sunshine early in the season: many, for pleasure in the prime of life. After one day lost in idleness at Naples, if intense and incessant thoughts (however fruitless) may be called so, I proceeded by water to Sorento, and thence over the mountains to Amalfi. Here, amid whatever is most beautiful and most wonderful in scenery, I found the Seniscalco. His palace, his gardens, his terraces, his woods, abstracted his mind entirely from the solicitudes of state; and I was gratified at finding in the absolute ruler of a kingdom, the absolute master of his time. Rare felicity! and he enjoyed it the more after the toils of business and the intricacies of policy. His reception of me was most cordial. He showed me his long avenues of oranges and citrons: he helped me to mount the banks of slippery short herbage, whence we could look down on their dark masses, and their broad irregular belts, gemmed with golden fruit and sparkling flowers. We stood high above them, but not above their fragrance, and sometimes we wished the breeze to bring us it, and sometimes to carry a part of it away: and the breeze came and went as if obedient to our volition. Another day he conducted me farther from the palace, and showed me, with greater pride than I had ever seen in him before, the pale-green olives, on little smooth plants, the first year of their bearing. "I will teach my people here," said he, "to make as delicate oil as any of our Tuscans." We had feasts among the caverns: we had dances by day under the shade of the mulberries, by night under the lamps of the arcade: we had music on the shore and on the water.

When next I stood before him, it was afar from these. Torches flamed through the pine-forest of the Certosa:[3] priests and monks led the procession: the sound of the brook alone filled up the intervals of the dirge: and other plumes than the dancers' waved round what was Acciaioli.


## 43   *from* Fifth Day's Interview

*Boccaccio*  I prayed; and my breast, after some few tears, grew calmer. Yet sleep did not ensue until the break of morning, when the dropping of soft rain on the leaves of the fig-tree at the window, and the chirping of a little bird, to tell another there was shelter under them, brought me repose and slumber. Scarcely had I closed my eyes, if indeed time can be reckoned any more in sleep than in heaven, when my Fiametta seemed to have led me into the meadow. You will see it below you: turn away that branch: gently! gently! do not break it; for the little bird sat there.

*Petrarca*   I think, Giovanni, I can divine the place. Although this fig-tree, growing out of the wall between the cellar and us, is fantastic enough in its branches, yet that other which I see yonder, bent down and forced to crawl along the grass by the prepotency of the young shapely walnut-tree, is much more so. It forms a seat, about a cubit above the ground, level and long enough for several.

*Boccaccio*   Ha! you fancy it must be a favourite spot with me, because of the two strong forked stakes wherewith it is propped and supported!

*Petrarca*   Poets know the haunts of poets at first sight; and he who loved Laura[1] . . . O Laura! did I say he who *loved* thee? . . . hath whisperings where those feet would wander which have been restless after Fiametta.

*Boccaccio*   It is true, my imagination has often conducted her thither; but here in this chamber she appeared to me more visibly in a dream.

"Thy prayers have been heard, O Giovanni," said she.

I sprang to embrace her.

"Do not spill the water! Ah! you have spilt a part of it."

I then observed in her hand a crystal vase. A few drops were sparkling on the sides and running down the rim: a few were trickling from the base and from the hand that held it.

"I must go down to the brook," said she, "and fill it again as it was filled before."

What a moment of agony was this to me! Could I be certain how long might be her absence? She went: I was following: she made a sign for me to turn back: I disobeyed her only an instant: yet my sense of disobedience, increasing my feebleness and confusion, made me lose sight of her. In the next moment she was again at my side, with the cup quite full. I stood motionless: I feared my breath might shake the water over. I looked her in the face for her commands . . and to see it . . to see it so calm, so beneficent, so beautiful. I was forgetting what I had prayed for, when she lowered her head, tasted of the cup, and gave it me. I drank; and suddenly sprang forth before me, many groves and palaces and gardens, and their statues and their avenues, and their labyrinths of alaternus[2] and bay, and alcoves of citron, and watchful loopholes in the retirements of impenetrable pomegranate. Farther off, just below where the fountain slipt away from its marble hall and guardian gods, arose, from their beds of moss and drosera[3] and darkest grass, the sisterhood of oleanders, fond of tantalising with their bosomed flowers and their moist and pouting blossoms the little shy rivulet, and of covering its face with all the colours of the dawn. My dream expanded and moved forward. I trod again the dust of Posilipo,[4] soft as the feathers in the wings of Sleep. I emerged on Baia;[5]

I crossed her innumerable arches; I loitered in the breezy sunshine of her mole; I trusted the faithful seclusion of her caverns, the keeper of so many secrets; and I reposed on the buoyancy of her tepid sea. Then Naples, and her theatres and her churches, and grottoes and dells and forts and promontories, rushed forward in confusion, now among soft whispers, now among sweetest sounds, and subsided, and sank, and disappeared. Yet a memory seemed to come fresh from every one: each had time enough for its tale, for its pleasure, for its reflection, for its pang. As I mounted with silent steps the narrow staircase of the old palace, how distinctly did I feel against the palm of my hand the coldness of that smooth stone-work, and the greater of the cramps of iron in it!

"Ah me! is this forgetting?" cried I anxiously to Fiametta.

"We must recall these scenes before us," she replied: "such is the punishment of them. Let us hope and believe that the apparition, and the compunction which must follow it, will be accepted as the full penalty, and that both will pass away almost together."

I feared to lose anything attendant on her presence: I feared to approach her forehead with my lips: I feared to touch the lily on its long wavy leaf in her hair, which filled my whole heart with fragrance. Venerating, adoring, I bowed my head at least to kiss her snow-white robe, and trembled at my presumption. And yet the effulgence of her countenance vivified while it chastened me. I loved her . . . I must not say *more* than ever . . . *better* than ever; it was Fiametta who had inhabited the skies. As my hand opened toward her,

"Beware!" said she, faintly smiling; "beware, Giovanni! Take only the crystal; take it, and drink again."

"Must all be then forgotten?" said I sorrowfully.

"Remember your prayer and mine, Giovanni? Shall both have been granted . . . O how much worse than in vain?"

I drank instantly; I drank largely. How cool my bosom grew; how could it grow so cool before her! But it was not to remain in its quiescency; its trials were not yet over. I will not, Francesco! no, I may not commemorate the incidents she related to me, nor which of us said, "I blush for having loved *first*;" nor which of us replied, "Say *least*, say *least*, and blush again."

The charm of the words (for I felt not the encumbrance of the body nor the acuteness of the spirit) seemed to possess me wholly. Although the water gave me strength and comfort, and somewhat of celestial pleasure, many tears fell around the border of the vase as she held it up before me, exhorting me to take courage, and inviting me with more than exhortation to accomplish my deliverance. She came nearer, more tenderly, more earnestly; she held the dewy globe with both hands, leaning forward, and sighed and shook her head, drooping at my pusillanimity. It was only when a ringlet had touched the rim, and perhaps the water (for a sun-beam on the surface could never have given it such a golden hue) that I took courage, clasped it, and exhausted it. Sweet as was the water, sweet as was the serenity it gave me . . . alas! that also which it moved away from me was sweet!

"This time you can trust me alone," said she, and parted my hair, and kissed my brow. Again she went toward the brook: again my agitation, my weakness, my doubt, came over me: nor could I see her while she raised the water, nor knew I whence she drew it. When she returned, she was close to me at once: she smiled: her smile pierced me to the bones: it seemed an angel's. She sprinkled the pure water on me; she looked most fondly; she took my hand; she suffered me to press hers to my bosom; but, whether by design I can not tell, she let fall a few drops of the chilly element between.

"And now, O my beloved!" said she, "we have consigned to the bosom of God our earthly joys and sorrows. The joys can not return, let not the sorrows. These alone would trouble my repose among the blessed."

"Trouble thy repose! Fiametta! Give me the chalice!" cried I . . . "not a drop will I leave in it, not a drop."

"Take it!" said that soft voice. "O now most dear Giovanni! I know thou hast strength enough; and there is but little . . . at the bottom lies our first kiss."

"Mine! didst thou say, beloved one? and is that left thee still?"

"*Mine,*" said she, pensively; and as she abased her head, the broad leaf of the lily hid her brow and her eyes; the light of heaven shone through the flower.

"O Fiametta! Fiametta!" cried I in agony, "God is the God of mercy, God is the God of love . . . can I, can I ever?" I struck the chalice against my head, unmindful that I held it; the water covered my face and my feet. I started up, not yet awake, and I heard the name of Fiametta in the curtains.

*Petrarca*   Love, O Giovanni, and life itself, are but dreams at best. I do think

> Never so gloriously was Sleep attended
> As with the pageant of that heavenly maid.

But to dwell on such subjects is sinful. The recollection of them, with all their vanities, brings tears into my eyes.

*Boccaccio*   And into mine too . . they were so very charming.

*Petrarca*   Alas, alas! the time always comes when we must regret the enjoyments of our youth.

*Boccaccio*   If we have let them pass us.

*Petrarca*   I mean our indulgence in them.

*Boccaccio*   Francesco! I think you must remember Raffaellino degli Alfani.

*Petrarca*   Was it Raffaellino who lived near San Michele in Orto?[6]

*Boccaccio*   The same. He was an innocent soul, and fond of fish. But whenever his friend Sabbatelli sent him a trout from Pratolino, he always kept it until next day or the day after, just long enough to render it unpalatable. He then turned it over in the platter, smelt at it closer, although the news of its condition came undeniably from a distance, touched it with his forefinger, solicited a testimony from the gills which the eyes had contradicted, sighed over it, and sent it for a present to somebody else. Were I a lover of trout as Raffaellino was, I think I should have taken an opportunity of enjoying it while the pink and crimson were glittering on it.

*Petrarca*   Trout, yes.

*Boccaccio*   And all other fish I could encompass.

*Petrarca*   I have had as many dreams as most men. We are all made up of them, as the webs of the spider are particles of her own vitality. But how infinitely less do we profit by them! I will relate to you, before we separate, one among the multitude of mine, as coming the nearest to the poetry of yours, and as having been not totally useless to me. Often have I reflected on it; sometimes with pensiveness, with sadness never.

*Boccaccio*   Then, Francesco, if you had with you as copious a choice of dreams as clustered on the elm-trees where the Sibyl led Aeneas,[7] this, in preference to the whole swarm of them, is the queen dream for me.

*Petrarca*   When[8] I was younger I was fond of wandering in solitary places, and never was afraid of slumbering in woods and grottoes. Among the chief pleasures of my life, and among the commonest of my occupations, was the bringing before me such heroes and heroines of antiquity, such poets and sages, such of the prosperous and the unfortunate, as most interested me by their courage, their wisdom, their eloquence, or their adventures. Engaging them in the conversation best suited to their characters, I knew perfectly their manners, their steps, their voices: and often did I moisten with my tears the models I had been forming of the less happy.

*Boccaccio*   Great is the privilege of entering into the studies of the intellectual; great is that of conversing with the guides of nations, the movers of the mass, the regulators of the unruly will, stiff, in its impurity and rust, against the finger of the Almighty Power that formed it: but give me, Francesco, give me rather the creature to sympathise with; apportion me the sufferings to assuage. Ah, gentle soul! thou wilt never send them over to another; they have better hopes from thee.

*Petrarca*   We both alike feel the sorrows of those around us. He who suppresses or allays them in another, breaks many thorns off his own; and future years will never harden fresh ones.

My occupation was not always in making the politician talk politics, the orator toss his torch among the populace, the philosopher run down from philosophy to cover the retreat or the advances of his sect; but sometimes in devising how such characters must act and discourse, on subjects far remote from the beaten track of their career. In like manner the philologist, and again the dialectician, were not indulged in the review and parade of their trained bands, but, at times, brought forward to show in what manner and in what degree external habits had influenced the conformation of the internal man. It was far from unprofitable to set passing events before past actors, and to record the decisions of those whose interests and passions are unconcerned in them.

*Boccaccio*   This is surely no easy matter. The thoughts are in fact your own, however you distribute them.

*Petrarca*   All can not be my own; if you mean by *thoughts* the opinions and principles I should be the most desirous to inculcate. Some favourite ones perhaps may obtrude too prominently, but otherwise no misbehaviour is permitted them: reprehension and rebuke are always ready, and the offence is punished on the spot.

*Boccaccio*   Certainly you thus throw open, to its full extent, the range of poetry and invention; which can not but be very limited and sterile, unless where we find displayed much diversity of character as disseminated by nature, much peculiarity of sentiment as arising from position, marked with unerring skill through every shade and gradation; and finally and chiefly, much intertexture and intensity of passion. You thus convey to us more largely and expeditiously the stores of your understanding and imagination, than you ever could by sonnets or canzonets, or sinewless and sapless allegories.

But weightier works are less captivating. If you had published any such as you mention, you must have waited for their acceptance. Not only the fame of Marcellus, but every other,

Crescit occulto velut arbor aevo;[9]

and that which makes the greatest vernal shoot is apt to make the least autumnal. Authors in general who have met celebrity at starting, have already had their reward; always their utmost due, and often much beyond it. We can not hope for both celebrity and fame: supremely fortunate are the few who are allowed the liberty of choice between them. We two prefer the strength that springs from exercise and toil, acquiring it gradually and slowly: we leave to others the earlier blessing of that sleep which follows enjoyment. How many at first sight are enthusiastic in their favour! Of these how large a portion come away empty-handed and discontented! like idlers who visit the seacoast, fill their pockets with pebbles bright from the passing wave, and carry them off with rapture. After a short examination at home, every streak seems faint and dull, and the whole contexture coarse, uneven, and gritty: first one is thrown away, then another; and before the week's end the store is gone, of things so shining and wonderful.

*Petrarca*   Allegory, which you named with sonnets and canzonets, had few attractions for me, believing it to be the delight in general of idle, frivolous, inexcursive minds, in whose mansions there is neither hall nor portal to receive the loftier of the Passions. A stranger to the Affections, she holds a low station among the handmaidens of Poetry, being fit for little but an apparition in a mask. I had reflected for some time on this subject, when, wearied with the length of my walk over the mountains, and finding a soft old molehill, covered with grey grass, by the way-side, I laid my head upon it, and slept. I can not tell how long it was before a species of dream or vision came over me.

Two beautiful youths appeared beside me; each was winged; but the wings were hanging down, and seemed ill adapted to flight. One of them, whose voice was the softest I ever heard, looking at me frequently, said to the other,

"He is under my guardianship for the present: do not awaken him with that feather."

Methought, hearing the whisper, I saw something like the feather on an arrow; and then the arrow itself; the whole of it, even to the point; although he carried it in such a manner that it was difficult at first to discover more than a palm's length of it: the rest of the shaft, and the whole of the barb, was behind his ankles.

"This feather never awakens anyone," replied he, rather petulantly; "but it brings more of confident security, and more of cherished dreams, than you without me are capable of imparting."

"Be it so!" answered the gentler . . "none is less inclined to quarrel or dispute than I am. Many whom you have wounded grievously, call upon me for succour. But so little am I disposed to thwart you, it is seldom I venture to do more for them than to whisper a few words of comfort in passing. How many reproaches on these occasions have been cast upon me for indifference and infidelity! Nearly as many, and nearly in the same terms, as upon you!"

"Odd enough that we, O Sleep! should be thought so alike!" said Love, contemptuously. "Yonder is he who bears a nearer resemblance to you: the dullest have observed it." I fancied I turned my eyes to where he was pointing, and saw at a distance the figure he designated. Meanwhile the contention went on uninterruptedly. Sleep was slow in asserting his power or his benefits. Love recapitulated them; but only that he might assert his own above them. Suddenly he called on me to decide, and to choose my patron. Under the influence, first of the one, then of the other, I sprang from repose to rapture, I alighted from rapture on repose . . and knew not which was sweetest. Love was very angry with me, and declared he would cross me throughout the whole of my existence. Whatever I might on other occasions have thought of his veracity, I now felt too surely the conviction that he would keep his word. At last, before the close of the altercation, the third Genius had advanced, and stood near us. I can not tell how I knew him, but I knew him to be the Genius of Death. Breathless as I was at beholding him, I soon became familiar with his features. First they seemed only calm; presently they grew contemplative; and lastly beautiful: those of the Graces[10] themselves are less regular, less harmonious, less composed. Love glanced at him unsteadily, with a countenance in which there was somewhat of anxiety, somewhat of disdain; and cried, "Go away! go away! nothing that thou touchest, lives."

"Say rather, child!" replied the advancing form, and advancing grew loftier and statelier, "Say rather that nothing of beautiful or of glorious lives its own true life until my wing hath passed over it."

Love pouted, and rumpled and bent down with his forefinger the stiff short feathers on his arrow-head; but replied not. Although he frowned worse than ever, and at me, I dreaded him less and less, and scarcely looked toward him. The milder and calmer Genius, the third, in proportion as I took courage to contemplate him, regarded me with more and more complacency. He held neither flower nor arrow, as the others did; but, throwing back the clusters of dark curls that over-shadowed his countenance, he presented to me his hand, openly and benignly. I shrank on looking at him so near, and yet I sighed to love him. He smiled, not without an expression of pity, at perceiving my diffidence, my timidity: for I remembered how soft was the hand of Sleep, how warm and entrancing was Love's. By degrees, I became ashamed of my ingratitude; and turning my face away, I held out my arms, and felt my neck within his. Composure strewed and allayed all the throbbings of my bosom; the coolness of freshest morning breathed around; the heavens seemed to open above me; while the beautiful cheek of my deliverer rested on my head. I would now have looked for those others; but knowing my intention by my gesture, he said consolatorily,

"Sleep is on his way to the Earth, where many are calling him; but it is not to these he hastens; for every call only makes him fly farther off. Sedately and gravely as he looks, he is nearly as capricious and volatile as the more arrogant and ferocious one."

"And Love!" said I, "whither is he departed? If not too late, I would propitiate and appease him."

"He who can not follow me, he who can not overtake and pass me," said the Genius, "is unworthy of the name, the most glorious in earth or heaven. Look up! Love is yonder, and ready to receive thee."

I looked: the earth was under me: I saw only the clear blue sky, and something brighter above it.

# Notes

Full details of editions and studies of Landor cited below in an abbreviated form are given in Life and Publications, Principal Editions and the Selected Bibliography.

## Introduction
### *I   The Neo-Classical Rôle*

[1] Forster, *Landor*, II, 531.

[2] Landor to Rose Paynter in 1840 (*Letters, Private and Public*, ed. Wheeler, p. 58).

[3] See Elwin, *A Replevin*, p. 38.

[4] See Ernest de Selincourt, 'Landor's Prose', *Wordsworthian and Other Studies*, Oxford, 1947, p. 80.

[5] 'To Shelley', *Poetical Works*, ed. Wheeler, II, 417, ll. 13–15.

[6] See Yeats: 'He had perhaps as much Unity of Being as his age permitted' (*A Vision*, London, 1938, p. 145); and Pound: 'You go to Crabbe for England of 1810, you go to Landor for an epitome; all culture of the encyclopedists reduced to manageable size, in the *Imaginary Conversations*' (*ABC of Reading*, London, 1961, p. 185).

[7] 'The Abbé Delille and Walter Landor', *Landor as Critic*, ed. Proudfit, p. 147.

[8] *Poems*, London, 1795, p. 208. Translated from the Latin.

[9] 'Marcus Tullius and Quinctus Cicero', *Conversations*, ed. Crump, II, 42.

[10] See 'Alfieri and Salomon the Florentine Jew', *Conversations*, ed. Crump, IV, 19–20. In 1838 he referred to himself as an 'aristocratic radical'; see Elwin, *A Replevin*, p. 325.

[11] [Fragment], *Poetical Works*, ed. Wheeler, II, 477, ll. 8–9. Thaddeus Kosciusko, 1746–1817, was the champion of Polish independence; Andrew Hofer, 1767–1810, led the Tyrolean peasants against Bavaria and the French.

[12] I use this expression in the sense established by Raymond Williams: 'this structure of feeling is the culture of the period: it is the particular living result of all the elements in the general organization' (*The Long Revolution*, London, 1961, p. 48). Williams sees it as expressed, consciously or not, in the arts of a period.

[13] 'Milton and Andrew Marvel', *Conversations*, ed. Crump, III, 332.

[14] See the 'Advertisement to the Story of Crysaor' in the note on POETRY **5**, **Crysaor**.

[15] R. I. Goldmark, *Studies in the Influence of the Classics on English Literature*, New York, 1918, p. 44.

[16] See Elwin, *A Replevin*, p. 48.

[17] *Selections*, p. xxvii.

[18] See Kelly, 'The Latin Poetry of Walter Savage Landor', p. 181. The poem was published in 1858.
[19] See Boccaccio on this distinction in *The Pentameron*, *Longer Prose Works*, ed. Crump, II, 134.
[20] Preface, *Heroic Idyls*, 1863.

## II  Landor's Art of Imitation

[1] 'Tradition and the Individual Talent', *Selected Essays*, London, 1951, p. 14.
[2] *Commentary on Memoirs of Mr. Fox*, *Landor as Critic*, ed. Proudfit, p. 57.
[3] 'Shelley and Keats', *The Use of Poetry and the Use of Criticism*, London, 1933, p. 88.
[4] In Sarah Austin's *Characteristics of Goethe*; quoted by Super, *Biography*, p. 377.
[5] 'Post-Script to "Gebir" ', *Landor as Critic*, ed. Proudfit, p. 47.
[6] 'Landor, English Visitor, and Florentine Visitor', *Landor as Critic*, ed. Proudfit, p. 159.
[7] Landor to Alexander Dyce in 1850; see Elwin, *A Replevin*, p. 64.
[8] 'The Poems of Catullus', *Longer Prose Works*, ed. Crump, II, 213.
[9] This account of the derivation of the Imaginary Conversation form is based on that of Prasher, *Imaginary Conversations*, pp. 92–107.
[10] See 'Gebir', Book VI, ll. 238–308, *Poetical Works*, ed. Wheeler, I, 46–7.
[11] See note on POETRY **9**, **[Wish for Ianthe]**.
[12] In 1839; see Forster, *Landor*, II, 298.
[13] See Forster, *Landor*, II, 373.
[14] Quoted by Super, *Biography*, p. 236.
[15] 'Greece! Be Tolerant', *Poetical Works*, ed. Wheeler, II, 365, ll. 11–12.
[16] Quoted by Colvin, *Landor*, p. 86.
[17] The Preface to the first edition of Arnold's *Poems*, 1853; *The Poems of Matthew Arnold*, ed. Kenneth Allott, London, 1965, p. 593.
[18] Landor to Lady Blessington in 1839; quoted by Super, *Biography*, p. 35.

## III  The Classical Structure of Feeling

[1] Forster, *Landor*, II, 530.
[2] 'The Idyls of Theocritus', *Landor as Critic*, ed. Proudfit, p. 278.
[3] Landor to Forster; quoted in Forster, *Landor*, II, 446.
[4] 'The Idyls of Theocritus', *Longer Prose Works*, ed. Crump, II, 174.
[5] Preface to *Simonidea*, London, 1806, p. vi.
[6] A part of this collection is kept at the Picture Gallery, Christ Church, Oxford.
[7] 'Lysander, Alcanor, Phanöe', *Poetical Works*, ed. Wheeler, II, 178, ll. 28–33.
[8] See *Imaginary Conversations*, ed. Prasher, pp. 160–6.
[9] 'Milton and Marvel', Second Conversation, *Conversations*, ed. Crump, V, 48.
[10] Cf. *Paradise Lost*, IV, ll. 304–11; and Landor's remarks on these lines in 'Southey and Landor I', *Landor as Critic*, ed. Proudfit, p. 236.
[11] *Pericles and Aspasia*, *Longer Prose Works*, ed. Crump, I, p. 189.
[12] 'Landor, English Visitor, and Florentine Visitor', *Landor as Critic*, ed. Proudfit, p. 160.
[13] 'Marcus Tullius and Quinctus Cicero', *Conversations*, ed. Crump, II, 63.

[14] 'Landor, English Visitor, and Florentine Visitor', *Landor as Critic*, ed. Proudfit, p. 159.

[15] 'To Layard, Discoverer of Ninevah', *Poetical Works*, ed. Wheeler, II, 420, ll. 31–5.

## IV    The Poetic Style

[1] *Pericles and Aspasia, Longer Prose Works*, ed. Crump, I, 189.

[2] 'Aeschines and Phocion', *Conversations*, ed. Crump, I, 169.

[3] *ABC of Reading*, p. 185.

[4] 'The Poems of Catullus', *Longer Prose Works*, ed. Crump, II, 200.

[5] 'The Hard and Soft in French Poetry', *Literary Essays of Ezra Pound*, ed. T. S. Eliot, London, 1954, p. 285.

[6] *Landor's Poetry*, p. 7.

[7] Landor to Southey, 8 May 1808; *Landor as Critic*, ed. Proudfit, p. 66.

[8] 'Milton and Marvel', *Conversations*, ed. Crump, V, 39.

[9] *A History of English Prosody*, 3 vols., London, 1910, III, 89.

[10] 'The Poems of Catullus', *Longer Prose Works*, ed. Crump, II, 213.

[11] Landor to Southey, February 1809; *Landor as Critic*, ed. Proudfit, p. 67.

[12] 'Walter Savage Landor', *The Romantic Movement in English Poetry*, London, 1909, p. 178.

[13] See Joseph Kestner, 'The Genre of Landor's *Gebir*', *The Wordsworth Circle*, V (1974), 46.

[14] Forster, *Landor*, II, 514.

[15] *Count Julian, Poetical Works*, ed. Wheeler, I, 210, IV, sc.ii, ll. 43–4.

[16] 'Milton and Marvel', *Conversations*, ed. Crump, III, 339.

[17] Pound to Mary Barnard, 13 August 1934; *The Letters of Ezra Pound*, ed. D. D. Paige, London, 1951, p. 346.

[18] Forster, *Landor*, II, 530.

[19] *ABC of Reading*, p. 70.

[20] For a lively debate on the nature of Landor's poetic diction, see the items under Davie, Donald A., in the Selected Bibliography, and Pinsky's *Landor's Poetry*, pp. 12–22.

[21] See *Landor as Critic*, ed. Proudfit, p. 93.

[22] See 'Southey and Landor I', *Landor as Critic*, ed. Proudfit, p. 222.

[23] *Commentary on Memoirs of Mr. Fox, Landor as Critic*, ed. Proudfit, p. 53.

[24] See POETRY **14**, **To Corinth**, and **15**, **Regeneration**.

[25] 'One morning in the spring I sate', *Poetical Works*, ed. Wheeler, II, 462, ll. 21–2.

[26] *Pericles and Aspasia, Longer Prose Works*, ed. Crump, I, 173.

[27] 'Francesco Petrarca', *Landor as Critic*, ed. Proudfit, p. 295.

## V    The Imaginary Characters

[1] Landor to Browning in 1845; quoted by Super, *Biography*, p. 355.

[2] 'Milton and Marvel', Second Conversation, *Conversations*, ed. Crump, V, 46.

[3] 'Marcus Tullius and Quinctus Cicero', *Conversations*, ed. Crump, II, 56.

[4] Quoted by Ian Jack, *English Literature 1815–1832*, Oxford, 1963, p. 344.

[5] See entry for 13 August 1812, *Henry Crabb Robinson on Books and their Writers*, ed. Edith J. Morley, 3 vols., London, 1938, I, 107; 'a happy term to express

that common fault of throwing the feelings of the writer into the body, as it were, of other personages, the characters of the poems'.

[6] 'Diogenes and Plato', *Conversations*, ed. Crump, I, 99.

[7] See, for example, notes on the Conversation 'Southey and Porson', PROSE **2**, 25 and 36.

[8] Southey to Landor; quoted by Forster, *Landor*, II, 103.

[9] Forster, *Landor*, I, 292–3. Cf. the speech of Petrarca in *The Pentameron*, PROSE **43**, p. 208.

[10] 'Dante and Beatrice', *Conversations*, ed. Crump, V, 139–40.

[11] 'Epicurus and Metrodorus', *Conversations*, ed. Crump, I, 259.

[12] Landor to Southey; see Super, *Biography*, p. 251.

[13] Landor to Southey; quoted by Elwin, *A Replevin*, p. 124.

[14] 'Landor, English Visitor, and Florentine Visitor', *Landor as Critic*, ed. Proudfit, pp. 158–9.

[15] See Robert Langbaum, *The Poetry of Experience*, London, 1972, pp. 75–108.

[16] Keats to George and Thomas Keats, 21 December 1817; *The Letters of John Keats*, ed. Maurice Forman, Oxford, 1952, p. 71. It is associated with his view expressed in a letter to Richard Woodhouse of 'the poetical Character' which 'has no character', and 'has as much delight in conceiving an Iago as an Imogen' (27 October 1818; *ibid.*, pp. 226–7).

[17] See note introducing PROSE **18**, p. 256.

[18] 'Rémy de Gourmont', *Literary Essays of Ezra Pound*, ed. T. S. Eliot, London, 1954, p. 344.

[19] *The Joyful Wisdom*, translated by Thomas Common, *The Complete Works of Friedrich Nietzsche*, ed. Oscar Levy, 18 vols., Edinburgh and London, 1909–13, II, 126.


# The Poetry

**1 Invocation to the Muse**    1 *Helicon*: a mountain in Boeotia which was sacred to the Muses, the goddesses of literature and the arts. On its slopes two fountains united in a stream. 5 Hayley: William, 1745–1820, author of numerous poems, including the continually reprinted *The Triumph of Temper*, 1781. 6 Peter Pindar: *nom-de-guerre* of the satirist John Wolcot, 1738–1819. 7 Mason: William, 1724–97, noted for academic odes and dramas in a magnificently classical style. 8 Crowe: William, 1745–1829, published his descriptive poem, 'Lewesdon Hill', in 1788. 16 George III: 1738–1820. His attempt to break the power of the Whigs, to restore the royal prerogative, and his support of the wars against the American colonists and revolutionary France were bitterly resented by Landor.


**Gebir**    The text is that of the second, revised edition, 1803, from which the relevant Arguments and footnotes are selected. Book I is printed in entirety; the extract from Book IV comprises ll. 182–223, and that from Book V ll. 1–13. Main variants in later editions are indicated below.

The full work is a heroic poem in seven books, parts of which were originally written in Latin. The chief source was 'The History of Charoba, Queen of Aegypt', in Clara Reeve's *Progress of Romance*, 1785. It was probably written in its first form in autumn, 1796.

Landor summarizes the story in the extended Preface to the 1803 edition: 'In the moral are exhibited the folly, the injustice, and the punishment of

Invasion, with the calamities which must ever attend the superfluous coloni-
zation of a peopled country. Gebir, the sovereign of Boetic Spain, is urged by
an oath, administered in childhood, to invade the kingdom of Egypt. He
invades it. Passions, the opposite to those which he has cherished, are excited
by his conference with the queen Charoba. On the other hand, *her* apprehen-
sions, of which at the first alarm she had informed her attendant Dalica, from
whom, as having been her nurse, she implores advice and assistance, decrease
at this interview with Gebir. But women communicate their fears more will-
ingly than their love. Dalica, all this time, intent on one sole object, and never
for a moment doubting that the visible perturbation of Charoba's mind pro-
ceeded, as at first, from her terrors, is determined to restore her tranquillity.
She executes the plan which she had long been forming, nor discovers the love
of Charoba but by the death of Gebir'.

**2  Book I**  1–11 Omitted in the editions of 1831 and 1846. 1 *Silenus*: an old
forest god, celebrated for drunkenness and prophetic wisdom. He was the
foster-father and boon-companion of *Bacchus* (3), god of wine, who loosens
care and inspires to music and poetry. In religious processions, he was attended
by troops of goat-like *Satyrs* (1). In Virgil's Sixth Eclogue he demonstrates his
twin rôle of philosophical entertainer; cf. **128 Silenus.** 7 *Cambria*: Wales. The
original poem was principally written at Swansea. 8 *fame*: Landor's note: 'I
believe, almost every hill in that country has its descriptive name; and it often
happens that the name alone is remaining of its history, and the history is
apparently that of some preternatural personage. This explains the words
"hide in heaven" '. 15 *name*: Landor's note: 'Tho' *Gibraltar* may not in strict
etymology be derived from *Gebir*, nor even be correlative, yet the fiction, as it
does not violate probability, is just as pardonable as the Teucro-latin names
in Virgil'. 17 Landor's note: 'Primeval wrongs – in not possessing, as it appears
his ancestors had, the throne of Egypt'. 42 *a city*: Landor conflates the legendary
gardens of Irem, possibly modern Damascus, constructed in the desert near
Aden by Sheddâd (*Sidad*, 43), son of Ad (*Gad*, 44), with *Gades* (44), modern
Cadiz, a famous colony of the Phoenicians on an island close to the SW coast
of Spain, in order to fabricate an origin for this international dispute; see the
Koran, Surah LXXXIX. 49 Landor's note: 'Dalica, to discover the sentiments
of the Queen, makes an indirect proposal of an union with Gebir; to which
she not only objects, but at first refuses to hold any conference with him'. 60–
254 Reprinted in 1859. 69 *Diana*: the moon goddess who fell in love with the
shepherd, Endymion, while he was sleeping on Mount Latmos (70). 88 *Tamar*:
named after a Cornish river. 127 *spring-tide*: Landor's note: 'It must be re-
membered that along the Mediterranean coasts the tides are sensible of hardly
any variation. But the coasts of Egypt are so flat, particularly the most fertile
parts, and the water so very nearly on a level with them, that Tamar may be
supposed to fancy it arising from spring-tide. Those who have ever from a low
and even country looked upon the sea, will have observed that the sea seemed
higher than the ground where they stood'. 139–40 *assum'd The sailor*: i.e. put
on the appearance of a sailor. 148 Landor's note: 'I make no apology for the
comparison. The *Scuttle-shell*, tho' the name be inharmonious and harsh, so as
not to be admissible in poetry, is of an elegant form and of a brilliant white-
ness'. 158 Landor's note: 'Tamar tho' aware of her sex, affects, from the
character she assumed, to consider her a sailor, that he might with more
propriety accept her challenge'. 170-7 Landor believed that Wordsworth had

plagiarized this extended image of the shell to illustrate one of the Wanderer's sermons in *The Excursion*, IV, 1132–40, published 1814. 190 Landor's note to 226 claims this verse represents the farthest he has ventured in taking metrical liberties: 'where the fastidious reader might make an elision, if he chose . . . "*If struggle* and equal strength, &c" '.

**3   Book IV**   42 *be with you peace*: Landor's note: 'Such has been precisely the eastern salutation for several hundred and even thousand years, and amongst several millions of people'.

**4   Book V**   7 *Masar*: modern Cairo.

**5   Crysaor**   The volume containing this poem was originally printed in 1800, and published two years later. The text is that of 1859. The extract comprises ll. 150–84 of the 207 line poem.

It is a heroic poem whose genesis is linked to that of 'The Phocaeans', projected as a much longer poem, two fragments of which (possibly written before 'Gebir') were published in this volume of 1802. The fragments revolve around the Persian invasion of Ionia, and the consequent flight of one of its nations to hospitality in Iberia, the Greek name for Spain. The chief sources for this poem are the universal histories of Diodorus Siculus and Justin, and the *Bibliothēkē* attributed to Apollodorus of Athens. Crump also suggests that Landor had in mind the story of Ajax Oileus 'who was shipwrecked, and taking refuge on a rock thence defied the gods. Neptune split the rock, and the hero perished miserably' (ed., *Poems*, II, 370).

In the 1802 edition Landor provided an 'Advertisement to the Story of Crysaor': 'Hardly any thing remains that made ancient Iberia classic land. We have little more than the titles of fables – than portals, as it were, covered over with gold and gorgeous figures, that shew us what once must have been the magnificence of the whole interior edifice. Lucan has wandered over Numidia, and Virgil too at the conclusion of his Georgics, has left the indelible mark of his footstep near the celebrated pharos of Egypt. But, in general, the poets of Greece and Italy were afraid of moving far from the latest habitations of their tutelar gods and heroes. I am fond of walking by myself; but others, who have gone before me, may have planted trees, or opened vistas, and rendered my walks more amusing. I had begun to write a poem connected in some degree with the early history of Spain; but doubtful whether I should ever continue it, and grown every hour more indifferent, I often sat down and diverted my attention with the remotest views I could find. The present is a sketch'.

In the full poem, Crysaor is described as the last survivor of the 'race of earth-born giants', and is associated with the Titans, the old order of gods being routed by Zeus (Jove), as he takes over the rule from Cronos. To Landor, the giant embodies the forces of reactionary tyranny, attempting to defy the inevitability of moral progress. The extract describes his death through the power of Neptune, god of the sea, at Jove's behest.

1 *the Sacrilege*: Crysaor has refused to adore Jove. 10 *Phlegethon*: a river of flame in Hades. 18 *Tethys*: a Titaness, the consort of the Titan Ocean (21). They are personifications, respectively, of a south European sea, including the Mediterranean, and a river supposed to encircle the plain of the earth. They have been imprisoned by the victorious Jove.

**6–11** The texts of these poems are those of 1846.

**6 [Rose Aylmer]** The 1846 text printed here is the final one. The version of the 1806 edition is as follows:
Ah what avails the sceptred race,
Ah what the form divine!
What, every virtue, every grace!
For, Aylmer, all were thine.

Sweet Aylmer, whom these wakeful eyes
May weep, but never see,
A night of sorrows and of sighs
I consecrate to thee.
The 1831 edition has *and* for *and of* (7).
Rose Aylmer was born in 1779, and died aged twenty in 1800. Landor may have first met her 'walking on the burrows at Swansea' with her younger half-sister, probably in 1796. Landor became acquainted with her family who lived at Laugharne, Carmarthen, and achieved a delicately gallant intimacy with Rose. She accompanied her aunt to Calcutta in 1799 where her uncle was judge in the Supreme Court of Bengal. She died there of the cholera.
1 *the sceptred race*: Super notes: 'The Aylmer family was very old and derived its name from a descendant of the elder brother and predecessor of Alfred the Great. Rose Aylmer was descended in the twenty-third generation from Edward I and might also have claimed the blood of Charlemagne and three other royal ancestors' (*Biography*, p. 517). 4–5 *Rose*: The repeated first name in the revision was perhaps a specific identification originally restrained by social discretion.

**7 [Imitation from Sappho]** Prompted by a two-line fragment from Sappho, the seventh-century BC poetess from Lesbos.

Γλύκηα μᾶτερ, οὔ τοι δύναμαι κρέκην τὸν ἰστὸν
πόθῳ δάμεισα παῖδος βραδίνῳ δἰ 'Αφροδίταν.
J. M. Edmonds translates:
'Sweet mother, I truly cannot weave my web; for I am o'erwhelmed through Aphrodite with love of a slender youth' (ed., *Lyra Graeca*, 3 vols., London, 1922–7, I, 277).

**9 [Wish for Ianthe]** 'Ianthe' is Jane Sophia Swift whom Landor met at Bath probably in 1802, and with whom he fell desperately in love. She married a cousin, in the tradition of her family, in 1803; but Malcolm Elwin has speculated on the possibility of a liaison extending into this marriage. The invention of the pseudonym owes something to discretion as well as euphony. She was widowed in 1814, and married Comte Pelletier de Molandé. She again became a widow about 1827, and by then in possession of a large fortune was wooed by the Duc de Luxembourg. Her path recrossed Landor's at Florence in 1829 and at Bath in 1839 and 1849–50. She remained his great passion, dying at Versailles in 1851.
Though Landor sometimes addresses poems inspired by one person to another, nearly all those naming 'Ianthe', or classed under her name in the 1831 edition, do relate to Jane Swift.

**10 [Ianthe Awaited]** 8–12 A reference to Nancy Jones, the 'Iöne' of Landor's earlier verse. He met her on vacation at Tenby, in Wales, as an undergraduate, and later lived with her at Swansea. They had a child who died, as did Nancy herself (probably from TB), at some time in or before 1806. 16 *Hesper*: the evening star (the planet Venus), already bright in early evening.

**Count Julian** The text is that of 1846. The first extract comprises the entire scene; the second ll. 3–27 of the original.

It is a verse tragedy in five acts. Landor wrote it between November 1810 and January 1811, at Bath. It was probably prompted by the arrival of the first instalment of the MS of Southey's new 'Tragic Poem', *Roderick, The Last of the Goths*, in July 1810 (published 1814); and the historical framework may derive from Gibbon's *The Decline and Fall of the Roman Empire*, Chapter LI.

Gibbon tells how, in AD 709, Musa ibn Nusair (Landor's 'Muza'), the Khalif's governor in Mauritania, attempting to complete the Saracen conquest of northern Africa, 'was repulsed from the walls of Ceuta by the vigilance and courage of count Julian, the general of the Goths. From his disappointment and complexity Musa was relieved by an unexpected message of the Christian chief, who offered his place, his person, and his sword to the successors of Mahomet, and solicited the disgraceful honour of introducing their arms into the heart of Spain. If we enquire into the cause of his treachery, the Spaniards will repeat the popular story of his daughter Cava (Landor's 'Covilla'); of a virgin who was seduced, or ravished, by her sovereign (Landor's 'Roderigo'); of a father who sacrificed his religion and country to the thirst of revenge'. The first invasion was commanded by a Saracen under-chieftain, Tarif, and the second by one named Tarik. Landor conflates them in his 'Tarik'.

In the 1846 edition, it was printed together with other pieces under the heading 'Acts and Scenes' with the following note: 'None of these poems of a dramatic form were offered to the stage, being no better than *Imaginary Conversations* in metre'.

**12   Fourth Act: First Scene** The dialogue takes place after the defeat and capture of Roderigo. 14–20 Gibbon writes (chapter LI): 'After the decease or deposition of Witiza, his two sons were supplanted by the ambition of Roderic (Landor's 'Roderigo'), a noble Goth, whose father, the duke or governor of a province, had fallen a victim to the preceding tyranny. . . . It is probable that Julian was involved in the disgrace of the unsuccessful faction; that he had little to hope and much to fear from the new reign; and that the imprudent king could not forget or forgive the injuries which Roderic and his family had sustained. The merit and influence of the count rendered him an useful or formidable subject . . . and it was too fatally shewn that, by his Andalusian and Mauritanian commands, he held in his hand the keys of the Spanish monarchy'. 19 *Ceuta*: the fortress of Septem on the Mauritanian coast opposite the nearest point of Europe. It belonged to the Roman emperor, not the Visigothic king. Julian was historically an Imperial, not a Gothic general. 72, 107 *Barbary*: the Saracen countries along the coast of north Africa. 134 *bell*: A better early reading is 'cell': cf. Nicholas A. Joukovsky, 'Southey on Landor: An Unpublished Letter', *The Wordsworth Circle*, VII (1976), 14). 140ff. The original edition gives a series of stage directions as footnotes: 140 *Roderigo*: 'Much agitated – after a pause'; 156 *Upon*: 'Julian greatly moved, goes towards him'; 157 *feet*: 'Starts back'; 168 *peace*: 'Julian looks sternly on the ground and does not answer'. 179 *thy end be peace*: Gibbon records (chapter LI) that Roderic actually drowned fleeing from battle.

**13 Fifth Act: Second Scene** In this dialogue between Tarik and Hernando, a Spanish officer, the Spaniard explains his chief's tragic predicament to their victorious ally.

**14 To Corinth** It was originally appended to the Conversation 'Maurocordato and Colocotroni' in *Imaginary Conversations*, 1824, in lieu of notes. The text is that of 1859.

The Conversation, between noted insurgents, concerns the Greek War of Independence.

1 Corinth is situated on the isthmus between the Aegean and the Adriatic. 1–2 Poseidon is god of earthquakes and water. One of the chief trades of this great commercial centre was shipbuilding. 4–8 *Theseus*, the legendary King of Athens, slew the brigand *Sciron* by throwing him into the sea, where, according to Ovid, his bones turned into the cliffs bearing his name. 9 *Isthmian games*: Theseus (or Poseidon himself) was the reputed founder of the festival celebrated on the Isthmus of Corinth in the spring of every second year. It included athletic, equine and musical contests. 13–14 *those words Divine*: probably an allusion to Titus Quinctius Flaminius, who proclaimed the liberty of Greece at the Isthmian games in 196 BC, after defeating Philip V of Macedon. 15–16 *that ridge So perilous*: The road from Athens to Megara ran along a ledge on the Scironian Cliffs, high above the sea. 15–31 Euripides' tragedy *Medea* is based on the story of Jason and Medea, daughter of the King of Colchis (17), who fled to Corinth after Medea had killed Jason's uncle for his sake. There Jason arranged to marry the daughter of the King of Corinth, and Medea, under sentence of banishment, killed the king, his daughter, and the two children she had by Jason, leaving him childless. 20 *the Eumenides*: the Furies or avenging deities. 36–9 The Corinthian order of architecture was the latest and most ornate. The capitals show delicately foliated details, typically of acanthus leaves. The Temple of Zeus at Athens was the most notable structure in this style. 40ff Corinth had been captured by Greek insurgents in 1822.

**15 Regeneration** It was originally appended to *Imaginary Conversations*, 1824, 'as a voluntary to close the work'. The text is that of 1847.

10 form: possibly should read 'foam'. 16–21 Italy, situated *between the seas* (17) of the Adriatic and Mediterranean, despite being a historical and natural unit, from Venice in the north to the southern heel, on opposite sides of which the towns of Taranto and Hydruntum (modern Otranto) are situated, had for long been fragmented and disorganized, recently under French domination (1797–1814), and thereafter under Austrian. Napoleon had proclaimed the end of the Venetian Republic (18) in 1797, and abandoned the territory to Austria. Landor was an enthusiast for the Risorgimento, the movement for reunification. 22–3 Cf. Genesis 1:26–8. 25 *Albion*: Great Britain. British policy at the Foreign Office under Castlereagh from 1812–22, and under Canning for long thereafter, was one of non-intervention and compromise with the liberal and despotic states of Europe. 26–9 Cf. John 19: 29–30; 34. 37 *golden Hermus and Melena's brow*: The Hermus is a river on the west coast of Asia Minor, flowing into the eastern Aegean behind the promontory of Melaena, which faces the island of Chios. The gold-bearing Pactolus is one of its tributaries. 41–2 The island of *Chios* was one of the reputed birthplaces of Homer who is said to have become blind. 44–5 Themes from the *Iliad:– a disdainful youth*: Achilles, who sulked in his tent as a result of a quarrel with *a lawless king*:

Agamemnon, who, forced to surrender the maiden who was his prize, to avert a *pestilence* that had broken out in the Greek camp, took a slave-girl belonging to Achilles in her place. Achilles was reconciled and rejoined the fight when his friend Patroclus was slain. A solemn funeral and games were held at which his friend's body was burnt on a huge *pyre*. 46–50 Possibly an allusion to a relatively minor incident in the Greek War of Independence. After the Massacre of Chios by the Turks in February 1822, the situation was partially redeemed by a daring raid of fire-ships from Psara, the small island off the NW coast of Chios, under the command of Miaoulis and Kanaris. The Turkish fleet, sustaining much damage, was driven back from the open sea into the shelter of the Dardanelles. 50 Landor notes: 'Reduced now by the *Holy Alliance* into worse slavery than before'. 52–3 *Elis*: a state in the NW of the Peloponnese in which the small plain of Olympia is situated where the *Olympian* Games were held every fourth year. 54 Marathon is the plain near Athens where the invading Persians were defeated by Miltiades in 490 BC. 55 *Salamis*: an island in the Saronic Gulf overlooking a strait in which the Persian fleet was crushingly defeated in 480 BC. 56–7 *Plataea*: It was alone of the Boeotian towns in being allied to Athens at an early date, and was the only ally to render assistance at Marathon. It was the scene of the great battle in 479 BC in which the Greeks under Pausanias defeated the Persian army. 57–60 *Anthela*, near Thermopylae, was the site of the temple of the Greek corn goddess, Demeter (*Ceres*). The Amphictyony was a religious association of Greeks worshipping at the same shrine. It met each year at Anthela which is situated at the base of Mount Callidromos. On the coastal plain were some hot springs consecrated to Hercules. 63 *Perfidious Ilion*: Paris, son of the King of Troy (*Ilion*), carried off Helen, the wife of Menelaus, thus bringing about the Trojan War. *parricidal Thebes*: Oedipus killed his father before becoming King of Thebes. 67–70 *Enna* is a vale in Sicily in which Demeter's daughter, Persephone, was gathering flowers when she was carried off by Hades to his kingdom. Though Zeus finally yielded to Demeter's pleas, the daughter could not be entirely released from the lower world, as she had eaten some pomegranate seeds there. It was arranged that she should spend eight (or six) months of each year on earth, and the remainder with Hades. The myth with which the cult was associated is symbolic of the burying of the seed in the ground and the growth of the corn. 71 Landor was then living at Florence. 82–5 *Leonidas*: the King of Sparta who defended the pass of Thermopylae at the time of the Persian invasion of 480 BC. An allusion may also be intended to Marco Bozzaris, known as 'The Leonidas of Modern Greece', who with 1,200 men put to rout 4,000 Turco-Albanians at Kerpenisi, being killed in the attack, in 1823. 86–93 Gelon was ruler of the city of Syracuse on the coast of Sicily, a colony founded by Corinth. He gained power by suppressing a democratic revolt against the founding aristocracy, and made the city the greatest Hellenic power of the time. His greatest achievement was to defeat completely a massive army of Carthaginian invaders under Hamilcar at the battle of Himera in 480 BC.

**16  On Seeing A Hair of Lucretia Borgia** First published in *The New Monthly Magazine and Literary Journal*, July 1825. The text is the final one of 1846. A text of 1825 gives:

> BORGIA, thou once wert almost too august,
> And high for adoration;– now thou'rt dust!

> All that remains of thee these plaits infold–
> Calm hair, meand'ring with pellucid gold!

A text of 1837 gives 'meandring' (4).

It was originally introduced in a note by Leigh Hunt: 'A solitary hair of the famous Lucretia Borgia ... was given me by a wild acquaintance (Byron) who stole it from a lock of her hair preserved in the Ambrosian library at Milan ...'. It inspired Landor's poem.

Lucrezia Borgia, 1480–1519, became a by-word for extravagant and splendid vice. She was the daughter of Pope Alexander VI whose first marriage was annulled, whose second husband was murdered at the behest of her brother, and who, as the wife of the Duke of Ferrara, attracted to her brilliant court many famous artists and poets.

**17 [Burns]** First published in 1828. The text is that of 1846.

Robert Burns, 1759–96, was a Scottish poet famous for warm-hearted intemperance.

**18 [Godiva]** First published in *Imaginary Conversations*, 1829, where it was appended to the Conversation 'Leofric and Godiva'; see note on PROSE **17**. The text is that of 1846.

Landor notes that he wrote it during his school-days at Rugby.

**19–37** The texts of these poems are those of 1846.

**19 [To a Portrait Painter]** The portrait was of 'Ianthe', done in 1808 when the poem was written in its original form. The painter was probably T. Langdon, miniature painter at Bath.

**21 [Ianthe's Name]** The original version of 1831 gives a final stanza:

> The tear for fading beauty check,
>   For passing glory cease to sigh;
> One form shall rise above the wreck,
>   One name, Ianthe, shall not die.

1 See note on **15 Regeneration,** 63. 2 Apollo persuaded the fates into granting Admetus, King of Pherae in Thessaly, longer life if at the appointed hour someone else would die for him. His wife *Alcestis* consented, and so died. But Heracles took her back from the messenger of Hades and restored her to her husband. *Alcestis* is a drama by Euripides based on this story.

**23 [Ianthe Leaves]** She was on her return to Ireland where her marriage had been arranged.

**25 Fiesolan Idyl** The title is Landor's MS correction in 1831 for the original 'Faesulan Idyl'. Landor moved to Fiesole, above Florence, where he had a villa on the hillside from 1829.

**26 [First Wrinkles]** The first line is a translation of Ovid's *Metamorphoses*, XV, 232, where the reference is to Helen of Troy.

**27 [William Gifford]** The critic and poetaster, 1756–1826. He was a savage early critic of *Gebir*, and as editor of the Tory *Quarterly Review* he pruned much of Southey's praise in his review of *Count Julian*. 3 *Scheld . . . Don*: rivers, the first in Belgium and the Netherlands, the second in Russia.

**28  Dirce**   The title name is unspecific. 3 *Charon*: the ferryman who took the souls of the dead over the river Styx (1) to the infernal regions.

**29  [Needwood Forest]**   An extensive tract of oaks and hollies in Staffordshire. It is intersected by the road from Rugeley (where the estates inherited from Landor's father lay) to Burton.

**30  [Towards Florence]**   Written in 1819.

**31  Old Style**   In 1831 the triplets are divided into separate stanzas. That version has 'three' for *six* (3).
    1   An imitation of Catullus's Carmen XXI. 2 *Catullus*: Gaius Valerius, *c.* 84 – *c.* 54 BC, the Roman lyric poet. 9 For *Lucullus* and *Cesar*, see note on the Conversation 'Lucullus and Caesar', PROSE **12**. Catullus wrote political lampoons on Caesar from the aristocratic standpoint, but later became reconciled.

**32  [Fiesolan Musings]**   The title is Sidney Colvin's. 2 For *aërial Fiesole*, see note on **25 Fiesolan Idyl.** 22 *Castlereagh*, Viscount: Robert Stewart, second Marquis of Londonderry, 1769–1822. See note on **15 Regeneration,** 25. 32 *Latian muse*: his Latin poetry. 35–40: References to the improvements Landor had introduced on his Llanthony estate, Monmouthshire (59). 37 Segovia: a province of central Spain. The sheep imported were the hardy Merino. 52 *Morning Post*: the oldest London daily newspaper; Coleridge, Southey and Wordsworth wrote for it. 59–62 The thirteenth-century Austin priory at Llanthony was ruined.

**35  On a Poet in a Welsh Church-Yard**   Possibly on Henry Vaughan, buried at Llansaintffraed, Brecknock, 1695.

**36  Another Urn at Thoresby Park**   In 1846 it follows several poems after the poem entitled **For an Urn in Thoresby Park**, printed below, **100**. There it is sub-titled 'The Residence of the Late Earl Manvers'. The park referred to is the largest in the Dukeries, at Ollerton, Nottinghamshire.

**37  On the Dead**   2 *Dorothea*: Dorothy Lyttleton who lived with her uncles, neighbours to the Landors, at Ipsley Court, eighteen miles west of Warwick. She acted as a mediator during Landor's estrangement from his father in 1795. She died in 1811, and the poem was written two years later.

**38  For an Epitaph at Fiesole**   The text is that of 1831. 4 'Ianthe'.

**39–42**   The texts of these poems are those of 1846. **To the Owlet, The Maid's Lament,** and **[Leaves and Girls]** were all first published in *Examination of Shakspeare*, 1834, where they were offered as examples of Shakespeare's juvenilia.

**42  To Wordsworth**  First published in *The Athenaeum*, 1 February 1834. In that version there is a space between ll. 24–5, but none between ll. 36–7. For Landor's relationship with Wordsworth, see note on the Conversation 'Southey and Porson', PROSE **2**, 2.

28 *Grace*: The three goddesses personifying loveliness or 'grace' were called the Graces. 46–8 In Wordsworth's 'Laodamia', published in 1815, the heroine follows the spectre of her husband who has been killed at Troy (*the Dardan strand*) to the shades. Their fate is symbolized by cypress trees:

A knot of spiry trees for ages grew
From out the tomb of him for whom she died;
And ever, when such stature they had gained
That Ilium's walls were subject to their view,
The trees' tall summits withered at the sight;
A constant interchange of growth and blight! (ll. 169–73)

See the Conversation 'Southey and Porson,' PROSE **2**, for Landor's criticism of the poem.

**43–56**  These poems were all published originally in *Pericles and Aspasia*, 1836; see note on this work, introducing PROSE **22–41**. They are all free imitations in the spirit of the whole work, attributed either to characters in the work or to poets known in antiquity.

**43  Corinna to Tanagra**  The text is that of 1859.

In her letter to 'Cleone' with which the poem is sent 'Aspasia' writes: '. . . the exterior of the best houses in Tanagra is painted with historical scenes, adventures of the Gods, allegories, and other things; and under the walls of the city flows the Thermodon . . .' (XLIV).

Corinna was a lyric poetess of the sixth century BC of whose work only a few fragments remain. She came from Tanagra, the chief town of east Boeotia, and wrote about the legends of her native country.

15–16 Apollo, *Latona's son* by Jupiter, was the god of lyric poetry. 25 *Dirce*: a fountain near Thebes, from where Pindar came who was referred to as 'The Swan of Dirce'. He was said to have received instruction in poetical composition from Corinna. 40 *the Delphic bays*: The chief festival for verse recitation was the Pythian Games held at Apollo's shrine at Delphi every third year of each Olympiad. The prize was a crown of bay leaves cut in the vale of Tempe.

**44  [Verses from Mimnermus]**  The text is that of 1846.

Mimnermus of Colophon in Ionia flourished in the second half of the seventh century BC. He left fragments of elegiac love poems concerned with the passing pleasures of youth.

1 *Thasos*: an island off the coast of Thrace famous for its gold mines. 2 *Naxos*: the largest and most fertile of the Cyclades, the islands round Delos. It was famous for its wine. 3 The island of *Crete* had a reputation as the home of lawgivers. *Samos*, an island off western Asia Minor, was the birthplace of Pythagoras. On it also was situated the temple of Hera, built *c*.560, the largest of its time in the Greek world. 5–8 *Lydia* was a territory in the west of Asia Minor, famous for the musical innovation of the Lydian mode, a scale appropriate to soft pathos. 8 *dedal*: skilful, fertile of invention, from Daedalus, the legendary Athenian craftsman who constructed the Cretan Labyrinth. 11–12 *Priapus*, the son of Dionysus and Aphrodite, was a god of fertility. His attribute was the phallic club, and his statue was often placed in gardens.

**45   Hegemon to Praxinoe**   The text is that of 1846.

In her letter to 'Aspasia' which includes this poem 'Cleone' explains that these 'loose Dithyrambics' arose from the fact that Hegemon's 'cousin Praxinoë, whom he was not aware of loving, until she was betrothed to Callias, a merchant of Samos, was married a few months ago' (XLIX).

**46   [Artemia: from Myrtis]** and **47   [Pentheusa: from Myrtis]**   The texts are those of 1846, where **47** was entitled 'From Myrtis'. Myrtis is a Boeotian poetess no fragment of whose work remains. She is said to have been the instructress of Corinna and Pindar. The other names are unspecific.

**47**   11 *Eros*: god of love.

**48   [War]**   The text is that of 1846. The war on which this poem is a comment is that between Athens and the island of Samos in 440 BC; see note on *Pericles and Aspasia*, introducing PROSE **22–41**, and Pericles's speech, PROSE **37**.

**49   [The Rites of Bacchus: from Alcaeus]**   The text is that of 1846.

Bacchus is the god of wine; Alcaeus, a lyric poet from Lesbos, of the seventh to the sixth century BC. His remaining fragments often concern the themes of wine and love.

**50   A Moral**   The text is that of 1846. Attributed to the philosopher 'Anaxagoras'; see note on *Pericles and Aspasia*, PROSE **39.**

**51   Ode to Miletus**   The text is that of 1859.

Attributed to 'Aspasia' who came from Miletus, the Ionian city with a famous harbour, on the coast of Asia Minor near the mouth of the Maeander. 1–4 Zeus (*Jove*) fell in love with Europa, daughter of the King of Tyre, and assuming the form of a bull enticed her on to his back, and so bore her away by swimming to Crete. There she gave birth to Minos, Rhadamanthus, and, according to some, Sarpedon. The dynasty of Minos is associated with the earliest European high civilization. 5–6 Phrixus and *Helle* escaped from the murderous intent of their step-mother on a winged and golden-fleeced ram, carrying them across the sea. Helle fell off into the part of the sea called accordingly the Hellespont. Miletus took the leading part in founding settlements in the region of the Hellespont and the Black Sea. 7–12 Leander, a youth of Abydos on the southern shore of the Hellespont, loved Hero, a priestess of Aphrodite at Sestos on the northern shore, where the strait is narrowest. Leander would swim across at night, until one tempestuous night he was drowned, and Hero in despair threw herself into the strait. The *Star* (9) is the lamp in Hero's tower which guided him. This and other details come from Musaeus's 'Hero and Leander'. 14 Byzantium is the famous city at the mouth of the Thracian Bosporus, on the shore of the Propontis, opposite the Hellespont. 21–4 Byzantium was actually established by Megarian colonists *c*. 657 BC, but other groups of colonists may also have contributed. 49–51 Arctinus of Miletus was an epic poet, *c*. eighth century BC. The other allusion is to blind, wandering Homer. 52 *Melesander* of Miletus wrote of the fight between the Lapiths and the Centaurs. It was Orpheus, the mythic poet, who was torn to death by Thracian women. 60 There is a popular belief that if a scorpion is surrounded by fire it will sting itself to death with its own tail.

**52 Erinna to Love** The text is that of 1846.
Erinna was a poetess of the Dorian island of Telos flourishing at the end of the fourth century BC.

**53 [From Sappho]** The text is that of 1846.
For Sappho, see note on **7 [Imitation from Sappho].**

**54 Sappho to Hesperus** The text is that of 1846.
For Hesperus, see note on **10 [Ianthe Awaited]**, 16.

**55 [Beauty]** The text is that of 1846.
Attributed to 'Anaxagoras'; see note on *Pericles and Aspasia*, PROSE **39**, 1.

**56 The Shades of Agamemnon and Iphigeneia** The text is that of 1859, where the speakers' names are capitalized and placed in the centre of the page above their speeches.
Attributed to 'Aspasia' who writes in her letter to 'Cleone': 'I imagine then Agamemnon to descend from his horrible death, and to meet instantly his daughter. By the nature of things, by the suddenness of the event, Iphigeneia can have heard nothing of her mother's double crime, adultery and murder' (CCXXV).
Iphigeneia was the daughter of Agamemnon and Clytemnestra. When the Greeks were on their way to the Trojan War they were detained at Aulis by contrary winds. Iphigeneia was required to be sacrificed to appease the wrath of Diana and, according to Aeschylus, was killed. On Agamemnon's return to Argos after the war, again in Aeschylus, he was murdered by his wife Clytemnestra and her paramour Aegisthus.
7 *Pallas* Athena was the patroness of Athens and of Greek cities in general. She ruthlessly pursued the good of the state. 35–42 After the overthrow of Cronos, Zeus and his brothers divided the universe by casting lots. Zeus (whose attribute was the eagle) obtained heaven, *Poseidon* the sea, and Hades (*Pluto*) the underworld. 58 *Incestuous Helen*: Helen became the wife of Paris after he carried her off from her original husband, Menelaus (the brother of Agamemnon), with whom she subsequently was reconciled. 64 Erebus is the primeval darkness; *Elysium* is the place where those favoured by the gods enjoy a pleasant life after death. 65–6 *Argos* was the country of which Agamemnon was king. It had *Mycenae* for its capital. 72–3 Agamemnon in Aeschylus is stabbed to death in a bath. 76 *Charon*: see note on **28 Dirce**, 3. 121 The daughter and son of Agamemnon, *Electra* and *Orestes*, subsequently avenged their father's death by killing Clytemnestra and Aegisthus. 128/9 *The Hours*: three season goddesses who, according to Hesiod, bring law, justice and peace. 132 *Lethèan spring*: Lethe is a river in Hades which bestows oblivion on those who drink its waters. 133 Agamemnon was a son of Atreus. 149–50 Persephone; see note on **15 Regeneration**, 67–70. 166 The Scamander is a river flowing past Troy into the Hellespont. 181 *Pelides*: Achilles was the son of Peleus. 188 *Dardans*: the Trojans who followed Priam, son or grandson of Dardanus. 189, 207 *Io Paean*: an invocation in a hymn of thanksgiving addressed to Apollo which formed the refrain. 194–205 An obscure passage. In the *Iliad* Diomedes,

the son of *Tydeus* (197), exchanged his for the golden arms of the *Lycian* (195) leader Glaucus. (He and *Ajax* also shared the arms of the other Lycian leader, Sarpedon, after duelling for them). After the death of Achilles (203), the arms which his mother *Thetis* (202) had had made for him by Hephaestus were claimed by both Ajax and Odysseus. When the latter was awarded them by the vote of the Trojan captives Ajax went mad with disappointment, and later killed himself, according to the *Odyssey* and, later, Sophocles and Ovid. There is probably an allusion (198–9) to the legend related by Pausanias that, when Odysseus was shipwrecked off the coast of Sicily, the arms of Achilles were cast up on the tomb of Ajax, on the promontory of Rhoeteum at the entrance to the Hellespont. The idea of Diomedes throwing the arms of Glaucus to his friend Ajax seems to be Landor's addition.

**57–64**  The texts of these poems are those of 1846.

**57  Farewell to Italy**  Originally published in *The Book of Beauty* for 1837. It commemorates his return to England in 1835. 7 *Fiesole*: see note on **25 Fiesolan Idyl**. *Valdarno*: the valley of the river Arno onto which Landor's garden at Fiesole looked out. 8–9 *Affrico* is a stream in the garden at the Villa Gherardesca at Fiesole. There Boccaccio's ladies bathed at the end of the First Day in the *Decameron*. 13 See **38 For an Epitaph at Fiesole.**

**58  To My Child Carlino**  Originally published in *The Pentameron and Pentalogia*, 1837.
Carlino is Landor's third and youngest son, Charles, born 1825. 40 *Walter* is Landor's second son, born 1822. 58 Calypso is the nymph of the island of Ogygie in the *Odyssey* who kept Odysseus for seven years, and promised him perpetual youth and immortality if he would stay with her; but Odysseus left her.

**59  Walter Tyrrel and William Rufus**  Originally published in *The Pentameron and Pentalogia*, 1837, where the scene is set: 'The New Forest, August 2, 1100'.
William II, d. 1100, was King of England from 1087 till his death. Walter Tyrrel was actually the son of the Lord of Poix in Picardy. He held the manor of Langham, Essex. Tyrrel's responsibility for the death of William II has never been finally established. The see of Winchester, as with many sees and abbeys during William's reign, had in fact been left vacant, so that the king could enjoy their revenues.

**60  [The Message]**  Originally published in *The Examiner*, 12 August 1838.

**61  [To Psyche]**  Originally published in *The Examiner*, 23 September 1838. In *The Book of Beauty* for 1842 it was entitled 'To . . . 1808' and dated June 1808; but Landor actually set sail to volunteer in the Spanish revolt two months later, on 9 August.

**62  To a Painter**  Originally published in *The Examiner*, 23 September 1838.
It is addressed to William Fisher, whose portrait of Landor is in the National Portrait Gallery.

**63 Henry The Eighth and Anne Boleyn. Scene in Richmond Chase**  Originally published in *The Book of Beauty* for 1839, where Landor gives the date as 'May 19, 1536'.

It is the second of 'Two Dramatic Scenes' entitled jointly **Henry The Eighth and Anne Boleyn** in the 1846 edition. The first is set on the day before the second, in the Tower of London. Anne Boleyn is presented with the Writ of Execution by the Constable of the Tower.

Anne Boleyn, 1507?–36, was the second wife of Henry VIII, 1491–1547, for whom he divorced Katharine of Aragon in 1527. They married in 1533, but the birth of a daughter in September failing to provide a male heir deeply disturbed Henry, who soon became involved with Jane Seymour. In 1536, after the miscarriage of a son, Anne was brought to trial for adultery and incest. She was condemned and beheaded; cf. the Conversation 'Henry VIII and Anne Boleyn', PROSE **7**.

8 *The Lady Katharine Parr*: Catherine Parr, 1512–48, was to become Henry's sixth and final queen. 23 Jane Seymour, 1509?–37, was lady-in-waiting to Henry's first two queens and became his third. They were married less than two weeks after Anne's execution, and she died giving birth to a son (later Edward VI), in 1537.

**64  On Seeing a Lady Sit for Her Portrait**  Originally published in *The Book of Beauty* for 1840, where there is an engraving of the portrait in question. It was of Miss Rose Paynter by William Fisher. She was the daughter of Rose Aylmer's half-sister, Sophia Price, (see the note on **6 [Rose Aylmer]**) and came to know Landor well in his later days at Bath.

**Fra Rupert**  The text is that of 1846. The scenes are printed in entirety. The full original title continues: 'The Last Part of a Trilogy: The First Being Andrea of Hungary, the Second Being Giovanna of Naples'.

This sequence of plays took its inception from Landor's reading of Anna Jameson's *Memoirs of Celebrated Female Sovereigns*, 1831.

In this final part, Giovanna, Queen of Naples, 1326–82, has taken as her third husband Otho of Brunswick, and has been excommunicated by Pope Urban VI. The Pope persuades her adopted son, Charles of Durazzo, to usurp, and he is duly crowned as King of Naples. According to Landor's version, Otho desperately attempts to rescue his wife, is wounded and dies in her arms. (He was actually imprisoned and released after her death). Giovanna refuses to abdicate and is murdered. Fra Rupert, the villainous, Iago-like monk, whose machinations Landor involves in these disasters, stabs himself on her funeral day to escape justice. The scandalous Giovanna of history is idealized into an embodiment of suffering femininity.

**65  [Act V] Scene IV**  The castle of Muro Lucano is sixty miles from Naples on the road to Brindisi, where Giovanna was actually suffocated in 1382.

**66  [Act V] Scene V**  Maximin and Stephen are shepherds from Hungary. Maximin has been misled into deserting his guard over Giovanna at Muro.

25 *Santa Chiara* is the great early fourteenth-century church and Franciscan convent at Naples.

**68  [From Moschus] and 69  [Imitation from Catullus]**  They were originally published in 'An Essay on Catullus' in *The Foreign Quarterly Review*, July 1842. The texts are those of 1853.

Moschus, *c.* 150 BC, was a pastoral poet of Syracuse. The first is a 'translation' of his Idyl III, 99–104. For Catullus, see note on **31 Old Style**, 2. The second is 'offered as a kind of paraphrase' of his Carmen IV.

**70  The Hamadryad**  Originally published in *The Foreign Quarterly Review*, October 1842, where it was introduced with the following note: 'In the poem we subjoin we claim no merit of imitation. The subject was taken from a short note of the scholiast on Pindar; and our readers may wonder and regret that it attracted no earlier and abler pen. Our hope is that it will be found of that order of simplicity which is simple in the manner of Theocritus'. The text is that of 1859.

The note referred to is in the volume Forster sent him to review, *Pindar's Epinician and Triumphal Odes*: 'Charon of Lampsacus relates a singular story about Rhoecus of Cnidus, who, having preserved an oak-tree from falling, was rewarded at his request by the love of the Hamadryad, whose life depended on that of the tree, on condition that he would abstain from all intercourse with mortal women; the goddess was to send a bee as her messenger when she intended to visit him. The messenger of love having on one occasion made its appearance while Rhoecus was engaged in a game of draughts, he uttered a peevish remark which incensed the Nymph . . .' (ed. J. W. Donaldson, London, 1841, p. 386).

A Hamadryad is a tree nymph. There is a sequel to the poem: 'Acon and Rhodope; or, Inconstancy'.

2 Cnidus is an ancient city of *Caria*, a region in SW Asia Minor. 7 *Pandion* is a small town on a headland in SW Caria. 8 *Athenè*: see note on **56 The Shades of Agamemnon and Iphigeneia**, 7. 12–22 *her Whose laws all follow*: Aphrodite, of whom one of the most famous statues of the ancient world by Praxiteles was located at Cnidus. She had an amorous intrigue with *Ares*, god of war. For *Zeus, Poseidon* and *Dis* (Hades), see **56 The Shades of Agamemnon and Iphigeneia**, 35–42. For the story of Dis and Persephone, see **15 Regeneration**, 67–70. For *Styx*, see note on **28 Dirce**, 3. 75–168 In 1859 the speakers' names are capitalized and placed in the centre of the page above their speeches. 94 *Cydonian bow*: from Cydonia, a city of NW Crete, the island famous for its archers. 132–5 Paris, brought up by shepherds on Mount Ida, south of the Hellespont, judged the contest between Hera, Athene and Aphrodite as to whom should be awarded the golden apple inscribed 'For the Fairest'. He gave the prize to Aphrodite who offered him the loveliest woman for his wife. With her help he accordingly carried off Helen, thus bringing about the Trojan War. 144 *Here*: the sister and consort of Zeus, she was the protectress of marriage. 243 *the Hours*: see note on **56 The Shades of Agamemnon and Iphigeneia**, 128/9.

**71  To My Daughter**  First published in *Blackwood's Magazine*, March 1843. The text is that of 1846.

Julia Landor was born in Pisa on 6 March 1819. The family did not move to Florence till the spring of 1821.

1–2 In the *Inferno*, Canto XXXIII, Dante has Count Ugolino recount how the Archbishop of Pisa had him and his four sons imprisoned in a tower and starved to death. 6 *the Hours*: see note on **56 The Shades of Agamemnon**

**and Iphigeneia**, 128/9. 13 Landor had a bust of Julia made by the sculptor Pozzi. 15–18 Julia visited her father in Bath from Florence in May 1843.

**72  On Southey's Death**  First published in *The Examiner*, 25 March 1843. The text is that of 1858.

For Southey, see note on the Conversation 'Southey and Porson', PROSE **2**. Southey died 21 March 1843.

9 *after saddest silence*: Since his second marriage in 1839 Southey's mind had failed him.

**73  To Robert Browning**  First published in the *Morning Chronicle*, 22 November 1845. The text is that of 1846.

Landor met the young Browning (1812–89) in London literary society in 1836, and became one of his most outspoken early admirers. Browning acknowledged his encouragement publicly in *Sordello*, 1840, and dedicated the final number of *Bells and Pomegranates*, 1846, containing 'Luria' and 'A Soul's Tragedy', to Landor.

10–13 Browning had been in the south of Italy in the autumn of 1844, arriving at Naples by ship. 13–14 One of the Sirens (fabulous creatures accredited with the power of drawing men to destruction by their songs), Parthenope, was supposed to have been washed ashore in the bay of Naples.

**74  [One Year Ago]**  Originally published in *The Keepsake* for 1846, where it is entitled 'Lines'. The text is that of *Works*, 1846.

**75  [Shakespeare]**  Added to the Conversation 'Abbé Delille and Walter Landor' in 1846. The text is that of 1846.

**76  The Death of Artemidora**  First published in two different versions in *Works*, 1846. The first version is in the text of the reprinted *Pericles and Aspasia*; the second, which is the basis of the later version printed here, in the 'Hellenics' section of the poems. The text is that of 1859.

The first version is introduced in a letter from 'Cleone' to 'Aspasia': 'Artemidora of Ephesus was betrothed to Elpenor, and their nuptials . . . were at hand . . .' (LXXXV).

11 *Iris*: the messenger of the gods. 19 After this line, the first version has three extra lines:

> With her that old boat incorruptible,
> Unwearied, undiverted in its course,
> Had plash'd the water up the farther strand.

**77  [Lethe's Water]**  First included in *Pericles and Aspasia* (CCXIX), *Works*, 1846, where it is attributed to 'Aspasia'. For Lethe, see note on **56 The Shades of Agamemnon and Iphigeneia**, 132.

**78  Thrasymedes and Eunöe**  The text is that of 1859.

Landor's immediate source was probably J. A. St John's *The History of the Manners and Customs of Ancient Greece*, 3 vols., London, 1842, I, 417. Wheeler notes that the story occurs also in Plutarch, Polyaenus, Dante and *The Spectator*, 4 November 1712 (ed., *Poetical Works*, II, 511). 20 *Cecropian port*: Cecrops was the mythical first king of Athens whose tomb was on the Acropolis. He

instituted marriage. 31 *the Parthenon*: the temple of Athene Parthenos (Pallas),
'the maiden', on the Acropolis at Athens. 35 For *Pallas*, see note on **56 The
Shades of Agamemnon and Iphigeneia**, 7. *Artemis*: the moon goddess, a
virgin huntress, to whom a sanctuary was dedicated on the Acropolis. 36
*Aphrodite*: the goddess of love; for *Herè*, see note on **70 The Hamadryad**, 144.
45 *Pisistratos*: the Tyrant of Athens, 560–27 BC. 52 *Piraeus*: a fortified promon-
tory with three harbours, near Athens.

**79   Icarios and Erigonè**   The text is that of 1859.
   The immediate source was probably J. A. St John's *The History of the Manners
and Customs of Ancient Greece*, I, 354. The story occurs in Nonnus, 'Apollodorus',
and Plutarch.
   Icarios was an Athenian who hospitably received Dionysus when he came
to Attica and in return was taught the cultivation of the vine. When he was
murdered, he was thrown into a well where he was discovered by his daughter
and her dog.
   5 *Pallas*: see note on **56 The Shades of Agamemnon and Iphigeneia**, 7.
106 *Moera*: her dog. 114–15 Erigonè in despair hanged herself and was changed
into the constellation Virgo, her father into the star *Boötes* and the dog into
the star named Canicula. 116 *the Eumenides*: see note on **14 To Corinth**, 20.
125–8 In the original story a pestilence fell on Ceos where the murderers were
received. Landor evokes another feast, that of the Lapiths, to which the
Centaurs were invited, and which resulted in carnage.

**80   Iphigeneia and Agamemnon**   The text is that of 1859. See note on **56
The Shades of Agamemnon and Iphigeneia.**
   5 *Calchas*: the seer who declared that Artemis required the sacrifice of
Iphigeneia. 13 *Olympus*: the mountain on the northern boundary of Greece
whose summit was regarded as the seat of the gods. 26–36 J. A. St John
explains that, before marriage, girls were regarded as belonging to the train
of Artemis, whose permission was sought with baskets of offerings to transfer
their worship to Hymen. The future bride was conducted to a sacrifice in the
citadel offered up to Athena. On her altar, and on those of several other gods,
she deposited a lock of her hair, 'in remoter ages, perhaps, the whole of it'
(*The History of the Manners and Customs of Ancient Greece*, II, 13). 27 *Artemis*: see
note on **78 Thrasymedes and Eunöe**, 35. 33 *Hymen* is the god of marriage.
35–6 *Athena*: Landor notes: 'Pallas Athena was the patroness of Argos'. She is
depicted with blue eyes.

**81–126.** Except where otherwise indicated, the texts of these poems are those
of 1846.

**81   [Proem]**   This poem was prefixed to 'Miscellaneous' poems in *Works*,
1846.

**82   [The Torch of Love]**   1 *torch*: Wheeler corrected the 1846 misprint,
'touch'.

**84   [Chill Beauty], 86   [Love for Life], 88   Ianthe's Troubles,** and
**90   [Ianthe Threatened]**   For 'Ianthe', see note on **9 [Wish for Ianthe].**

**88 Ianthe's Troubles** The text is that of 1858.

**91 [The Duller Olive]** 2 *Myrtle*: made into wreaths for victors at the Olympian games. 3 *olive*: Besides being the symbol of peace, it was also made into a crown which was the highest prize at the Olympian games, and the highest distinction bestowed upon a citizen deserving well of his country.

**100 For an Urn in Thoresby Park** See note on **36 Another Urn at Thoresby Park** 15–16 Riou: Captain Edward, 1758?–1801, was cut in two by cannon-shot as, severely wounded, he encouraged his men at the Battle of Copenhagen. Parliament voted a monument to his memory in St Paul's Cathedral.

**102 [Return]** Written at Bath in 1839 to Lady Graves Sawle (i.e. Rose Paynter; see note on **64 On Seeing a Lady Sit for Her Portrait)** who had spent the previous winter in Paris.

**105 [Favourite Painters]** 1 Raphael, 1483–1520, *Titian* (4), *c*. 1490–1576, and *Correggio* (5), *c*. 1494–1534, are Italian Renaissance painters. 7 Rubens: Peter Paul, 1577–1640, a Flemish painter. 8 Rembrandt, 1606–69, a Dutch painter. 9 Poussin, Nicolas, 1594–1665, and *Claude* Lorrain (12), 1600–82, are French neo-classical painters. 12 Ausonia is an ancient name for Italy.

**107 [War in China]** Written *c*. 1840. Great Britain had provoked the Opium War in China, 1839–42, to obtain commercial concessions.
  2 *Kong-Fu-Tsi*: the Chinese sage Confucius, *c*. 551–479? BC.

**108 [Ternissa]** See note on the Conversation 'Epicurus, Leontion and Ternissa', PROSE **16**. 10 For *Persephone* and Pluto (Hades) (12), see note on **15 Regeneration**, 67–70.

**109 [What Remains]** 7–8 Horace (*Satires* II, iii) writes of Clodius, son of Aesop the tragedian, who drew a pearl of great value from his ear, melted it in vinegar, and drank to the health of Cecilia Metella. 11 For *the myrtle*, see note on **91 [The Duller Olive]**, 2; for *the bay*, see note on **43 Corinna to Tanagra**, 40.

**111 [Memory and Pride]** See note on **9 [Wish for Ianthe]**.

**112 To J. S.** The text is that of 1858.
  To Jane Sophia Swift, 'Ianthe'; see note on **9 [Wish for Ianthe]**.

**113 [Sedater Pleasures]** 31 *Essex*: Robert Devereux, second Earl of Essex, 1567–1601, English courtier and favourite of *Queen Bess* (32), Elizabeth I, 1533–1601.

**114 Malvolio** Ostensibly addressed to the joyless Puritan in Shakespeare's *Twelfth Night*; but references to the moon, daffodil, daisy, and thrush probably allude to subjects of Wordsworth's lyric poetry.

**115 Good-Bye** The text is that of 1858.

**117   [The Fiesolan Villa]**   See note on **25 Fiesolan Idyl**. 2 *that villa with its tower*: Landor's own Villa Gherardesca. 16 *Valdarno*: see note on **57 Farewell to Italy**, 7. 18 *The abbey*: The unfinished façade of the fifteenth-century Badia Fiesolana is dark green and white. 20 *the Doccia's font*: The *Doccia* was a fifteenth-century convent. 21 *two ruin'd castles*: Castel di Poggio and Castello di Vincigliata. 22 Maiano is a village; the mill is Podere Molinaccio. 31 *The graceful tower of Giotto*: Giotto, *c.* 1266–*c.* 1337, the Florentine painter and architect, began the bell tower at the side of the west front of the Duomo (32), the Cathedral of Florence.

**119   [For a Grave in Widcombe Church-Yard]**   At Bath *c.* 1842 Landor bought a plot of land for his grave at Widcombe nearby.

**121   Plays**   The text is that of 1858.

**122   To Julius Hare with 'Pericles and Aspasia'**   Landor was friendly with three of the four Hare brothers – Francis, Augustus and their younger brother Julius, 1795–1855. Julius became Archdeacon of Lewes and was a specialist in German literature and the classics, enthusiasms which coalesced in his translation, with Thirlwall, of Niebuhr's *History of Rome*. For *Pericles and Aspasia*, see note introducing PROSE **22–41**.
   12 *Phidias*: the Greek sculptor, *c.* 490–*c.* 48 BC, commissioned by Pericles to contribute to the adornment of *the Parthenon* (15); see note on **78 Thrasymedes and Eunöe**, 31. 15–16 The frieze from the outside walls of the Parthenon and some of the metopes were acquired by Lord Elgin and sold to the British Government. 17 Landor wrote the original *Pericles and Aspasia* at Fiesole in 1835. 21–5 Francis Hare died at Palermo, Sicily, in 1842. 39 The Prussian Field-Marshal, Gebhard Leberecht von Blucher, 1742–1819, was an outstanding opponent of Napoleon and the leader in the War of Liberation, 1813–14. 40 Tyrtaeus was a Spartan poet, *c.* the middle of the seventh century BC. His war-songs encouraged his countrymen in their war against the Messenians. Ernst Moritz *Arndt*, 1769–1860, was a German nationalist poet one of whose popular songs was 'Was blasen die Trompeten?'. He wrote a quatrain in praise of 'Freiheit' to Landor after he had met him at Bonn in 1832.

**123   To Southey**   For Southey, see note on the Conversation 'Southey and Porson', PROSE **2**. 10–11 In the *Odyssey*, Book VI, Nausicaa describes the poplar wood of her father Alcinous, King of the Phaeacians. It is sacred to Athene and comprises a royal park and vegetable garden. 12–14 In the *Iliad*, Book VI, Hector's son, Astyanax, is frightened by his father's horse-hair helmet plume. His mother was Andromache, and he was thrown from the Trojan battlements after the capture of the city. 15 *Olympus*: see note on **80 Iphigeneia and Agamemnon**, 13. 17 *Simöis*: a river flowing past Troy into the Hellespont. 19–21 Pindar, the choral lyric poet, was born near Thebes in 522 or 518 BC. He is chiefly famous for his odes celebrating athletic victories.

**124   Lines on the Death of Charles Lamb**   Landor met Lamb the essayist, 1775–1834, whose pseudonym was 'Elia', in 1832, at Enfield near London.

**125   To Miss Isabella Percy**   Wheeler identifies the addressee as the daughter of Lord Charles Percy, of Guy's Cliffe, near Warwick (ed., *Poetical Works*, III, 25).

**126 To a Bride, Feb. 17, 1846**  Rose Paynter (see note on **64 On Seeing a Lady Sit for Her Portrait**) married Charles B. Graves Sawle, the eldest son of a Cornish baronet, on 18 February 1846. Landor attended the wedding at Walcot.

**127 Pan and Pitys**  The text is that of 1847. This is the first of two English translations of the Latin original published in 1815.

Landor probably derived the story from Pierre Bayle's *Historical and Critical Dictionary*. It is also referred to by Lucian. Pan is the nature god, half-goatish in shape, and especially concerned with the fertility of flocks, who comes from Arcadia (4), the district in the Peloponnesus which was, according to Virgil, the home of pastoral simplicity and happiness. Pitys is the nymph of the fir-tree.

5 *Styx*: See **28 Dirce**, 3. It was also the name of a little river falling down a cliff on Mount Aroanius in Arcadia. 7 *Boreas*: the north wind, depicted as winged, with rough hair and beard. 18 *he who rules Olympus*: Zeus. 23–9 This story is referred to in Virgil's *Georgics*, III, 391 ff., and in the commentaries of Servius and 'Probus'. *Cynthia* is the moon-goddess. 34 *Selinos*: a river of Elis, sometimes referred to as part of Arcadia. 42–6 This incident seems to have been invented by Landor. 67 *philomel*: the nightingale, according to Latin authors. 68 *Padan glades*: The Padus (modern Po) is Italy's longest river. 71 *Cytoros*: a mountain in Paphlagonia, covered, according to Virgil, with box-trees. 73 *Lycaean Knolls*: Lycaeus is a mountain of Arcadia. 76 *Hesperus*: see **10 [Ianthe Awaited]**, 16. 77 *Tethys*: see **5 Crysaor**, 18. 104–5 *that lynx-skin down Which Bacchus gave me*: Pan was identified by the Romans with Faunus. Fauns and leopards are often depicted in the train of *Bacchus*; cf. note on **Gebir, 2 Book I**, 1–11. 150 *Jove's brother*: Poseidon; see note on **56 The Shades of Agamemnon and Iphigeneia**, 35–42. 151–4 *Ismaros* is a mountain on the south coast of Thrace – a haunt of Orpheus, the legendary poet, who went down to Hades to recover his dead wife, Eurydice, and lost her again by disobeying the condition that he should not look back. Landor may also be evoking the story of Orithyia from Ovid. She was the daughter of the King of Athens whom Boreas carried away by force to Thrace. *The Manes* are the spirits of the dead.

**128 Silenus**  The text is that of 1847.

1–6 See **Gebir, 2 Book I**, 1-11. The first six lines of these pieces are similar. This piece proceeds to refer more exactly to Virgil's Sixth Eclogue from which *Chromis* (24) and *Mnasylos* (28) are taken.

**129–152** The texts of these poems are those of 1853.

**129 To Verona**  Originally published in *The Examiner*, 16 September 1848.

11 *that theater*: probably the Arena, the largest Roman amphitheatre in existence after the Colosseum. (There also remains a Roman Theatre, founded under Augustus). 13–18 Verona was the birth place of Catullus; (see note on **31 Old Style**, 2). *Coelius* and *Aufilena* appear in the poems of Catullus. *Lesbia* is the name he gave his mistress, and her sparrow is the subject of Carmina

II and III. 19 ff *One there is. . . :* Shakespeare. 21–3 *Romeo and Juliet* is set 'In fair Verona'. 25–6 *This lone tomb One greater than you walls have ever seen:* The fourteenth-century Tomb of Juliet remains. 27 Manto was the prophetess daughter of Tiresias from whom Mantua, situated between Cremona and Verona, derives its name. Mantua is the birth place of Virgil who studied at Rome and was to celebrate the Empire.

**130 Dying Speech of an Old Philosopher** Originally published in *The Examiner*, 3 February 1849. The text is punctuated as in 1853, where it was reprinted as an epigraph in capitals. The capitalization here is that of the MS facsimile in Forster's *Landor*, II, 464.

Written on the night of the day that Forster and Dickens had visited Landor at Bath to celebrate his seventy-fourth birthday.

**131 To the Author of 'Festus' on the Classick and Romantick** In 1853 it was published in the 'Epistles' section. ll. 35–51, 63–4, 86–7, 90–2, 97–101, 112, and 134 were added in 1853.

Philip James Bailey, 1815–1902, was the author of *Festus*, a cosmic blank verse poem on the lines of *Faust*.

15 *cestus:* a contrivance of leather loaded with metal and wound round the hands of Roman boxers to weight their blows. 24–6 Cf. Genesis 1;2:1–3. 48–9 Ovid's grave is at Tomis, on the Black Sea, where he died AD 18. In his exile, he gave a picture of the Getae, a fierce, long-haired Thracian nation, learnt their language and composed in it a song of triumph for Augustus. 50–1 Cardinal Pietro Bembo, 1470–1547, the Italian humanist and historiographer of Venice who wrote prose and verse in Latin as well as Italian. 60 *Marmion:* 'A Tale of Flodden Field', 1808, the romantic epic by Walter Scott. 62 *Achaians:* Greek followers of the Homeric kings, Agamemnon and Menelaus. 63–4 Thomas Campbell, 1777–1844, wrote the 'Battle of Hohenlinden', commemorating the defeat of the Austrians by the revolutionary French in Bavaria, and 'The Battle of the Baltic'. 72 *Pheidias:* see note on **122 To Julius Hare with 'Pericles and Aspasia'**, 12. 73–8 Milton, with allusion to his *Paradise Lost* and *Samson Agonistes.* Landor suggests that Milton was influenced by Italian writers such as Tasso, in the choruses and lyrical passages of *Aminta* (see note on **136 On Swift Joining Avon Near Rugby**, 10–12), Guarini and Andreini. 78 *Sampson:* sic. 82 *Belial:* a Biblical personification of evil and worthlessness. 85 *Goldsmith:* Oliver, 1728–74; *Gray:* Thomas, 1716–71. 86 *Collins:* William, 1721–59, became melancholic and finally insane. 87 *Shelley,* 1792–1822, and *Keats,* 1795–1821, both died in Italy. 88 *Cowper:* William, 1731–1800. 91 *Canning:* George, 1719–96, became Prime Minister in 1827. He was the leading spirit behind the *Anti-Jacobin,* started in support of the English Constitution, a parodist and poet. *Frere:* John Hookham, 1769–1846, was a diplomat, translator of Aristophanes, and author of the burlesque poem *Arthur and the Round Table. Smith:* Robert Percy, 1770–1845, the lesser known brother of Sydney Smith, was a writer of fine epitaphs. 93–6. Felicia Dorothea Hemans, 1793–1835, the poetess. Among her works are 'Ivan the Czar' and 'Casabianca' ('The boy stood on the burning deck'). 98 Aphrodite was worshipped at Paphos, a city in Cyprus. The Amazons were a race of female warriors from Scythia. 101 *bays:* see note on **43 Corinna to Tanagra**, 40. 104–12 A reference to *The Excursion*, published 1814, and its principal character, the Wanderer, who is a *pedlar.* 116–17 The quotation marks, wrongly omitted in 1853, are

restored. The words come from *Paradise Lost*, Book I, 460–1, and refer to the Philistine god, Dagon, cast down and mutilated in the presence of the ark of the Lord. 119 *Southey*: see note on the Conversation 'Southey and Porson', PROSE **2**. 133 *The graceful son of Maia*: Hermes who invented the lyre and is the patron of literature. 136 For *Apollo*, see note on **43 Corinna to Tanagra**, 15–16.

**132  To The Reverend Cuthbert Southey**  Originally published in *The Examiner*, 26 January 1850. In 1853 it was published in the 'Epistles' section.

Charles Cuthbert Southey was the only surviving son of Robert Southey, for whom see note on the Conversation 'Southey and Porson', PROSE **2**.

5–8 Landor met Robert Southey in April 1808 at Bristol where Southey was born. Perhaps Landor had read some of Southey's early translations from Bion and Moschus (1794), the epic *Joan of Arc* (1796), or the *Letters Written during a Short Residence in Spain and Portugal* (1797). He had reviewed 'Gebir' in 1799; see note on **154 Apology For Gebir**, 17–24. 9–10 Southey visited Landor at Llanthony (see note on **32 [Fiesolan Musings]**, 35–40) for two days in August 1811. 13 *Hondy*: a river rising in Breconshire and flowing into Monmouthshire past Llanthony. 17 *Comioy*: Cwmiou is a hamlet. 18–22 Landor claimed that his house was alone in Tours in not being used for the billeting of French troops defeated at Waterloo. 25–7 Southey visited Landor at Como for three days in June 1817. The previous year Southey had lost his first-born son. 29 *Bellagio*: a resort on Lake Como. *Valintelvi*: Val d'Intelvi, between Lake Lugano and Lake Como. 30 *Monterosa*: the Alpine mass separating Italian Piedmont from the Swiss Valais. *Helvetia*: the Roman name for the western part of modern Switzerland.

**133  [In Memory of Lady Blessington]**  Originally published in *The Examiner*, 23 March 1850.

Marguerite Power, a young Irish widow, married Charles, Earl of Blessington, in 1818. Landor met them when they visited Florence in 1827. They were the centre of a scandalous entourage. For some time in the 1830s she acted as Landor's unofficial literary agent, and in 1836 took Gore House, Kensington, where Landor frequently stayed, attending her salon, while in London. She died in June, 1849.

20 *Where the man-queen was born*: Elizabeth I, born at Greenwich. 22 *Where . . . man*: Oliver Cromwell who died in Whitehall. 23–4 She was buried at Chambourcy, near St Germain-en-Laye, outside Paris.

**134  Remonstrance and Reply**  Originally published in *Leigh Hunt's Journal*, 15 February 1851.

**135  To Age**  Originally published in *The Examiner*, 5 June 1852.

**136  On Swift Joining Avon near Rugby**  Originally published in *The Examiner*, 21 August 1852.

8 For *Fiesole*, see note on **25 Fiesolan Idyl**. 10–12 Milton's elegy 'Lycidas' was probably influenced by the irregularly rhymed passages in the *Aminta* of Torquato *Tasso*, 1544–95. 17 *Latian feet*: Latin metre. 37–8 'Ianthe', Jane Sophia Swift; see note on **9 [Wish for Ianthe]**. 45 *that sacred River*: the Avon, running through Shakespeare's native Stratford. 47–8 *Maenads*: the female

attendants on Bacchus; io-evohe is the cry of their frenzied rites. 49–56 John Wycliffe, 1330/2–84, the theologian and reformer, was buried in the churchyard at Lutterworth, Leics. But in 1428, his body was exhumed and burnt, and his ashes cast into the Swift by order of a Papal commission. He denied the doctrine of transubstantiation, maintained the sole authority of scripture, and the right of the laity to confiscate church property.

**137–147**   These poems were published in the 'Epigrams' section in 1853.

**138   On Catullus**   For Catullus, see note on **31 Old Style**, 2. 2 *Sirmio*: a promontory on the southern shore of Lake Garda where Catullus had a villa. 3–4. There are three Graces, goddesses who bestow beauty and charm, one of whom is Thalia, the muse of comedy. 6 *nectar*: the drink of the gods, conferring immortality.

**139   [Pure Pleasures]**   1 *Bacchus*: See **Gebir**, **2 Book I**, 1.

**140   [Ireland]**   5 *Tara*: a hill in county Meath, where the Kings of Ireland were enthroned.

**141   [To Mazzini]**   Giuseppe Mazzini, the Italian patriot and revolutionary, 1805?–72. After imprisonment for political conspiracy he later lived in London, plotting the liberation of Italy and union under a liberal government. He returned to Rome in 1848 during the revolutionary movement, but was driven into exile as he attempted to foment risings in Italian cities, and impeded the policy of Cavour to reunite Italy under King Victor Emmanuel II.

**143   [Mutability]**   1 Ulysses underwent a series of adventures on his way home to Ithaca from Troy, as told in the *Odyssey*. *Myrrha* is unspecific.

**149   [The Genius of Greece]**   17 *Dircè*: see note on **43 Corinna to Tanagra**, 25. 18 *Ilissus*: a river flowing near Athens.

**150   To Verona**   4 *Garden or theater*: see note on **129 To Verona**, 11. 6–9 Austria ruled the province of Venetia of which Verona was the capital until the Austro-Prussian War, 1866, when it joined the Kingdom of Italy. 10–11. The city of Naples was founded on the site of a monument to the Siren, *Parthenopè*. The Parthenopean Republic was set up in 1799 after Ferdinand IV had fled before the French revolutionary army. In the course of his shifting fortunes, the Bourbon King was restored in 1815 when he merged Naples with Sicily, styling himself King of the Two Sicilies. 13 *Sybarites*: the inhabitants of a city of Calabria, given to pleasure and effeminacy. 17 *Benacus*: the largest Italian lake, the modern Lake Garda. 20–21 In 1848, Verona was the only town in the north of Italy not to join in the anti-Austrian uprising of that year. The revolution collapsed everywhere in the north except in Venice, which remained independent until August 1849. These lines suggest that the poem may have originally been written during the period of temporary independence, when Venice and its waters (*the dolphin* and *the Adrian wave*) were the only areas over which the Austrian toad had no control.

**152   To Shelley**   2 *We knew each other little*: Shelley had been an early enthusiast for 'Gebir', but when Shelley wished to make his acquaintance at Pisa in 1819 Landor refused, because of the rumours of Shelley's mistreatment of his first wife. He later revised his opinion of Shelley after meeting his friend, the biographer John Trelawny, and the poet's second wife, Mary. 3–5 At *Lucca*, 1818, Shelley translated Plato's *Symposium*; at Pisa, 1819, he wrote 'Epipsychidion', 'Adonais', and 'Hellas'; and at San Terenzo, on the coast near *Lerici*, 1822, he composed 'The Triumph of Life'. 15 *Hellas*: ancient Greece.

**153 March 24** Originally published in *The Examiner*, 22 April 1854. The text is that of 1858.

Landor's sister, Elizabeth Savage Landor, died 24 February 1854. 4 *The cushat*: the wood-pigeon.

**154 Apology for Gebir** Originally published in *The Examiner*, 9 September 1854. The text is that of 1858. Cf. the note introducing **Gebir, 2–4**.

1 *Fidler*: Landor notes: 'A Welsh pony'. 2–4 *Bala moor* is the area around the outlet of the River Dee from Bala Lake, Merionethshire. A noted spot for grouse-shooting. 11 *Tawey's sands*: Landor notes: 'Swansea river'. 17–24 For *Southey*, see note on the Conversation 'Southey and Porson', PROSE **2**. He reviewed 'Gebir' most enthusiastically in the *Critical Review* for September 1799. 38 *the northern star*: probably Sir Walter Scott, 1771–1832. 39 *Bloomfield*: Robert, 1766–1823, started his career as an agricultural labourer and became famous as the author of 'The Farmer's Boy', of which it is said 26,000 copies were sold in less than three years. 50 *Cardigan*: James Thomas Brudenell, seventh Earl of Cardigan, 1797–1868, was the general in command of a cavalry brigade in the Crimean War. He led the light brigade at the attack on Balaclava. Lord Robert Edward Henry *Somerset*, 1776–1842, together with Lord Uxbridge, led the household brigade of cavalry at Waterloo. Sir James Whitley Deans *Dundas*, 1785–1862, was the admiral who held chief command at the bombardment of Sebastopol. 51 Sigaeum is a promontory on which the Greeks based their naval camp during the Trojan War. It was the object of a long war between the cities of Athens and Mytilene. Nearby was a tumulus believed to be the tomb of Achilles. 54 *Corinthian*: see note on **14 To Corinth**, 36–9. 58 Gainsborough: Thomas, 1727–68, English painter. *Watteau*: Jean Antoine, 1684–1721, French painter. 60 *Hudibras*: a satire in the burlesque heroic metre of octosyllabic couplets by Samuel Butler, 1612–80. 64 *Young*: Edward, 1683–1765, became rector of Welwyn. His *The Complaint, or Night Thoughts on Life, Death and Immortality* is a didactic poem of some 10,000 blank verses. 70 *the syrinx*: the pan-pipe. 79. *Gades*: see note on **Gebir, 2 Book I**, 42.

**155 The Georges** The text is as originally published in *The Atlas*, 28 April 1855. Possibly suggested by Thackeray's lectures on the *Four Georges* delivered 1855–6.

1 *George the First*: 1660–1727. 2 *George the Second*: 1683–1760. 4 *George the Third*: 1738–1820. 5 *the Fourth*: 1762–1830. His only legitimate child – a daughter – died in childbirth. He was succeeded by his brother William IV.

**156 Europa and Her Mother** The text is that of 1859, where the speakers' names are capitalized and placed in the centre of the page above their speeches. Cf. note on **51 Ode to Miletus**, 1–4.

10 *ox*: Landor notes: 'Bulls are never at large in those countries; Europa could never have seen one'. 39 *Hades*: the underworld.

**157–160**. The texts of these poems are those of 1858.

**157 Voyage to St Ives, Cornwall, from Port-Einon, Glamorgan, 1794** This voyage was undertaken when Landor was in Wales, the summer after his rustication.

**158 Death of the Day** Wheeler quotes a letter from Landor to Forster, 8 April 1854: 'This evening, I took my usual walk a little earlier, and sitting afterwards without candles for about an hour as I always do . . . I watched the twilight darken on my walls and my pictures vanish from before me' (ed., *Poetical Works*, III, 56).

**160 My Homes** 2 *Arrowe*: a stream which runs near the estate at Ipsley in Landor's mother's family. It is about eighteen miles west of Warwick. 5–6 For *Llantony*, see notes on **32 [Fiesolan Musings]**, 35–40 and 59–62. 7 Landor had visited *Paris* in the summer of 1802 after the Peace of Amiens. When Landor abandoned Llantony in 1814, he rode through Brittany to *Tours* where he stayed one year. 8 *Ronsard*: Pierre de, 1524–85, a French lyric poet. 9 Bérenger: Pierre Jean de, 1780–1857, a French poet noted for light satire. 12 *at Arno's side*: see note on **71 To My Daughter** for the beginning of his residence at Florence. 13 *the Medicaean palace*: The Landors rented apartments in the palace of the Marchese de' Medici-Tornaquinci at Florence from November 1821 to the end of 1827. 14 *Lares*: the spirits of the dead who had the special care of house and household. 15 For *Fiesole*, see note on **25 Fiesolan Idyl**. 16 *Doccia's dell*: see note on **117 [The Fiesolan Villa]**, 20. 17 For *Affrico* and *Boccaccio's Fair Brigade* (23), see note on **57 Farewell to Italy**, 8–9. 28 Landor left his family at Fiesole in 1835.

**161 Coresus and Callirhoë** The text is that of 1859. This is the later of two translations of Landor's Latin original, written 1809, published 1815.

The story derives from Pausanias. Wheeler notes its reoccurrence in Sir George Wheeler's *Journey into Greece*, and in a poem on the same subject by William Thompson, 1712?–66? (ed., *Poetical Works*, II, 524).

1 *Calydon*: the leading city of Aetolia which boasted a celebrated statue of *Bacchus* (3); see note on **Gebir, 2 Book I**, 1. 28 *Hesper*: see note on **10 [Ianthe Awaited]**, 16. 34 *an ilex*: the evergreen oak. 64 Erythrae was an Ionian city, on a bay opposite the island of Chios in the Aegean. 114 For *olive*, see note on **91 [The Duller Olive]**, 3; for *bay*, see note on **43 Corinna to Tanagra**, 40. 124 *Saturn*: Astrologers considered Saturn an evil planet to be born under: its influence was sluggish and gloomy. 146 *Dodona*: a town in Epeiros, celebrated for its oracle of *Jupiter* (155). 156 *the son of Semele*: Bacchus, by Zeus.

**162 Leontion, on Ternissa's Death (Epicuros also Departed)** The text is that of 1859. Cf. note on the Conversation 'Epicurus, Leontion, and Ternissa', PROSE **16**.

7 *this garden*: Epicurus taught in a garden after which his school was named.

**163–175** The texts of these poems are those of 1863.

**163   A Friend to Theocritos in Egypt**   Theocritus, the Greek lyric poet, *c.* 300 – *c.* 260 BC, was a native of Syracuse in Sicily. He moved to Alexandria to enjoy the patronage of Ptolemy Philadelphus. Wheeler quotes Landor's essay, 'The Idyls of Theocritus': 'Among his friends in Egypt was Aratus . . . Philetus the Coan was another . . . Aratus was more particularly his friend' (ed., *Poetical Works*, II, 540). 26 *Pan and Pitys*: see note on **127 Pan and Pitys**.

**165   An Old Poet to Sleep**   The second of two versions published in the same volume, 1863. The first is entitled 'Eucrates to the God Sleep', where the poet's name is unspecific.

5 *Pactolos*: a small river in Lydia, once famous for the particles of gold in its sand, due, in legend, to Midas having bathed there. 20–3. In the earlier version seven lines:

While thou wert hovering round about the couch
Until he stoopt and said, close over it,
"Sleep often plays with me, as once he used,
"Refreshing in his way the vernal flowers,
"Flowers that had droopt and but for him had died.
"He now departs from thee, but leaves behind
"His own twin-brother beauteous as himself.

23 Landor notes: 'There is an ancient statue of a Genius representing *Death* in the form of a beautiful youth. Dr Young has introduced the God, in full feather, to the *world*, leading him to a seat of eyelashes not damp under him'. For Young, see note on **154 Apology for Gebir**, 64. The references are to a statue in the Uffizi, Florence, and to *Night Thoughts*, I, 1–6.

**166   On the Death of Admiral Sir Sidney Smith**   Smith, 1764–1840, was famous for the defence of Saint Jean d'Acre against the French in their progress east. He died in Paris and was buried at Père-Lachaise where there is a monument to his memory. 2–3 Cf. note on the Conversation 'Lord Brooke and Sir Philip Sidney', PROSE **1**, referring to Sir Philip *Sidney*.

**167   [Shakespeare]**   10 The confusion of tongues at *Babel* (Genesis, 11). 11 *Raleigh*: Sir Walter, 1552?–1618, explorer, statesman, historian and poet. *Bacon*: Francis, 1561–1626, philosopher and statesman.

**168   [Ye Who Have Toil'd Uphill]**   4 *Pelasgic*: The Pelasgi were an ancient race believed to have occupied Greece before the Hellenes.

**169   [Unruly Pegasus]**   2 *Pegasus* is the winged horse which by striking the *sacred mount* Helicon (4) with its foot gave rise to the *fount* Hippocrene (3), representing poetic inspiration. The Muses were originally worshipped at Pieria (3) on the slopes of Mount Olympus.

**170   [Ianthe's Name on Sand]**   See note on **9 [Wish for Ianthe]**.

**171   [New Authors]**   6 *Ben* Jonson, 1573–1637. 8 *Waller*: Edmund, 1606–87. 12 Alludes to *Paradise Lost*, I, 26: 'And justify the ways of God to men'.

**172   Invitation of Petronius to Glycon**   Gaius Petronius Arbiter, d. AD 65, was a companion of the Emperor Nero and director of entertainments at the imperial court. He was famous for his *Satyricon*, a satirical prose romance, interspersed with verse, which survives in a fragmentary state. The central episode is the 'Cena Trimalchionis', the sumptuous dinner to which an upstart invites the hero. Glycon is unspecific.

1 *Tryphoena*: a courtesan in the *Satyricon*. 2 *Tusculum*: a fashionable resort for wealthy Romans. 14 *Epictetus*: *c.* AD 60–140, a Stoic philosopher. Poor and lame, he taught at Rome for a time. 16 *Seneca*: Lucius Annaeus, d. AD 65, was a Stoic philosopher and the tutor of Nero. Condoning Nero's crimes he became wealthy. 20 For *Epicurus*, see note on the Conversation 'Epicurus, Leontion, and Ternissa', PROSE **16**. 22 In 1863, six lines which do not belong to this poem were printed here.

**173 [To Julius Hare: on Fame]** See note on **122 To Julius Hare with 'Pericles and Aspasia'**.

**174 Tibullus** Albius Tibullus, *c.* 60?–19 BC, a Roman elegiac poet contemporary with Virgil and Horace.

1–2 Tibullus either refused or did not attract the patronage of Augustus or Maecenas, his impresario. 3 *Delia* is his mistress in the first of the three books of elegies he wrote. 5–6 Tibullus set out to the east in the entourage of *Messalla*, his aristocratic Roman patron, but fell ill and returned to Italy. It is uncertain whether he served under Messalla in Gaul when the latter became proconsul, but he celebrated his exploits in poetry. 7 *Nemesis*: both the divine spirit of vengeance for insolence and the name of his later mistress. 8 Ovid's, in *Amores*, iii, 9.

**175 [The Laurel Bears a Thorn]** For the bay-tree, see note on **43 Corinna to Tanagra**, 40. 6 For *Ilissus*, see note on **149 [The Genius of Greece]**, 18.

**176 [At Wordsworth's Desire]** Originally published in Forster's *Landor*. The title is probably Forster's. Dora Wordsworth commissioned the verses for her album in 1832, though they were not copied there until 1836. The text is that of the album MS, a facsimile of which is printed in F. V. Morley's *Dora Wordsworth, Her Book*, London, 1924, p. 112. 4 The question-mark is editorial.

**177 [An Invitation]** The text is that of Forster's *Landor* where it was originally published. It was written January 1856. 2 *Forster*: John, 1812–76, historian, friend and biographer of Landor.

**178–82** The texts of these poems are those of *Letters and Unpublished Writings*, edited by Wheeler, 1897, where they were first published.

**178 [Smiles and Tears]** Dated by Landor 1801, the year in which, Wheeler records, 'he narrowly escaped marrying a rich heiress' (ed., *Letters and Unpublished Writings*,1897, p. 185).

**179 [On the Heights]** Wheeler's title. 7 *laurel*: the bay tree; see **43 Corinna to Tanagra**, 40.

**180 [Thomas Paine]** 1737–1809, the Anglo-American political theorist and writer of *The Rights of Man*. His deism and antagonism to Washington led to his ostracism in America where he died in poverty.

**181 [Daniel Defoe]** The first of two poems printed on this subject in 1897. Defoe, 1661?–1731, was a journalist and novelist. His *The Shortest Way with the Dissenters* led to his being fined, imprisoned and put in the pillory. His *Robinson Crusoe* appeared in 1719.

13 *Rodney*: George Brydges, first Baron, 1719–92, was the admiral who, amongst other services rendered during the Seven Years' War, captured Martinique in the West Indies. *Nelson*: Viscount Horatio, 1758–1805, destroyed the French fleet at Aboukir, defeated the Danes at Copenhagen and the combined fleets of the French and Spanish at Trafalgar.

**182 [Apology for the *Hellenics*]** Wheeler's title. The 'Hellenics' is the name Landor gave to his poems on Greek themes in the volumes of 1846, 1847 and 1859. 5 *Alfieri*: Vittorio, 1749–1803, the Italian neo-classical dramatist. He wrote two tragedies on *Brutus* (8). 9 *Corneille*: Pierre, 1606–84, the French neo-classical dramatist. 11 *Racine*: Jean, 1639–99, the French neo-classical dramatist, depicted the loves and intrigues of the fashionable world of Louis XIV's Paris in the guise of classical characters. 13–20 Shakespeare. 28–30 Themes from the *Iliad*. For *Andromache*, see note on **123 To Southey**, 12–14. 32 Achilles was the son of *Peleus*.

# The Prose

*Imaginary Conversations* Though Landor claimed to have written 'two or three' Conversations in 1797, one of which was refused for the *Morning Chronicle*, the impetus towards this form of composition was Southey's announcement in a letter of 14 August 1820, that he was commencing a 'series of dialogues'. Landor probably started composition soon after in 1820, though the first published, the first of two Conversations entitled 'Southey and Porson', did not come out (by way of advertisement for the succeeding book publication) until 1823. The last Conversations in English were published in 1856.

**1 Lord Brooke and Sir Philip Sidney** The text is that of 1846.

Fulke Greville, Lord Brooke, 1554–1628, poet and statesman, became Chancellor of the Exchequer. He went to school and to court with Sidney. With Sidney, Spenser and others he belonged to a literary côterie interested in creating a new English poetry. Sidney's pastoral 'Join, mates, in mirth with me' is addressed to him and Sir Edward Dyer. His own works, mostly published after his death, include tragedies, sonnets and poems on political and moral themes. Landor notes: 'His style is stiff, but his sentiments are sound and manly'. He was murdered by a servant, and buried in Warwick. He composed his own epitaph: 'Fulke Greville, servant to Queen Elizabeth, counsellor to King James, friend to Sir Philip Sidney'.

Sir Philip Sidney, 1554–86, travelled extensively in his youth in France (where he witnessed the massacre of St Bartholomew in 1572), Austria and the Italian city states. He was later in Ireland and undertook several diplomatic commissions on the continent. He met his death in the war in the Low Countries, at Zutphen, from a wound in the thigh. Despite his dashing career, his temperament was one of Puritan sobriety. He enjoyed only uncertain health and was disappointed in his love for Penelope Devereux, the mistress addressed in his sonnet sequence *Astrophel and Stella*. He wrote also the *Arcadia*, a pastoral romance, *Apolgie for Poesie*, the first major critical essay in Renaissance England, and a translation of the Psalms.

The Conversation takes place at Penshurst, the country house near Tonbridge where Sidney was born and which he later inherited. Prasher suggests that the time 'may be the summer of 1585, before Philip left for the Netherlands' (ed., *Imaginary Conversations*, p. 562).

The primary source is Greville's own *Life of the Renouned Sir Philip Sidney*, 1652.

[1] The *Via Sacra* in Rome is the street approaching the most sacred parts of the city, the temples of Vesta and the Penates, the Forum and the Capitol. [2] The five lines from 'We' to 'us' were added in 1826. [3] The two lines from 'It' to 'stores' were added in 1826. [4] The five lines from 'Afterward' to 'Death!' were added in 1826. [5] The six lines from '*Brooke*' to '*Sidney*' were added in 1846. [6] Medusa was one of the Gorgons, represented with hideous face, glaring eyes and serpents in her hair. [7] The allusion is to Sidney's oak, under which the Conversation is supposed to be taking place, planted at Penshurst to commemorate his birth. [8] The allusion is to Sidney's *Arcadia* and its pastoral framework. [9] Prasher points out that this allusion is to Sidney's allegiance to Aristotle's principle that art is imitation. She quotes from *Apologie*: 'Nature never set foorth the earth in so rich Tapistry as diverse Poets have done . . . her world is brasen, the Poets only deliver golden' (ed., *Imaginary Conversations*, p. 567). [10] Alexander the Great, 356–23 BC, conquered Persia in 331 BC. [11] The three lines from 'We' to 'life' were added in 1846. [12] Sidney did not value his own writings highly. None of his works appeared in his own lifetime, and he expressed the wish that his *Arcadia* should be destroyed. He came to distrust the moral effect of literature. [13] Sonnets XXXVIII and XXXIX of *Astrophel to Stella* are on this subject. [14] For the story of *Alcestis*, see note on POETRY **21**, **[Ianthe's Name]**, 2. [15] The allusion is to Icarus, the son of Daedalus, who made wings for both to escape from the Cretan labyrinth; but Icarus flew too near to the sun, and the wax from which the wings were made melted, so that he fell into the sea and was drowned. [16] This passage, from '*Sidney*' to 'was', and the next, from '. . . Let' to 'rest', were added in 1846.

**2  Southey and Porson**  The first Conversation to be published, it appeared in the *London Magazine*, July 1823. The text is that of 1846. It is the first of two Conversations between the same persons. Southey is also the interlocutor in two Conversations in which Landor takes part in his own person.

Robert Southey, 1774–1843, the poet and biographer, was Landor's most important literary friend. An early enthusiast for 'Gebir' (see note on POETRY **154**, **Apology for Gebir**, 16–17) he met Landor in 1808 (see note on POETRY **132**, **To The Reverend Cuthbert Southey**, 5–8). It was Southey who introduced Landor to his friend Wordsworth's poetry and who stimulated him to write dialogues. They met only on rare occasions (see note on POETRY **132**, **To The Reverend Cuthbert Southey**, 9–10; 25–7); for the last time at Clifton and Bristol in 1836; but their fruitful and mutually supportive correspondence (Landor encouraged Southey to resume writing poetry in 1808) preserved Landor's self-esteem in exile. Landor honoured him with several poetic tributes; see, for example, POETRY **72**, **On Southey's Death**, and **123**, **To Southey**.

Richard Porson, 1759–1808, the noted Greek scholar and critic, was appointed Professor of Greek at Cambridge in 1792 and later principal librarian at the London Institution. He became known for intemperate habits. Both Southey and Porson were known as reviewers unperverted by personal animus. Southey was noted for fair-minded civility, and Porson for exacting scholarship.
¹ The first fifteen lines to 'inquiry' were added in 1846. ² The Conversation owes its origin to Landor's decision to withdraw his projected dedication of the original volumes of *Imaginary Conversations* to Wordsworth. Landor feared Wordsworth would be embarrassed by his own political views as expressed in several of the Conversations, and acknowledged him instead by this dialogue largely devoted to a consideration of his poetry. Landor's earlier admiration for Wordsworth (see POETRY **42**, **To Wordsworth**) was later substantially qualified. Super attributes the change to a combination of a chivalric impulse to defend Southey (of whom Landor believed Wordsworth had remarked, '. . . I would not give five shillings for all that (he) has ever written'), resentment at Wordsworth's fancied coolness towards himself, and even jealousy of Wordsworth's reputation (see *Biography*, p. 276). He attacked Wordsworth several times: in *A Satire on Satirists, and Admonition to Detractors*, 1836 (where he accused Wordsworth of plagiarizing his own extended image of the shell in 'Gebir', Book I; see note on POETRY **2**, 170–7); in his essay 'The Idyls of Theocritus', 1842; and especially in the second Conversation 'Southey and Porson', *Blackwood's*, December 1842. Yet the original version of this Conversation, except for the clipping of some passages of exaggerated praise, remained unaltered in the edition of 1846. ³ Cf. Colossians 3:9–10. ⁴ *Lazarettos* are leper-houses. ⁵ The eighteen lines from '*Porson*' to 'with the broken stalks in' were added in 1846. ⁶ *Percy*: Thomas, 1729–1811, antiquary and poet, collected and edited numerous ancient ballads in *Reliques of Ancient Poetry*, published 1765. ⁷ *the Wartons*: Joseph, 1722–1800, critic and poet, published two volumes of *Odes*, 1744 and 1746, showing an unusual susceptibility for nature, revolting against the school of Pope. His brother Thomas, 1728–90, poet and literary historian, became Professor of History at Oxford, and is best known for his *History of English Poetry*, 1774–81. ⁸ *Cowper*: William, 1731–1800, author of *The Task*, published in 1785, noted for its evidence of a love of nature, and a translation of Homer, published in 1791. ⁹ In 279 BC. ¹⁰ Prasher notes: 'This may be an inaccurate reference to 1. 185 ff., Book xxiii, of the *Iliad*, in which Aphrodite keeps the dogs and Apollo keeps the sun from destroying Hector's body' (ed., *Imaginary Conversations*, p. 638). ¹¹ *Swift*: Jonathan, 1667–1745, on George Frederick *Handel*, 1685–1742, in 'Directions for a Birth-day Song, October 30, 1729', 275–80, and on John Churchill, first Duke of *Marlborough*, 1650–1722, in the *History of the Four Last Years of the Queen*, 1758. ¹² *Pope*: Alexander, 1688–1744, on Richard *Bentley*, 1662–1742, the classical scholar and verbal critic, in 'An Epistle from Mr Pope to Dr Arbuthnot', 164, and in 'First Epistle of the Second Book of Horace Imitated', 103–4. ¹³ *Gray*: Thomas, 1716–71, on Anthony Ashley Cooper, third Earl of *Shaftesbury*, 1671–1713, in a letter to Richard Stonhewer, 18 August 1758, and on Jean-Jacques *Rousseau*, 1712–78, in two letters to the Revd William Mason, 22 January 1761, and November 1764. ¹⁴ The First Folio of Shakespeare's plays appeared in 1623, seven years after his death. ¹⁵ Several lines of inflated praise of Wordsworth are here omitted from the original. ¹⁶ *Jeffrey*: Francis, 1773–1850, who edited the *Edinburgh Review* from its commencement in 1802 until 1829, was an

inveterate and personal critic of Wordsworth and his poetry. [17] The four lines from 'In' to 'taken' were added in 1846. [18] The fourteen lines from 'I' to 'them?' were added in 1846. [19] *Coleridge*: Samuel Taylor, 1772–1834, Wordsworth's friend, collaborated with him in *Lyrical Ballads*, 1798. [20] *Morland*: George, 1763–1804, an English landscape painter. [21] In *Specimens of the Table Talk of the Late Samuel Taylor Coleridge*, 2 vols., London 1835, I, 147–8. [22] See note on POETRY **15**, **Regeneration**, 52–3. [23] Porson edited several works by this tragedian, *c.* 480–406 BC. [24] The eleven lines from 'Some' to 'indiscriminately' were added in 1826. [25] In 1826, the three lines from 'Clear' to 'profound' come after 'size' (two lines lower) as part of Porson's speech. [26] The four lines from 'Our' to 'ages' were added in 1846. [27] Aeschylus, Sophocles and Euripides. [28] For 'Laodamia', see note on POETRY, **42 To Wordsworth**, 46–8. It was written in 1814, six years after the death of Porson. [29] *Ennius*: Quintus, 239–169 BC, a Roman poet, was an intimate friend of the elder *Scipio, c.* 236–184/3 BC, the soldier and literary patron, and he introduced the epic hexameter in the Homeric manner into Roman poetry. [30] *Cato*: Marcus Porcius, 234–149 BC, the censor, who applied himself to the moral reform of the Roman nobility, and the checking of luxury. He took Ennius to Rome. [31] A street off Leadenhall Street, Aldgate, London. At that time merchants and brokers met at two coffee-houses there. [32] Landor notes: 'The memory of Porson was extraordinary, and quite capable of this repetition'. Wordsworth revised the poem in the light of Landor's criticism. He wrote to Landor, 21 January 1824: 'You have condescended to minute criticism upon the *Laodamia*. I concur with you in the first stanza, and had several times attempted to alter it upon your grounds. I cannot, however, accede to your objection to the "second birth", merely because the expression has been degraded by Conventiclers. I certainly meant nothing more by it than the *eadem cura*, and the *largior aether*, &c, of Virgil's 6th Aeneid. All religions owe their origin or acceptation to the wish of the human heart to supply in another state of existence the deficiencies of this, and to carry still nearer to perfection whatever we admire in our present condition; so that there must be many modes of expression, arising out of this coincidence, or rather identity of feeling, common to all Mythologies; and under this observation I should shelter the phrase from your censure; but I may be wrong in the particular case, though certainly not in the general principle' (*The Letters of William and Dorothy Wordsworth: The Later Years 1821–1850*, edited by E. de Selincourt, 3 vols., Oxford, 1939, I, 134). Wordsworth accordingly altered this stanza to read:

> With sacrifice before the rising morn
> Vows have I made by fruitless hope inspired;
> And from the infernal Gods, 'mid shapes forlorn
> Of night, my slaughtered Lord have I required.

[33] A tragedy by the Scottish poet, John Home, 1722–1808. The quotation is from Act V, sc. i. [34] Despite his comments above, Wordsworth changed the last two lines to read:

> Spake of heroic hearts in graver mood
> Revived, with firmer harmony pursued.

The original edition has after this quotation four lines of exalted praise for the poem which it refers to as 'a composition such as Sophocles might have exulted to own'.[35] *ratafia*: a fruit-flavoured cordial. [36] Originally and in 1826 this speech was part of Porson's preceding speech. [37] For *Pindar*, see note on POETRY

**123**, **To Southey**, 19–21. [38] *Herculaneum* is a small city at the foot of Vesuvius which was buried beneath an eruption in AD 79. Excavations began in 1738, yielding works of art and over 1800 papyri from the library of a rediscovered villa.

**3 Aeschines and Phocion** The text is that of 1853. The extract is the beginning of the Conversation.

Aeschines, *c.* 390–30 BC, was an Athenian orator noted for his exchanges with Demosthenes in the courts. Phocion, *c.* 402–318 BC, the Athenian general and statesman, noted for his splendid contempt of the people's fickleness and of popular leaders. Both were opposed to the policy of Demosthenes, who warned his fellow-countrymen of the ominous significance of the rise to power of an autocratic Macedonia in the *Philippics*. In his Third Philippic, 'On the Embassy', he attacked Aeschines whom he accused of having betrayed the best interests of Athens in his advocacy of a common peace. Phocion realized the insuperable military strength of Macedonia and advised Athens to treat for terms when out-manoeuvred before the battle of Chaeronea. After the crushing defeat of Athens he helped preserve peace with Philip and Alexander.

The chief sources are Plutarch's *Life of Phocion* and *Life of Demosthenes*.

[1] The anecdote behind this passage is taken from Plutarch's *Life of Phocion*, but there is no reference to Aeschines (VIII, 163): 'Indeed, when an oracle from Delphi was read out in the assembly, declaring that when the rest of the Athenians were of like mind, one man had a mind at variance with the city, Phocion came forward and bade them seek no further, since he himself was the man in question; for there was no one but he who disliked everything they did' (quoted by Prasher, ed., *Imaginary Conversations*, p. 728). Prasher suggests this incident is conflated with Aeschines' speech 'On the Embassy', in reply to Demosthenes, 'in which he called upon Phocion to witness he did not speak falsely about his service in the battle of Tamynae, and . . . to endorse his plea' (ed., *Imaginary Conversations*, p. 728). [2] *Demosthenes*, 383–22 BC, was the greatest of Athenian orators. [3] Both Aeschines and Phocion served in the Euboean campaign. [4] *Demades*: 350–19 BC, a shifty and venal orator. [5] *Polyeuctus*: a luxurious friend of Demosthenes, for Sphettus. [6] Prasher lists the following victories from Plutarch's *Life*: in the Euboean campaign, in aid of Megara and of the allies on Hellespont and at Byzantium (ed., *Imaginary Conversations*, p. 729). [7] Plutarch writes 'forty-five' times. [8] *Aristides*: d. *c.* 468 BC, the democratic Athenian leader known as 'The Just'. [9] *Epaminondas*: *c.* 420–362 BC, the Theban commander, noted for military strategy and nobility of character. [10] *Miltiades*, *c.* 550–489 BC, among many military exploits commanded the Athenian force at Marathon. [11] *Cimon*: d. 449 BC, the son of Miltiades. His chief exploit was the defeat of the Persian fleet at the mouth of the Eurymedon *c.* 468 BC.

**4 King James I and Isaac Casaubon** The text is that of 1846. The extract is the end of the Conversation.

James I, 1566–1625, issued his *An Apology for the Oath of Allegiance* in 1606. There he refuted the claim of the Papacy to exert authority over the English crown. He invited the French Huguenot scholar and theologian Isaac Casaubon, 1559–1614, to London, as the latter's respect for the authority of the Fathers, together with his rejection of papal dominion, had brought him close to the position of the Anglo-Catholics. He became a naturalized Englishman and was buried in Westminster Abbey. The eucharistic doctrine of James's early Calvinism is similar to that of his subsequent Anglicanism, contained in the Twenty-Eighth Article of the Church of England, which condemns the Roman Catholic doctrine of Transubstantiation: 'the Body of Christ is given, taken, and eaten in the Supper, only after an heavenly and spiritual manner'. The Conversation is supposed to be one of James's regular Sunday theological discussions with Casaubon.

¹ Prasher notes: 'One of the great triumphs of the pontificate of Gregory XIII was the arrival in Rome in 1585 of four Japanese ambassadors sent by converted Japanese kings to thank the pope for sending them Jesuit missionaries' (ed., *Imaginary Conversations*, p. 826).

### 5   General Kleber and French Officers   The text is that of 1846. The whole Conversation is printed.

Jean-Baptiste Kléber, 1753–1800, was left in command of the French in Egypt when Napoleon deserted his army and returned to France in 1799. He was assassinated after breaking a·Turkish army which had entered from Syria.

¹ Napoleon took an illustrious team of scientists and men of letters to Egypt with him. ² *ophthalmia* is inflammation of the eye. ³ See notes on POETRY **166**, **On the Death of Admiral Sir Sidney Smith**, and on the Conversation 'Lord Brooke and Sir Philip Sidney', PROSE **1**. ⁴ See note on POETRY **181**, **Daniel Defoe**, 13. ⁵ Nelson utterly destroyed the French fleet in Aboukir Bay, in 1798. ⁶ Memnon, the King of Ethiopia, was supposed to have lived in Egypt. The Greeks gave his name to the great statue of Amenophis III at Thebes which was said to make a musical sound at daybreak when Memnon greeted his mother, the goddess of dawn. ⁷ Nelson, whose personal initiatives often put him at odds with his superiors and the Admiralty, was largely responsible, acting boldly and without orders, for the victory over the Spanish off Cape St Vincent in 1797. He defeated the Danes at Copenhagen in 1801, ignoring the order to cease action by putting his telescope to his blind eye and saying he could not see the signal. Smith was snubbed by the British government and left without well-defined authority for attempting to override diplomatic protocol and deliver a direct message from the King of Sweden. ⁸ On his own initiative, Smith helped at the evacuation of *Toulon* in 1793, burning the French ships which had to be left behind. Sir Gilbert *Elliot*, 1751–1841, had been appointed civil commissioner there, but when Toulon ceased to be a British possession, he left for Florence where he attempted to set the Italian states against the French. Smith's action at *Acre*, ultimately holding the breach till the arrival of the Turkish troops, effectively checked the progress of French arms in the East. ⁹ After the French defeat at Aboukir, Turkey, whose power the French had been ostensibly establishing in Egypt, also declared war on France. ¹⁰ Jacques François, baron de *Menou*, 1750–1810, was to succeed Kléber in command. Styling himself 'Abdallah' and adopting the Moslem faith, he was to aim at an Egyptian kingdom and ruin his army.

### 6   Middleton and Magliabechi   The text is that of 1846.

Conyers Middleton, 1683–1750, scholar and divine, visited Rome for a great part of 1724–5, and published his *Letter from Rome* in 1729 about the incorporation of pagan beliefs and ceremonies into the Catholic church. He could never have met Antonio Magliabechi, 1633–1714, the keeper of the Palatine Libary at Florence. Middleton is said to have left a manuscript treatise doubting the efficacy of prayer which was burnt.

¹ The lines from 'I' to the end were added in 1826.

**7  Henry VIII and Anne Boleyn**  The text is that of 1846. The extract is the beginning of the Conversation. Cf. note on POETRY **63**, **Scene in Richmond Chase**. Henry has come disguised.

¹ Landor notes: 'Henry was not unlearned, nor indifferent to the costlier externals of a gentleman; but in manners and language he was hardly on a level with our hostlers of the present day. He was fond of bear-baitings and other such amusements in the midst of the rabble, and would wrestle with Francis I. His reign is one continued proof, flaring and wearisome as a Lapland summer day, that even the English form of government, under a sensual king with money at his disposal, may serve only to legitimatize injustice . . . The government was whatever the King ordered; and he a ferocious and terrific thing, swinging on high between two windy superstitions, and caught and propelled alternately by fanaticism and lust. In Anne Boleyn, the frank and unsuspicious gayety of her temper, the restless playfulness of high spirits, which we often saw formerly in the families of country gentlemen, first captivated the affections and afterwards raised the jealousy of Henry. Lightness of spirit which had made all about her happy the whole course of her life, made her so the last day of it. . .'. ² Landor notes: 'She miscarried of a son, January 29th, 1536: the King concluded from this event that his marriage was disagreeable to God. He had abundance of conclusions for believing that his last marriage was disagreeable to God, whenever he wanted a fresh one, and was ready in due time to give up this too with the same resignation; but he never had any *conclusions* of doing a thing disagreeable to God when a divorce or decapitation was in question'.

**8  Lord Chesterfield and Lord Chatham**  The text is that of 1846. The extract is the end of the Conversation.

Philip Dormer Stanhope, fourth Earl of Chesterfield, 1694–1773, was a politician, wit and letter-writer. His *Letters* to his natural son, Philip Stanhope, written almost daily from 1737 onwards, were designed for the education of the young man. They are full of sensible information on matters of worldly good-breeding.

William Pitt the elder, first Earl of Chatham, 1708–78, served as war minister under George II and led Britain to victory over the French in the Seven Years War. He was a political individualist, forming a rapid succession of alliances in parliament. When he was eventually given the opportunity of forming an independent administration, illness prevented him from taking an active lead. After an attack of insanity in 1767, his political career declined during the last ten years of his life. The outbreak of the American War reawakened something of the old vigour as he fought to preserve the colonies for Britain. While speaking in parliament on this subject he fell ill, and died one month later. He was buried in Westminster Abbey.

¹ *Cervantes*: Miguel de, 1547–1616, the Spanish novelist, dramatist and poet, author of *Don Quixote de la Mancha*. ² The eight lines from 'The' to 'positions' were added in 1826. ³ For Bacon, see note on POETRY **167**, **[Shakespeare]**, 11. The *Essays* came out 1597–1625. ⁴ For *Plato*, see note on the Conversation 'Diogenes and Plato', PROSE **14**. ⁵ The nineteen lines from '*Chesterfield*' to 'it' were added in 1826.

**9  Marcus Tullius and Quinctus Cicero**  The text is that of 1853.

Marcus Tullius, 106–43 BC and Quintus (whom Landor misnames 'Quinc-tus'), *c.* 102–43 BC, were brothers. They were educated in philosophy and rhetoric at Rome and later in Greece.

Marcus Tullius became Rome's greatest orator and was also a prolific writer of verse, letters, and works on philosophy, politics and rhetoric. He achieved the highest political office of consul, and refused to become the fourth member of what became the first dictatorial Triumvirate of Caesar, Pompey and Crassus. He was exiled for his public disapproval of Caesar's violent methods. After Pompey's death, he took no further part in politics and devoted himself to writing works on philosophy and rhetoric. After a quarrel, he and his impetuous brother became reconciled. His was among the first names pros-cribed by the new dictatorial Triumvirate of Antony, Octavian and Lepidus. He did not whole-heartedly attempt to escape, and met his death at the hands of Antony's agents with courage and dignity. Among his many surviving letters are three books addressed *Ad Quintum Fratrem*.

Four short letters from Quintus to his brother also remain. Quintus was an able administrator and a brave soldier. He was also a victim of the proscription of 43, and was betrayed with his son by his slaves.

[1] *Critobulus* is unspecific. [2] *Atticus*: Titus Pomponius, 109–32 BC, was the intimate friend of Cicero. He spent a long time at Athens acquiring perfect Greek. Correspondence between him and Cicero survives. [3] Two beautiful youths: *Hylas* fetching water found a spring and was pulled into it by the nymphs who fell in love with him; *Narcissus*, who loved no one till he saw his own reflection in water, fell in love with that, pined and died, to become the flower of the same name. [4] The two lines from 'Certainly' to 'you' were added in 1826. The following four lines from 'Consciousness' to 'Marcus!' were added in 1846. [5] The seven lines from 'In' to 'truth' were added in 1846. [6] The title of *praetor* originally belonged to the Roman consul as leader of the army; that of *proscriber* to the official who published the names of those condemned to death. [7] The twenty-four lines from 'Two' to 'departed' were added in 1826. 8 Cicero's adored daughter, *Tulliola*, died in 45 BC. [9] The twenty-one lines from 'I' to 'state' were added in 1846. [10] This work is concerned with the problems of death, grief, passion and other mental disorders, and the question of what is essential for happiness. Cicero aimed to give the Romans a philo-sophical literature of their own to rival the Greeks'. [11] As well as absorbing the writings of the Greek philosopher Aristotle, 384–22 BC, Cicero reproduced the theories of many Greek thinkers who came after him but whose own works have not survived. On moral questions he owed much to the Stoics and the teachings of Epicurus. [12] *Epicurus*: see note on the Conversation 'Epicurus, Leontion and Ternissa', PROSE **16**. [13] *Pollio*: Gaius Asinius, 76 BC–AD 5, was active in politics and literature. A sharp critic, he corrected Cicero, Caesar, Sallust and Livy. [14] In the *Tusculan Disputations*, Cicero tells how, when he was quaestor in Sicily in 75 BC, he discovered the tomb of *Archimedes*, *c.* 287–12 BC, the mathematician and inventor, near one of the gates of Syracuse, overgrown with brambles and forgotten. In his *Life of Marcellus*, Plutarch tells of the death of Archimedes who, during the invasion of Syracuse, was intent upon a diagram, and asked an enemy soldier to wait for him to arrive at the solution before he would accompany him. The enraged soldier slew him. [15] Cicero had villas at both these resorts for wealthy Romans. At *Tusculum* he composed several philosophical treatises, and at nearby *Formiae* he was to be murdered.

**10 Marcellus and Hannibal** The text is that of 1853. The whole Conversation is printed.

Crump quotes Appian, *De bello Annibalico*, L, describing the skirmish in which Marcellus was killed at Venusia: 'Claudius Marcellus, the conqueror of Sicily, then for the fifth time Consul, and Titus Crispinus pitched their camps opposite to Hannibal's, but declined battle. But Marcellus, seeing some of the Numidians carrying off some plunder, and thinking that there were but few of them, charged them with only three hundred men with his wonted courage and impetuosity. But, unexpectedly, the Carthaginian troops attacked the Romans on all sides, and put the rear rank of them to flight. But Marcellus, thinking that his men still followed him, fought on bravely until he fell, pierced by a javelin. And when Hannibal came up to the body and saw him lying with his wounds all in front, he praised him for a good soldier though a bad general. He took the ring from the Roman's finger, gave his body a noble funeral, and sent the ashes to the dead man's son in the Roman camp' (ed., *Conversations*, I, 337).

Hannibal, 247–182 BC, was the Carthaginian leader against Rome in the Second Punic War. After entering Italy by crossing the Alps he was joined by the Gauls of northern Italy.

The incident in which Marcellus's son is borne off by Marcellus's fleeing entourage is derived from Plutarch's *Life of Marcellus*.

[1] Plutarch tells of Marcellus's victory over the Gauls at Clastidium and of the single combat between Marcellus and the Gaulish king, Veredomarus. Thereby he won the 'opima', the special spoils which are the reward of such a personal combat between generals. [2] The Fortunate Islands; see note on *Pericles and Aspasia*, PROSE **36**, 2. [3] Despite many victories, Hannibal was never to take Rome. 4 *Minos* was an ancient King of Crete supposed to rule among the dead.

**11 Peter the Great and Alexis** The text is that of 1846. A section from the middle of the Conversation only is omitted.

Landor's characterization of Peter I, 1672–1725, Czar of Russia, is too harsh; and that of his son by his first, arranged marriage, Alexis, too sympathetic. The weak-willed son conspired with his mother against his father's westernizing reforms and, opposing his anticlerical policy, renounced his own right of succession and left St Petersburg in 1716. From there he was sent to Naples for his own safety; but his father, discovering his whereabouts, enticed him back to St Petersburg where he was arrested, brutally treated, and probably died under the lash shortly before his scheduled execution, in 1718.

[1] Emperor Charles VI, 1685–1740. [2] A Mongolian tribesman. [3] Peter himself created this body which conferred on him the title of 'Emperor' and 'The Great'. [4] By the Treaty of Nystad, 1721 (three years after the death of Alexis), Sweden ceded territories to Russia, including Livonia.

**12 Lucullus and Caesar** The text is that of 1853.

Lucius Licinius Lucullus, *c.* 114–57 BC, was an able general and statesman in Asia and an honest and humane pro-praetor in Africa. He became a consul, and later retired from active life to live in the refined luxury which the wealth amassed in Asia afforded. He was an Epicurean, a lover and generous patron of literature and the arts.

The meeting is supposed to take place *c.* 49 BC, actually after Lucullus's death, when Caius Julius Caesar, 102–44 BC, after Pompey had taken his stand against him and the Senate had commanded Caesar to lay down his command, is imagined as secretly visiting Lucullus, a consistent opponent of Pompey, to seek his help.

The description of Lucullus's villa derives from Plutarch's *Life of Lucullus*.
[1] *Luni* was an ancient city of Etruria. [2] *Antiochia* (in Syria) and *Alexandria* (in Egypt) were considered centres of luxurious living at that time. [3] *Marcipor* is an Ethiopian slave. [4] Landor notes: 'The raspberry and gooseberry are not cultivated in Italy, but grow plentifully on many parts of the Alps and Apennines. In one garden, belonging to a Florentine, are currants introduced by a French family. None of these fruits are known at Rome. Where the climate does much for fruit, the people do little'. [5] Baiae was a fashionable resort on an inlet of the Bay of Naples, with a mild climate. Caesar had a villa there. [6] Proudfit notes that, according to Pliny, 'Before the victory of Lucius Lucullus in the war against Mithridates, that is up to 74 BC, there were no cherry-trees in Italy. Lucullus first imported them from Pontus' (ed., *Selected Imaginary Conversations*, p. 32). Pontus was a well-watered and fertile region of north Asia Minor, with a mild climate on the coast and in the valleys. [7] The modern Lake Como. [8] Plutarch writes of Lucius's deep affection for his younger brother, Marcus Terentius Varro. Lucius refused to hold office until his brother was himself of a proper age to do so. Plutarch notes: 'Nor did (Marcus) himself long survive Lucullus, but, as in age and reputation he came a little behind him, so did he also in the time of his death, having been a most affectionate brother' (quoted by Proudfit, ed., *Selected Imaginary Conversations*, p. 32). [9] *Faesulae*: Fiesole; see note on POETRY **25**, **Fiesolan Idyl**. [10] Sylla: Lucius Cornelius Sulla, 138–78 BC, the Roman military dictator, treated harshly those municipalities which had opposed his rise to power, notably in Etruria where Faesulae was situated.

**13  Mr Pitt and Mr Canning**  The text is that of 1846.

William Pitt the Younger, 1759–1806, was the second son of the first Earl of Chatham; see note on the Conversation 'Lord Chesterfield and Lord Chatham', PROSE **8**. He acquired a reputation for inhumane pragmatism on the principle that it was better to do the best possible in any situation rather than surrender office. Although he was scrupulously honest in regard to his own conduct and financial dealings, contemptuous of those who sold votes and political influence, he resorted on several occasions to jobbery and bribery to achieve the necessary support on important issues. From his appointment as Chancellor of the Exchequer at the age of twenty-three, he became adept in the practice of winning a parliamentary majority. He became Prime Minister, in 1783, and first provoked Landor's bitter opposition by entering the war against revolutionary France. He left tremendous debts, but no children to pay them.

George Canning, 1770–1827, orator and statesman, was the consistent supporter of Pitt from his entering parliament in 1793. He served as Treasurer of the Navy, 1804–6. After his leader's death, he became Foreign Secretary in the Portland administration, 1807–9. He was recalled to the Foreign Office in 1822 (see note on POETRY **15**, **Regeneration**, 25), and became Prime Minister for the last few months of his life in 1827. He is the chief Tory butt of Landor's writings, appearing in many disguises.

The Conversation is supposed to take place shortly before Pitt's death.

[1] *Sheridan*: Richard Brinsley, 1751–1816, the Whig dramatist and orator. As later references in this Conversation indicate, he was constantly troubled by financial problems, and for the last few years of his life was harassed by creditors. [2] Turkish slaves who served as horsemen in the army of Saladin. After revolting they established their own dynasties in Egypt. [3] *Wesley*: John, 1703–91, the founder of the Methodist church. [4] Whitefield: George, 1714–70, a powerful evangelical preacher. [5] *Fox*: Charles James, 1749–1806, a statesman and orator, was of his day the outstanding parliamentary proponent of liberal reform. [6] Napoleon. During the Napoleonic Wars, Pitt's military coalitions against France were unsuccessful on land. Shortly before his death, Britain's allies were defeated at Austerlitz. [7] In 1805 Napoleon proclaimed himself King of Italy and annexed Genoa to France; but it was not until after Pitt's death, in 1810, that, after having his marriage to the empress Josephine annulled, Napoleon married Marie Louise, daughter of the Austrian emperor. [8] Canning composed the verses 'The Pilot that Weathered the Storm' for Pitt's birthday, May 28 1802. [9] The Prince Regent, the future George IV. [10] Nymphs of the Mohammedan paradise. [11] Canning entered Christ Church, Oxford, in 1788; Landor Trinity College, 1792. [12] Tooke: John Horne, 1736–1812, radical politician and philologist, was arrested in 1794. Landor believed Pitt perjured himself when he was examined for the defence at Tooke's trial for high treason, 'in order to prove that the meeting at the Thatched House Tavern, in 1782, of which he was a Member, had the same objects in view, as the Seditious Societies of the present time. His evidence, however, totally failed to establish this laboured point' (Gifford's *William Pitt*, quoted by Proudfit, ed., *Selected Imaginary Conversations*, p. 59). [13] *Dundas*: Henry, Viscount Melville, 1742–1811, was Pitt's Secretary for War, 1794–1801, and became First Lord of the Admiralty in 1804. In 1806 he was impeached for misappropriation of public money, but was acquitted. Landor's poetic comment was:

> GOD's laws declare,
> Thou shalt not swear
> By aught in heaven above or earth below.
> *Upon my honour*! Melville cries . .
> He swears, and lies . .
> Does Melville then break God's commandment? No.

(*Poetical Works*, ed. Wheeler, II, 269)

[14] *Burke*: Edmund, 1729–97, orator and statesman, held the office of Paymaster of the Forces in two ministries. [15] In 1829, the following lines were printed: 'shew, as lady D. did at lady A.'s, while she was arranging the flowers in her bosom, talking to an admirer and forgetting she was on the stairs, until she fell down them. This is . . .'. [16] Canning was educated at Eton. [17] Landor notes: 'Pitt's father never made it: but it was necessary to attribute it to some other person than Pitt himself'. [18] Pitt had opposed the coalition of the Tory Lord North and the Whig Shelburne, leaving the only workable alternative of the mixed administration of North and Fox, 1783. When this unpopular ministry was dismissed, North acted with the opposition, against Pitt, for the rest of his life. [19] The eight lines from 'Employ' to 'author' replace twenty-two lines on minor political personalities in the original edition of 1829. [20] *Bolingbroke*: Henry St. John, First Viscount, 1678–1751, statesman and philosopher. His *The Idea of a Patriot King*, 1749, was considered by Whigs as a Tory textbook for the kind of infringement of parliamentary government operated by George III. [21] This bill was introduced to cover Pitt's advance to

a private business house of £40,000 with the idea of supporting public credit. The loan was repaid, but a law had to be passed to authorize the irregularity.

## 14  Diogenes and Plato   The text is that of 1853.

Diogenes, *c.* 400–*c.* 325 BC, founded the Cynic sect of philosophy. His main principles were that happiness is attained by satisfying only natural needs, and by satisfying them in the cheapest and easiest way. Whatever is natural cannot be dishonourable or indecent, and so can and should be done publicly. These straightforward theories he demonstrated by pointed utterances and drastic actions.

The Conversation is a sustained attack on Plato, 427–348 BC, the idealist philosopher. Landor's antipathy to Plato, more or less informed, is evidenced throughout his writings. He particularly objected to what he saw as the philosopher's bent towards merely metaphysical conjecture, his advocacy of the legal restriction of personal liberty, and his support of political tyranny. Landor had made a special study of Plato before writing this dialogue. Forster writes: 'He had been so bent . . . upon finding for himself what there was in the famous philosopher, that he went daily for several weeks or months into the Magliabechian library at Florence, and, refreshing his neglected Greek, read the whole of the dialogues in the original from beginning to end' (*Landor*, II, 192).

The Conversation owes much, as Landor's long terminal note to the original indicates, to Diogenes Laertius's *Lives of Eminent Philosophers*, where several meetings in Athens between the two philosophers are recorded.

[1] Diogenes is said to have lived in a large earthenware tub in the Sanctuary of the Mother of the Gods at Athens. [2] See note on POETRY **51**, **Ode to Miletus**. The city was famous for woollen cloth of a high quality. [3] See Plato's *Timaeus*, XL. [4] Proudfit quotes Diogenes Laertius's *Lives of Eminent Philosophers*: 'Plato had defined Man as an animal, biped and featherless, and was applauded. Diogenes plucked a fowl and brought it into the lecture-room with the words, "Here is Plato's man." In consequence of which there was added to the definition, "having broad nails" ' (ed., *Selected Imaginary Conversations*, p. 160). [5] Landor notes: 'Parts of knowledge which are now general, but were then very rare, and united in none'. [6] Plato's school, the Academy, was situated in a garden outside the walls of Athens. [7] Timon of Athens, *c.* 500–429 BC. [8] Diogenes was a native of Sinope on the Euxine. [9] A reference to the death of Socrates who was sentenced to die by drinking hemlock when convicted of corrupting the youth and introducing new deities, in his disinterested search for truth. [10] *Socrates*: 469–399 BC. [11] Proudfit quotes Diogenes Laertius's *Lives of Eminent Philosophers*: 'They say that, on hearing Plato read the *Lysis*, Socrates exclaimed, "By Heracles, what a number of lies this young man is telling about me!" For he has included in the dialogue much that Socrates never said' (ed., *Selected Imaginary Conversations*, p. 166). [12] The seven lines from 'Keep' to 'within' were added in 1846. [13] The forty-seven lines from 'Thou' to 'Virtue?' and the following twenty-nine lines from '*Diogenes*' to the end were added in 1846. [14] Among many contenders, Chios and Smyrna in Asia Minor have the strongest claims to be the birthplace of *Homer*. [15] *Herodotus, c.* 480– *c.* 25 BC, was the first historian to make the events of the past the subject of research and verification. He wrote in the Ionian dialect, in a clear and simple style. [16] Aristotle, 384–22 BC, was Plato's pupil for twenty years. [17] Proudfit notes that Aristotle composed the *Scolion*, or drinking song, according to

Diogenes Laertius, while at the court of Hermias Atarneus, and quotes it from *Lives of Eminent Philosophers*: 'O virtue, toilsome for the generation of mortals to achieve, the fairest prize that life can win, for thy beauty, O virgin, it were a doom glorious in Hellas even to die and to endure fierce, untiring labours. Such courage dost thou implant in the mind, imperishable, better than gold, dearer than parents or soft-eyed sleep. For thy sake Heracles, son of Zeus, and the sons of Leda endured much in the tasks whereby they pursued thy might. And yearning after thee came Achilles and Ajax to the house of Hades, and for the sake of thy dear form the nursling of Atarneus too was bereft of the light of the sun. Therefore shall his deeds be sung, and the Muses, the daughters of Memory, shall make him immortal, exalting the majesty of Zeus, guardian of strangers, and the grace of lasting friendship' (ed., *Selected Imaginary Conversations*, p. 197). [18] This speech is a parody of Plato's allegory of the cave in *The Republic*, vii. [19] *Pericles* and [20] *Aspasia*: see note on *Pericles and Aspasia* introducing PROSE **22–41**.

## 15 Barrow and Newton    The text is that of 1846.

Isaac Barrow, 1630–77, the divine, scholar and mathematician, occupied the Chair of Greek at Cambridge and the Gresham Professorship in Geometry. He later became the first Lucasian Professor of Mathematics there, publishing two mathematical works, the first on Geometry, the second on Optics. He became the Master of Trinity, Cambridge, where he founded the library, and wrote famously eloquent sermons and a brilliant specimen of ecclesiastical controversy, the *Pope's Supremacy*.

His pupil, Sir Isaac Newton, 1642–1727, the natural philosopher, is remarkable for a series of discoveries in mathematics, optics, and physics. Barrow resigned the Lucasian Professorship in his favour in 1669. He became a Fellow of the Royal Society in 1672, and was to preside over that body for twenty-five years from 1703. His law of universal gravitation was not published until 1687. He sat in parliament for his university and was knighted in 1705. Beside his scientific writings he also produced several theological works. Personally, he was remarkable for simplicity, humility and gentleness, with a distaste for controversy.

Crump points out that the Conversation is supposed to take place in 1668, on the day before Newton went up for his master's degree, when he had already provided material and corrections for Barrow's work on Optics (see *Conversations*, IV, 108). Barrow resigned the Lucasian Professorship to him the following year and devoted the rest of his life to theology.

[1] See note on the Conversation 'Diogenes and Plato', PROSE **14**. [2] See note on the Conversation 'Diogenes and Plato', PROSE **14**, 16. [3] See notes on POETRY **167**, **[Shakespeare]**, 11, and on the Conversation 'Lord Chesterfield and Lord Chatham', PROSE **8**, 3. [4] See note on the Conversation 'Marcus Tullius and Quinctus Cicero', PROSE **9**. [5] Polyphemus, the chief of the Cyclopes, a race of gigantic shepherds in Sicily. [6] *Montaigne*: Michel de, 1533–92, French essayist. [7] *Erasmus*: 1466?–1536, Dutch humanist. [8] *Galileo*: 1564–1642, Italian astronomer, mathematician and physicist. [9] *Wentworth*: Thomas, first Earl of Strafford, 1593–1641. A firm supporter of royal prerogative, he enforced despotic reforms in financial administration that doubled the state's revenue; but was eventually the object of a bill of attainder brought against him by the opposition. Charles I after long hesitation signed the bill, and Strafford was beheaded. Landor notes: 'He far excelled in energy and

capacity the other councillors of Charles; but there was scarcely a crueller or (with the exception of his master) a more perfidious man on either side. Added to which, he was wantonly oppressive, and sordidly avaricious'. [10] *Mazarin*: Jules, 1602–61, French statesman and cardinal. [11] *Richelieu*: Armand Jean du Plessis, duc de, 1585–1642, cardinal and chief minister of France under Louis XIII. [12] *Lycophron* of Chalcis, born *c.* 325 BC, a Greek poet of the late Hellenistic age. [13] *Euclid*, the Greek mathematician, flourished *c.* 300 BC. [14] Cf. note on the Conversation 'Marcus Tullius and Quinctus Cicero', PROSE **9**, 14. [15] *Xenophon, c.* 430 – *c.* 355 BC, the Athenian soldier and writer, composed his *Memorabilia* of Socrates by means of an imaginary conversation between Socrates and various persons, and invented speeches for Socrates in his *Apology* and for the characters in his *Symposium*. Landor wrote two Conversations – between Xenophon and the younger Cyrus, and Alcibiades and Xenophon. [16] Phoebus *Apollo* was the god of light, sometimes identified with the sun. In myth, his first feat was the taking of Delphi for his abode by the destruction of its guardian, the dragon *Python*, embodying the dark forces of the underworld. [17] *propylaea*: the building forming the imposing entrance of the Athenian Acropolis. [18] For *the Graces*, see the note on POETRY **138**, **On Catullus**, 3–4. [19] Girdles. [20] The girdle of Venus, fabled to excite love. [21] The aged statesman and counsellor of the Greeks in the *Iliad*. [22] I cannot discover which militarist pope: Julius II?.

### 16   Epicurus, Leontion, and Ternissa   The text is that of 1853.

Epicurus, 341–270 BC, was the founder of the Epicurean school of philosophy. He taught that wise conduct derived from the evidence of the senses, rejecting superstition and belief in the supernatural. He held that pleasure (or absence of pain) is the only good known to the senses, and is obtainable by plain living and virtue conducing to harmony of body and mind. Landor notes: 'Certain it is, that moderation, forbearance and what St Paul calls *charity*, never flourished in any sect of philosophy or religion so perfectly and so long, as among the disciples of Epicurus'.

In this Conversation he is presented talking with two girl pupils: Leontion, who married Metrodorus, and the invented 'Ternissa'; (see POETRY **162**, **Leontion, on Ternissa's Death (Epicuros also Departed)**). In the Preface to 1853 Landor refers to 'Themisto': 'we called her Ternissa, and she preferred the name'. Crump suggests that Landor associated the name with that of the wife of an intimate friend of Epicurus called 'Thermista' (ed., *Conversations*, I, 208). Landor also composed a Conversation between Epicurus and Metrodorus, and two others with Menander.

The chief source is Diogenes Laertius's *Lives of Eminent Philosophers* which contains the titles of Epicurus's treatises, three epistles summarizing his system and a collection of forty of the most important articles of his doctrine.

[1] Crump quotes Epicurus's letter to Menoecos from Diogenes Laertius's *Lives of Eminent Philosophers*, X: 'Accustom yourself therefore to regard death as something that concerns you not at all; seeing that all good and evil exist alone in the perception of them; and death is the loss of all perception . . . Therefore that most terrible of all dread evils, death, can touch us not at all, seeing that while we live, death is away from us, and when we die, we are then away from him' (ed., *Conversations*, I, 212). [2] A kind of large lemon, according to Pliny. [3] *the Styx* and [4] *Charon*: see note on POETRY **28**, **Dirce**, 3. [5] The two lines from 'Whenever' to 'it' were added in 1846. [6] Crump quotes

from the letter cited in 1: 'The man who deprives men of their belief in God is not so impious as he who attributes to God the passions of men' (ed., *Conversations*, I, 214). [7] Landor notes: 'Seneca quotes a letter of Epicurus, in which his friendship with Metrodorus is mentioned, with a remark that the obscurity in which they had lived – so great indeed as to let them rest almost unheard of in the midst of Greece – was by no means to be considered as an abatement of their good fortune'. Crump identifies the letter as Senec. Epist. 79. 15 (ed., *Conversations*, I, 215).

## 17  Leofric and Godiva  The text is that of 1846.

Lady Godiva, fl. *c.* 1040–80, the wife of Leofric, Earl of Mercia, was the benefactress of several monasteries, including the Benedictine abbey of Coventry, which she and her husband founded in 1043. The legend on which this Conversation is based first appeared in the *Chronicle* of Roger of Wendover. Cf. POETRY **18, [Godiva]**, the poem Landor appended to this Conversation.

The Conversation is supposed to take place as Godiva and Leofric approach the walls of Coventry.

[1] The church of St Michael's at Coventry was actually a fourteenth-century foundation. [2] Cf. Ephesians 4:26. [3] *Godwin*: d. 1053, the powerful Earl of Wessex, who, exiled for his defiance of King Edward the Confessor, led an armed invasion of England and forced a settlement on the king restoring him to his former importance.

## 18  Fra Filippo Lippi and Pope Eugenius the Fourth  The text is that of 1846.

Filippo Lippi, *c.* 1406–69, one of the foremost Florentine painters of the early Renaissance, was temperamentally unsuited for the life of a monk. He left the convent of the Carmelites where, orphaned, he had spent much of his youth, and became celebrated for religious painting marked by keen observation and human interest. Browning's poem 'Fra Lippo Lippi', which owes some of its characterization to this Conversation, was published in *Men and Women*, 1855.

Pope Eugenius IV, 1383–1447, was noted for his ascetic habits.

Crump quotes the chief source, Vasari's *Life of Filippo Lippi*: 'While upon the coast of Ancona he was amusing himself on the sea in company with some friends; and one day they were all carried off together by the Moorish galleys which scour the sea in those parts, and so conveyed to Barbary, where they were all put on the chain and enslaved; and there, with much discomfort, he remained eighteen months. But one day, having had much familiarity with his master, he took it into his head to make a picture of him; he therefore took a burnt stick from the fire, and made on the white wall a picture of him at full length in Moorish garments. This was told to his master by the other slaves; and so marvellous a feat did it seem to those people, who neither draw nor paint, it was the occasion of his being set free from the chain, where he had so long been kept . . . After he had executed some little paintings for his master, he was sent safely to Naples' (ed., *Conversations*, II, 373).

The occasion of the meeting between the painter and the Pope is given also by Vasari who writes that Fra Filippo was sent from Cosimo de Medici to present a gift of some of his pictures.

[1] *ortolans*: small birds considered a table delicacy. [2] A small, rather stunted variety of fig. [3] In Islam, *Gabriel* revealed the Koran to Muhammad, becoming

the angle of truth. [4] From the West European coast of France and N W Spain. [5] See note on POETRY **12,   Count Julian**, 72. [6] A country holiday. [7] A village north of Florence. [8] See note on POETRY **25,   Fiesolan Idyl**. [9] See note in POETRY **117, [The Fiesolan Villa]**, 20. [10] In the 1450s (actually after the pope's death) Fra Lippo was at *Prato*, the Tuscan city in central Italy, decorating the choir of the Cathedral with frescoes representing scenes from the lives of St John the Baptist and St Stephen. [11] The painter Filippino Lippi, a student of Botticelli, was their son. [12] A papal decree made on the personal initiative of the pontiff. [13] The pope's office is in succession to St Peter, a fisherman.

**19   Aesop and Rhodopè**   Originally in *Heath's Book of Beauty* for 1844, published 1843. The text is that of 1853.

Aesop, fl.*c*. the middle of the sixth century BC, the composer of Greek animal fables, is said by Herodotus to have been a slave in the house of Iadmon, a Thracian.

Rhodopè, a Greek courtesan of great beauty, was his fellow slave. Crump notes that she was brought to Egypt by Xantheus the Samian, but that Landor invented the circumstances (ed., *Conversations*, I, 7).

[1] See note on POETRY **42, To Wordsworth**, 46–8. [2] See note on POETRY **70, The Hamadryad**, 132–5. [3] The wife of Tyndareus, King of Sparta, seduced by Jupiter, who visited her in the form of a swan.

**20   Second Conversation**   Originally in *Heath's Book of Beauty* for 1845, published in 1844. The text is that of 1853.

[1] *chlamys*: A short mantle usually worn by men in ancient Greece. [2] See POETRY **174, Tibullus**, 7. [3] See note on POETRY **14, To Corinth**, 20.

**Citation and Examination of William Shakspeare**   The text is that of 1846. It was written in 1834. The full title continues '. . . Euseby Tree, Joseph Carneby, and Silas Gough, before the Worshipful Sir Thomas Lucy, Knight, touching deer-stealing on the 19th day of September in the year of grace 1582, now published from original papers'.

It is an extended Imaginary Conversation in which Shakespeare is supposed to be tried at Charlecote, Lucy's seat on the road between Warwick and Stratford-upon-Avon, for his legendary deer-stealing. Shakespeare is accused by two of Sir Thomas's keepers and the witness, a chaplain, Silas Gough. It is full of Warwickshire allusions calling on Landor's own local associations.

As Crump notes, the idea may have arisen from Landor's reading of James White's *Letters of Falstaff*, 1796, which Charles Lamb had loaned to Landor in 1831: 'This may have turned his thoughts back to an old subject; in one of the conversations, burned in his quarrel with Mr Taylor [the original publisher of the first volumes of *Imaginary Conversations*, 1824], the speakers were Shakespeare and Sir Thomas Lucy, and doubtless something of the old work survives in the present book' (ed., *Longer Prose Works*, I, vii–viii).

**21   [Dr Glaston's Warning]**   In the extract, Shakespeare is supposed to be relating the after-dinner discourse of an unhistorical 'preacher at Oxford, who had preached at Easter in the chapel-royal of Westminster' called 'Dr. Glaston'. Shakespeare alleges that he walked to Oxford to hear him preach at the university church of St. Mary's, and afterwards accosted him.

[1] 'A young gentleman' in the same company 'who, from his pale face, his abstinence at table, his cough, his taciturnity, and his gentleness, seemed already more than half poet'. 'Dr. Glaston' is advising him against that vocation. [2] The *Cherwell* is a tributary of the Thames running by Oxford. [3] *Godstow* is on the Thames, three and a half miles NW of Oxford. [4] The Fair Rosamond, according to Higden, monk of Chester (*c.* 1350), 'was the fayre daughter of Walter, Lord Clifford, concubine of Henry II, and poisoned by Queen Eleanor, AD 1177 . . . She was buried at Godstow, in an house of nunnes . . .'. [5] A perennial herb. [6] *Hawkins*: Sir John, 1532–95, English admiral. In the defeat of the Spanish Armada he commanded the 'Victory'. [7] 'John Wellerby who sought glory in letters now sees the glory of God'.

**Pericles and Aspasia**   The text is that of 1846. It was originally composed in 1835 and published in 1836. It was republished with much additional material in 1846.

It is an evocation of the greatest period in Greek life when the powerful character and oratory of Pericles, *c.* 500–429 BC, dominated Athens. It was his ambition to make Athens an ideal democracy and the leader of all Greece, but he was consistently impeded by the jealousy of Sparta. Nevertheless, under him, the Delian confederacy of Ionian states, founded to combat the Persian invasions, became a kind of Athenian empire. He subdued a revolt of the island of Samos, off the coast of Asia Minor, in 439, but in 431 he was faced with the Peloponnesian War, in which Sparta led the southern and western cities of Greece against him. With some difficulty he held his own, but the war was still in progress when he died. His vision of Athens was of a state embodying the highest attainments of human culture, and he was on intimate terms with the greatest artists, poets and philosophers of the day. His faithful consort was the courtesan Aspasia of Miletus (see note on POETRY **51, Ode to Miletus)**, noted for her intellectual distinction. As she was not an Athenian citizen, they were unable to marry.

The genesis and sources of the work Landor indicates in a letter to Southey: 'I began a conversation between Pericles and Aspasia, and thought I could do better by a series of letters between them, not interrupted; for the letters should begin with their first friendship, should give place to their conversations afterwards, and recommence on their supposed separation during the plague of Athens. Few materials are extant: Bayle, Menage, Thucydides, Plutarch, and hardly anything more' (quoted by Super, *Biography*, p. 251). The original format was altered by sustaining the epistolary form almost throughout, and by extending the circle of correspondents, especially by including among them an imaginary confidante of Aspasia from Miletus called 'Cleone'. The letters and speeches are also diversified by interspersing them with prose fragments and verses supposed to come from various ancient writers (see POETRY **43–56**).

Though his conception of the work is deeply imbued in the period and physical location of Periclean Athens, Landor deliberately emancipates himself from the attempt at historical reconstruction. He himself points out: 'The characters, thoughts, and actions are all fictions. Pericles was somewhat less amiable, Aspasia somewhat less virtuous . . .' (quoted by Super, *Biography*, p. 263), and in the orations he wrote for Pericles he avoided using those recorded by the historians.

**22   Aspasia to Cleone**
[1] An allusion to the close of her previous letter, which Aspasia concludes by announcing her arrival at Athens, but without any details. [2] See note on the Conversation 'Lord Brooke and Sir Philip Sidney', PROSE **1**, 15. [3] March. 4 See note on POETRY **2, Gebir, Book I**, 1. The festival of the Urban Dionysia was held in March, and was attended by visitors from all parts of Greece. It included a sumptuous procession in which a statue of the god was carried on a chariot, and the performance on three consecutive days of new tragedies and comedies. [5] A large island in the north of the Aegean. [6] In the *Prometheus Bound* of *Aeschylus*, 525–456 BC, the Titan has incurred the wrath of *Zeus* by becoming the champion of mankind and giving men fire and the arts. He is nailed to a rock in the wilderness of Scythia where an eagle daily feeds on his liver which is restored each night. He is comforted by the chorus of Oceanides, daughters of Oceanus, and together with them is hurled into the abyss.

**23   Aspasia to Cleone**   [1] 'The venerable and good-natured old widow' whom Aspasia is visiting.

**24   Xeniades to Aspasia**   [1] Letters XX–XXX recount the infatuation of Xeniades with Aspasia, and his death from love-sickness. In XVII, 'Cleon' had written that he had left Miletus, supposedly to superintend his silver mines at Lemnos.

**25   Aspasia to Cleone**   [1] This letter was not in the first edition.

**26   Aspasia to Xeniades**   [1] See the *Odyssey*, VI, 40–7: 'So spake grey-eyed Athene, and departed to Olympus, where, as they say, is the seat of the gods that standeth fast for ever. Not by winds is it shaken, nor ever wet with rain, nor doth the snow come nigh thereto, but most clear air is spread about it cloudless, and the white light floats over it. Therein the blessed gods are glad for all their days. . .' (translated by S. H. Butcher and A. Lang, London, 1922, p. 93).

**35   Cleone to Aspasia**   [1] See note on POETRY **7, [Imitation from Sappho]**. [2] Landor is referring to the stanzas beginning Φαίνεταί μοι κῆνος ἴσος θέοισιν, not the later discovered, so-called letter to, or ode on, Anactoria. It is translated by J. M. Edmonds: 'It is to be a God, methinks, to sit before you and listen close by to the sweet accents and winning laughter which have made the heart in my breast beat fast, I warrant you. When I look on you, Brocheo, my speech comes short or fails me quite, I am tongue-tied; in a moment a delicate fire has overrun my flesh, my eyes grow dim and my ears sing, the sweat runs down me and a trembling takes me altogether, till I am as green and pale as the grass, and death itself seems not very far away; – but now that I am poor, I must fain be content . . .' (ed., *Lyra Graeca*, 3 vols., London, 1922–7, I, 187). [3] *Sophocles*, 495–406 BC, and *Euripides*, 480–406 BC, Greek tragic poets.

**36   Aspasia to Cleone**   [1] Their native city of Miletus was situated at the mouth of the *Maeander*. [2] The Fortunate Islands was an ancient name for the Canary Islands, or any imaginary land set in distant seas.

**37 Oration of Pericles to the Soldiers round Samos** Placed unnumbered between CXV and CXVI.
[1] The place of assembly for all the citizens in Athens. [2] See note on POETRY **51, Ode to Miletus**, 14. Crump notes that Thucydides records that *Byzantion* also revolted with Samos (ed., *Longer Prose Works*, I, 244). [3] Crump notes that Thucydides records: 'Certain of the Samians . . . entered into a confederacy with Pisuthnes, son of Hystaspes, who at that time was in power at Sardis' (ed., *Longer Prose Work*, I, 245). [4] In 480 BC, *Xerxes* followed in the steps of his father Darius to attempt to win Greece for the Persian empire. After some initial successes his fleet was defeated near the island of Salamis. [5] *Salamis*: see also note on POETRY **15, Regeneration**, 55.

**38 Oration of Pericles** [1] Supposedly spoken in 431 BC when the Spartans (Lacedaemonians) invaded Attica. [2] See note on POETRY **14, To Corinth**, 1. The Corinthians incited the Spartans to declare war on Athens inspired basically by commercial rivalry. Athens had assisted *Corcyra* and formed a defensive alliance with her. It was one of the immediate causes of the war. [3] *Corcyra*: A Corinthian colony (modern Corfu). [4] *Piraeus*: see note on POETRY **78, Thrasymedes and Eunöe**, 52. [5] As the Dorian city of *Megara* had assisted Corinth at the battle of Sybota, the Athenians passed a measure excluding the Megarians from the markets and ports of their empire. [6] The first ten years of the war were indecisively waged by this king who led the invasion. [7] Thucydides had accused Pericles of squandering the resources of the state and of misappropriating the money of the Confederacy for such purely Athenian purposes. Pericles had replied that the allies had no reason to complain as long as Athens defended them efficiently. [8] The policy practised by Pericles was to allow the Spartans to ravage Attica and risk no land engagement, confining himself to naval operations. [9] *Marathon* and [10] *Plataea*: see notes on POETRY **15, Regeneration**, 54 and 56–7. [11] *Miltiades*: see note on the Conversation 'Aeschines and Phocion', PROSE **3**, 10. [12] After Marathon, Miltiades, on his own proposal, was commissioned to attack the island of *Paros* which had furnished a trireme to the Persians. He besieged the city of Paros for twenty-six days, but without success, and then returned home wounded, was condemned for criminal conduct and soon died. [13] See note on POETRY **56, The Shades of Agamemnon and Iphigeneia**, 7.

**39 Anaxagoras to Aspasia** [1] In the philosopher and scientist Anaxagoras, *c.* 500–428 BC, Landor is said to have felt he was in part depicting himself. [2] The Greek city on the Hellespont to which Anaxagoras retired after being fined for propagating impious doctrines, though defended by Pericles. [3] See note on POETRY **161, Coresus and Callirhoë**, 146. [4] An Athenian astronomer who devised a calendar. Anaxagoras was also interested in this subject, and was the first to explain solar eclipses.

**40 Anaxagoras to Aspasia** [1] The promontory of Thrace was an Athenian colony.

**41 Pericles to Aspasia** [1] The plague which fell on Athens in 430 BC intensified the ordeal of the war. [2] *Hippocrates*, *c.*460–*c.* 370 BC, and *Acron*, fl. fifth century, were physicians. [3] *Damon*: an Athenian musician and teacher of Pericles. [4] See note on the Conversation 'Aeschines and Phocion', PROSE **3**,

8. He was ostracized but returned from exile when the expedition of Xerxes was threatening, holding a command at Salamis and leading the Athenian contingent at Plataea. [5] *Pindar*: see note on POETRY **123, To Southey**, 19–21. [6] *Empedocles*, b. the first quarter of the fifth century BC, the philosopher and scientist of Acragas. [7] *Aeschylus*, 525–456 BC, the Greek tragic poet, went to Sicily to live at the court of Hiero I, and died at Gela. [8] *Protagoras*: born *c.* 485 BC, a professional sophist. [9] *Democritus*: born *c.* 460 BC, an atomistic philosopher. [10] *Herodotus*, *c.* 480–25 BC, visited Athens. See note on the Conversation 'Diogenes and Plato', PROSE **14**, 15. Book I of his *History* tells, in part, of the creation of the Persian empire by Cyrus. Book II is a description of Egypt, and Book III begins by relating the conquest of Egypt by Cambyses. [11] *Cyrus*: died 529 BC, was the founder of the Persian Empire. [12] *Thucydides*: *c.* 460–400 BC, wrote a history of the Peloponnesian War. [13] *Phidias*: see note on POETRY **122, To Julius Hare with 'Pericles and Aspasia'**, 12. [14] Phidias's two statues, of Athena Parthenos and Zeus of Olympia, made from gold and ivory, were reckoned the finest of the ancient world.

**The Pentameron and Pentalogia**   The extracts given here are from 'The Pentameron'. The text is that of 1846. Landor began it during the three months he spent in Germany in 1836, and it was first published in 1837.

It is a series of five day-long interviews between Giovanni Boccaccio, 1313–75, whose *Decameron* (a collection of tales represented as having been told over ten days) gave Landor the idea for the framework of this work, and Francesco Petrarch, 1304–74, the poet and humanist. Petrarch is supposed to pay Boccaccio a visit at his villa at Certaldo, between Florence and Siena. They met in Florence in 1350 and became life-long friends. Boccaccio was influenced by Petrarch into becoming a Greek scholar and working to re-introduce Greek literature.

The conversation dwells largely on lengthy criticisms of Dante's *Divine Comedy* and Boccaccio's *Decameron*, and on close analysis of the poetry of Virgil and Horace.

**42   Second Day's Interview**   [1] *Acciaioli*: Niccolo, was the seneschal of Joanna I, 1343–82, Queen of Naples. [2] At Naples he had met Maria d'Aquino, the illegitimate daughter of King Robert, whom he was to immortalize in prose and verse as 'Fiammetta', and who is said to have urged him to write. [3] The Italian name for a Carthusian monastery. The one referred to here was founded by Acciaioli on the Arno near Florence.

**43   Fifth Day's Interview**   [1] Petrarch first saw Laura (probably Laura de Noves, 1308?–48, wife of Hugo de Sade), who was to inspire his great vernacular love lyrics, at Avignon in 1327. [2] An ever-green shrub. [3] A white-flowered plant. [4] *Posilipo* and [5] Baiae: on the coast near Naples. [6] Now known as Orsanmichele, in Via dei Calzaiuoli. [7] In Book VI of the *Aeneid*, Aeneas visits the Cumaean *Sibyl* and descends with her into the nether world. Just inside hell,

> Full in the midst of this infernal Road,
> An Elm displays her dusky Arms abroad;
> The God of Sleep there hides his heavy Head:
> And empty Dreams on ev'ry Leaf are spread.

(Dryden's translation, ll. 394–7)

[8] A shorter version of the next section, to the end, was originally published separately under the title 'The Dream of Petrarca' in *Heath's Book of Beauty* for 1838, published 1837. When first composed Landor had called it 'The Dream of Gnomon of Priene' and intended it for insertion in *Pericles and Aspasia*.

[9] *Marcellus*, born 43 BC, was the son of Octavia the sister of Augustus. He was adopted by Augustus and married to his daughter Julia. He died two years later and was considered a national loss. The quotation is from Horace, *Odes*, I, 12, referring to the lustre of Marcellus's name which 'grows with each generation'. [10] See note on POETRY **42, To Wordsworth**, 28.

# Selected Bibliography

## Bibliographies

*A Bibliography of the Writings in Prose and Verse of Walter Savage Landor*, Thomas James Wise and Stephen Wheeler, London, 1919.
*A Landor Library: A Catalogue of Printed Books, Manuscripts and Autograph Letters by Walter Savage Landor*, Thomas James Wise, privately printed, London, 1928.
*The Publication of Landor's Works*, R. H. Super, London, 1954.

## Secondary Sources

ALDINGTON, RICHARD, 'Landor's "Hellenics" ', in his *Literary Studies and Reviews*, New York, 1924.
BRADLEY, WILLIAM, *The Early Poems of Walter Savage Landor*, London, 1914.
BUXTON, JOHN, 'Walter Savage Landor', in his *Grecian Taste: Literature in the Age of Neo-Classicism 1740–1820*, London, 1978.
COLVIN, Sir SIDNEY, *Landor* (English Men of Letters), London, 1881.
DAVIE, DONALD A., 'The Shorter Poems of Landor', *Essays in Criticism*, I (1951), 345–55 (repeated in his *Purity of Diction in English Verse*, London, 1952).
'Eminent Talent', *Essays in Criticism*, XX (1970), 446–72.
DILWORTH, ERNEST, *Walter Savage Landor*, New York, 1971.
ELWIN, MALCOLM, *Savage Landor*, New York, 1941 (revised and enlarged as *Landor: A Replevin*, London, 1958).
FLASDIECK, HERMANN M., 'Walter Savage Landor und seine "Imaginary Conversations" ', *Englische Studien*, LVIII (1924), 390–431.
FORSTER, JOHN, *Walter Savage Landor: a biography*, 2 vols., London, 1869.
KELLY, ANDREA, 'The Latin Poetry of Walter Savage Landor', in *The Latin Poetry of the English Poets*, ed. J. W. Binns, London and Boston, 1974.
LEAVIS, F. R., 'Landor and the Seasoned Epicure', *Scrutiny*, XI (1942), 148–50.
LEE, VERNON, 'The Rhetoric of Landor', in her *The Handling of Words*, New York, 1923.
MERCIER, VIVIAN, 'The Future of Landor Criticism', in *Some British Romantics: a collection of essays*, ed. J. V. Logan, J. E. Jordan, and Northrop Frye, Columbus, Ohio, 1966.
NITCHIE, ELIZABETH, 'The Classicism of Walter Savage Landor', *The Classical Journal*, XIV (1918) 147–66.
PINSKY, ROBERT, *Landor's Poetry*, Chicago and London, 1968.
POUND, EZRA, *ABC of Reading*, London, 1934.

PROUDFIT, CHARLES L., 'Landor on Milton: The Commentator's Commentator', *The Wordsworth Circle*, VII (1976), 3–12.

SELINCOURT, E. de, 'Classicism and Romanticism in the Poetry of Landor', in *England und die Antike*, ed. F. Saxl, Berlin, 1932.

STEPHEN, Sir LESLIE, 'Landor's Imaginary Conversations', in his *Hours in a Library*, Third Series, London, 1879.

SUPER, R. H., *Walter Savage Landor: a biography*, London, 1954.

'The Fire of Life', *Cambridge Review*, LXXXVI (1965), 170–5.

'Walter Savage Landor', in *The English Romantic Poets and Essayists: a review of research and criticism*, ed. C. W. and L. H. Houtchens, revised edition, New York and London, 1966.

'Landor and Catullus', *The Wordsworth Circle*, VII (1976), 31–7.

SYMONS, ARTHUR, 'Walter Savage Landor', in his *The Romantic Movement in English Literature*, London, 1909.

VITOUX, PIERRE, *L'Oeuvre de Walter Savage Landor*, Paris, 1964.

WILLIAMS, STANLEY T., 'Walter Savage Landor as a Critic of Literature', *PMLA*, XXXVIII (1923), 906–28.

# Index of titles and first lines
# (Poetry)

# Index of persons (Prose)

Italics indicate that the person is not referred to
by name in the text.